J.M. COETZEE'S AUSTERITIES

J.M. Coetzee's Austerities

Edited by

GRAHAM BRADSHAW
Chuo University, Japan, and University of Queensland, Australia

and

MICHAEL NEILL
University of Auckland, New Zealand

ASHGATE

Published by
Ashgate Publishing Limited
Wey Court East
Union Road
Farnham
Surrey, GU9 7PT
England

Ashgate Publishing Company
Suite 420
101 Cherry Street
Burlington
VT 05401-4405
USA

www.ashgate.com

British Library Cataloguing in Publication Data
J.M. Coetzee's austerities.
    1. Coetzee, J. M., 1940- –Criticism and interpretation.
    I. Bradshaw, Graham. II. Neill, Michael.
    823.9'14–dc22

Library of Congress Cataloging-in-Publication Data
J. M. Coetzee's austerities / edited by Graham Bradshaw and Michael Neill.
        p. cm.
    Includes bibliographical references and index.
    ISBN 978-0-7546-6803-9 (alk. paper) – ISBN 978-0-7546-9905-7 (ebook : alk. paper)
    1. Coetzee, J. M., 1940—Criticism and interpretation. I. Bradshaw, Graham. II. Neill,
Michael.

    PR9369.3.C58Z74 2010
    823'.914–dc22

                                                                    2009027380
ISBN 9780754668039 (hbk)
ISBN 9780754699057 (ebk)

Mixed Sources
Product group from well-managed
forests and other controlled sources
www.fsc.org Cert no. SA-COC-1565
© 1996 Forest Stewardship Council

Printed and bound in Great Britain by
MPG Books Group, UK

Contents

Contributors

Derek Attridge is the author of *J.M. Coetzee and the Ethics of Reading* (2004), *The Singularity of Literature* (2004) and many other books on literary theory, poetic form, and James Joyce. He recently completed *Reading and Responsibility: Deconstruction's Traces* (for Edinburgh University Press) and is currently editing, with David Attwell, *The Cambridge History of South African Literature* and, with Jane Elliott, *Theory after "Theory"* (for Routledge). He is Professor of English at the University of York and a Fellow of the British Academy.

David Attwell is the editor, with J.M. Coetzee, of *Doubling the Point: Essays and Interviews* (1992), and the author of *J.M. Coetzee: South Africa and the Politics of Writing* (1993). His more recent work is *Rewriting Modernity: Studies in Black South African Literary History* (2005). Formerly of the Universities of Natal and Witwatersrand, he is the Head of the Department of English and Related Literature at the University of York.

Graham Bradshaw is the author of *Shakespeare's Scepticism* (1987), *Misrepresentations: Shakespeare and the Materialists* (1993), and *Shakespeare's Peculiarity* (forthcoming); he is also co-author (with Tetsuo Kishi) of *Shakespeare in Japan* (2005), and Senior Editor of the *Shakespearean International Yearbook*. In addition, he has published extensively on modern literature and music. Formerly Professor of English at Chuo University, Tokyo, he is now Honorary Professor of English and Fine Arts at the University of Queensland.

Carrol Clarkson is the author of *J.M. Coetzee: Countervoices* (2009). Her main research interests are in philosophy of language and in post-apartheid South African literature and art. She has published essays on law and literature, and her second book, *Drawing the Line: Towards an Aesthetics of Post-Apartheid Justice*, is under contrct with Fordham University Press. She is an Associate Professor and Head of the Department of English at the University of Cape Town in South Africa.

Barbara Dancygier is Associate Professor in the English Department of the University of British Columbia. Her research interests include cognitive linguistics, cognitive narratology and cognitive poetics. She is the author of *Conditionals and Prediction* (1998) and co-author (with Eve Sweetser) of *Mental Spaces in Grammar* (2005). Her forthcoming book, *The Language of Stories*, proposes a cognitive linguistic account of fictional narratives.

Lindiwe Dovey is the author of *African Film and Literature: Adapting Violence to the Screen* (2009). She is lecturer in African Film and Performance Arts at SOAS, University of London, and the Founding Director of the Cambridge African Film Festival.

Teresa Dovey has written on J.M. Coetzee since the mid-1980s. She lives in Sydney and is interested in the reception of Coetzee's recent work in Australia.

Lars Engle is Professor and Chair of English at The University of Tulsa. He is the author of *Shakespearean Pragmatism: Market of His Time* (1993) and numerous essays on Renaissance literature (in, for example, *PMLA*, *Shakespeare Quarterly*, *SEL*, *MP*), and is an editor of *English Renaissance Drama: A Norton Anthology* (2002). His articles on contemporary South African literature have appeared in *The Threepenny Review*, *The Yale Journal of Criticism*, *Pretexts*, *English Studies in Africa* and several edited volumes.

Myrtle Hooper is Senior Professor in English at the University of Zululand where she has taught for more than twenty years. Her doctorate was on silence in Southern African fiction, and she has published on various South African writers, notably Mofolo, Plaatje, Smith, Paton, Head and Rooke, as well as on Joseph Conrad. Present research interests include cross-culturality and identity; privacy, politeness and power; and the ethics of reading. Her work on Coetzee dates back to the early 1990s, and has mainly been comparative.

Jonathan Lamb, the Andrew W. Mellon Professor of the Humanities at Vanderbilt University, was the Stanton Avery Distinguished Fellow at the Huntington Library in 2005–6. Following *Preserving the Self in the South Seas, 1680–1840* and *Exploration and Exchange: A South Seas Anthology* (both 2001) , he has published a number of articles in peer-reviewed journals. His most recent books are *The Evolution of Sympathy in the Long Eighteenth Century* (2009) and *The Things Things Say* (forthcoming). He was formerly a professor of English at Princeton University, and was a visiting Fellow at King's College Cambridge (2008–9).

Michael Neill is Emeritus Professor of English at the University of Auckland. He is the author of *Issues of Death* (1997) and *Putting History to the Question* (2000), and has edited *Anthony and Cleopatra* (1994) and *Othello* (2006) for the Oxford Shakespeare. Among his many published essays are articles on postcolonial fiction from a number of regions, including South Africa.

Zoë Wicomb is Professor of English Studies at the University of Strathclyde, Scotland. She is the author of numerous essays on South African writing and culture, and her latest work of fiction, a collection of short stories, is *The One That Got Away* (2008).

Laurence Wright is Director of the Institute for the Study of English in Africa at Rhodes University and Honorary Life President of the Shakespeare Society of Southern Africa. His research interests include Shakespeare and the history of Shakespeare in South Africa, South African Language Policy, African literature in English and language education for teachers. Recent work includes *"Disgrace* as J.M. Coetzee's *Tempest"* in *Renaissance Drama and Poetry in Context* (2008), "Ecological Thinking: Schopenhauer, J.M. Coetzee and who we are in the world" in *Toxic Belonging?: Identity and Ecology in Southern Africa* (2008) and *Stimela: Railway Poems of Southern Africa* (2008). His latest publication is an edited special issue of *The Shakespearean International Yearbook* (2009) on South African Shakespeare in the twentieth century (with general editors Graham Bradshaw and Tom Bishop).

Introduction

After "Disgrace": Lord and Lady Chandos in Cape Town and Adelaide

Graham Bradshaw

"We think we understand the universe, but we only understand 4 percent of everything," said James Watson Cronin, who won the 1980 Nobel for physics by proving that certain subatomic reactions escape the laws of fundamental symmetry.

According to the most recent models, he said, 73 percent of cosmic energy seems to consist of "dark energy" and 23 percent of "dark matter," the pervasive but unidentified stuff that holds the universe together and accelerates its expansion.

The remaining 4 percent consists of so-called "normal matter" such as atoms and molecules.

AFP report on the Amsterdam conference on astro-particle physics in September 2007.

Coetzee as a "Late Modernist"[1]

Philip, Lord Chandos, and the letter he wrote to Lord Bacon on "22 August 1603" exist only as non-non-fictional creations, like the novel in which Coetzee's Elizabeth Costello rewrote *Ulysses* from Molly Bloom's point of view, and like Lady Chandos and her own letter to Bacon. The famous Chandos Letter was written in 1902 by Hugo von Hofmannsthal, and was originally just called "A Letter" ("*Ein Brief*"). Later, after Hofmannsthal's death, this short work came to be regarded as a seminal European modernist text; it anticipated both Wittgenstein's concern with the limits of language and thought and the kind of linguistic and philosophical, as well as fictional and existential, crisis that Jean-Paul Sartre recycled in *La Nausée*. As for Lady Chandos: although Hofmannsthal's Lord Chandos refers to their four-year-old daughter Katherina Pompilia by name, he never names his wife. She received her name a century later, in 2002, when Intermezzo Press published Coetzee's "Letter of Elizabeth, Lady Chandos".

Although the 1902 and 2002 publication dates suggest that the second, Coetzeean "Letter" was some kind of centennial tribute from a "late modernist" writer to a pioneering predecessor, it was also an advance publication that

---

[1] Coetzee is content to be described as a "late modernist". See Derek Attridge , *J.M. Coetzee and the Ethics of Reading: Literature in the Event* (Chicago: University of Chicago Press, 2004), 2–6.

reappeared, in 2003, as the "Postscript" to *Elizabeth Costello: Eight Lessons*. When Coetzee's "Elizabeth, Lady Chandos" signed her letter to "Elizabeth C." she became Coetzee's third Elizabeth, or "E.C.", after Elizabeth Costello and Elizabeth Curren in *Age of Iron* (1990), a novel that takes the form of a very long letter from Mrs Curren to her daughter that may or may not be delivered to – and then may or may not "find", in Coleridge's deeper sense – its intended recipient. The three Elizabeths all express strong beliefs, that are being given a "voice" (a crucial notion for Coetzee) but are also framed and questioned within the fictions they inhabit. When Coetzee was asked in an interview how far his own beliefs coincided with those of Elizabeth Curren he austerely replied:

> There is no ethical imperative that I claim access to. Elizabeth is the one who believes in *believes in*. As for me, the book is written, nothing can stop it. The deed is done, what power was available to me is exorcised.[2]

There speaks the "late modernist", and when Michael Neill and I were planning the present collection one of our two main aims was to align or realign the South African Coetzee with the "late modernist" Coetzee whose South African critics have so often chided or attacked him for playing games that, like the Chandos Letter, question the relation between language and reality (and "realism") instead of demonstrating some less complicated, more overtly political "solidarity". Our other chief aim in planning this collection was that it would pay particular attention to Coetzee's most recent fiction, even if practical exigencies then dictated that there would be no room for separate essays on important earlier novels like *Foe* or Coetzee's fascinating third-person memoirs, *Boyhood* and *Youth*. Fortunately, some of the omissions were relative, not absolute; for example, Lindiwe and Teresa Dovey's essay on "Coetzee on Film" provides new perspectives on *Waiting for the Barbarians* and *Life & Times of Michael K* and *In the Heart of the Country*. The prospective omissions also seemed easier to countenance because, as anybody who follows the progress of a living writer knows, each new work can bring some shift in our sense of earlier works, and in Coetzee's case there is the further, important question of how his work has developed since he left South Africa for Australia in 2002. In this collection David Attwell, writes, or fears, that "The Australian provenance of *Elizabeth Costello*, *Slow Man*, and *Diary of a Bad Year* will be distinctive and striking but it is unlikely to produce so rich a harvest".[3] That may or may not be true, and in comparison with the furore that followed the publication of *Disgrace* Coetzee's "Australian" novels have been quietly or coolly received. And yet they already provide a standpoint from which it seems clear that *Disgrace* was not only the culmination of Coetzee's engagement with South Africa: it also looks forward to the "Australian" novels where, as Derek Attridge writes in this

---

[2]   J.M. Coetzee, *Doubling the Point: Essays and Interviews*, ed. David Attwell (Cambridge, Mass.: Harvard University Press, 1992), 250.

[3]   Chapter 8, 176.

collection, Coetzee is more than ever concerned to "represent the practice of art, in terms both of its coming-into-being and of its role in the world once it is produced, in his post-apartheid fictions and what we might call his semi-fiction".[4]

Certainly, Coetzee has been playing strange games with names ever since *Dusklands*; in that work, as in his most recent novel, *Diary of a Bad Year*, the grim games with his own family name were entangled with the profoundly vexed and disturbing issue of complicity. In *Age of Iron* Coetzee's first "E.C", who is so tortured by her sense of complicity, is never actually identified as "Elizabeth" within the novel. In *Life & Times of Michael K* the Kafkaesque "K" must suffice since we never learn Michael's family name, just as we never learn the names of the magistrate or the "barbarian" woman in *Waiting for the Barbarians*. As Derek Attridge observes in his indispensable *J. M. Coetzee and the Ethics of Reading*, the question of naming is "central to any question of the relation to, and the resistance of, the other"; there is even some doubt or confusion, which Coetzee himself may have chosen not to resolve, about whether the "M" in "J.M. Coetzee" stands for "Michael" or "Maxwell".[5] In *Disgrace* one of Lucy's rapists is unexpectedly called Pollux, which prompts Laurence Wright's breathtaking conclusion to his essay in this collection: if we then look for Castor, "the more spiritually or intellectually-minded of the 'heavenly twins'" in that foundation myth, the terribly ironic "implication is that David Lurie, the artist-rapist, fits the bill".[6] In *Diary of a Bad Year*, the protagonist's name turns out to be "John", and his initials are "J.C"; he is a South African novelist who attended the same Marist brethren school as the author Coetzee, had a father whose forename also began with "Z", wrote a novel called *Waiting for the Barbarians* and a book on censorship that sounds very like *Giving Offense*, and eventually emigrated to Australia. However, unlike his creator, John is single and childless, and had a sister not a brother; he takes no exercise, his hands are arthritic, his eyesight "shot", "teeth even worse", and his handwriting is a "half-blind scrawl" because Parkinson's disease is destroying his motor control. He has lived alone for years in an apartment in Sydney, whereas Coetzee has lived in Adelaide with his partner since he emigrated to Australia in 2002. We also learn that in the period covered by the first part of the *Diary*, "12 September – 31 May 2006", John is 72, so that he is several years older than his creator, who was born in 1940. That John also broods, like his creator, on the "impostures of authorship" is then assimilated to this game with names, which simmers for a long while before we even learn that the protagonist's name is "John" and that his initials are "J.C."

Before considering how the Chandos Letter matters in *Elizabeth Costello*, it is worth noticing its importance for another major contemporary and "late modernist" novelist. In the section of George Hughes's *Reading Novels* that discusses novels that "move off from the first with pronouns", Hughes observes that the opening

[4] Chapter 1, 28.
[5] Attridge, *J.M. Coetzee and the Ethics of Reading*, 94–95.
[6] Chapter 7, 162.

of John Banville's *Doctor Copernicus* (1976) initially refrains from naming the protagonist even as it "overtly plays with the concept of naming".[7] Overtly and covertly, if we notice how Banville's incipit also plays variations on the more famous opening of *A Portrait of the Artist as a Young Man*. In each case the infant scientist or artist – Banville's young Nicolas Copernicus, Joyce's young Stephen Daedalus – is learning to identify himself through things and names that existed before him; *infans*, the Latin root for "infant", means being unable to speak. "At first" the "big tree" outside "had no name": "It was the thing itself, the vivid thing. It was his friend."[8] Later, he learns the names of things as he learns his own name, from others: "Look Nicolas, look. See, the big tree!" Just as Joyce's Stephen keeps registering "nice" or "queer" words and feelings, Nicolas – Banville's first Portrait of the Early Modern Scientist – is fascinated by the "strange" relation between words and things:

> Tree. That was its name. And also: the linden. They were nice words. He had known them a long time before he knew what they meant. They did not mean themselves, they were nothing in themselves, they meant the dancing singing thing outside. In wind, in silence, at night, in the changing air, it changed and yet was changelessly the tree, the linden tree. That was strange.

The "big tree" leaves such an imprint on young Nicolas's wondering imagination that he recalls it when he is dying, as "a part of the world" that became "almost a part of himself". The adult Nicolas never discovers in "himself" any comparably rooted sense of national or political identity, although he tries to oblige the nationalist uncle who urges him not to think of himself as a German, Pole or Prussian: "You are an Ermlander, simple. Remember it."

> And so, meekly, he became what he was told to be. But it was only one more mask. Behind it he was that which no name or nation could claim to be. He was Doctor Copernicus. (94)

Later, when "Doctor Copernicus" has worked out the first heliocentric model of the solar system but is unable to reconcile his revolutionary correction of the Ptolemaic error with his rage for order and his need for a supreme fiction,[9] he loses his belief that "the physical world was amenable to physical investigation", that it is "possible to say the truth", or that "the thing itself could be said" (116). The relation between "things" and words or names that had fascinated young Nicolas breaks down, in the way that Nicolas's dead brother describes when he appears to the dying Nicolas in a dream or nightmare:

---

[7]   George Hughes, *Reading Novels* (Nashville: Vanderbilt University Press, 2002), 30–31.

[8]   John Banville, *Doctor Copernicus* (London: Minerva, 1990), 3.

[9]   Banville incorporates the phrases from Wallace Stevens in his text.

We know the meaning of the singular thing only so long as we content ourselves
with knowing it in the midst of other meanings: isolate it, and all meaning drains
away. It is not the thing that counts, you see, only the interaction of things; and,
of course, the names … (239)

Lord Chandos hovers behind this dream, or Copernican nightmare; six years
later, in 1982, when Banville published *The Newton Letter: An Interlude* as the
third novel in his "scientific" tetralogy,[10] the eponymous "Newton letter" (or
Newtonian nightmare) turned out to be Banville's appropriation of the letter
that Hofmannsthal's Lord Chandos wrote to Francis Bacon, "apologizing for his
complete abandonment of literary activity", and explaining that for the last two
years he has been living "a life of scarcely credible emptiness" in which he can
no longer connect words with things.[11] As Banville notes in his introduction to
the most recent translation of the Chandos Letter: "Words are not only bound to
things but are at the same time separate from them. Horse may be the horseness
of allhorse, as Joyce declared, but the horse remains itself even if we call it a
zebra."[12]

Hofmannsthal's Chandos explains to Bacon that one result of his affliction –
which, he concedes, might be regarded as a "mental disease" – was that the
"abstract words" needed to "bring out an opinion" crumbled "in my mouth
like rotten mushrooms"; single words "turned into eyes which stared at me", or
became "dizzying whirlpools which spun around and around and led into the void"
(121–2). And now, things – disconnected things, like "a watering can, a harrow left
in a field, a dog in the sun, a shabby churchyard, a cripple" – suddenly fill him with an
"absurd", almost mystical but ethically vacuous rapture in which "everything" has
"meaning" (123). The "whirlpools" of language cannot carry this incommunicable
meaning and instead lead into "the void", just as his earlier "religious ideas" of a
"well-designed plan of a divine providence" no longer have "power over me", and
"belong to the cobwebs through which my thoughts pass as they shoot out into
the void, but upon which so many others are snagged and remain" (120). In short,
the warning in Nicolas Copernicus' nightmare and the Newton letter became true
for Lord Chandos much earlier, in "1603" or 1902: Isolate the singular thing and
meaning drains away. For Hofmannsthal's Lord Chandos his quasi-mystical, glad-
animal exaltations provide no consolation or escape from what he calls "a life of
scarcely credible emptiness" and what he suspects Bacon will regard as a "mental

[10]   Tetralogy or trilogy: *Mefisto*, the next novel that followed *Doctor Copernicus*,
Kepler and *The Newton Letter*, was usually regarded as the completion of a "scientific"
tetralogy, until the three earlier novels were reprinted by Picador in 2000 as *The Revolutions
Trilogy*.

[11]   Hugo von Hofmannsthal, *The Lord Chandos Letter and Other Writings*, introduced
by John Banville and translated by Joel Rotenberg (New York: New York Review Books,
2005), 125. The "Letter" appears at the end of this collection (117–28).

[12]   *The Lord Chandos Letter*, ix.

disease", because their "meaning" remains incommunicable and provides him with
nothing to live by, or from. In this respect his abject "misery" follows from his
human need to communicate through language, and perhaps, although this is more
ambiguous, from some residual reluctance to surrender human responsibility.

Elizabeth, Lady Chandos, Coetzee's third "E.C.", is also in great misery
for different yet complementary reasons, which are marital, religious, and also
linguistic. In the passage from Hofmannsthal's "Letter" that Coetzee chose to
prefix to his own "Letter", Lord Chandos refers to a "mistress":

> At such moments even a negligible creature, a dog, a rat, a beetle, a stunted
> apple tree, a cart track winding over a hill, a mossy stone, counts more for me
> than a night of bliss with the most beautiful, most devoted mistress. These dumb
> and in some cases inanimate creatures press toward me with such fullness, such
> presence of love, that there is nothing in range of my rapturous eye that does not
> have life. It is as if everything, everything that exists, everything my confused
> thinking touches on, means something.

Of course a nobleman in Elizabethan England or Hofmannsthal's Vienna could
be expected to have a beautiful and devoted mistress or two, but the effect of that
comparative reference to extra-marital "bliss" in the Chandos Letter might prompt
us – and seems to have prompted Coetzee – to reflect that for Hofmannsthal's
Chandos "everything that exists" has "meaning" *except* his wife and her
unconditional devotion. He tells Bacon that he has concealed his affliction from
her, but Coetzee's Lady Chandos proudly assures Bacon, three fictional weeks (or
a century) later, that "No husband can succeed in concealing from a loving wife
distress of mind so extreme" (227). Her own "distress" is no less extreme because
her love for her husband is so helplessly faithful and so fiercely erotic that she is a
traviata in the double sense the Italian word balances, a betrayed woman who also
betrays herself by being utterly abandoned in her "raptures" and her "distress":

> A time of affliction I call the present time; yet in the company of my Philip I
> too have moments when soul and body are one, when I am ready to burst out
> in the tongues of angels. *My raptures* I call these spells. They come to me; with
> no other man would I know them. Soul and body he speaks to me, in a speaking
> without speech; into me, soul and body, he presses what are no longer words but
> flaming swords.
>
> We are not meant to live thus, Sir. *Flaming swords* I say my Philip presses
> into me, swords that are not words; but they are neither flaming swords nor are
> they words.

Although her husband has evidently abandoned his own "religious ideas", such
ideas compound Elizabeth's "distress" when she considers how we are "meant
to live", and then feels guilty about her sexual "raptures". In this respect she is
both a victim and a fictional embodiment of the historically unhappy convergence

between the anti-sexual, anti-feminine tendencies in Christianity (or Paulinity) and the Cartesian tradition that separates the body from the mind or "soul", reason from imagination, and cognition from emotion.

Elizabeth's affliction is also linguistically complementary, as Jonathan Lamb succinctly observes in his contribution to the present volume:

> Everything experienced by her husband as an embodied meaning has turned for her into a metaphor: *"Always it is not what I say but something else"*... Her husband and she have been divided, he operating within the zone of saying only what things mean, and she in the zone of meaning only what her words say.[13]

Since our thinking about abstractions (like Time or the Self or a Nation, or Race) always involves metaphorical "mappings" or cognitive "blends", Philip's own earlier attempts to think abstractly would always have been ineluctably metaphorical; Elizabeth's affliction is complementary not because she cannot stop using metaphors (none of us can) but because she keeps catching herself in the process:

> Always it is not what I say but something else. Hence the words I write above:
>
> *We are not meant to live thus.* Only for *extreme souls* may it have been intended to live thus, where words give way beneath your feet like rotting boards (*like rotting boards* I say again, I cannot help myself; not if I am to bring home to you my distress and my husband's, *bring home* I say, where is home, where is home?)

Coetzee's "Letter" could even be considered as an oblique commentary on cognitive linguistics, which, surprisingly, he never directly discusses in his numerous essays on language and linguistics. As one of the several contributors to this volume who attend very closely to the relation between Coetzee's fictional and non-fictional writings, Barbara Dancygier also goes furthest in questioning the assumptive basis for the distinction between fiction and non-fiction. She notes that Coetzee's most recent novels, *Elizabeth Costello*, *Slow Man* and *Diary of a Bad Year*, are all "novels about the multiple agencies involved in producing fiction", and are constructed as "commentaries on the relationship between fact and fiction and on the role of our fiction in our lives". Dancygier goes on to show how, by "uncovering the conceptual underpinnings of the processes of meaning construction", recent work in cognitive science and cognitive poetics illuminates the "narrative choices" and "conceptual constructs" in these "Australian" novels and makes it necessary to "re-think" some "basic assumptions about narrative discourse".

---

[13]   Chapter 9, 189.

Apart from some searching pages in an essay by Lucy Graham on "Textual Transvestism" Coetzee's "Letter" has barely been discussed, and when it became the "Postscript" to *Elizabeth Costello* one reviewer complained that it had no connection with that work.[14] That is untrue, although it would be true to say that Costello herself couldn't have written the "Letter" and wouldn't see why it is a fitting "Postscript". The first chapter of *Elizabeth Costello* originally began as a lecture on " Realism" that Coetzee presented as a fiction with Costello as its newly invented protagonist. Costello is also giving a lecture on "Realism", and what she says is enough to suggest that her creator may have made her an Australian novelist because making her South African might have started too many unhelpful "Who does he mean? Could it be Nadine?" hares.

In her lecture on "Realism", and in one of her all too many touchingly weary but irritably impatient short cuts, Costello insists that she is an old woman who no longer has time to say anything she does not mean or make remarks that do not mean what they say. Unlike Stanley Cavell in *Must We Mean What We Say?* or those cognitive linguists who have shown how frequently the meaning of a sentence or utterance depends upon pragmatic knowledge of its speaker and context, Costello supposes that meaning what she says is somehow just the same as saying what she means. But meaning what you say, or what your words mean, can be very punishing if you have failed to say what you mean. Whenever English speakers revise something they have written they know what it means to think, "That is not what I meant to mean", although not all languages resemble English in allowing this verbal play on the meanings of "mean". (Dutch does not, so probably nor does Afrikaans.) Although Costello is so sensitive and brave in confronting our heartbreakingly brutal human world, she is altogether untouched by the late modernist anxieties about language that trouble her creator, or a writer like Banville. The brief but laden "Postscript" to *Elizabeth Costello: Eight Lessons* then delivers a ninth lesson, and a kind of last word on "Realism": unlike Elizabeth Costello, Elizabeth Chandos is tortured and maddened by her sense that what she says always means "something else, always something else" (229).

Jonathan Lamb goes to the heart of this contrast between Lady Chandos and Costello when he observes:

> Saying what one means, if what one means is a distinct idea from a sense impression, is Locke's version of bald empiricism and the 'real' non-metaphorical language Newton desired. The word serves the idea. Meaning what you say, on the other hand, puts words first and they or the persons using them decide what they are saying. Humpty Dumpty is the tyrannical exemplar of this option ... Meaning what you say endows language with a limitless metaphorical potential,

---

[14]   See Lucy Graham, "Textual Transvestism: The Female Voices of J.M. Coetzee", in Jane Poyner, ed., *J. M. Coetzee and the Idea of the Public Intellectual* (Athens: Ohio University Press, 2006), 217–35. Adam Mars-Jones complained that the "Postcript" adds nothing relevant to *Elizabeth Costello* in his review for the *Observer*, 14 September 2003.

because any word can stand for any other, unconstrained by loyalty to definitions or to the reality of things on which they depend.[15]

Later, when Costello is lecturing within Coetzee's two lectures on "The Lives of Animals", she claims again that she says what she means, and also claims that her remark "I feel like [Kafka's monkey] Red Peter" means what it says. On the contrary, to quote the vigilant Lamb again:

> The possibility that the remark means something different from Costello herself troubles the meaning of the word "like", which spins between the alternatives of "resemble" and "identical with." The first person pronoun is likewise disturbed, referring equally to Costello, Red Peter and the remark.[16]

Since Coetzee is habitually precise about linguistic matters, Costello's wearily assertive imprecision shows why we should not regard her as an *alter ego* through whom Coetzee can ventriloquize.

"Foundational Fictions"

Within this volume, Carrol Clarkson considers the relationship between language and reality by taking as her starting point the artist Robert Smithson's profoundly suggestive essay, "A Sedimentation of the Mind: Earth Projects". Smithson's geological metaphor answers to his sense that "Words and rocks contain a language that follows a syntax of splits and ruptures". That sentence and the geological metaphor recall Nietzsche's philological and etymological project in *The Genealogy of Morals*, while Smithson's next sentence might have been taken from the Chandos Letter, when Chandos found the "whirlpools of language" leading into a "void": "Look at any word long enough," Smithson warns, "and you will see it open up into a series of faults, into a terrain of particles each containing its own void."[17] As Clarkson wryly observes, such "etymological forays" never hit "reassuring bedrock".[18] Rather, Smithson's concept of "sedimentation" extends to language when the mind has become "silted up with words which have become naturalized": the words "assume their power over us" when the "foundational fictions" they carry (like undeclared baggage) have also become "naturalized" – although "linguistic scrutiny" of the "word or phrase" often "unearths contradictory meanings that threaten to undermine the entire edifice" (50). Clarkson then notes

---

[15] Chapter 9, 181.

[16] Ibid., 181.

[17] Robert Smithson, *The Collected Writings*, ed. Jack Flam (Berkeley: University of California Press, 1996), 107. Quoted here by Clarkson in Chapter 2 at p. 43.

[18] Chapter 2, 43–4.

how many of Coetzee's characters "find themselves looking long and hard at words":

> Characters like Mrs Curren, Elizabeth Costello and Paul Rayment pick out isolated words, reconfigure them in declension, compare related words in different languages, trace the etymological roots. A question of language in general, and its capacity to articulate the truth, is a central preoccupation in Coetzee. (43)

In *White Writing*, Coetzee himself observes that "language, consciousness and landscape are interrelated" (7), and explores the "burden of finding a home in Africa for a consciousness formed in and by a language whose history lies on another continent" (173); in *Disgrace*, David Lurie comes to believe that "English is an unfit medium for the truth of South Africa" (117). Perhaps it is time to reconsider the Whorf-Sapir thesis about language.

Be that as it may, Clarkson presses further than most of Coetzee's critics and reviewers when she directs attention to the significance of Coetzee's own references to "foundational fictions" and "constructs", as in this passage from *Giving Offense*:

> Affronts to the innocence of our children or to the dignity of our persons are attacks not upon our essential being but upon constructs – constructs by which we live, but constructs nevertheless. This is not to say that affronts to innocence or dignity are not real affronts … the infringements are real; what is infringed, however, is not our essence, but a foundational fiction to which we more or less wholeheartedly subscribe, a fiction that may well be indispensable for a just society, namely, that human beings have a dignity that sets them apart from animals and consequently protects them from being treated like animals. (14)

The point I am wishing to add to Clarkson's very acute analysis is that such a passage very well suggests the "late modernist" provenance of Coetzee's austere, admonitory declaration that "There is no ethical imperative that I claim access to. Elizabeth is the one who believes in *believes in*."

Coetzee's references to "constructs" and to "foundational fictions" that may be "indispensable for a just society" would be as unacceptable to contemporary foundationalists and fundamentalists as Nietzsche's view (in *The Twilight of the Idols*) that "There are no moral facts whatsoever", or Wittgenstein's constant view (in *Philosophical Investigations* as well as the *Tractatus*) that values can never be "read off" as part of the world's fabric and furniture. Clifford Geertz very well suggests what is at issue in *Islam Observed*, when he reconsiders the familiar anthropological distinction between *mythos* and *ethos*. Noting that *mythos* or "world view" is the "usual term for "the collections of notions a people has of how reality is at base put together", while the people's "general style of life, the way they do things and like to see things done" is called their *ethos*, Geertz goes on to argue that the "heart" of the religious perspective, or way of looking at the world, is not the theory that beyond the visible world lies an invisible one, and not the doctrine that some divine presence broods over this world, but "the conviction that the values one holds are grounded in the structure of reality, that between the way one ought to live and the way things really are there is an unbreakable inner connexion".[19] So, what "sacred symbols do for those to whom they are sacred is to formulate an image of the world's construction and a program for human conduct that are mere reflexes of one another", since the *mythos* and the *ethos* are mutually confirming:

> Such symbols render the world believable and the ethos justifiable, and they do it by invoking each in support of the other. The world view is believable because the ethos, which grows out it, is felt to be authoritative; the ethos is justifiable because the world view, upon which it rests, is held to be true. Seen from outside the religious perspective, this sort of hanging a picture from a nail driven into its frame appears as a kind of sleight of hand. Seen from inside, it appears as a simple fact. (97)

For many modernist writers like Joyce, Conrad, Beckett and Hofmannsthal himself, who gave up writing poetry after writing the "Letter", there is no corresponding conviction that "the values one holds are grounded in the inherent structure of reality", and no "unbreakable inner connexion" of the kind that Geertz locates at the "heart" of the "religious perspective".

In this respect a comparison between Coetzee and the earlier "J.C" seems instructive. In *Heart of Darkness*, *Lord Jim* and *Nostromo*, Joseph Conrad constantly accentuates the rift between *mythos* and *ethos* – between "seeing from inside", in Geertz's sense, and "seeing from outside", in a helplessly or vigorously sceptical fashion. In the two earlier works Marlow, Conrad's narrator, will never surrender his concern to "live decently" – that is, his concern with conduct or *ethos* – although he becomes increasingly uncertain what to *believe*. Coetzee's references to "foundationalist fictions" looks in exactly the same two sharply opposed directions (the collapse of *mythos*, the subsequently more urgent need for *ethos* or some code of conduct) as Conrad's references to "saving" or "sustaining illusions" in *Heart of Darkness* and *Nostromo*. These two works also bear witness to a remarkable shift, from Conrad's concern with the hitherto dominant forms of British and European imperialism in *Heart of Darkness* to his astonishingly prescient concern, in *Nostromo*, with the new or emergent form of imperialism that was inaugurated by the Republican governments of Presidents McKinley and Roosevelt. In his correspondence, above all with Cunninghame Graham, Conrad was both unequivocally fierce and remarkably well-informed in his condemnations of what the "Yankee Conquistadores" were doing in the years that separated *Heart*

---

[19]   Clifford Geertz, *Islam Observed: Religious Development in Morocco and Indonesia* (Chicago: University of Chicago Press , 1971), 97.

of Darkness from *Nostromo*. Like "J.C." in Coetzee's *Diary*, Conrad had "Strong Opinions" that clearly directed the "shift" I have described, as he moved from Kurtz to Holroyd. And yet, when these passionately held and seemingly firm personal or political beliefs entered his fiction, they were never provided with some kind of special pass or exemption, to spare them from Conrad's anti-foundationalist scepticism about what the no less radically sceptical Coetzee calls "fundamental fictions" to which we "more or less wholeheartedly subscribe" because they "may well be indispensable for a just society". The undeniable political concerns cannot be detached from the epistemological troubles.

However, one striking difference between Conrad's situation and that of Coetzee is no less instructive and is discernible in the marked contrast between the first reviews of *Nostromo* (which made Conrad despair) and reviews of novels like *Waiting for the Barbarians* and *Foe*. Since *Nostromo* now appears so politically prescient, it seems all the more astonishing that (so far as I could discover) not one contemporary reviewer of *Nostromo* mentioned the topical relationship between what happens in the fictional state of Costaguana and what had been happening in Panama only months before Conrad completed his novel, when American warships were sent to secure the Panamanian revolution and the future of the Panama Canal. Like Tolstoy in the final book of *Anna Karenina*, Conrad had revised his novel's projected ending to keep pace with recent political events. Conrad even brought in his own American warship to guarantee the "independence" of his fictional state, and gave it the name of a real American warship that was by then out of service but had been used to protect US interests in Latin America for many years. The reviewers' political pococurantism was doubtless to some extent accidental: it was unfortunate that no editor wanting a review of *Nostromo* thought of asking Cunninghame Graham to review it, or J.A. Hobson, whose fascinating 1902 study of *Imperialism* also tracked the differences between the older, British and European forms of imperialism and the emergent, soon to be dominant and no less deadly US version. Still, there could be no sharper contrast with what happened when Coetzee's *Waiting for the Barbarians* appeared in 1980, and almost every South African reviewer was striving to relate that novel's fictional state to South Africa in some more or less allegorical fashion, as though novels only matter when they can be assimilated to or swallowed by some prevailing political discourse.[20]

When *Life & Times of Michael K* was published in 1983, Nadine Gordimer complained that "Coetzee's heroes are those who ignore history, not make it."[21] In 1986 the South African response to *Foe* was even more dismayed and sometimes acrimonious, as Michael Marais recalls:

[20]   Different difficulties are likely to confront non-South African readers who are in no position to reflect that the nameless magistrate's duties largely coincide with those of a South African magistrate, and may not even register the signs in *Disgrace* that Melanie is not a "white" student.
[21]   Nadine Gordimer, "The Idea of Gardening", *New York Review of Books* 2 (February 1984), 3–6 at pp. 3–4.

While the country was burning, quite literally in many places, the logic went, here was one of our most prominent authors writing about the writings of a somewhat pedestrian eighteenth-century English novelist. Nothing could have seemed further removed from the specificities and exigencies of life in the eighties in South Africa. Michael Chapman probably summed up the mood and sentiments of many South African readers and critics when he dismissed the novel in the following terms: "In our knowledge of the human suffering on our own doorstep of thousands of detainees who are denied recourse to the rule of law, *Foe* did not so much speak to Africa as provide a kind of masturbatory release, in this country, for the Europeanising dreams of an intellectual coterie".[22]

Fortunately, critics as diverse as Gayatri Spivak, Derek Attridge, and Benita Parry have shown how such criticisms missed the point of Coetzee's ethical rigour. In his unusually aggressive 1988 talk/essay on "The Novel Today" (which he has chosen never to reprint, although it could easily have been included in *Doubling the Point*), Coetzee himself protested against the powerful, "perhaps even dominant tendency, to subsume the novel under history, to read novels as what I will loosely call imaginative investigations of real historical forces and circumstances; and to treat novels that do not perform this investigation as lacking in seriousness". This "argument", Coetzee warned:

is only peripherally an argument about greater or lesser truth. It is an argument about supplementarity: in times of intense ideological pressure like the present, when the space in which the novel and history normally coexist, like two cows on the same pasture, each minding its own business, is squeezed almost to nothing, the novel has only two options: supplementarity or rivalry. It cannot be both autonomous and supplementary.[23]

Nevertheless the "argument" has continued since Coetzee left for Australia, and in a 2006 interview in Johannesburg Gordimer returned to the attack by complaining that "In the novel 'Disgrace' there is not one black person who is a real human being". She went on:

I find it difficult to believe, indeed more than difficult, having lived here all my life and being part of everything that has happened here, that the black family protects the rapist because he's one of them. If that's the only truth he could find in the post-apartheid South Africa, I regretted this very much for him."[24]

[22]   Michael Marais, "Death and the Space of the Response to the Other in J.M. Coetzee's *The Master of Petersburg*", in Poyner, *J.M. Coetzee and the Life of the Public Intellectual*, 83–99, at pp. 83–4.
[23]   J. M. Coetzee, "The Novel Today", *Upstream* 6.1 (1988): 2–5.
[24]   Reported in *The New York Times*, 16 December 2007.

This unpleasant charge about how Coetzee presents "one of them" rests on an all too "sedimented" set of assumptions about the conditions of being – to recall Marlow's beleaguered phrase in *Lord Jim* – "one of us".

Recall again Coetzee's austere comment on Elizabeth Curren: "There is no ethical imperative that I claim access to. Elizabeth is the one who believes in *believes in*." In *Henry IV, Part Two*, Shakespeare's play persistently suggests some relation between the state of Falstaff's diseased, decaying body and that of the State, or common weal, although such a thought never occurs to Falstaff. As Michael Neill observes in the present collection, Elizabeth Curren thinks of the cancerous swellings in her body as "physical symptoms of the shame aroused by her complicity in apartheid", with a metaphorical counterpart in "the morbid condition of the state itself".[25] In her desperate situation, any remaining advance must be heuristic or teleological, not a matter of being pressed forward from behind. When this teacher of classics and dying, disillusioned humanist discovers that she has given a false etymology for "caritas" or charity, she is not too troubled by her genealogical mistake: she is far more urgently concerned to discover what "taking care of" might mean – not in what Clarkson calls "etymological forays" but in what remains of her own life. As Clarkson notes, this concern with "caring" is very important to Paul Rayment in *Slow Man*, and becomes unexpectedly important to David Lurie in *Disgrace*. Ironically, and tragically, the very intensity of Mrs Curren's concern with *ethos* and the conditions of community makes her – like Coetzee's magistrate, Costello and "J.C." in the *Diary*, or like the other J.C.'s Marlow – an ever more isolated, lonely figure.

It should by now be clear why, when Michael Neill and I were planning this collection, we hoped that it might realign the South African Coetzee with the "late modernist" Coetzee, who has never abandoned or forgotten or ceased to care about that modernist, linguistic and epistemological battlefield where the Viennese Elizabethan Lord Chandos met his end. In this respect Coetzee has more in common with Kafka and Beckett, or contemporary Irish writers like Banville and Derek Mahon, or Polish writers like Zbigniew Herbert and Czeslaw Milosz, than with other South African novelists; *Inner Workings*, his latest collection of critical essays, begins with essays on Italo Svevo, Robert Walser, Robert Musil, Walter Benjamin, Bruno Schulz, Sandor Marai and Paul Celan.

Complicities and the Interplay of "Voices"

The "Strong Opinions" of Coetzee's three Elizabeths or EC's, and "John" or "J.C", the protagonist of *Diary of a Bad Year*, make them ready to rush in where Coetzee does not fear to tread, but treads more warily. This helps to explain the sad, finely calibrated shock when Coetzee went on to publish *Slow Man* in 2005, and for the first time included examples of Elizabeth Costello's fictional prose. The examples

---

[25]   Chapter 4, 98.

are not only and predictably "realistic" but tired or old-fashioned. Paul Rayment, the protagonist of *Slow Man*, is not impressed when he glances through Costello's award-winning *The House on Eccles Street* and *The Fiery Furnace*. He soon "snaps *The Fiery Furnace* shut": "He is not going to read any more of the colourless, odourless, inert and depressive gas given off by its pages" (120). Readers who agree with Paul are then immediately involved in an Escher-like puzzle, since Paul Rayment is not only a fictional character but the ostensible creation of the novelist Elizabeth Costello, who is also a fictional character in Coetzee's novel.

Since Paul never doubts that he had a prior life before Costello's novel begins, he can never suppose that his only "real" life begins on the unforgettable first page of her (or Coetzee's) novel, and he is sufficiently independent as a character to refuse to accept the plot or fictional space into which Costello wishes to plant him. After Costello's plottily contrived liaison between Paul and Marianna – between the "halt" and the "blind" – fails to work in fictional terms and becomes nothing more than a functionally satisfactory fiasco, or spilling of seed, Marianna disappears without ever being created as a convincing character, and Paul insists on finding his own way. As I suggest later in this volume, the idea of a fictional character going his own way might conceivably make sense in Bakhtinian or Dostoevskean terms, but the baffled Costello blames her character for being cold, slow and passionless. In this collection's two final essays Zoë Wicomb and Barbara Dancygier both incline more than I do to Costello's view of Paul and his limitations, but Wicomb also emphasizes that Costello herself is "not up to the job".[26] As one of the most powerful and impressive of later South African novelists, Wicomb's own sense of what the "job" involves leads her to propose an enthralling account of the ways in which the novelist's relation to the character can be (in a lived, not merely figural sense) "intersubjective".[27]

In this respect *Slow Man* looked forward to *Diary of a Bad Year*, but do these "Australian" novels modify or sharpen our sense of the novelist's relation to his character in the last and most fiercely controversial South African novel? Estate agents speak of "deceptively spacious" apartments, and *Disgrace* might at first seem deceptively simple. The chapters are short, each with a single focus that advances a linear storyline, so that it would be relatively easy to give the chapters titles – "Soraya", "Melanie" and so on. Yet the novel's difficulties and challenges appear as soon as we find ourselves trying to grasp the non-linear relations between its different constituents. What, for example, is the relation between Lurie's idea that what he did to Melanie was "not quite a rape" and his horror when his daughter is not only gang-raped but decides to keeps the baby and submits to Petrus's offer of protection (or else) by becoming one of his wives? And what is the relation between David's way of regarding his own selfish behaviour and his intellectual pursuits – his fascination with Romantic poetry, especially Byron, and his increasing commitment to the chamber opera that eventually "consumes him

---

[26] Chapter 11, 219.
[27] Ibid., 250.

night and day" (214), in which Byron is gradually effaced or displaced by the longings of a middle-aged, grieving and even Bev Shaw-like Teresa Guiccioli?

As Derek Attridge observes in this collection, the "experience of creation" becomes, for Lurie as for Coetzee's Dostoevsky in *The Master of Petersburg*, "one of a mysterious otherness making itself felt":

> Lurie, in particular, seems unaware of what the reader must surely be conscious of: that his developing narrative of the love between Byron and Teresa Guiccioli touches at many points on his own sexual history, and that his coming to terms with that history occurs in part through creative identification with the middle-aged, miserable heroine of his opera.[28]

So, in *Disgrace* as in *The Master of Petersburg*, "the connection between the aesthetic and the erotic is profound, if resistant to analysis: both forces take one unawares, as if touched by a god, and lead one into unknown territory, for good or ill".[29] Freud (who so notoriously argued that a woman never resists rape with her full strength) included this remarkable final footnote to the first of his *Three Contributions to a Theory of Sex*:

> The most pronounced difference between the sexual life [*Liebesleben*] of antiquity and ours lies in the fact that the ancients placed the emphasis on the impulse itself, while we put it on its object. The ancients extolled the impulse and were ready to ennoble through it even an inferior object, while we disparaged the activity of the impulse as such and only countenance it on account of the merits of the subject.[30]

It suits Lurie all too well to regard and even explain himself as a worshipper of Eros, like one of Freud's "ancients", although (as his secretary could confirm, after their one-night stand) he is incapable of, and even dislikes, passionate abandon. But is he also telling a truth, or at least being more truthful than he knows? Just as the very articulate Lurie is unaware of the sources of his creative impulse, he cannot articulate or explain, even to himself, whatever impulse prompts him to care for the dogs, even when they are dead dogs.

Critics and readers will go on arguing about Lucy's sense of having been complicit in the disgraces of South African history, or about Coetzee's real or alleged creative complicity with his protagonist. In the present collection Myrtle Hooper's essay is sharply critical of the novel, of its male author, and also of male critics like Attwell and Attridge who, she argues, follow Coetzee in taking a view

---

[28]   Chapter 1, 37.

[29]   Ibid., 37.

[30]   Siegmund Freud, *Three Contributions to the Theory of Sex*, in *The Basic Writings of Siegmund Freud*, translated and edited by A.A. Brill (New York: The Modern Library, 1938), 563.

of David Lurie that is "so hard to swallow".[31] Like many of this controversial novel's South African critics and reviewers, Hooper is primarily concerned with (what counts as) rape and with associated racial and gender issues in post-apartheid South Africa. Lars Engle's thoughtful comparison of *Disgrace* with Gordimer's *None to Accompany M* challenges us to approach these last issues from a very different perspective, while some of the objections that Hooper enters with such passion and force are directly addressed in David Attwell's discussion of what happened when *Disgrace* became a set text in South African high schools. Attwell's essay began as a public address and is concerned with what almost inevitably gets "left out" in schoolroom discussions, including the novel's "self-consciousness", "its inter-textuality" and "layered sense of history", the significance of its dealings with Romantic poets, the way in which "current students are positioned as uncritical consumers of globalized culture", and the novel's dwelling on death, in the course of developing its particular ethical consciousness" – "everything, in other words, that gives the novel its intelligence, once the obviously controversial issues have been stripped away".[32] Laurence Wright's suggestive and original essay then concentrates on the critical significance of some of the issues that are usually "left out"--on the novel's intertextual dealings with Kant and Schopenhauer and Goethe, as well as Byron and Wordsworth, and the increasing significance of music in the disgraced protagonist's life. Of course Hooper might well disagree with Attwell's suggestion that the "obviously controversial" issues can be "stripped away". This, one might say, goes with the territory, since the issues (including different "constructs" and "foundational fictions") are framed in ways that present no obvious solution that is not, arguably, part of the problem. As Wright slyly observes, his own essay might "come closest to being a discussion of some of the things the character David Lurie might want us to think about, were he in a position to know that we are engaged in reading *Disgrace*".[33]

Coetzee's most recent novel, *Diary of a Bad Year*, looks back to *Dusklands* and *Age of Iron* in its harrowing concern with historical "complicity", and is also concerned to explore the question of what might be called creative "complicity" if we suppose that the protagonist's viewpoint is privileged. The very layout of the new novel works against that supposition. Each page is divided into different voices or polyphonic parts, like a *partitur* or musical score that groups and then travels down from the woodwind, wind and percussion to the fiddles. To start at the top: Part One of the *Diary* is called "Strong Opinions", and the top part (which quite often means most) of each page presents one of the strong or opinionated essays that Bruno Geistler of Mittwoch Verlag GmbH has commissioned the award-winning "John" or "J.C." to write. Old men often deliver strong opinions too readily and cry too easily; John is all the more willing to accept the German commission because he feels so keenly "the dishonour, the disgrace of being alive

---

[31]   Chapter 6, 145.

[32]   Chapter 8, 163.

[33]   Chapter 7, 147.

in these times" (112–13), but also feels that he no longer has the "endurance" to write another novel.

Coetzee's new novel begins when John has recorded his first "Strong Opinion", on "The Origins of the State", and has also just had his "first glimpse of her" (1) – that is, of Anya, the wonderfully desirable and (as it turns out) intelligent Filipina who is young enough to be John's granddaughter but immediately compels his imagination, so that he pursues her and employs her as his secretary. This way of launching the novel might well recall the aged (but not so old) W.B. Yeats's response in the late poem "Politics" to Thomas Mann's suggestion that "In our time the destiny of man presents its meaning in political terms":

> How can I, that girl standing there,
> My attention fix
> On Roman or on Russian
> Or on Spanish politics?
> Yet here's a travelled man that knows
> What he talks about,
> And there's a politician
> That has read and thought,
> And maybe what they say is true
> Of war and war's alarms,
> But O that I were young again
> And held her in my arms!

John's responses to Anya and their developing relationship are then recorded in the diary entries that appear lower on each page of the novel, beneath the commissioned essays that Anya must prepare for the publisher. Once Anya enters John's life as his *segretaria* and "secret aria", her own thoughts and responses appear at the bottom of the score-like pages, which also record her changing impressions of the strong opinions of Alan, the confident and amoral investment advisor who is her lucky lover. A conventional sort of plot emerges when Alan has designs on John's savings, but this is far less gripping than what happens when the issue of complicity nearly destroys the relationship between John and Anya.

John's own "Strong Opinions", on matters ranging from terrorism and paedophilia to Christian liars like Bush and Blair, are indeed so forceful (like Costello's) that reviewers who identify "John" with Coetzee have already become incensed – for example, by John's views of "terrorism". Not only does John protest that, although "dropping bombs from high altitude upon a sleeping village is no less an act of terror than blowing oneself up in a crowd, it is perfectly legal to speak well of aerial bombing ('Shock and Awe')", he goes on to ask,

> Whose heart is so hardened as to feel no sympathy at all for the man who, his family having been killed in an Israeli strike, straps on the bomb-belt in full knowledge that there is no paradise of houris waiting for him, and in grief and

rage goes out to destroy as many of the killers as he can? No other way than death is a marker and perhaps even a definition of the tragic. (21)

John's invocation of a "sleeping village" movingly conveys the innocence of the victims, and the murderous inadequacy of all those stipulative definitions of "terrorism" in which the crucial stipulation is always left out: for instance, those who promote the "war on terror" never say that a "terrorist" is *any non-American or non-Israeli* who kills and maims innocent civilians in pursuit of a political objective. But are "we" as innocent? The question of complicity enters once again if it is argued that in a democracy we are all responsible for whatever "our" elected leaders do over our names, even if we did not vote for them or were too young to vote, like many of the victims in the "sleeping village". The very first of John's essays argues that "From the moment of our birth we are subject":

> What the Hobbesian myth of origins does not mention is that the handover of power to the state is irreversible. The option is not open to us to change our minds, to decide that the monopoly on the exercise of force held by the state, codified by the law, is not what we wanted after all, that we would prefer to go back to a state of nature. (2–3)

For John, "We are born subject" (1), but we are also complicit.

John's position then resembles that described by Albert Memmi when he writes of "the colonizer who refuses":

> He may openly protest, or sign a petition, or join a group hostile towards the colonizers. This already suffices for him to recognize that he has simply changed difficulties and discomfort. It is not easy to escape mentally from a concrete situation, to refuse its ideology while continuing to live within its actual relationships. From now on, he lives his life under the sign of a contradiction which looms at every step, depriving him of all coherence and tranquillity.[34]

As Memmi also observes, somewhat gloatingly, "Colonial relations do not stem from individual good will or actions; they exist before his arrival or birth, and whether he accepts them or rejects them matters little", since the "colonizer who refuses" is still "part of the oppressing group and will be forced to share its destiny, as he shared its good fortune":

> No matter how he may reassure himself, 'I have always been this way or that with the colonized', he suspects, even if he is in no way guilty as an individual, that he shares a collective responsibility by the fact of membership in an oppressor group (38–39).

---

[34]   Albert Memmi, *The Colonizer and the Colonized* (London: Souvenir Press, 1974), 20.

Thinking like Memmi rather than Mandela, John agonizes over his own sense of complicity, even when he is writing, in his essay "On Zeno", that "the order we see in the universe may not reside in the universe at all, but in the paradigms of thought we bring to it" (79). In an earlier essay, "On National Shame", he asks:

> Is dishonour a state of being that comes in shades and degrees? If there is a state of deep dishonour, is there a state of mild dishonour too, dishonour lite? The temptation is to say no: if one is in dishonour one is in dishonour. Yet if I heard today that some American had committed suicide rather than live in disgrace, I would fully understand; whereas an Australian who committed suicide in response to the actions of the Howard government would risk seeming comical. (39)

But then, in the very next paragraph, John writes that

> The generation of white South Africans to which I belong, and the next generation, and perhaps the generation after that too, will go bowed under the shame of the crimes that were committed in their name. (39)

Strong opinions often emerge from a parley of different, conflicting or more doubtful views or inner voices, and John himself has different voices. Later, when Anya questions some of his "Strong Opinions", he warns her that they "do not necessarily come from my inmost depths". She then repeats softly, "Dishonour descends upon one's shoulders", and he (not she) reflects, "That sounds like the inmost depths to me": "I sat shaken, speechless" (73–74). Anya asks, "What are you going to do about your kind of shame?" and John replies, "I have no idea":

> I was going to say (I said) that when you live in shameful times shame descends upon everyone, and you simply have to bear it, it is your lot and your punishment. Am I wrong? Enlighten me. (79)

At the bottom of this same page Anya is arguing with Alan, who insists that John cannot understand the "managerial state" and "can't think structurally", because "he can't get away from Africa": "That is where he came from, that is where he is stuck, mentally." This complicating counterpoint continues when Anya, who evidently finds John's notion of complicity too metaphysical but would like to relieve his real distress, tells him a story – while her lover is sneering in the paginal basement that for John everything is a "morality play", "good versus evil": "What he fails to see or refuses to see is that individuals are players in a structure that transcends individual motives, transcends good and evil" (80).

"It may help, it may not", Anya says, before telling John how she and a girlfriend were raped by three "American college boys" who "had invited us to come and have a look at their boat":

They seemed nice, so what the hell, we went with them. Then they said, How about we go for a sail? Well, they took us for a sail, and I won't go into the details but there were three of them and two of us, and they must have decided that we were just a couple of bimbos, a couple of *putas*, whereas they were sons of doctors and lawyers and what have you, they were taking us cruising on the Caribbean, so we owed them, so they could do what they liked with us. Three of them. Three strapping young males.

We didn't return to port all that day. The second day out at sea my girlfriend broke down and tried to jump overboard, and that gave them a fright, so they put in at some little fishing village down the coast and dumped us there. The end of one little adventure, they thought, now let's go look for another one.

But they were wrong. It wasn't the end. We got back to Cancún and we laid charges with the police, we had all the names, all the particulars, and they issued a warrant and those boys were arrested at the next port where they stopped and their yacht was impounded and the story hit the papers back in Connecticut or wherever and they were in deep shit.

So why am I telling you this story? Because when we went to the police, the *jefe*, the police captain, a very nice man, very sympathetic, said to us, You are sure you want to do this (meaning, are you sure you want this story to get out), because, you know, dishonour, *infamia*, is like bubble gum, wherever it touches, it sticks.

You know what I said? I said, This is the twentieth century, *capitano* (it was still the twentieth century then). In the twentieth century, when a man rapes a woman it is the man's dishonour. The dishonour sticks to the man, not to the woman. At least that is how it is where I come from …

… When you tell me you walk around bent under your load of dishonour, I think of those girls from the old days who had the bad luck to get raped and then had to wear black for the rest of their lives – wear black and sit in a corner and never go to parties and never get married. You have got it wrong, Mister C. Old thinking. Wrong analysis, as Alan would say. Abuse, rape, torture, it doesn't matter what: the news is, as long as it isn't your fault, as long as you are not responsible, the dishonour doesn't stick to you. So you have been making yourself miserable over nothing. (80–88)

When Anya finishes her story in the central stream of text on page 88, she is arguing with Alan again at the bottom of the same page, about John's essay "On Probability", which had appeared at the top of pages 80–85. Alan too is declaring that John is "a hundred years out of date": "We live in a probabilistic universe, a quantum universe. Schrödinger proved it. Heisenberg proved it." "And before the quantum universe?", the irrepressible Anya asks: "Before a hundred years ago? Did we live in another kind of universe?"

John's essay "On Apology" appears at the top of those pages in which he records his jarringly insensitive response to Anya's story. He insists that "dishonour" cannot be "washed away" or "wished away" and still "has its old power to stick", and even tells Anya that he feels complicit with the rapists: "Your three American boys – I have never laid eyes on them, but they dishonour me nevertheless." Worse, he suggests that she must or should feel some kind of shame that she is refusing to acknowledge: "And I would be very surprised if in your inmost depths they did not continue to dishonour you" (90–91). Before she leaves the apartment the hurt, furious Anya hisses at him, "Don't you tell me how I feel!" In the morning John finds the latest computer disc in his letterbox together with a note "in her plump, rather schoolgirlish hand": "This is the last typing I can do for you. I cannot stand your undermining of me. A."

John's sense of complicity has become so much a part of his "inmost being" that we can readily understand when he reacts angrily to what he sees as Anya's challenge – which issues from her own no less deeply felt sense that she belongs to herself and will not accept responsibility for something that herself did not do, for something done by others to others, or done by others to her. She cannot understand why she should feel guilt, or shame, when she was a victim not an agent, or why John insists that the next two – rather than just one or three – generations of white South Africans must be bowed by an historical burden of shame. This terrible clash, in which each of these good people is "undermining" so much more than the other's "strong opinion", nearly brings their relationship to an end – but who is right, or wrong?

The novel does not answer that question. Instead, the interplay of voices frames questions about how far "complicity" is historically and morally inescapable. For Anya, the notion of complicity remains unreal or metaphysical; for John, as for Elizabeth Curren and (eventually) the magistrate in *Waiting for the Barbarians*, it is inescapably real. It is right *for* John, though not necessarily right *of* him, to feel and take on that terrible burden. The right *for*/right *of* distinction flies against the orthodox argument that moral judgments are universalizable. But would it be right for, let alone right of, Anya *or us* to feel complicity with what morally dysfunctional politicians like John Howard, Bush or Blair do over our names – and could it be right in any sense for Anya to feel that being raped dishonoured *her*? John's answer to both of these questions, according to his "Strong Opinions", is Yes: Australians and the British and especially Americans should all feel as dishonoured as South Africans. In her quarrels with Alan as well as John, the relatively uneducated but intelligent Anya holds out a different, pragmatic possibility: the wrongs that we can change we should fight to change, but each of us has only one life and should learn to live with wrongs that cannot be changed, for the sake of those we love as well as our own sake. In its staging of these alternatives *Diary of a Bad Year* is as dialogical as any novel by Dostoevsky – and no less "great-souled", without the extra pan-slavic-messianist baggage. In Coetzee's novel, Anya's voice and "world-view" are accorded no less life, cogency and respect than John's "Strong" but frequently self-contradictory "Opinions", just as Shakespeare frames the issue of "honour" by keeping faith with the beliefs of a Hal, Falstaff and Hotspur.

When John adds a longer "PS" to his message begging Anya to return, *Diary of a Bad Year* takes another very subtle and moving turn – since John is so clearly dying, like Elizabeth Curren, and feels ever more pressed to distinguish real from fancied needs. It is typical of this novel's extraordinary way of taking the reader by surprise that the "*PS*" only appears on page 119, when the original message or appeal had appeared to finish on page 98. The original message had been brief and to the point:

> Dear Anya,
>
> You have become indispensable to me – to me and the present project. I cannot imagine handing over the manuscript to someone else. It would be like taking a child away from its natural mother and putting it in a stranger's care. I urge you, please reconsider.
>
> Yours,
>
> J.C.

The "PS" doesn't "urge", it begs and woos:

> Some news. I am beginning to put together a second, gentler set of opinions. I will be happy to show them to you if that will persuade you to return. Some of them take up suggestions that you let drop. A gentle opinion on birds, for example. A gentle opinion on love, or at least on kissing between a gentleman and a lady. Can I induce you to take a look?

In the intervening pages John has not changed his "Strong Opinions": instead, he observes, "What has begun to change since I moved into the orbit of Anya is not my opinions themselves so much as my opinion of my opinions" (106). He thinks he "should have heard her out on the subject of honour, let her have the rhetorical victory she was after" (109); he could "go upstairs" and say, "*You are right, I concede, honour has lost its power, dishonour is dead, now come back to me*" (110). Then he thinks, "I should thoroughly revise my opinions, that is what I should do" (117) – and then writes the "PS". The essays he goes on to write, including the two final essays in "Strong Opinions" as well as the 24 "gentle" essays in "2. Second Diary", abound in references to the "soul" and thoughts of the last things, that are refracted through essays "On The Erotic Life" and "On Ageing" ("All old folk become Cartesians": 147), as well as essays "On the Mother Tongue" and "On J. S. Bach" as "the best proof we have that life is good" (173).

D.H. Lawrence's idea of the novel as a "thought-adventure" is appropriate in this case, but answers no less well to the other novels in which issues are framed by the collisions between different voices and sometimes, as with the barbarian woman, Friday and even Melanie, different silences. In the *Diary* the games with names become especially provoking but always work to undercut, not underscore, any notion of authorial authority. This is all the more remarkable if, as seems very likely, Coetzee's own view of "complicity" is closer to John's than to Anya's, whose opposed views are so convincingly recorded in her youthful voice. Instead of asking what Coetzee thinks, or expecting one character's voice to be privileged, we might locate a thinking process at work within the interplay of different voices. For some readers, Coetzee's austere recoiling from more clubbable commitments may seem glacially withdrawn; others may reflect that Coetzee, like the modernist writers Peter Heller discusses so well in *Dialectics and Nihilism*, presents a thesis and antithesis with no possibility of synthesis; others may think, as I myself have been suggesting, that Coetzee is observing and accentuating the rupture between *mythos* and *ethos* even as he refuses, against all the odds, to surrender his passionate concern with human responsibility.

Chapter 1
Coetzee's Artists; Coetzee's Art

Derek Attridge

So this is art, he thinks, and this is how it does its work! How strange! How
fascinating!

(Coetzee, Disgrace, 185)

Although the question of art's functions and responsibilities was at the centre of
much debate during the apartheid years in South Africa, representations of artists
are rare in the country's fiction from this period. If characters with an artistic
career are depicted, they are less likely to be painters or poets than journalists (like
the would-be writer Mouse and her associates in Bessie Head's *The Cardinals*
(1995, but written 1960–62) or photographers (like the hero of Mandla Langa's
Tenderness of Blood (1987), committed to reflecting as directly as possible the
injustices around them. One gets the strong sense that the lives and works of artists
were not of commanding interest, and that the natural tendency for the writer to be
concerned with his or her own profession, or its analogues in the other arts, was for
the most part suppressed. There were, of course, exceptions, the most consistent
probably being André Brink, who as a novelist and as a critic has, throughout his
prolific career, been fascinated by the social and individual significance of story-
telling. *States of Emergency* (1988) asks whether a love story can be responsibly
written in a time of political crisis; *The First Life of Adamastor* (1993; Afrikaans
version 1988) and *On the Contrary* (1993) continue this concern with the power
of narrative in both its mythic and its literary forms. After the end of apartheid,
Brink remained interested in the ways in which stories can both obscure and
reveal the past – a topic given new urgency by the uncoverings of the Truth and
Reconciliation Commission – as evidenced by *Imaginings of Sand* (1996), *Devil's
Valley* (1998), *The Other Side of Silence* (2002) and *Before I Forget* (2004). There
is an early example of a novel with a painter at the centre, Nadine Gordimer's
Occasion for Loving (1963), but not much is made of the fact that Gideon Shibalo
is an artist other than the somewhat unusual lifestyle it allows him to adopt and
the added interest it gives him as a character and an object of sexual passion. Zoë
Wicomb's *You Can't Get Lost in Cape Town* (1987) presents episodes in the life of
a girl, then young woman, who by the end of the book has become a writer – the
writer, it seems, of the earlier stories in the collection – but we learn little about
this decision or what it entails beyond its impact on her immediate family.

Performers probably figure in fiction of this period more prominently than
those who write, paint, sculpt or compose, especially when their lives are entwined

with those of the community – examples would be the troupe of actors in Brink's *Looking on Darkness* (1974) and Njabulo Ndebele's descriptions of the ne'er-do-well Lovington's trumpet-playing in his story "Uncle". Interestingly, Ndebele includes a brief vignette of a visual artist in the story as well: "brother Mandla" draws Lovington in the act of playing, and the boy narrator, accustomed only to realistic representation, is surprised to see the distorted image he produces. But the collection in which "Uncle" appeared – *Fools and Other Stories* – was itself an exception in 1983, especially for a black writer: it turned away from scenes of racial conflict and political struggle to examine some of the trials and triumphs of daily township life. (And of course Ndebele himself argued influentially for a fiction of the ordinary.)[1]

Since the democratic elections of 1994, however, there has been a noticeable increase in depictions of artists, as if the lifting of the burden of apartheid and the obligation to deal with its daily ravages allowed writers greater freedom to turn, self-reflexively, to the production and purpose of art as issues worth pursuing in fiction. The result has not always been a happy one; Athol Fugard, for instance, who created some of the finest plays of the apartheid era, notably in collaboration with the Serpent Players, turned to sentimental rewritings of his own life as an author in *Valley Song* (1996), *The Captain's Tiger* (1999), and *Sorrows and Rejoicings* (2002).

But other writers have been more inventive. In Zakes Mda's *Ways of Dying* (1995), the hero, Toloki, is not just a performer, offering his services as "Professional Mourner", but a visual artist as well, winning a national art competition as a boy and helping to make the shack he builds with Noria, his childhood acquaintance, a colourful collage that would be "at home in any museum of modern art"[2] – the shack that they then cover with beguiling images from *Home and Garden* magazines. But the role of art in this novel is not only to provide pleasure and solace in the midst of suffering; in Toloki's father, Jwala the blacksmith, Mda gives us a less comprehensible and comforting image of the artist – a man whose iron figurines surprise even the creator himself and baffle those who see them. The ending of the novel leaves the significance and fate of these puzzling works of art, now bequeathed to Toloki, challengingly uncertain: they may be sold to an art dealer for a significant sum or kept to entertain local children. In *The Madonna of Excelsior* (2002), Mda again makes visual art a significant presence, mediating his narrative of the Free State village Excelsior from apartheid to democracy through descriptions of actual paintings by the Belgian-South African artist Frans Claerhout, and making visits to Claerhout's studio an important part of the fictional life-story of the central characters Niki and Popi. Another fine writer who has turned his

---

[1]   See Njabulo Ndebele, *South African Literature and Culture: Rediscovery of the Ordinary*, intro. Graham Pechey (Manchester: Manchester University Press, 1994), especially "Turkish Tales and Some Thoughts on South African Fiction" and "The Rediscovery of the Ordinary".

[2]   Zakes Mda, *Ways of Dying* (Cape Town: Oxford University Press, 1995), 67.

attention to the production and consumption of art in post-apartheid South Africa is Ivan Vladislavić. In one of the four stories that make up *The Exploded View* (2004), 'Curiouser', Vladislavić depicts a successful visual artist, Simeon Majara, who is caught in the compromising toils of the art market in a way that would have been highly unlikely – for a black artist – during the apartheid years. Vladislavić's sardonic representation of the changed relation between art and politics reveals the newly complex context in which the artist has to work, now that the old simple binaries have disappeared.

Other indications of this turn in post-apartheid South African fiction would include the artists in two novels originally published in Afrikaans: Etienne van Heerden's solitary sculptor Jonty Jack Bergh in *The Long Silence of Mario Salviati* (2002; first published as *Die Swye van Mario Salviati*, 2000), who is visited by a gallery curator anxious to purchase a mysterious piece called "The Staggering Merman" for her "rainbow" collection of contemporary South African art; and, in a very different key, Marlene van Niekerk's epileptic Lambert Benade in *Triomf* (1994), who dedicates hours to painting and repainting an epic mural representing South Africa overlaid with many of his private demons. The figure of the writer comes to the fore in Zoë Wicomb's complex novel *David's Story* (2000), one of the most important post-apartheid novels, in which the narrator faces the task of piecing together – and elaborating on – the fragmentary details of an acquaintance's experiences as a member of the ANC during the guerrilla campaign and then in the transitional period.

The most striking example of this shift is in J.M. Coetzee's oeuvre, although it would be difficult in his case to ascribe it to an instrumental view of art challenged by the ending of apartheid. It is not surprising that Coetzee – one of the finest critics of South African literature in English and Afrikaans – should have raised in his fiction the question of the writer's function and authority at a time when most other novelists in the country were concerned with questions of political and military power and resistance to it. I'm thinking in particular of *Foe* (1987), which goes back to the beginnings of the English novel to explore the processes whereby certain narratives become canonized while others fail to gain a foothold. But the eponymous writer in that novel, better known as Daniel Defoe, is an inscrutable figure we see from the outside; the novel's focus is on Susan Barton's attempt to gain access to the authority of authorship rather than on the author himself, and the writing for which he is known is understood as true reporting rather than fiction. Barton, too, is concerned with truth, not fiction, though one could certainly see her as an artist in spite of herself.[3] It is not until the year of the first democratic elections themselves, 1994, that Coetzee publishes a novel – his seventh – that

---

[3]   Patrick Hayes, in "'An Author I Have Not Read': Coetzee's *Foe*, Dostoevsky's *Crime and Punishment*, and the Problem of the Novel", *Review of English Studies* 57 (2006): 273–90, argues that she represents the values and assumptions of the novel genre (see esp. 282–5).

gives us the immediately present consciousness of a professional writer, and no less a writer than Fyodor Dostoevsky, the "master" of *The Master of Petersburg*.

Whether or not it has anything to do with the ending of apartheid, from then on the figure of the artist is never far away from Coetzee's most important writing. The two memoirs, *Boyhood* (1997) and *Youth* (2002), track, with a certain degree of licence, the early years of the writer himself, and thus cannot escape being read as studies of the artist in embryo. In the former, it is only at the very end of the work that the possibility of a writer's vocation announces itself; in the latter, gleams of a future as a writer of fiction shine through the dismal tale of John's futile efforts as a poet. *Disgrace* (1999) follows the fortunes of a teacher of literature whose creative energies are devoted no longer to criticism but to an opera. In the lectures of *The Lives of Animals* (1999) and the book within which they were later incorporated, *Elizabeth Costello* (2003), we find Coetzee foregrounding – like Fugard and Brink – the successful but now aging writer, and in the latter work the question of art's role is raised in several different ways. Two short fictions, the Nobel Lecture "He and His Man" (2003) and "As a Woman Grows Older" (2004) continue this probing of the artist's life, and *Slow Man* (2005) explores at length the relationship between a writer (Elizabeth Costello once more) and the character she is creating. Most recently, *Diary of a Bad Year* (2007) features an elderly writer who has engaged on a series of opinion pieces as he feels he no longer has the strength to write a novel (54).

Of course Coetzee, more than most writers we label "South African", is entirely at home in the tradition of the European novel, and it is here, rather than in previous South African writing, that his predecessors in the fictional representation of artists are to be found – not so much in the conventional *Künstlerroman*, with its pattern of growing maturity and final creative triumph, but some of the darker accounts of what it means to be an artist. The most obvious example is Thomas Mann's exploration of the cost of creative achievement in *Doctor Faustus* and *Death in Venice*; while Coetzee's interest in the faltering steps of the young artist bear a clear relation to the ironies of Joyce's *Portrait of the Artist as a Young Man*. A more oblique heritage can be traced from James, Kafka, Woolf, Proust, Nabokov, and many others.

*   *   *

How, then, does Coetzee represent the practice of art, in terms both of its coming-into-being and of its role in the world once it is produced, in his post-apartheid fictions and what we might call his semi-fictions?

Let us begin with thirteen-year-old John in *Boyhood*, enquiring of his mother after the death of his great-aunt Annie, "What has happened to Aunt Annie's

books?"[4] The books in question are the multiple unsold copies of her father's –
John's great-grandfather's – pious autobiography *Ewige Genesing* ("eternal
healing") that weigh down the shelves in her storeroom. He receives no answer,
and can only ask: "How will he keep them all in his head, all the books, all the
people, all the stories? And if he does not remember them, who will?" The memoir
ends with these questions, with this first inkling that authorship is not something
you choose but something that makes demands on you – understood by young John
as the obligation to preserve and memorialize. It is not so much a door opening on
an enticing prospect as a heavy responsibility which cannot be shared.

The sequel *Youth* opens with John now aged nineteen, living a life of willed
austerity as he completes his university studies. We quickly learn that the early
intimation of an artistic vocation evident in the first memoir has blossomed into a
whole-hearted commitment, but the irony in Coetzee's use of hackneyed Romantic
rhetoric – though not evident to his young protagonist – cannot be mistaken by the
reader:

> For he will be an artist, that has long been settled. If for the time being he must be
> obscure and ridiculous, that is because it is the lot of the artist to suffer obscurity
> and ridicule until the day when he is revealed in his true powers and the scoffers
> and mockers fall silent.[5]

In place of a somewhat unwilling response to an obscure demand, John's
commitment is now all too deliberate. The caustic irony at his expense persists to
the end of the book, lightened only by our knowledge that this John is – to some
not quite verifiable degree – also the John who is writing the work we are reading,
the internationally lauded novelist whose understanding of the artist's calling is far
removed from the naive romanticism assumed by his earlier self.

The conception of the artist that dominates *Youth*, then, is not one we are
invited to endorse. Take, for instance, John's belief, frequently reiterated, that for
the male artist a key to creative release is a sexual connection with a woman (or
sexual connections with a number of women). One of the many hilarious moments
that arise from this conviction is his invocation of Picasso: "Out of the passion that
flares up anew with each new mistress, the Doras and Pilars whom chance brings
to his doorstep are reborn into everlasting art. That is how it is done" (11). But
there are bleak consequences as well, since all the sexual relationships he embarks
on are failures, and his notion that they serve the greater good of his art turns out
to be a poor excuse for cowardice and selfishness.

Another belief that is made fun of is that huge tracts of the literary tradition
can be ignored as worthless on the say-so of admired writers – in this case, Eliot
and Pound:

---

[4]   J.M. Coetzee, *Boyhood: Scenes from Provincial Life* (New York: Viking, 1997),
166.
[5]   J.M. Coetzee, *Youth* (London: Secker & Warburg, 2002), 3.

On their authority he dismisses without a glance shelf after shelf of Scott, Dickens,
Thackeray, Trollope, Meredith. Nor is anything that came out of nineteenth-
century Germany or Italy or Spain or Scandinavia worthy of attention. Russia
may have produced some interesting monsters but as artists the Russians have
nothing to teach. (25)

Given the importance of Dostoevsky to the mature Coetzee, the last sentence in
particular is brims with irony. Something else that John feels he has to dismiss
is his own background: his attempts to write prose founder on his discovery
that prose requires a specific setting, and the only one with which he is familiar
enough is South Africa (62–3). This is a repeated pattern: again and again, we
find John rejecting what will become important for J.M. Coetzee – he even tries
reading Dutch poetry, and writes it off as worthless: but more than forty years
later Coetzee will publish *Landscape with Rowers*, his translations of a selection
of Dutch poems.[6]

However, towards the end of the book a different understanding of the literary
artist's task is hinted at. Bored with work on his MA thesis on Ford Madox
Ford in the British Library Reading Room, John "allows himself the luxury of
dipping into books about the South Africa of the old days" (136–7). The word
"luxury" is surprising, for this activity goes against all he has been telling himself
about his vocation; but he is "captivated by stories of ventures into the interior,
reconnaissances by ox-wagon into the desert of the Great Karoo, where a traveller
could trek for days on end without clapping eyes on a living soul" (137). And as a
result, he imagines himself writing a fictional account of such a journey that would
be so convincing it would be taken as a true report. This is another false starting
point, naively assuming that fiction aspires to the condition of historiography, but
it is one that will lead eventually to the second novella of Coetzee's *Dusklands*,
in which he will use historical sources to convey something of the reality of the
early exploration of South Africa. The dream of fiction that can be passed off
as historical truth, however, will itself become one of the notions staged and
undermined in that work.

There is a second epiphanic moment in *Youth*, in which John chances upon a
work that will – we know from Coetzee's later career – serve as a more fruitful
source than the limited pantheon decreed by Pound and Eliot, and will complicate
the newly found attachment to realism. Attracted by the Olympia Press binding,
John buys a copy of Beckett's *Watt* from a second-hand bookseller. "From the
first page he knows he has hit on something. Propped up in bed with light pouring
through the window, he reads and reads ... When he comes to the end he starts

---

[6]   J.M. Coetzee, *Landscape with Rowers: Poetry from the Netherlands* (Princeton:
Princeton University Press, 2004). Some of these translations were first published a good
deal earlier; see *Doubling the Point: J.M. Coetzee, Essays and Interviews*, ed. David Attwell
(Cambridge: Harvard University Press, 1992), 400.

again at the beginning" (155).[7] What links these two moments is that they happen unexpectedly, arriving athwart the calculated route he has set himself. Nothing comes of them within the pages of *Youth*, however. The memoir ends with John regretting that he can no longer write poetry (though he programmes a computer to do it for him),[8] and he still associates his artistic failure with his failure as a lover.[9] Coetzee is determined to leave his earlier self still trudging along on a false path.

We may turn for further representations of the artist to the hybrid work published the year after *Youth*, *Elizabeth Costello*, much of which consists of lectures given in a fictional setting. Here we find another figure of the writer, an Australian novelist, this time near the end rather than at the beginning of a life. A passage in the later work establishes a connection with the earlier one by hinting at a period in North London that is reminiscent of John's unhappy sojourn there:[10]

> "*This woman*," her son imagines himself saying, "*is the same woman who, forty years ago, hid day after day in her bedsitter in Hampstead, crying to herself, crawling out in the evenings into the foggy streets to buy the fish and chips on which she lived, falling asleep in her clothes.*"[11]

There is no simple identification of Costello with Coetzee, however, notwithstanding the shared letters in their names. Whereas the events of John's life in *Boyhood* and *Youth* bear a strong resemblance to those of Coetzee's life, insofar as they can be verified, there is not much in the specifics of Elizabeth Costello's past or present that matches those of her creator. In general terms there are, of course, similarities: a colonial background, literary success, prizes, vegetarianism, invitations to give talks, a novel written as a feminist counterpart to an English classic (in Coetzee's case *Foe*, in Costello's case Joyce's *Ulysses*), and a style and set of concerns that have clear affinities. But in discussing Costello as a representation of the artist one must not make the mistake of taking her to be Coetzee's model or self-image; the distance between the two writers is as

---

[7] I have discussed some of the implications of this moment in "Sex, Comedy and Influence: Coetzee's Beckett", in Elleke Boehmer, Robert Eaglestone and Katy Iddiols, eds, *J.M. Coetzee in Context and Theory* (London: Continuum, 2009), 71–90.

[8] Coetzee's own effort was published as "A Computer Poem," *The Lion and the Impala* (Dramatic Society of the University of Cape Town) 2.1 (1963): 12–13.

[9] In an interview in *Doubling the Point* we find him recalling this period: "As I remember those days, it was with a continual feeling of self-betrayal that I did not write. Was it paralysis? Paralysis is not quite the word. It was more like nausea: the nausea of facing the empty page, the nausea of writing without conviction, without desire" (19).

[10] In fact, the lecture "What is Realism?" was first given in 1996, so *Youth* may be a later development of this passage; see Derek Attridge, *J.M. Coetzee and the Ethics of Reading: Literature in the Event* (Chicago: University of Chicago Press, 2004), 194.

[11] J.M. Coetzee, *Elizabeth Costello: Eight Lessons* (London: Secker & Warburg, 2003), 30.

important as the similarities.[12] Costello does, however, pose in moving terms some of the central problems and predicaments that are likely to beset a writer such as Coetzee in the early twenty-first century.

The question of the relation between a fictional account of an artist's life and autobiography is raised, in fact, early in *Elizabeth Costello*: a radio interviewer puts it to Costello in the following form: "'Your most recent novel, ... called *Fire and Ice*, set in the Australia of the 1930s, is the story of a young man struggling to make his way as a painter against the opposition of family and society. Did you have anyone in particular in mind when you wrote it? Does it draw upon your own early life?'" (11–12). And Costello replies, "No, *Fire and Ice* isn't autobiography. I made it up" (12). Coetzee here seems to be both inviting the reader to make the connection *and* problematizing it. In any case, she has already conceded in the same response that "we draw upon our own lives all the time – they are our main resource, in a sense our only resource", and this is perhaps a more reliable guide to the relation between Coetzee's representations of artists and his own artistic practices.

In the opening lesson, "Realism", from which I have been quoting, the Costello we see is far from the confident author revelling in the abundant evidence of her success. Her prize lecture is on the loss of faith in representation (the faith that young John acquired in the British Library), and in it she confesses that she is "less than certain" about herself, and predicts a time when her books will be forgotten. Thirteen-year old John's sense of authorship in *Boyhood* is recalled when she remarks that "there must be some limit to the burden of remembering that we impose on our children and grandchildren" (20). It is left to her son to voice a different view of her: he feels that he does not know the truth of his mother as artist, but he worships her as "a mouthpiece for the divine" – not, he adds in a puncturing of the conventional image typical of Coetzee, in "the Greco-Roman mould", but rather like a Tibetan or Indian god, "incarnated in a child, wheeled from village to village to be applauded, venerated" (31). A later chapter, "The Problem of Evil", provides a counterpart: if the artist can be touched by a god, he or she can also be brushed by the leathery wing of the devil (167–8) – at least that is what Costello, with characteristic hesitancy and self-questioning, feels is necessary to explain the horribly vivid evocation of evil in the novelist Paul West's description of the execution of the Stauffenberg plotters. Another kind of counterpart is provided by the alternative view of the divine offered by Costello's sister Blanche: the suffering Christ in "The Humanities in Africa", represented in the repetitive crucifixes of the Zulu woodcarver Joseph. The only kind of artist this god recognizes is the one whose work is devoted entirely to depicting his anguish: not an artistic career one can imagine either Costello or her author embracing, yet one that Coetzee has made intensely present as if to clarify the implications of choosing the other path.

---

[12]   We might note that her son, who in some ways offers a counter-image, is, like her author, called John.

In the final section of this fifth lesson, Costello herself speaks of worship, with some ambiguity as to its object. She is imagining a scene in Correggio's studio, as he shows his model how to lift her nipple with her fingertips for his painting of the Virgin and Child; all the men in the room are not only erotically aroused but also "worship the mystery that is manifested to them: from the body of the woman, life flowing in a stream" (150). It seems that it is the beauty of the female breast that is being worshipped, and the analogy Costello is drawing is with her own act of exposing her breasts to a dying man; yet when she goes on, "Mary blessed among women smiles her remote angelic smile and tips her sweet pink nipple up before our gaze" we seem to be in the presence of the painting, not the model. Here is a different conception of the aesthetic, in which it is inseparable not only from the divine but also from the erotic, as if the youthful John was not entirely wrong in associating art and sex. A similar association occurs in the lessons "The Novel in Africa", which ends with Costello's memory of three nights spent with a Nigerian writer, and "Eros", which begins with her attraction to the poet Robert Duncan.

The fullest exploration of the artist's vocation occurs in the final lesson, "At the Gate", a Kafkaesque – Costello's own adjective – account of the writer's entry into the afterlife, or into a kind of limbo or purgatory. Pressed to state her beliefs in order to be admitted through the gate, Costello first argues that as a writer she cannot afford beliefs, and that her role is to act as "secretary of the invisible" (a phrase she takes from Miłosz), using only her heart to guide her. "That is my calling: dictation secretary. It is not for me to interrogate, to judge what is given me. I merely write down the words and then test them, test their soundness, to make sure I have heard right" (199). When this proves insufficient to satisfy her judges, she describes to them the life-cycle of the mud frogs of the Dulgannon River in Australia. "What do I believe? I believe in those little frogs" (217).

Neither of these attempts to describe the operation of art carries full conviction; Costello is aware as she speaks of their inadequacy. Once again, she seems baffled by what she has committed her entire life to. One thing that emerges strongly from Coetzee's exploration of art is that we cannot expect artists to be able to justify what they do. (His own reluctance to comment on his work is well-known.) The nearest Costello comes to an account of the sources of art is in the further description of the process of "testing the soundness" of the words that come to her. After her passionate avowal of the reality of the frogs, the following passage occurs:

> She tries a test that seems to work when she is writing: to send out a word into the darkness and listen for what kind of sound comes back. Like a foundryman tapping a bell: is it cracked or healthy? The frogs: what tone do the frogs give off? (219).

Of course this account is still perplexing – what does it mean to "send out a word into the darkness"? What could the "tone" of a word be? In this case, the answer turns out to be: "no tone at all". But this it seems, is not the end of the story –

"She is too canny, knows the business too well, to be disappointed just yet. The mud frogs of the Dulgannon are a new departure for her. Give them time: they might yet be made to ring true." Later, leaving the courthouse and crossing the square, "she gives the frogs a tap with her fingernail. The tone that comes back is clear, clear as a bell" (222). She also tests the word *belief*, and finds that although the sound that it returns is not as clear, it is clear enough. "Today, at this time, in this place, she is evidently not without belief" (222). That "evidently" is typical of the mental world of many of Coetzee's characters: it signals the slight sense of surprise with which they discover their own feelings and capabilities. Although this account of the creative process is not without the self-ironizing quality that runs through the chapter, it is one that, in its very oddness, asks to be taken seriously.

A different version of what we might call the dictation theory occurs in "He and His Man," Coetzee's Nobel lecture (2003). Robinson Crusoe, now living alone in Bristol, sits every evening composing accounts of extraordinary happenings around Britain. He can do this only by imagining – if that is the right word for an experience in which he seems entirely passive – that he is receiving reports from a man travelling about the country. At one point, he muses over the phrase "Death himself on his pale horse": "those are words he would not think of. Only when he yields himself up to this man of his do such words come."[13] (That the language Crusoe is admiring is that of Revelations, and that his man's reports are taken verbatim from Daniel Defoe's *Tour through the Whole Island of Great Britain* and *Journal of the Plague Year*, compound the ironies.) The final image of the piece – Crusoe and "his man" passing one another at sea, each oblivious to the other's presence – seems to figure the writer's necessary ignorance of the sources of his or her inspiration.

*   *   *

When we turn to the novels, we find some of these versions of the artist's vocation conveyed in even more extreme forms. Coetzee's darkest picture of the artist is his version of Dostoevsky in *The Master of Petersburg*.[14] The gestation and birth of a work of art – the work that we recognize as *The Possessed* – is portrayed as slow, difficult, without joy or affirmation; the moment of creativity is arrived at at the end of a long, tortuous path, with none of the conventional trappings of the artist gathering material or seeking inspiration. The extraordinary final chapter "Stavrogin" – named after the character in *The Possessed* whom we begin to see literally taking shape – is one of the strangest descriptions of the creative process we have. In it the imagery of epilepsy that has run through the book, and which

---

[13]   J.M. Coetzee, "He and His Man", The Nobel Lecture in Literature, 2003 (London: Penguin, 2004), 15.

[14]   I have discussed this picture further in chapter 5 of *J.M. Coetzee and the Ethics of Reading*.

the historical Dostoevsky suffered from, reaches its culmination: to begin writing is to allow oneself to fall, to give up the norms of taste, morality, justice, to let oneself be taken over by an implacable exterior force. Writing is gambling, testing, betrayal, perversion, a surrendering of the soul. "He sits with the pen in his hand, holding himself back from a descent into representations that have no place in the world, on the point of toppling, enclosed within a moment in which all creation lies at his feet, the moment before he loosens his grip and begins to fall."[15] At the centre of the betrayal is the innocent young daughter of his landlady; his capacity to write depends on her corruption.

What are we to make of this? Is Coetzee suggesting that *The Possessed* is a work that represents human evil and folly with such power that one can only imagine it coming into being in this way, by a process akin to epilepsy, a taking over of the mind by a force it cannot control or comprehend? Or are we to take it as paradigmatic of all creative activity? What it has in common with the more benign accounts of creativity we have seen is the giving over of oneself to an other, without any certainty about the outcome. To this degree, at least, *The Master of Petersburg*'s representation of art is consistent with what we have seen in Coetzee's other works. And if the artist cannot know in advance where the commitment to the new work coming into being will lead him or her, its beneficence or wholesomeness is something that cannot be guaranteed.

Although the representations of writers in *Foe* and *The Master of Petersburg* might have led to expectations that any depictions of art in Coetzee's fiction would be far from straightforward, nothing could have prepared readers for the work of art we see being created in *Disgrace*. Lurie's opera is one of the most unexpected elements of the novel, and it is not surprising that, although it plays an increasingly important part in the narrative, it is often given short shrift in accounts of the book. We first hear of it on the fourth page of the novel, after learning that Lurie, the author of three books, is tired of prose. "What he wants to write is music: *Byron in Italy*, a meditation on love between the sexes in the form of a chamber opera."[16] A little later on, in the course of his seduction of his student Melanie, he mentions that he is working on Byron's time in Italy (15). He describes his current project to his daughter Lucy, after the termination of his university post and his arrival at her smallholding, as: "Something on the last years of Byron. Not a book, or not the kind of book I have written in the past. Something for the stage, rather. Words and music. Characters talking and singing" (62–3). And he offers a reason for writing it: "I thought I would indulge myself. But there is more to it than that. One wants to leave something behind" (63).[17] We also learn that he intends to borrow the music, and that his ideas about orchestration have moved towards something meagre –

---

[15]   J.M. Coetzee, *The Master of Petersburg* (London: Secker & Warburg, 1994), 241.

[16]   J.M. Coetzee, *Disgrace* (London: Secker & Warburg, 1999), 4.

[17]   Although this cannot be all there is to an artistic vocation, it is interesting that Elizabeth Costello has a similar thought: "If I, this mortal shell, am going to die, let me at least live on through my creations" (*Elizabeth Costello*, 17).

"violin, cello, oboe or maybe bassoon". The opera is mentioned again when Lurie and his daughter are recovering from the attack on the smallholding, and we get a clearer sense of the three characters he is envisaging: Byron, his mistress Teresa Guiccioli, and her husband. A little later "the project is not moving" (141); the characters he had imagined are slipping away, and "their loss fills him with despair" (142).

The first hint that a genuine creative process is beginning occurs when Lurie is with Bev Shaw at the end of a day of dog-killing. "In his head Byron, alone on the stage, draws a breath to sing ... *Sunt lacrimae rerum, et mentem mortalia tangunt*: those will be Byron's words, he is sure of it. As for the music, it hovers somewhere on the horizon, it has not come yet" (162). An odd way of proceeding, it would seem: a Vergilian tag for the words to be sung, and an expectation that the music will arrive from somewhere else. Finally, back in Cape Town, the work begins to take a shape of its own, and the story of Lurie's disgrace pauses while Coetzee devotes six-and-a-half pages (180–86) to the evolving opera. Lurie acknowledges that the plan he had formulated is not working; the phrase he uses looks forward to the response by Elizabeth Costello I have already cited: "There is something misconceived about it; something that does not come from the heart" (181). The metaphor recurs when he asks himself, in reconceiving the work as a study of Teresa in middle age: "Will an older Teresa engage his heart as his heart is now?" (181) and "Can he find it in his heart to love this plain, ordinary woman?" (182). The answer turns out to be yes: Teresa's emptiness and longing grip him, and the language repeatedly affirms that the creative process, once it is underway, is a matter of listening and being led – the artist as what Costello, after Miłosz, calls the secretary of the invisible. Teresa and the dead Byron "demand a music of their own":

> And astonishingly, in dribs and drabs, the music comes. Sometimes the contour of a phrase occurs to him before he has a hint of what the words themselves will be; sometimes the words call forth the cadence; sometimes the shade of a melody, having hovered for days on the edge of hearing, unfolds and blessedly reveals itself. As the action begins to unwind, furthermore, it calls up of its own accord modulations and transitions that he feels in his blood even when he has not the musical resources to realize them. (183–4).

Finding the sonorities of the piano at which he is composing too rich, he fetches a township-fabricated banjo, and, "to his surprise" (184), he finds its music inseparable from his female character. He is not sure if he is inventing the music or the music is inventing him (186). When another voice emerges "from the dark", it is one "he has not counted on hearing" – the voice of Allegra, Byron's five-year old daughter. "From where inside him does it come?" (186), he asks.

In the final phase of the novel, in the time of waiting for the birth of Lucy's baby, Lurie works on Teresa's music on the banjo in a compound behind the animal clinic. The opera now "consumes him night and day" (214). Teresa is fully realized, and Lurie's creation is described as if he were listening to her rather than bringing her into being. Yet the opera, it seems, "is going nowhere" (214); he feels he is failing Teresa, and, in yet another use of a now familiar metaphor, "hopes she will find it in her heart to forgive him". The most Lurie can hope for is that "somewhere from amidst the welter of sound there will dart up, like a bird, a single authentic note of immortal longing". And this hope itself is a highly circumscribed one: even if he does succeed in creating this note, he knows he will not hear it himself. The final reference to the opera is the observation that the dog that has become particularly attached to Lurie responds to Teresa's music with what seems like a desire to participate (215).

As in *The Master of Petersburg*, Coetzee shows us the slow birth of a work of art. In both instances, the work emerges out of the most intense elements in the personal histories of the artists; yet the experience of creation is one of a mysterious otherness making itself felt – and doing so only after a period of waiting, of trial and error, of what could be called preparation if the artists were not so much in the dark about what they should be doing or what lies beyond the horizon. Lurie, in particular, seems unaware of what the reader must surely be conscious of: that his developing narrative of the love between Byron and Teresa Guiccioli touches at many points on his own sexual history, and that his coming to terms with that history occurs in part through creative identification with the middle-aged, miserable heroine of his opera. (Where the younger Teresa reminded the reader of Melanie – she is nineteen, Melanie twenty – her older, "dumpy" and "stocky" incarnation sounds more like Bev Shaw.) He does, however, recognize that Teresa has become more important to him than a mere product of his imagination: when he finds that his sense of honour denies him Lucy's ability to accommodate to the changed circumstances, he turns to her: "Teresa may be the last one left who can save him. Teresa is past honour" (209). In both novels, too, the connection between the aesthetic and the erotic is profound, if resistant to analysis: both forces take one unawares, as if touched by a god, and lead one into unknown territory, for good or ill. As in *Youth*, Coetzee leaves us in no doubt that this trope can be an excuse for irresponsible and selfish behaviour; but it also seems to be the only way to understand the forces at work in desire and artistic invention.

Another surprise awaits us at the heart of *Slow Man*. For 78 pages the novel seems to have little to do with questions of art – the nearest we get to this topic is Paul Rayment's interest in photography, but his passion is documentation, not art. (He is outraged when the function of the photograph as trustworthy record is challenged by Drago's digital manipulation.) Then, unexpectedly, we have to deal with the entry into the novel of its own author, in the guise of Elizabeth Costello, and engage in a difficult double reading: the story of Rayment's new life without a leg continues, but superimposed on it is the story of Elizabeth Costello's struggle to fashion a novel out of the unpromising materials she has been landed with. (This is not the first time an author and his or her characters have occupied the same fictional space in Coetzee's oeuvre – we might think of the individuals who populate Foe's house, or of Robinson and "his man".) Again, the artist is portrayed as subject to forces outside herself; Costello becomes a somewhat pathetic figure, unable to escape from the world that seems to have come to her unbidden, but unable also to generate the fictional developments she feels are necessary. The novel stages a huge "as if": when one writes a novel, it is as if one were to find oneself living with one's characters, prodding them and pushing them to do what characters in novels are supposed to do, but without real power over them.[18]

In *Diary of a Bad Year* we encounter a novelist who has more traits in common with Coetzee than Costello has: his initials are J.C. and his first name is apparently "John"; he has moved to Australia from South Africa; he has been a university professor and is known as a critic as well as a writer of fiction; he is the author of a novel entitled *Waiting for the Barbarians*.[19] But: he was born in 1934, whereas Coetzee was born in 1940 (and he is therefore seventy-two in 2006, when the novel is set and when Coetzee was sixty-six); he lives alone in Sydney and not with a partner in Adelaide; he is writing a series of opinion pieces for a German collection entitled *Strong Opinions* and is not producing a strange work that fuses opinions and fiction entitled *Diary of a Bad Year*. Very little of the book is concerned with J.C.'s work as a novelist, and we learn more about the huge labour of such work than of its rewards.[20] But in two of the opinion pieces, he offers a more positive view. In "On the writing life", he quotes Gabriel Garcia Márquez on inspiration as a mutual relationship between writer and theme – "'You spur the theme on and the theme spurs you on too'" (192); and in "On the mother tongue", he challenges the notion that writing is a matter of searching for words until one succeeds in saying what one had wanted to say, asking if an alternative description isn't more accurate – "I fiddle with a sentence until the words on the page 'sound' or 'are' right, and then stop fiddling and say to myself, 'That must be what you wanted to say'" (196). He continues with a question that complicates the account of writing given by Costello in "At the Gate": "If so, who is it who judges what sounds or does not sound right? Is it necessarily I ('I')?"

*   *   *

By far the largest part of Coetzee's evocation of the artist's work in his fictional and semi-fictional writing is devoted to the process of creation; we need to turn to his critical prose to find extensive commentary on finished works and, by implication

---

[18] For further discussion of the structural complexity produced by this conceit, see Barbara Dancygier's essay in this collection (Chapter 12).

[19] J.M. Coetzee, *Diary of a Bad Year* (London: Harvill Secker, 2007), 171.

[20] "To write a novel you have to be like Atlas, holding up a whole world on your shoulders and supporting it there for months and years while its affairs work themselves out. It is too much for me as I am today" (54); "I read the work of other writers, read the passages of dense description they have with care and labour composed with the purpose of evoking imaginary spectacles before the inner eye, and my heart sinks" (192).

at least, their importance for readers. There are a few places in the fictions and semi-fictions where the question of art's function is raised, however.[21] Elizabeth Costello, from the vantage point of the elderly writer, expresses doubt in many places about art's value to individuals or to society. She listens to her own voice explaining the significance of the novel and finds she is not sure if she believes any longer in what she is saying (*Elizabeth Costello*, 39). Once, it seems, she thought of literature as a force for good in the world, now "she is no longer sure that people are always improved by what they read" (160). In "As a Woman Grows Older", Costello, now seventy-two, is ready to disparage her own life's work: "The residue of wine is, excuse the word, piss; what is the residue of beauty? What is the good of it? Does beauty make us better people?" Once again, it is one of her children who values her creativity more highly than she does herself: what she has written, her daughter Helen says, has "changed the lives of others, made them better human beings, or slightly better human beings ... Not because what you write contains lessons but because it *is* a lesson." And she reaches for a word that plays an important part in Coetzee's ethical and aesthetic terminology: "You teach people how to feel. By dint of grace. The grace of the pen as it follows the movements of thought" (12). She may mean only grace in the sense of beauty, but there is also a suggestion of grace in the sense of a freely given gift, given to and by the artist.[22] However, Costello is not convinced, and Helen's view cannot be said to be endorsed by the piece as a whole.

The significant exception to Costello's sceptical view of the value of art is her endorsement of certain kinds of animal poetry. Writers, she argues in "The Poets and the Animals",

> teach us more than they are aware of. By bodying forth the jaguar, Hughes shows us that we too can embody animals – by the process called poetic invention that mingles breath and sense in a way that no one has explained and no one ever will. He shows us how to bring the living body into being within ourselves. (97–8).

Even this approbation is qualified by what she calls the "terrible irony" of the ecological philosophy that governs poetry like Hughes', leaping uncritically from the individual animal to the idea of the species. There is little sense that Costello believes literature to be a powerful instrument in advancing the cause she is espousing, however; rather that some works, read with the right kind of attention,

---

[21]   The opinion pieces in *Diary of a Bad Year* end with two that deal with artists, Bach and Dostoevsky; although they are both accolades, and the second expresses gratitude for the examples Tolstoy and Dostoevsky provide for the artist, they do not engage with the question of art's function in society (226).

[22]   On the importance of grace in Coetzee, see Michael Neill's essay in this collection (Chapter 4), and Attridge, *J.M. Coetzee and the Ethics of Reading*, 177–83.

may afford a glimpse of genuine otherness – upon which ethical action *could* be built.

In *Disgrace*, Lurie's dedication to his opera seems to have remarkably little to do with its potential effects. There is, however, one moment when this issue surfaces: Lurie rebukes himself for devoting his time and effort to dead dogs when there are other ways of serving the world – "Even sitting down more purposefully with the Byron libretto might, at a pinch, be construed as a service to mankind" (146). That wry, Beckettian, "at a pinch" gives the game away: there is no solid conviction here about the usefulness of art, or at least of his own art.

*   *   *

Surveying these various representations of the creative process in Coetzee's post-apartheid writing, one notes their variety but also a consistent pattern. Art is not a game, or a project, or a business enterprise: it is a burden laid upon the artist, a burden whose source remains uncertain; an obligation to find ways of doing justice to otherwise unheard voices; a giving of oneself over to other modes of being.[23] It cannot be planned in advance, and a successful outcome cannot be guaranteed; indeed, the very notion of "success" remains a doubtful one.[24] It is always a matter of finding the right forms – the words, the timbres, the melodies, the colours and shapes – and rejecting those that don't ring true, in a process that, although it belongs to the ancient tradition of inspiration by the Muse, is more dogged and circuitous. Coetzee does not emphasize the work of patient revision and re-revision that one must nevertheless assume to be part of his own practice, but it is worth noting the comment on his discovery of some of Beckett's manuscripts at the University of Texas when he was a PhD student there: "It was heartening to see from what unpromising beginnings a book could grow: to see the false starts, the scratched-out banalities, the evidences of less than furious possession by the Muse."[25] Sometimes the artistic impulse is entangled with the erotic urge, which also makes its uncompromising demands from a place that cannot be apprehended, and which cannot be securely channelled in a positive direction.

---

[23] In an interview, Coetzee speaks of the duty the writer is under, and enters a "tiny demurral" against the prioritizing of the duty imposed by society over the duty imposed by a "transcendental imperative" (*Doubling the Point*, 340).

[24] Coetzee gives a clear statement of the writing process as undetermined in advance: "Writing reveals to you what you wanted to say in the first place. In fact, it sometimes constructs what you want or wanted to say. What it reveals (or asserts) may be quite different from what you thought (or half-thought) you wanted to say in the first place" (*Doubling the Point*, 18).

[25] *Doubling the Point*, 25. One gets a sense of his own practice from his remark about Doris Lessing: she "has never been a great stylist – she writes too fast and prunes too lightly for that" (*Stranger Shores: Essays 1986–1999*. London: Secker & Warburg, (2001), 291).

With the possible exception of the youthful John, we are made to feel the seriousness and genuineness of the artistic impulse: these works would have little interest if Coetzee did not succeed in persuading us that the kind of art we see emerging matters in the world. But how does it matter? Not, as we have seen, in any utilitarian sense. The Costello pieces are filled with doubts about the usefulness of art; Dostoevsky makes no claims about the novel he is beginning or the ones he has published; Lurie's opera is destined to have no impact, barely any existence, in the wider world. Art matters because it does not matter in ways that can be assessed, harnessed, exploited; because it resists the drives of rationalization, increasing productivity, self-advancement and self-improvement. If in his treatment of artists and art Coetzee takes his bearings from a European forebear, it is not from the affirmations, however qualified, of Joyce or Mann, but, through the course of a long trajectory we saw beginning in *Youth*, from the mordant self-doubtings of Beckett.[26] And implicit in these stagings of the artistic process is the invitation to read Coetzee's works themselves in the same manner, looking not for moral profit or political edification, but alert to the ways in which they trouble the practices and goals that dominate much cultural and social life today. Like Levinas's Other, it is in its very powerlessness that the power of Coetzee's fiction lies.

The artists in Coetzee's fiction have less of direct value to offer the new South Africa, or the global cause of progress towards justice and material well-being, than most of those portrayed by his fellow countrymen and women;[27] and one could say the same of Coetzee's art in relation to their art, with the important qualification that in its resistance to the dominant currents of our time it does have something of immense significance to offer. If what it offered were a lesson, it would be the lesson that art can matter, and matter deeply, without having any lessons to offer. The reason this is *not* a lesson is the same as the reason why my summary is wholly inadequate: the importance of Coetzee's artists and of Coetzee's art is something that can be experienced only in the reading, in a committed and generous reading, in which the reader responds to the voice of the other resounding in the moving grace of the author's words. And this is why all Coetzee's tracings of the strange

---

[26]   It is interesting to note that in 1974 – the year of his first fictional publication – Coetzee published an article on Nabokov's *Pale Fire* in which he declared that, by contrast with Beckett, the Russian author's radicalism was "half-hearted", quoting the famous passage from *Three Dialogues* in which Beckett describes an art that prefers "the expression that there is nothing to express, nothing from which to express, no power to express, no desire to express, together with the obligation to express" ("Nabokov's *Pale Fire* and the Primacy of Art," *UCT Studies in English* 5 (1974): 1–7).

[27]   In his Jerusalem Prize Acceptance Speech in 1987, Coetzee asked: "What prevents the South African writer from … writing his way out of a situation in which his art, no matter how well-intentioned, is – and here we must be honest – too slow, too old-fashioned, too indirect to have any but the slightest and most belated effect on the life of the community or the course of history?" (*Doubling the Point*, 98–9). His answer at the time was that apartheid South Africa imposed itself too powerfully; but there is little to suggest that he feels art has any stronger effect in post-apartheid South Africa, or for that matter Australia.

processes of artistic creation are directly relevant to our understanding of his art (and perhaps of art more generally): because in opening ourselves to that otherness we are participating in the artist's own encounter with the obscure imperatives without which no invention at all can happen.

Chapter 2
Responses to Space and Spaces of Response in J.M. Coetzee[1]

Carrol Clarkson

I

In his essay, "A Sedimentation of the Mind: Earth Projects" (1968), the artist, Robert Smithson, writes:

> Words and rocks contain a language that follows a syntax of splits and ruptures. Look at any *word* long enough and you will see it open up into a series of faults, into a terrain of particles each containing its own void. This discomforting language of fragmentation offers no easy gestalt solution; the certainties of didactic discourse are hurled into the erosion of the poetic principle.[2]

Several of Coetzee's characters find themselves looking long and hard at words, exploring the possibility of a primal linguistic authenticity. Characters like Mrs Curren, Elizabeth Costello and Paul Rayment pick out isolated words, reconfigure them in declension, compare related words in different languages, trace the etymological roots. A question of language in general, and its capacity to articulate the truth, is a central preoccupation in Coetzee: one immediately thinks of David Lurie's conviction that "English is an unfit medium for the truth of South Africa"[3] and his yearning to sound, at the very least, "a single authentic note" in the opera he is composing.[4] Ever since Plato's *Cratylus*, the earliest existing philosophical text on names, we have come to recognize that linguistic – and especially etymological – enquiries never end in affirmative consolidations of a "correctness" of names by nature.[5] Differently put, in Smithson's terms, etymological forays do not

[1] Thank you to Stephen Clarkson and to Gail Fincham for incisive and encouraging comments on earlier drafts. Material included in this chapter also appears in my *J.M. Coetzee: Countervoices* (Houndmills: Palgrave, 2009).

[2] Robert Smithson, *The Collected Writings*, ed. Jack Flam (Berkeley, Los Angeles and London: University of California Press, 1996), 107.

[3] J.M. Coetzee, *Disgrace* (London: Secker & Warburg, 1999), 117.

[4] Coetzee, *Disgrace*, 214.

[5] I have discussed Plato's dialogue elsewhere in more detail, with specific reference to proper names in fiction. See my article, "Dickens and the *Cratylus*", *British Journal of*

hit reassuring bedrock. Yet (and this is my argument of here), despite the fact that linguistic foundations are demonstrably friable, that cultural beliefs (which depend on that language) are contingent constructs, Coetzee, through his fiction, reiterates the value of creating a space for voices to be heard – even in the instant of exposing the underlying faultline of splits and ruptures. The argument of this chapter develops in the interfold of the topographic and the textual. I begin with Coetzee's early consideration of the implications of writing about the African continent in English. The argument then hinges on the etymology of the word "care", especially as it arises in *Age of Iron* and *Slow Man*, and leads to questions about the ways in which language, rather than landscape, draws the limit between notions of "native" and "foreign". The chapter concludes with a reflection about the space of the literary artwork itself: on what terms can it become a *site* of engagement between writer and reader, and in what ways does the artwork have the potential to erode the very limits that the language of its own construction sets?

II

Smithson's provocative linking of "words and rocks" through a "syntax of splits and ruptures" is relevant to Coetzee in complex ways. In *White Writing* (1988), Coetzee speaks of the "quest for an authentic language" to depict the African landscape. He carefully formulates the question: "Is there a language in which people of European identity, or if not of European identity then of a highly problematical South African-colonial identity, can speak to Africa and be spoken to by Africa?"[6] The quest for this authentic language thus takes place within a framework in which "language, consciousness, and landscape are interrelated" (7). Further, the writer whose native tongue is English bears the "burden of finding a home in Africa for a consciousness formed in and by a language whose history lies on another continent" (173). The "burden is one that Coetzee recognizes in the writings of the nineteenth-century English botanist and explorer, William Burchell,[7] and in *Youth*, Coetzee cites Burchell as a source of his own literary inspiration:

> The challenge [Coetzee] faces is a purely literary one: to write a book whose
> horizon of knowledge will be that of Burchell's time, the 1820s, yet whose

Aesthetics 39.1 (January 1999): 53–61. References to the dialogue in this chapter are by paragraph number. As he launches into his extravagant etymological explanations, Socrates warns that his "notions of original names are truly wild and ridiculous" (426b) and that his "ignorance of these names involves an ignorance of secondary words" since he is "reduced to explaining these from elements of which he knows nothing" (426a).

  [6]   J.M. Coetzee, *White Writing: On the Culture of Letters in South Africa* (New Haven and London: Radix, in association with Yale University Press, 1988), 7–8.

  [7]   See Coetzee, *White Writing*, 36–44.

response to the world around it will be alive in a way that Burchell, despite his energy and intelligence and curiosity and sang-froid, could not be because he was an Englishman in a foreign country, his mind half occupied with Pembrokeshire and the sisters he had left behind.[8]

The writer using a European language and literary tradition is faced with a predicament: on the one hand, Africa can be named in negative relation to Europe, as in Burchell's opening comment on a sunrise viewed from the top of Table Mountain:

> I perceived in it nothing remarkable. I observed none of those streams of light which, in England, may often be seen radiating from the sun, just before it appears above the horizon, and which are so trite a feature in pictures of sunrise.[9]

As Coetzee points out (in a different context), it is a "self-defeating process" to "nam[e] Africa by defining it as non-Europe – self-defeating because in each particular in which Africa is identified to be non-European, it remains Europe, not Africa, that is named".[10] On the other hand, to name Africa without reference to Europe or to a European aesthetic of landscape presents tough challenges of its own. Thus Olive Schreiner (as Ralph Iron) writes in the 1883 preface to *The Story of an African Farm*: "Sadly … [the writer] must squeeze the colour from his brush, and dip it into the grey pigments around him. He must paint what lies before him."[11] What room does this leave for the aesthetic imagination? For Schreiner, "[t]hose brilliant phases and shapes which the imagination sees in far-off lands are not for him to portray" (40); Coetzee speaks of "a century of writing and overwriting (drab bushes, stunted trees, heat-stunned flats, shrilling of cicadas and so forth)". Whereas the imaginary landscape of *Waiting for the Barbarians* "represented a challenge to my power of envisioning … the Karoo threatened only the tedium of reproduction, reproduction of a phraseology in which the Karoo has been done to death".[12]

Within the fictional worlds of Coetzee's novels themselves, characters express misgivings that European languages and culture offer any legitimate space of response to Africa at all. Thus, for example, David Lurie mordantly reflects on his absolute incapacity to respond with efficacy to the situation in which he finds himself: he is locked in the lavatory while his daughter, Lucy, is being gang-raped in the bedroom on a smallholding outside Salem in the Eastern Cape:

---

[8] J.M. Coetzee, *Youth* (London: Secker & Warburg, 2002), 138.

[9] William Burchell, *Travels in the Interior of Southern Africa*, Vol. I (1822; facsimile reprint, Cape Town: Struik, 1967), 40.

[10] Coetzee, *White Writing*, 164.

[11] Olive Schreiner, *The Story of an African Farm* (London: Penguin, 1995), 40.

[12] J.M. Coetzee, *Doubling the Point: Essays and Interviews*, ed. David Attwell (Cambridge, MA, and London: Harvard University Press, 1992), 142.

He speaks Italian, he speaks French, but Italian and French will not save him here in darkest Africa. He is helpless, an Aunt Sally, a figure from a cartoon, a missionary in cassock and topi waiting with clasped hands and upcast eyes while the savages jaw away in their own lingo preparatory to plunging him into their boiling cauldron. Mission work: what has it left behind, that huge enterprise of upliftment? Nothing that he can see.[13]

Insistently in *Disgrace*, the socio-political aftermath of colonialism is indexed in the anachronistic disjuncture between a European language and the Africa it attempts to represent. The phrase "nothing that he can see" links the passage just cited to the following one. When Petrus uses the word "benefactor", Lurie reflects:

A distasteful word, it seems to him, double-edged, souring the moment. Yet can Petrus be blamed? The language he draws on with such aplomb is, if he only knew it, tired, friable, eaten from the inside as if by termites. Only the monosyllables can still be relied on, and not even all of them.

What is to be done? Nothing that he, the one-time teacher of communications, can see. Nothing short of starting all over again with the ABC. By the time the big words come back reconstructed, purified, fit to be trusted once more, he will be long dead. (129)

Yet if English is, according to Lurie, "an unfit medium for the truth of South Africa", unable to speak in an authentic way about the continent to which it is foreign, the language itself seems subject to the natural igneous processes that have formed those very continents in the first place, as Lurie goes on to comment:

Stretches of English code whole sentences long have thickened, lost their articulations, their articulateness, their articulatedness. Like a dinosaur settling in the mud, the language has stiffened. Pressed into the mould of English, Petrus's story would come out arthritic, bygone. (117)[14]

Lurie's near-obsessive interest in being articulate himself results in his unearthing of a number of European resonances in each English word he so carefully turns over. Here are just three examples:

A man of patience, energy, resilience. A peasant, a *paysan*, a man of the country (117)

---

[13]   Coetzee, *Disgrace*, 95.

[14]   I am reminded of a passage with similar metaphoric resonances in Thomas Hardy: "Medievalism was as dead as a fern-leaf in a lump of coal" (Thomas Hardy, *Jude the Obscure* (Harmondsworth: Penguin, 1985), 131). Coetzee often refers to the writings of Thomas Hardy in essays and interviews.

She loves the land and the old, *ländliche* way of life (113)

Modern English *friend* from old English *freond*, from *freon*, to love (102)

A curious tension arises in these examples. On a semantic level the words raise associations of chthonic rootedness ("paysan", "ländliche"), of home and community ("neighbour", "friend", "benefactor"). But the trans-lingual and etymological enquiry itself, regardless of what the words *mean*, recalls Smithson's "splits and ruptures" that are geological, as much as they are linguistic. The histories and etymological connections of these words recall a distant place and a time past;[15] to say these words *in Africa* is to re-enact, in language, a continental drift.

III

It is the fissile propensity of language (rather than a stabilized grounding in a unitary essence) that is reiterated in each elaborate etymology provided by Coetzee's characters. English words in Africa are diachronous in their evocation of another era and another continent. This is something that Coetzee consciously plays up in his writing. "[W]hat I like about English," Coetzee says in an interview with Jean Sévry,

> and what I certainly don't find in Afrikaans, is a historical layer in the language that enables you to work with historical contrasts and oppositions … there is a genetic diversity about the language, which after all is not only a Germanic language with very heavy romance overlays, but is also a language which is very receptive to imported neologisms so that macaronic effects are possible – you can work with contrasts in the etymological basis of words.[16]

What concerns me now are the ethical implications of internal semantic splits exposed in etymological quests. In Plato's *Cratylus*, Socrates provokes Hermogenes into agreeing that a "professor of the science of language should be able to give a very lucid explanation of first names, or let him be assured he will only be talking

---

[15]   Rita Barnard makes a related comment about the many foreign words in the novel. She singles out the word, "eingewurzelt" (rooted in): "The word, redolent with notions of organic community and peasant tradition, is intended to affirm the man's [Ettinger's] tenacity. But the very fact that it is a German word effectively undermines its dictionary definition: Ettinger's origins … may be too European for him to survive without a brood of sons on the post-apartheid platteland" (Rita Barnard, "J.M. Coetzee's *Disgrace* and the South African Pastoral", *Contemporary Literature* 14.2 (2003): 199–224, at 206–7).

[16]   J.M. Coetzee and Jean Sévry. "An Interview with J.M. Coetzee." *Commonwealth* 9 (1986): 1–7, at 2.

nonsense about the rest".[17] In Coetzee, however, the recognition of a "foundational fiction"[18] and "false etymologies"[19] does not necessarily invalidate the structures built on those foundations – even when it comes to matters of ethics. My example (from *Age of Iron* and *Slow Man*) is the phrase, "take care of".[20]

Elizabeth Curren, a professor of classics who has terminal cancer, gives a little lecture to Vercueil, the homeless man she has taken into her house:

> The spirit of charity has perished in this country … those who accept charity despise it, while those who give, give with a despairing heart. What is the point of charity if it does not go from heart to heart? What do you think charity is? Soup? Money? Charity: from the Latin word for the heart.[21]

In the first place, the value system and the language Mrs Curren invokes have no leverage in the totalitarian, apartheid South Africa of the 1980s. Hers is the "authority of the dying and the authority of the classics", as Coetzee puts it in an interview with David Attwell,[22] both of which "are denied and even derided in her world: the first because hers is a private death, the second because it speaks from long ago and far away" (ibid.). Yet for Coetzee, it is important that a voice such as Mrs Curren's is heard, despite the fact that she speaks "from a totally untenable historical position". The rationale for her having a say is that "even in an age of iron, pity is not silenced" (ibid.). Thus Coetzee creates a space for the "private", the "long ago" and the "far away" in the here and now. Coetzee himself does not offer programmatic ethical imperatives in the way that his characters often do (think of Elizabeth Costello, or of Mrs Curren – "How shall I be saved? By doing what I do not want to do. That is the first step: that I know. I must love, first of all, the unlovable"[23]). But even though Mrs Curren's position may be historically untenable, Coetzee's staging of it does not amount to a dismissal.[24] In fact, Coetzee

---

[17]   Plato "Cratylus", in *The Dialogues of Plato* vol. 3, trans. Benjamin Jowett (London: Sphere, 1970), 426a–b.

[18]   J.M. Coetzee, *Giving Offense* (London and Chicago: University of Chicago Press, 1996), 14.

[19]   J.M. Coetzee, *Age of Iron* (New York and London: Penguin, 1990), 22.

[20]   I have gained much from conversations with Arthur Rose about "taking care" in Coetzee. In his own post-graduate work, Rose questions the possibility and the limits of an "ethics of gratitude" in a care-relation. What are the responsibilities of the donor in *this* respect?

[21]   Coetzee, *Age of Iron*, 22.

[22]   Coetzee, *Doubling the Point*, 250.

[23]   Coetzee, *Age of Iron*, 136.

[24]   This is also true of David Lurie's preoccupation with Romantic poetry: "He must have a look again at Victor Hugo, poet of grandfatherhood. There may be things to learn" (Coetzee, *Disgrace*, 218). See my article, "'Done because we are too menny:' Ethics and Identity in J.M. Coetzee's *Disgrace*." *Current Writing* 15.2 (October 2003): 77–90.

suggests that a measure of the seriousness of a literary text is its capacity for dialogism. From the perspective of the writer it is "a matter of awakening the countervoices in oneself and embarking upon speech with them".[25] In *Slow Man* Paul Rayment has a childhood memory of mixing all his coloured plasticine bricks together until he has one huge ball of "leaden purple". The bright colours "will never return because of entropy, which is irreversible and irrevocable and rules the universe".[26] To let Mrs Curren have her say is to preserve one small chink of colour in the purple ball.

Almost immediately after Elizabeth Curren's pronouncement that caritas is "from the Latin word for the heart," she adds, "A lie: charity, *caritas*, has nothing to do with the heart. But what does it matter if my sermons rest on false etymologies? … Care: the true root of charity."[27] Mrs Curren's comment leads us to revisit, in a more nuanced way, Plato's *Cratylus*, and Coetzee's thoughts about linguistic reference (specifically in *White Writing*). The interlocutors in the *Cratylus* set out from the assumption that "the correct name indicates the nature of the thing" (428e), whereas Coetzee (whose views are perhaps subtly distinct from those of David Lurie) holds to a primal rift between signifier and signified: in no language do we find a case where "things are their names" by nature.[28] But, as we learn from the *Cratylus*, whether one can provide "a lucid explanation of first names" or not does not prove one's theory of reference either way. Further (I borrow Smithson's phrasing again), the fact that Mrs Curren's ethical view draws on a "poetic principle" (the fictive association of *caritas* and "heart") rather than on "the certainties of didactic discourse"[29] does not, in itself, make her view any less valid.

To extend the implications that arise from Smithson, and to bring us back to Coetzee – that one's ethical system is based on contingent social constructs, rather than on universal "essences," is, in practice, irrelevant. The exposure of a constructed, rather than a "natural" base, is certainly not reason enough to scrap the system.[30] Coetzee provides a graphic example of this in *Giving Offense*. The states of dignity and innocence, he points out, are elaborate social constructs – we are not born with dignity or innocence; we do not possess them "inherently." Thus:

> Affronts to the innocence of our children or to the dignity of our persons are attacks not upon our essential being but upon constructs – constructs by which

---

[25]   Coetzee, *Doubling the Point*, 65.

[26]   J.M. Coetzee, *Slow Man* (London: Secker & Warburg, 2005), 119.

[27]   Coetzee, *Age of Iron*, 22; my emphasis, except for *caritas*.

[28]   Coetzee, *White Writing*, 9. Coetzee seems to conflate "signified" and referent (*White Writing*, 8–9). The confusion has momentous implications – but this is not the place to discuss them.

[29]   Smithson, *Collected Writings*, 107.

[30]   Incidently, this is what Cratylus, in Plato's dialogue, maintains: "I cannot be satisfied that a name which is incorrectly given is a name at all" (Plato, 433c).

we live, but constructs nevertheless. This is not to say that affronts to innocence or dignity are not real affronts ... the infringements are real; what is infringed, however, is not our essence, but a foundational fiction to which we more or less wholeheartedly subscribe, *a fiction that may well be indispensable for a just society*, namely, that human beings have a dignity that sets them apart from animals and consequently protects them from being treated like animals.[31]

It is in this context that the title of Smithson's essay is interesting: "A Sedimentation of the Mind", as Stephen Clarkson pointed out to me, creates an image of the mind becoming silted up with words which have become naturalized. In this way words assume their power over us: the foundational fiction becomes naturalized". With an added ironic twist, it is precisely the recognition of the contingency of one's cultural belief, rather than an unswerving conviction that it represents the ultimate truth, that can provide the basis for an ethical response: "it is a good thing to remember that it might have been different".[32]

Foundational fictions are one thing – but often the linguistic scrutiny of a word or phrase unearths contradictory meanings that threaten to undermine the entire edifice – Robert Smithson again: "Look at any word long enough, and you will see it open up into a series of faults, into a terrain of particles each containing its own void."[33] It is this "series of faults", this "void", that confronts Paul Rayment as he stares at the words, "take care of". Marijana Jokić (the Croatian nurse employed to look after him following his cycling accident which results in his leg being amputated), asks an innocent enough question: "who is going to take care of you?"[34] But the question provokes mental crisis in Rayment. Echoes of *Age of Iron*, *Disgrace* and *Elizabeth Costello* remind us yet again that questions of ethics, as is so often the case in Coetzee, are intricately bound up in questions of language.[35] In the first place Marijana's question is not univocal, "presumably there is a more charitable way of interpreting the question – as Who is going to be your stay and support?, for instance"[36] While the spoken exchange that ensues has to do with his biographic circumstances, Rayment's internal monologue rages:

> her question echoes in his mind ... The more he stares at the words <u>take care of</u>, the more inscrutable they seem. He remembers a dog they had when he was

---

[31]   Coetzee, *Giving Offense*, 14; my emphasis.

[32]   Stephen Clarkson, email, 11 January 2006.

[33]   Smithson, *Collected Writings*, 107.

[34]   Coetzee, *Slow Man*, 43.

[35]   Elizabeth Costello tries out words for her sexual encounter with the old, bedridden Mr Phillips: "Not *eros*, certainly – too grotesque for that. *Agape*? Again, perhaps not. Does that mean the Greeks would have no word for it? Would one have to wait for the Christians to come along with the right word: *caritas*?" (J.M. Coetzee, *Elizabeth Costello: Eight Lessons* (London: Secker & Warburg, 2003), 154).

[36]   Coetzee, *Slow Man*, 43; Coetzee's italics.

a child in Lourdes, lying in its basket in the last stages of canine distemper ... "*Bon, je m'en occupe*," his father said at a certain point ... Five minutes later, from the woods, he heard the flat report of a shotgun, and that was that, he never saw the dog again. *Je m'en occupe*: I'll take charge of it; I'll take care of it; I'll do what has to be done. That kind of caring, with a shotgun, was certainly not what Marijana had in mind. Nevertheless, it lay englobed in the phrase, waiting to leak out.[37]

Instead of consoling him that Marijana's "care" is more than "just nursing" (33), Rayment's attempts to get to the bottom of the phrase call up chilling childhood memories and erode any certainties he may have had about meaningful communication with the one person in the world who seems to care about him now. Far from offering reassurance, the phrase brings to the linguistic surface of the dialogue a few bleak particulars: Rayment is a foreigner in Australia; he has no family in Adelaide; he has lost contact with his relatives in Europe. Further, "what of his reply: *I'll take care of myself*? What did his words mean, objectively?" As if despite the intentions of its speakers, meanings proliferate, and the phrase provokes Rayment's (extravagantly detailed) thoughts of suicide:

Did the taking care, the caretaking he spoke of extend to donning his best suit and swallowing down his cache of pills, two at a time, with a glass of hot milk, and lying down in his bed with his hands folded across his breast? (44)[38]

But if "taking care", at a psychological level, harbours contradictory and potentially destructive meanings, it is worth recalling Coetzee's own comments on Freudian psychoanalysis. Psychoanalysis, says Coetzee, "has scientific ambitions, and science has no ethical content". He goes on to elaborate:

What psychoanalysis has to say about ethical impulses may be illuminating (I give as an instance the link Freud points to between pity and destructiveness) but is ultimately of no ethical weight. That is to say, whatever one thinks the psychological origins of love or charity may be, one must still act with love

---

[37] Coetzee, *Slow Man*, 43–44, Coetzee's italics.

[38] The disruptive counter-meaning of "taking care" draws attention to the rift in communication between Lucy and her father, David Lurie, in *Disgrace* (197–8):

"'I don't understand. I thought you took care of it [Lucy's unborn child], you and your GP.'
'No.'
'What do you mean, no? You mean you didn't take care of it?'
'I have taken care. I have taken every reasonable care short of what you are hinting at. But I am not having an abortion'."

and charity. The outrage felt by many of Freud's first readers – that he was subverting their moral world – was therefore misplaced.[39]

Besides, the semantic waywardness of language is precisely what makes literary writing dialogic; the "countervoices" that are raised are a sign of the writer's "step[ping] down from the position of what Lacan calls 'the subject supposed to know'"[40]

"Care" is the "true root of charity", as Mrs Curren (of *Age of Iron*) points out[41] and these are her concerns: "the spirit of charity has perished in this country" (22); she is

> trying to keep a soul alive in times not hospitable to the soul.
> Easy to give alms to the orphaned, the destitute, the hungry. Harder to give alms to the bitter-hearted ... But the alms I give to Vercueil are hardest of all. What I give he does not forgive me for giving. No charity in him, no forgiveness. (*Charity?* Says Vercueil. *Forgiveness?*) Without his forgiveness I give without charity, serve without love. (130–31, Coetzee's italics).

It is not always easy to know what to make of Mrs Curren's meditations, especially given her own frequent retractions, qualifiers and reformulations: for instance, "I may seem to understand what I say, but believe me, I do not" (131). Yet, at the very least, this much is clear: her personal engagements are played out within a specific socio-political landscape, and her dilemmas arise in an aporetic ethical space – a space at once personal and political, inalienable and foreign:

> Now that child is buried and we walk upon him. Let me tell you, when I walk upon this land, this South Africa, I have a gathering feeling of walking upon black faces. They lie there heavy and obdurate, waiting for my feet to pass, waiting for me to go, waiting to be raised up again. (125–6).

Despite her abhorrence of the police violence that has led to Bheki's death, despite her own efforts to save the boy's life, Mrs Curren, in a passage such as the one above, gives intimations that she is implicated in the horrors of apartheid.

IV

Without making crude pronouncements about realism, it is possible to link Mrs Curren's life events and preoccupations (also those of the characters in *Disgrace*) to historic and geographic co-ordinates: calendars and maps are points of reference

---

[39]   Coetzee, *Doubling the Point*, 244.

[40]   Coetzee, *Doubling the Point*, 65.

[41]   Coetzee, *Age of Iron*, 22.

that, within the fictive worlds of these novels, determine the socio-historical moment, and that distinguish the native from the foreign. Yet even as regards his most "realistic" writing, a cautionary note must be sounded: in an interview with Coetzee in 1983, Tony Morphet comments on *Life & Times of Michael K*: "The location of the story is very highly specified. Cape Town – Stellenbosch – Prince Albert – somewhere between 1985–1990."[42] Coetzee's response draws attention to the danger of taking these reference points at face value:

> The geography is, I fear, less trustworthy than you imagine – not because I deliberately set about altering the reality of Sea Point or Prince Albert but because I don't have much interest in, or can't seriously engage myself with, the kind of realism that takes pride in copying the "real" world. (455)

This is something that Coetzee recognizes in William Kentridge's films. In an essay on *History of the Main Complaint*, Coetzee observes, "the streets belong to a bygone, more provincial age, the 1940s or 1950s. But it would be a mistake to conclude, from this and from Soho's office decor, that Kentridge's films are about a past era."[43] Thus even when the physical geography of the place, and historical moments in time are ostensibly legible in the text, the referents to space and time within an artwork operate differently, reminding me again of Smithson's "abstract geology".[44] Reflections about objective time and space thus cede ground to reflections about literary representation, to reflections about Coetzee's deployment of the logical operations of language within the worlds of his fiction. In Slow Man, questions arise not so much about the relation between language and topographic space, but about the relation between a language and its speakers. My focal point is still that of English, and even more specifically, the word "care". It is the characters' relation to the English language, rather than to a physical geographic location, that dictates the boundary between the native and the foreign, the chthonic and what Elizabeth Costello calls the "butterfly".[45]

Paul Rayment imagines writing a letter to Marijana, apologizing for his indiscretion, thanking her for the care she has given him, and pleading her to accept his offer to pay for her son's education. In the letter, he will write:

> You have taken care of me; now I want to give something back, if you will let me. I offer to take care of you … I offer to do so because in my heart, in my core, I care for you. (165, Coetzee's italics)

---

[42] J.M. Coetzee and Tony Morphet, "Two Interviews with J.M. Coetzee, 1983 and 1987," *TriQuarterly* 69, Special issue: *From South Africa* (Spring/Summer 1987): 454–64, at 455.

[43] J.M. Coetzee, "*History of the Main Complaint*", in *William Kentridge* (New York: Phaidon, 1999), 82–93, at 87.

[44] Smithson, *Collected Writings*, 100.

[45] Coetzee, *Slow Man*, 198.

But Rayment does not write this letter. "Care", he thinks,

> he can set the word down on paper, but he would be too diffident to mouth it,
> make it his own speech. Too much an English word, an insider's word. Perhaps
> Marijana of the Balkans, giver of care, compelled even more than he to conduct
> her life in a foreign tongue, will share his diffidence. (ibid.)

It is the English language, not Australia, that casts Rayment and Marijana as foreigners. In the English-speaking world, Rayment continues (the passage recalls *Age of Iron*) "caring should not be assumed to have anything to do with the heart". He contemplates adding a final comment in the imagined letter: "*Excuse the language lesson ... I too am on foreign soil*" (165, Coetzee's italics). Language, landscape and consciousness are thus more closely interrelated than before in Coetzee, to the extent that language itself appears to be the only ground. Elizabeth Costello, a character in *Slow Man* who seems to be the author of the very fiction we are reading, also thinks about English in this way. Rayment tells her:

> English has never been mine in the way it is yours. Nothing to do with fluency
> ... But English came to me too late. It did not come with my mother's milk. In
> fact it did not come at all. (197)

To this Costello responds: "You know, there are those whom I call the chthonic, the ones who stand with their feet planted in their native earth; and then there are the butterflies ... temporary residents, alighting here, alighting there. You claim to be a butterfly (198). The "burden," perhaps, facing the likes of Rayment and Marijana – to reformulate the sentence from *White Writing* that I cited near the outset of this chapter – is not to find a home in Australia, but to find one in the English language. Rayment, speaking English, feels like a "ventriloquist's dummy" (198), and Elizabeth offers to teach him to speak like a true native. "How does a native speak?" Rayment asks, to which Costello replies, "From the heart" (231).

If the novel warns us about the dangers of entropy, of subsuming differences into a totality, it is perhaps even more insistent in its appeal to reinstantiate Mrs Curren's "false etymology" – that is to say, to realign care, charity, *caritas*, and heart. Paul Rayment, since his accident, has been subjected to a ruthless "regimen of care" (32); to "indifferent ... motions of caring" (15); to the patronizing care of the welfare system (22); to an absence of "loving care" (261) and to the "care" of his leg, which amounts to its having been amputated without his informed consent (10). Elizabeth Costello seems to have been given the task of writing a book about Paul Rayment – she too looks upon him "with a sinking heart, with everything but love". Rayment would like to say to her, "*Have a little charity ... Then perhaps you may find it in you to write*" (162, Coetzee's italics). Is charity the space of art's response? In what way can it bring about an ethical engagement on the part of the viewer or reader?

V

In a striking incident in *Slow Man*, Paul Rayment shows Marijana's teenage son, Drago, his collection of Fauchery photographs – photographs of Australia's goldrush in the 1850s. On his death, Rayment will donate his collection: "It will become public property. Part of our historical record" (177). Without warning, Rayment finds himself close to tears, not because of the thought of his own death, but

> more likely it is because of *our. Our record, yours and mine.* Because just possibly this image before them, this distribution of particles of silver that records the way the sunlight fell, one day in 1855 ... may, like a mystical charm – *I was here, I lived, I suffered* – have the power to draw them together. (177, Coetzee's italics)

The two-dimensional paper card with its distribution of silver particles has an objective materiality in time and space – but the space of the artwork is not reducible to static spatio-temporal co-ordinates. The image of the "long-dead Irishwomen" provokes an empathetic response across centuries, and will continue to reach out to an illimitable future; far-off continents are reeled in to a small scrap of paper as Rayment, "the boy from Lourdes", and Drago, "son of Dubrovnik", meet, with understanding, the gaze of two Irishwomen in Australia. Geography and time are refracted through silver particles and effect what the artist and film-maker, William Kentridge, would call a "distant connectedness".[46] The artwork, in the moment of its reception, thus reconfigures ordinary conceptions of time and space, but that moment, in turn, rests on the responsiveness – or, shall we say, the charity – of its viewers.

---

[46]   William Kentridge, "Interview with Dan Cameron", in *William Kentridge* (Chicago: New Museum of Contemporary Art in association with Harry N. Abrams, 2001), 67–74, at 72.

Chapter 3
Coetzee on Film

Lindiwe Dovey and Teresa Dovey

> Though he goes to bioscope every Saturday afternoon, films no longer have the
> hold on him that they had in Cape Town, where he had nightmares of being crushed
> under elevators or falling from cliffs like the heroes of the serials. He does not see
> why Errol Flynn, who looks just the same whether he is playing Robin Hood or Ali
> Baba, is supposed to be a great actor. He is tired of horseback chases, which are all
> the same. The Three Stooges have begun to seem silly. And it is hard to believe in
> Tarzan when the man who plays Tarzan keeps changing. The only film that makes
> an impression on him is one in which Ingrid Bergman gets into a train carriage
> that is infected with smallpox and dies. Ingrid Bergman is his mother's favourite
> actress. Is life like that: could his mother die at any moment just by failing to read
> a sign in a window?

J.M. Coetzee, *Boyhood*, 45

In this passage from Coetzee's autobiography of his early years spent in the
Western Cape, the young boy is shown progressing from a relationship to cinema
in which he is in its thrall, to one in which he begins to suspend his belief and
become critical of its conventions, although it maintains the power to unsettle
him by casting a new light on the nature of signification, time and death. Coetzee
has had relatively little to say about the cinematic medium, but, according to a
filmmaker who has worked closely with him, "cinema has had an immense impact
on him" and the author "knows cinema very, very well, respects it, and is full of
admiration for it".[1]

Given this interest in cinema, and the widespread recognition accorded
Coetzee's novels, it seems surprising that, until recently, only one – *In the
Heart of the Country* – had been adapted to film. The adaptation of *Waiting for
the Barbarians* has been in preparation for some years, and the adaptation of
Disgrace is being released in different parts of the world as this book goes to press.
Interviews we have undertaken with filmmakers who have adapted or will adapt
the novels, or have attempted to do so, reveal that Coetzee has been cooperative,
and that he has expressed a desire for some control over the process, in different
cases offering to write the screenplay, insisting on having the right of veto over
the screenplay, or providing commentary on successive drafts. This suggests that
Coetzee is concerned that the films should be true to his vision of the novels in

---

[1]   Personal communication from Michael Fitzgerald, 20 August 2006.

at least certain respects – that he requires fundamental terms of fidelity in the adaptations. Given that the act of translating a novel to the filmic medium involves a form of interpretation, the nature of these terms can provide valuable insights into the novels, particularly with a writer like Coetzee, who is extremely reluctant to offer or to comment on interpretations of his own work.

In the case of *Waiting for the Barbarians*, Coetzee himself wrote the screenplay, commissioned to do so by the film producer and screenwriter Michael Fitzgerald, who optioned the novel in 1992. With *Life & Times of Michael K*, Coetzee read and commented on successive drafts by filmmaker Cliff Bestall, insisting that in the contract with the producers, Channel 4, he [Coetzee] should have a right of veto on the script. Coetzee was delighted with the first draft – and we will return to describe aspects of this draft later – but Channel 4 requested changes. Coetzee did not want to accede to Channel 4's demands for a more positive ending, but Bestall – in his own words – "stupidly tried to work between David Rose [at Channel 4] and Coetzee" and "made a mess of the screenplay", which Coetzee then rejected.[2] A third draft – based on the original one – never went into production because of changes in staff at Channel 4.

The process of translating *In the Heart of the Country* into the film *Dust* (made by Marion Hänsel),[3] as well as Coetzee's subsequent comments on the film and on the novel are, of course, the most illuminating. These comments, made in an interview with David Attwell, indicate that the novel itself was conceived in filmic terms. In response to a question about the *literary* influences on *In the Heart of the Country*, Coetzee replies:

> You are right to see similarities between (the novel) and the French *nouveau roman*, but behind both there is, I think, a more fundamental influence: film and/or photography.[4]

Our intention in this paper is to explore what the precise nature of this "fundamental influence" is, and how an understanding of the cinematic qualities of *In the Heart of the Country* can enrich the experience of reading it. In order to do this, we draw on Coetzee's quite detailed comments on how the novel references certain films and, as a way of teasing out what this might mean in relation to the reader's experience of the work, we compare the aesthetics visualized by Coetzee with the aesthetics of Hänsel's film. In doing this, we are also engaging, more broadly, in a discussion about different modes of reading, and how particular responses are invoked by the formal properties of different texts and films. We are interested, in

---

[2]   Personal communication from Cliff Bestall, 18 August 2006.
        [3]   *Dust* (1985). Dir. Marion Hänsel. Belgium/Spain/South Africa. Prod. Man's Films (Belgium) and Daska Film International. 87 min. Distr. Kino International (USA).
        [4]   J.M. Coetzee, "The Poetics of Reciprocity", in *Doubling the Point: J.M. Coetzee, Essays and Interviews*, ed. David Attwell (Cambridge, MA: Harvard University Press, 1992), 57–68, at 59.

particular, in how experiencing a novel through the aesthetics of a certain type of film can allow one to see and feel – and think – differently, can allow something to emerge which is perhaps not evident when one pays attention to the novelistic discourse alone.

In relation to this idea of how form impacts experience, we wish to take up and take further the argument developed in Derek Attridge's *J.M.Coetzee and the Ethics of Reading: Literature in the Event* (2004). Attridge proposes a mode of reading "that occurs as an event, a living-through or performing of the text that responds simultaneously to what is said, the way in which it is said, and the inventiveness and singularity (if there is any) of the saying".[5] This is an approach to reading which emphasizes the importance of form, in that the event is defined as what "used to be called 'form'" (31), and reading is described as *experiencing* the event, as *living* the text, as "re-staging the work's own performances" of "meanings and feelings" (9).

Attridge's choice of terms would at first seem to place his approach within the current move towards modes of criticism grounded in a sensory or embodied appreciation of the materiality of works of art rather than in the instrumental rationality of theory. This sensory approach is perhaps best exemplified in the work of film critics such as Laura Marks and Laleen Jayamanne, who draw on Adorno and Horkheimer's, and Benjamin's, notion of mimesis as a means of displacing the subject–object relations produced by abstract thought. Mimesis allows for a way of approaching the object in its full, sensuous particularity and, harnessed by criticism, gestures towards thinking through the body as a means of thinking *beyond* thought. Marks develops a theory of representation that is "auratic, embodied, and mimetic", and Jayamanne talks about how her own description of a film "begins not only to mimic the object, as a preliminary move, but also to redraw the object".[6]

The terms with which Attridge develops his idea of responsible readership appear to be quite similar to Jayamanne's description of how she attempts to be faithful to the object "in much the same way that a singer is true to the score in not singing a single wrong note".[7] Attridge argues that:

> A response that might be called "responsible," that simultaneously re-enacts and brings into being the work as literature and not as something else, and as *this* work of literature and not another one, is a response that takes into account as

[5] Derek Attridge, *J.M. Coetzee and the Ethics of Reading: Literature in the Event* (Chicago: University of Chicago Press, 2004), 60.

[6] Laura Marks, *The Skin of the Film: Intercultural Cinema, Embodiment, and the Senses* (Durham and London: Duke University Press, 2000), xiii; Laleen Jayamanne, *Toward Cinema and Its Double: Cross-Cultural Mimesis* (Bloomington and Indianapolis: Indiana University Press, 2001), xi.

[7] Jayamanne, *Toward Cinema*, xi.

fully as possible, by restaging them, the work's own performances – of, for example, referentiality, metaphoricity, intentionality, and ethicity. (9)

There are key aspects in which Attridge's and Jayamanne's approaches differ, however, these being the way in which Attridge insists upon a quite stringent exclusivity for the category of literature, and also the way in which he studiously avoids drawing on theory. Jayamanne draws on concepts as a "way of entering" films,[8] and Marks, too, draws extensively on theory, while also arguing that the films she examines are "themselves works of theory" and that "they are not waiting to have theory "done to" them, they are not illustrations of theory but theoretical essays in their own right".[9]

Coetzee's novels can be – and indeed have been – described as working in this way too, engaging with the philosophical debates of theory through the formal devices of fiction.[10] In that the novels allow for the performance of thought, as an alternative to the abstract discursive mode of philosophy, Attridge's call for a reading that requires an *experiencing* of the event, a *living* of the text, and "re-staging the work's own performances" of "meanings and feelings", would seem to be entirely appropriate. Like Jean-Luc Godard, we would argue, however, that the "evidence of the senses" is not enough,[11] that approaching the novels mimetically, refusing to go "outside" the novels except to draw on history, cannot guarantee a reading that does them justice. Both Hänsel's translation of *In the Heart of the Country* into film and Attridge's own reading of the novel provide examples of this inadequacy.

Hänsel's description of the way in which she approached the translation of the novel into film would appear to be, in many ways, exemplary of the kind of reading proposed by Attridge. In the first place, Hänsel says that she chose to adapt the novel in part because of the quality of the writing – she says that for her to be willing to adapt she needs "a very, very high quality of writing" and that she "cannot fall in love with badly written books".[12] This emphasis on the writing style – and not merely a "good story" – would seem to confirm Attridge's idea of the reader respecting the "singularity" of the text. Hänsel rejected Coetzee's proposal to write the screenplay, however, on the grounds that he "is not a film person" and that she had "to make the story [hers] to be able to direct it well". She mailed successive drafts of the screenplay to Coetzee, who commented – in characteristically terse fashion – by mail or telegram.

---

[8]   Ibid., xii.

[9]   Marks, *The Skin of the Film*, xiv.

[10]   Teresa Dovey, *The Novels of J.M. Coetzee: Lacanian Allegories* (Cape Town: A.D. Donker, 1988).

[11]   Cited by David Sterritt, *The Films of Jean-Luc Godard: Seeing the Invisible* (Cambridge: Cambridge University Press, 1999), 22.

[12]   Marion Hänsel, filmed interview with Lindiwe Dovey, 18 November 2002.

Hänsel describes how, having come to filmmaking from acting, her first step in the directing process during production is to spend time alone on the set, physically acting out each character's part. She says that she has to "feel physically … the rhythm of the story" – she has to live it in her body. This, in turn, allows her to undertake her storyboarding, at which point the screenplay "comes alive" for her. As far as the political context of South Africa is concerned, she says that she knew about apartheid and "was able to read all the metaphors … in *In the Heart of the Country* and the apartheid regime". She would thus appear to be an ideal reader in Attridge's terms – experiencing, living, and performing the meanings and feelings of the text, and being knowledgeable about the country's history. (Attridge argues that "Literal reading needs all the history – literary history, social history, political history, cultural history, intellectual history – it can get" (60).)

The first point that needs to be made about the film is that those physical aspects which film presents with an immediacy not available to writing, and which are able to evoke a mimetic response in viewers, are quite simply wrong in cultural terms. The physical setting is wrong, although this was not entirely the fault of Hänsel: sanctions against South Africa by European countries led to the film being shot in Spain, and the landscape, architecture and furnishings of the house are unplaceable, but are quite obviously not that of a farm in the Karoo. As Hänsel herself acknowledges, the South African reviews of the film were scathing, noting that even the sheep did not look South African. The choice of actors also means that the cultural embeddedness of the bodies we see and hear speaking is lost. We see Jane Birkin and Trevor Howard, and hear their English accents, while minor characters – the men on horseback and the boy who delivers the mail – speak English with strange accents, probably intended to sound like those of Afrikaners. The servants, who in the novel are clearly Coloured people, are played by John Matshikiza, a black South African in the role of Hendrik (to whom, notably, Hänsel refers as their "conscience" on set, thereby acknowledging a certain dis-ease in relation to the South African context), and Nadine Uwampa, a Ugandan-Belgian woman in the role of Klein-Anna.

The "South African-ness" of the film was clearly important to Coetzee, as one of the essential terms of fidelilty, and Hänsel speaks of how he was at first reluctant to agree to her request to option the novel, because, in her words, he saw her as "a Belgian girl who had nothing to do with South Africa, who had never been there". Coetzee's comments on Hänsel's drafts mainly concerned "South African truths … which [Hänsel] couldn't know" – for example, Hänsel wanted a scene with Magda playing the piano, but Coetzee informed her that this would have been unrealistic. When Hänsel travelled to South Africa to undertake location scouting, Coetzee arranged for her to travel to the Karoo to experience at first hand the setting of *In the Heart of the Country*, and, when she was not able to make this journey because she was ill, he spent a great deal of time showing her photographs and books of the Karoo.

More central to our argument is Hänsel's lack of attentiveness to the singularity of the novel's form. In spite of arguing that the most difficult task in adaptation is to find the "inner rhythm" of the novel, Hänsel says that she "knew" that she "could not cut the script or the film exactly in those little chapters which work in the book very well and give it a ... very special style". She acknowledges that the book is "written like a film" but says that she "could not keep exactly that pacing of the story". The pacing of the film is, in fact, very slow, and the film progresses from one carefully composed *mise-en-scène* to the next, each shot framed so as to stage a particular action or emotion. Although Hänsel speaks about the necessity of finding a motivation for the composition of each shot, the lighting, framing and camera movement clearly suggest that a primary motivation was an aesthetics less to do with translating the formal properties of the novel, and more to do with creating visual pleasure for the viewer. Hänsel's choice of Jane Birkin to play the role of Magda – although Coetzee had protested in a telegram that "Jane Birkin is beautiful, Magda is not" – is also representative of this desire to create visual pleasure for its own sake.

The film not only slows down the pace of the novel but also virtually silences the speaking voice. The film begins with Magda/Birkin saying in voice-over "To my father, I've been an absence all my life", with a slow tracking shot backwards that shows her standing with her back towards the camera as she looks out of a window at a landscape beyond. Dialogue between Magda and her father and Magda and the servants is reduced to a minimum (and is in English rather than Afrikaans), there are only a few monologues from Magda (one of them written by Birkin, adapted from a passage in the novel), and only short, isolated instances of voice-over. Often what begins as a voice-over, with Magda/Birkin's voice separated from her image, quickly changes (by means of a camera pan or tilt) into a shot showing Magda/Birkin speaking the words out aloud, in the manner of the stage drama monologue. What we hear are the sounds of wind, sheep, occasional grunting or laughing, and the intermittent extra-diegetic music of Hänsel's South American composer. Overall, sound is subordinated to the image, which altogether dominates in the film.

In terms of plot, Hänsel creates a quite conventional, linear narrative. She does include the repetitions of the killing of the father – although not the repetition of the shooting (numbered sections 118 and 119 in the novel) – and she does include the return of the father at the end. However, Hänsel provides a clear demarcation of her own sense of the boundaries between the "real" and the "fantastical". She signals the transitions from the "real" sequences to the "fantasy" sequences by means of the convention of a musical motif, and also by embedding the "fantasy" sequences *within* the sequences which depict "real" events. For example, the single rape sequence in the film (there are two rape sequences in the novel – numbered sections 206 and 209) cuts from the *mise-en-scène* of Hendrik thrusting himself against Magda, into a sequence of shots that clearly belong to another time and place, and then back into the *mise-en-scène* of Hendrik on top of Magda. The interposed sequence is composed of jump-cut shots, and is clearly shown to be Magda's fantasy of a more harmonious relationship – we see a close-up of a black man's back with a white woman's hand slowly caressing it, then a close-up of a white woman's back with a black man's hand stroking it. These shots are accompanied by the extra-diegetic music that tends to accompany each fantasy sequence in the film.

Hänsel tells of how, when she read the novel for the first time, she was fascinated by the fact that a man could describe "that well the feelings in the flesh, in the body, in the sex" of a woman, and says that her own feminist interpretation of the "uncertainties" of the novel derived from the process of "entering into the madness of the head of a woman in solitude and oppression". The repetitions are largely accounted for in narrative terms as the fantasies of a crazy woman; they are explained or naturalized through being reduced to the level of the individual psychology of madness. The tension that exists in the novel between the pull to respond mimetically to the characters, and the pull to reflect on how events and behaviours, and the *repetition* of these events, might signify more broadly, is thereby lost.

Also lost are the intertextual allusions, the self-referentiality, the complex layering of histories and discourses achieved by the novel. The work of the filmmaker is foregrounded only in the sense that *Dust* is very obviously intended to be an "art movie", and that the filmmaker shows herself to be an artist who is very competent at painting in light and sound and movement. Of course, one might argue that this kind of distortion of the text is very often what happens in film adaptations, that cinema does not have the means to render the discursive components of the written text, and that it is not fair to expect it to do so. But film *does* have these means at its disposal and we will, at a later point, draw on Coetzee's commentary concerning the type of film that he had in mind in order to illustrate how another type of film could have allowed us to see "differently" in a way that Hänsel's film does not.

First, however, we want to return to the idea of "responsible" reading, and argue that it is, ironically, because Hänsel has not adequately responded to the filmic qualities of the novel that her film does not offer such a reading. It needs to be said, in her defence, that she is first and foremost a filmmaker, and did not set out to perform the work of interpretation expected of a literary critic. Attridge's reading of the novel can be expected to be adequately responsive to the complexities of form – particularly since this kind of responsiveness is integral to his approach – but in many respects his reading works in a way that is similar to that of Hänsel. Although, like Hänsel, he recognizes the influence of film on the novel, like her, he underplays this influence, discounting the effects of the numbered segments in favour of the "illusion of immediacy" and what he calls a "readerly involvement" (22). He focuses on the "capacity of mimesis to overcome the metafictional apparatus" (26) and ways in which the realist narrative can be "saved" (27).

Attridge does pay lip service to the formal devices that create a "fissure" in the "prevailing discourses" as the means by which "otherness" is staged in the novel (30). His reading weaves back and forth between those moments of the novel that appear to encourage a mimetic response in the reader – always those moments capable of being read in the mode of realism – and those that disturb it. However, like Hänsel, the only formal device disruptive of realist conventions on which he focuses is the device of repetition, and, like her, he naturalizes the repetitions and contradictions of the novel by distinguishing between "fantasized" and "real" versions of the killing of the father and the rape, arguing that "the words are to be taken as referring to real events unless there is good reason, in a particular section of the novel, to take them as the outcome of fantasy or psychological derangement" (24).

In distinguishing between those moments in the narrative that invoke a mimetic response by representing actions or feelings with "painful vividness" (25), and the formal devices that create a "fissure" in the "prevailing discourses" of the novel, Attridge's reading overlooks what is most radical about Coetzee's fiction. What is most radical and remarkable about the novels – and *In the Heart of the Country* in particular – is the way in which they invoke a mimetic – rather than purely cognitive – response to *form* as event. It is in this way that Horkheimer and Adorno have described the workings of the formal properties of high modernism – as having a mimetic relationship to the conditions of modernity itself, and being able to evoke that effect in readers.[13]

If this is Attridge's experience of *In the Heart of the Country*, then – according to the terms he has laid down – there are no grounds for arguing with it. The problem is that his reading needs to allow *us* to experience the novel differently, needs to attempt, at least, to re-stage the "otherness" he only talks about. Otherwise – again according to his own terms – one has to ask what work his reading can do in the public domain of criticism. Because Attridge is so resolute in his desire to re-instate the exclusive category of the literary, and in his refusal to go "outside" literature, he does not do justice to the formal inventiveness of the novel. He overlooks the layered allusions within the novel to discourses other than the literary, and does not take seriously Coetzee's comments on the fundamental influence of film and/or photography on the novel. Our argument is that the novels "come alive" in more complex and interesting ways if one does go "outside" the text in order to understand how the formal devices work, and that this involves, among other things, an attempt to imagine the novel as a whole through the lens of film and film theory.

When Coetzee says that "*In the Heart of the Country* is not a novel on the model of a screenplay",[14] what he appears to imply is that it is *closer* to film than the screenplay's verbal mapping of dialogue and setting which then have to be translated into the audio-visual medium. Unlike the screenplay, the novel aims, through formal devices, to produce certain of the effects of film. That is to say, it mimics the form of film in order to have a mimetic effect on readers precisely through its form. The films which Coetzee references as imprinting the style of *In the Heart of the Country* are Chris Marker's *La Jetée* (1962), Andrzej Munk's

---

[13]   Max Horkheimer and Theodor W. Adorno, *Dialectic of Enlightenment*, trans. John Cumming (1947; London: Allen Lane, 1973).

[14]   Coetzee, "Poetics", 59.

The Passenger (1963), and – obliquely – Jean-Luc Godard's *Le Petit Soldat* (1960). We will turn in a moment to a discussion of the aesthetics of these films, and their effects, but it is significant to point out, in the first place, that these films could broadly be called "political" in terms of their themes. *La Jetée* and *The Passenger* deal with traumas related to world wars, and Godard's film is a response to the Algerian War of Independence (1956–62).

La Jetée is the complex futuristic tale of a prisoner of war whose memories make him the prime candidate to be sent, by means of time travel, to a time before the war (possibly World War III, although this is never clarified), to find "clues" for the present.[15] The film, only 28 minutes in length, is entirely composed of black-and-white stills (except for one brief, moving image), with the story narrated through voice-over. *The Passenger*, a one-hour film compiled by friends of Munk from footage he shot before his premature death in 1961, concerns the relationship between a female officer and a female prisoner from a Nazi concentration camp, who find themselves on the same ocean liner.[16] Although stills are used only at the beginning and the close of the film, a voice-over asks rhetorical questions throughout. *Le Petit Soldat* is one of Godard's most overtly political films, following Bruno Forestier, who is working as a Secret Agent for the French government and is ordered to kill an Algerian sympathizer.[17] The woman with whom Forestier falls in love is, unknown to him, working for the Algerian cause, making the film a complex interrogation – both through its themes and through its constant and questioning voice-over – of the ethics of war.

While conventionally political in content and theme, the style of these three films does not embrace the realism that one would usually associate with political cinema. Instead, the style is characterized by editing or montage that deliberately does not, in the tradition of classical cinema, attempt to link actions in a continuous or causal way. As Coetzee himself points out, *La Jetée* and *The Passenger* achieve their status as political or critical cinema largely through the use of stills and through the liberation of the sound track from the image track in the form of voice-over. It is significant that Coetzee talks about pleading for voice-over in the making of the films based on his novels, and also for "the independence of the voice".[18] He points out that "the irony is, doing the narration through dialogue keeps film tied to stage drama. It makes sound film more primitive than silent film" (ibid.). In visual terms, film that is tied to the tradition of stage drama is film that relies heavily on *mise-*

---

[15] *La Jetée* (1962). Dir. Chris Marker. France. Prod. Argos Films. 28 min. Distr. New Yorker Films (USA).

[16] *The Passenger* (1963). Dir. Andrzej Munk and Witold Lesiewicz. Poland. Prod. Zespol Filmowy. 62 min. Distr. Hen's Tooth Video (USA).

[17] *Le Petit Soldat* (1960). Dir. Jean-Luc Godard. France/Switzerland. Prod. Les Films Georges de Beauregard, Société Nouvelle de Cinématographie (SNC). 88 min. Distr. Winstar Video (USA).

[18] Coetzee, "Poetics", 60.

en-scène, on the composing of shots, as the equivalent of the dramatic scene – as Hänsel's film does.

The work of Marker, Munk and Godard has been characterized by film theorists both as constituting a radical intervention in viewers' experience of time and as an attempt to reflect a post-war shift in the human perception of time. Coetzee's use of certain of the formal devices of cinema can be said, likewise, to enact an engagement with issues relating to philosophies of time. *In the Heart of the Country* pre-dates the work of Gilles Deleuze, which has been described as "a philosophy of time" and as an attempt to "acknowledge philosophy's debt to film and film theory".[19] Deleuze introduced the terms "movement-image" cinema and "time-image" cinema to refer to the different forms of montage that he saw as operational pre-war and post-war respectively, with the work of Marker, Munk and Godard exemplifying time-image cinema. Discussing Marker's *La Jetée* in the context of Deleuze's theory, Rodowick says:

> there is now only linking through "irrational" divisions. According to mathematical definition, the interval dividing segmentations of space is now autonomous and irreducible; it no longer forms a part of any segment as the ending of one and the beginning of another. Image and soundtrack are relatively autonomous. While referring to each other, they nonetheless resist being reconciled into an autonomous whole. ... Inside and outside, mind and body, mental and physical, imaginary and real are no longer decidable qualities. (5)

Marker, Munk and Godard are not, however, interested in the philosophy of time for its own sake. Their work is – in Godard's words – profoundly connected to an ethical project of "making political films politically".[20] Responding to the violence of World War II, European colonialism in Africa, the Vietnam war, and the war in Algeria, their films are political not in the conventional sense, but in their exploration of the nature of power in particular contexts, not least in the context of filmmaking itself. In this respect it is significant that in an early interview Coetzee recognizes the affinity of his work with critical cinema, described by him as "a cinema that is in the first place critical of its own formal assumptions, which are reflections of an ideological position" (Thorold & Wicksteed n.d.: 5).[21]

Coetzee's concern with narrative temporality has been extensively discussed in an early reading of *In the Heart of the Country* and *Life & Times of Michael K*,[22] and is, of course, exemplified in his 1981 article on Kafka (included in *Doubling the*

---

[19]   David N. Rodowick, *Gilles Deleuze's Time Machine* (Durham and London: Duke University Press, 1997), xiii.

[20]   Cited in Sterritt, *The Films of Jean-Luc Godard*, 10.

[21]   Alan Thorold and Richard Wicksteed, "Grubbing for the Ideological Implications: A Clash (More or Less) with J.M. Coetzee", Interview with J.M. Coetzee, in *Sjambok. A Varsity* Publication (SRC, University of Cape Town, n.d.), 5.

[22]   See Dovey, *The Novels of J.M. Coetzee*.

Point). The disruption of narrative continuity in these novels marks an ambivalence concerning the subject's insertion into the Symbolic, which essentially involves an insertion into historical time. In the Kafka article, Coetzee draws on Roman Ingarden in his articulation of two kinds of awareness of time:

> The first, which we can call historical awareness, imputes reality to a past which it sees as continuous with the present. The second, which we can call eschatological, recognizes no such continuity: there is only the present, which is always present, separated from Ingarden's "dead past" by a moment of rupture, *the Entscheidende Augenbick*.[23]

It is these two kinds of awareness of time that Magda's narrative embodies, with the eschatological awareness representing the successive moments of enunciation, and the whole of the novel as "utterance" inevitably entering into the time of history.

One of the key points emphasized by Coetzee in his comments on the novel, on Hänsel's film, and on narrative more generally, is the effect of pacing, or rhythm. In the discussion with Attwell about the Kafka article, he says:

> by its nature narrative must create an altered experience of time. That experience can be heady for both writer and reader. For the reader, the experience of time bunching and becoming dense at points of signification in the story, or thinning out and skipping or glancing through non-significant periods of clock time or calendar time, can be exhilarating – in fact, it may be at the heart of narrative pleasure. As for writing and the experience of writing, there is a definite thrill of mastery – perhaps even omnipotence – that comes with making time bend and buckle, and generally with being present when signification, or the will to signification, takes control over time.[24]

Here Coetzee talks about an embodied experience of narrative temporality *per se*, regardless of content or context; about the pleasure, for the writer, of mastering time in the act of writing, and, for the reader, of living through the changing rhythms of the narrative. But for Coetzee the concern with time is not all, or even primarily, about play or pleasure, or about reflecting on the dilemmas of the narrating self. Later in the same interview, he says:

> time in South Africa has been extraordinarily static for most of my life. I think of a comment of Eric Auerbach's on the time-experience of Flaubert's generation, the generation that came to maturity around 1848, as an experience of a viscous,

---

[23] J.M. Coetzee, "Time, Tense, and Aspect in Kafka's 'The Burrow'", in *Doubling the Point*, 210–32, at 231.

[24] J.M. Coetzee, "Kafka" interview with David Attwell, in *Doubling the Point*, 197–209, at 203–4.

sluggish chronicity charged with eruptive potential. I was born in 1940: I was eight when the party of Afrikaner Christian Nationalism came to power and set about stopping or even turning back the clock. Its programmes involved a radically discontinuous intervention into time, in that it tried to stop dead or turn around a range of developments normal (in the sense of being the norm) in colonial societies. It always aimed at instituting a sluggish no-time in which an already anachronistic order of patriarchal clans and tribal despotisms would be frozen in place. ... So I am not surprised that you detect in me a horror of chronicity South African style. (209)

This "viscous, sluggish chronicity charged with eruptive potential" described here is the equivalent of the historical time that is challenged by the attempt to create the effect of eschatological time through the formal devices of *In the Heart of the Country*.

Coetzee talks about how "films that used montage effectively" influenced poets and novelists in the period of high modernism to make more "rapid transitions" (1992a: 59), and how this is reflected, too, in the brief, numbered sequences of the novel. Of *Dust* he says it "retains virtually none of the sequence divisions and indeed none of the quite swift *pacing* of the novel. It loses a lot of vitality thereby, in my opinion".[25] The divisions allow for moments of rapid pacing, as well as shifts in pacing, but what they allow Coetzee to *leave out* is also important – in his own words, "the kind of scene-setting and connective tissue that the traditional novel used to find necessary – particularly the South African novel of rural life that *In the Heart of the Country* takes off from".[26] The narrative is punctuated by spaces, or absences – silences which are "*significant* blanks",[27] in what might be seen as a Romantic gesture towards "a true deepdown I beyond words".[28] The division of the narrative into segments, then, calls for an embodied response to changes in rhythm, and requires the reader to fill in the gaps, to introduce his/her own "I" into the narrative as a means of bridging the gaps. The reader is deterred from lapsing into a routinized sensory-motor response, jolted out of the familiar conventions of cause-and-effect narrative connections.

There are moments where the pacing slows down, however. This can be felt when the present perfect is used to describe the rituals of life on the farm, as in Section 8, for example: "In a house shaped by destiny like an H I *have lived* all my life ... Sundown after sundown we *have faced* each other. ... Then we *have retired* to sleep" (*Heart*, 3, our emphasis). Certain sections narrated in the iterative tense are also slow with the tedium of a routinized existence and patterns of thinking, such as when Magda says, in Section 1, "I am the one who stays in her room reading or

---

[25]   Coetzee, "Poetics", 60.
[26]   Ibid., 59–60.
[27]   Dovey, *Novels of J.M. Coetzee*, 193.
[28]   J.M. Coetzee, *In the Heart of the Country* (Johannesburg: Ravan Press, 1978), 16 (hereafter *Heart* in parentheses).

writing or fighting migraines" (1). In section 12 Magda is made to talk explicitly about fighting "against becoming one of the forgotten ones of history" (3), and how she "[creaks] into rhythms that are [her] own" (8), while also acknowledging that her pulse "will throb with the steady one-second beat of civilization" (3). However, in *effect*, that is to say, in evoking a mimetic response in the reader, it is the shifting rhythms that convey the tension between the oppressive weight of teleology – of historical, patriarchal time – and the momentary violent attempts to break through or out of this time. These represent the kind of "violent phantasms" described by Coetzee in relation to South African writers,[29] and are enacted in the frenzied activity involved in successive killings of the father, first, and then in the repeated rape by Hendrik.

Coetzee's handling of narrative temporality means that time becomes politicized, and that the political is staged at the level of form in the novel. Although Coetzee is concerned primarily with the politics of apartheid South Africa, as is evident when he talks about "The *power* of the world [the South African writer's] body lives in to impose itself on him and ultimately on his imagination, which, whether he likes it or not, has its residence in his body",[30] the allusiveness of his novel means that it aligns itself with other discourses involved in similar attempts to evade the workings of power. The most obvious of these is the discourse of feminism – both the early feminism of Olive Schreiner, and the contemporary American feminism expressed most articulately in the poetry of Adrienne Rich, and in her essays, such as "When We Dead Awaken: Writing as Re-vision" (1971).[31] Rich talks about making "poems that *are* experiences", in which she says "something is happening, something has happened to me and, if I have been a good parent to the poem, something will happen to you who read it".[32] In the collection *The Will to Change* (1971),[33] she, like Coetzee, draws on film as a means to engage with the physical representation of temporality offered by this medium. This is made explicit in poems like "Pierrot le Fou" (the title of a Godard film), "Images for Godard" and "Shooting Script" – all made up of short numbered sections divided into discrete images conveyed in at most two or three lines. There are quite remarkable similarities between "Shooting Script" and *In the Heart of the Country*, which we do not have space to elaborate on here, our point being to show more broadly how the engagement of literature with film offers the means to engage a politics of the body.

---

[29]   J.M. Coetzee, Jerusalem Prize Acceptance Speech, in *Doubling the Point*, 96–9, at 98.

[30]   Ibid., 99.

[31]   Adrienne Rich, "When We Dead Awaken: Writing as Re-vision" (1971), in *Adrienne Rich's Poetry and Prose*, ed. Barbara Charlesworth Gelpi and Albert Gelpi (New York: Norton, 1975), 166–76.

[32]   Ibid., 89.

[33]   Adrienne Rich, *The Will to Change: Poems 1968–1970* (New York and London: Norton, 1971).

The earlier discussion of how the concern with narrative temporality is central to *In the Heart of the Country*[34] is conducted in linguistic terms, and takes the reader a long way away from the embodied experience of time offered by the formal devices of the novel – the separate numbered segments, the repetitions, the use of tense. A film could do this differently, but, in the absence of such a film – for which it would probably be impossible to raise the funding – we would like to imagine what it might look and feel like. This is a gesture towards an interpretation of the novel that "re-stages" the text, that calls on the rational or cognitive faculties of the readers of this interpretation, as well as attempting to evoke a new experiencing of the novel through the play of the senses along with the intellect.

We begin by going "outside" the novel, to re-read Coetzee's comments on the novel and the films by which it is influenced. We watch the films again, and read film criticism and theory. We are trying to escape our own clichéd sensory-motor responses to the novel as literature, trying to see it and feel it through film. We re-watch the filmed interview with Hänsel, and converse with filmmakers who have worked on adapting the novels. We need to draw on their different sensibilities.

We see – and understand – that we need to be able to draw on the audio-visual seductiveness of film, to enchant the viewer, to draw the viewer in, to re-create the passion for the place and the people that is expressed in the novel. We understand that without the means to evoke passion or pleasure, power has no foothold.

We imagine a film that opens with a few seconds of black leader followed by the words "Section 1" in white against a black background. This will be enough to defamiliarize the viewer before the action opens on a family drama: a bridal couple in early twentieth-century dress travel in a horse-drawn cart, clip-clopping across the backdrop of rural rusts and greys. This landscape would – to many South African viewers – be recognizable as that of the Karoo, beautiful in its arid minimalism. In the farmhouse, at a shuttered window, a woman watches them approach, introducing the threat – or promise – of jealousy and revenge. This appears to be the opening sequence of a film in the genre of an historical romance.

This sense of a pastoral paradise recurs intermittently throughout the film through sequences, in technicolour, of the idealized rituals of everyday life on a farm not yet changed very much by the technologies of the modern era. We imagine sequences showing, for example, the polishing of silverware outside in the shade of the gabled farmhouse; the rites of cooking and eating, of planting and harvesting; smoke rising from chimneys at sunset and animals being herded from the fields into the kraals, accompanied by the sound of lowing, pails clanking, crickets beginning their nightly chirping, distant voices and laughter.

The lure of a narrative thread is, likewise, maintained only intermittently. This is done through the conventions of shot and counter-shot, and eye-level matching, to show the simmering tensions between the characters in both the family drama, and in the drama involving the masters and the servants. We find that we have not

---

[34]   See Dovey, *The Novels of J.M. Coetzee*.

been able to entirely avoid imagining these kinds of sequences through scenes from Hänsel's film, which have imprinted themselves on our brains. We have to work hard to erase Jane Birkin and Trevor Howard from our mind's eye and imagine instead unknown actors who speak with South African English accents; and, in the place of Matshikiza and Uwampa, Coloured people speaking Afrikaans.

So much for the evoking of desire, for the need to lull the viewer into habituated modes of perception, in order to make the rupturing of these more strongly felt. The scenes we have described evoke what Magda refers to as the "steady one-second beat of civilization" (*Heart*, 3), but we now have to find a way to evoke the "viscosity" of time on the farm, to conjure up the "sluggish no-time" and "the horror of chronicity South African style" that Coetzee talks about. Here we have to start drawing on the films by Munk and Marker. Still images, which each play for several seconds, and which are perhaps shown more than once, might be able to achieve a slowing of the pace. We remember that Coetzee has commented on how still images can encourage "a remarkable intensity of vision (because the eye *searches* the still image in a way it cannot search the moving image)".[35]

We go back to Laura Marks, re-read what she says in *The Skin of the Film* about Deleuze's category of "optical images", which are characteristic of "time-image" cinema. Optical images are "still or thin-looking images" which are nevertheless "ultimately the richest" (42), since, they "bring the thing each time to an essential singularity" (46). Marks notes that these images are characterized by absence, that they "call on the viewer to search for their hidden history" (42). They seem to have the potential to be able to both conjure and confound thought. Optical images are not necessarily still images, are not necessarily images at all, but are often constituted simply of black or white leader.

Now we imagine imperfect images – mottled, blemished, grainy stills, or old movie footage, in sepia or in black-and-white. Black and white leader alternates with images of an H-shaped farm shown from above, set in a stony Karoo landscape, clearly demarcated by fences; old photographs of family patriarchs and matriarchs, posing alone or with family and servants arranged hierarchically around them; men posing for group photographs – committees or teams or hunting parties; perhaps figures recognizable as apartheid's policy-makers. We need images that conjure what Coetzee has described as, "the *crudity* of life in South Africa, the naked force of its appeals, not only at the physical level but at the moral level too, its callousness and its brutalities, its hungers and its rages, its greed and its lies" which "make it as irresistible as it is unlovable".[36] We are not sure that we can find the appropriate images – images that do not simply evoke standard responses in viewers saturated by media images of this kind.

We have to begin imagining a voice, or voices. We are sure about the passages of dialogue – they will be spoken in Afrikaans (with English subtitles), which is described by Magda as a "language of nuances, of supple word-order and delicate

---

[35]   Coetzee, "Poetics", 60.

[36]   Coetzee, Jurusalem Prize Acceptance Speech, 99.

particles, opaque to the outsider, dense, to its children, with moments of solidarity, moments of distance" (*Heart*, 30). The monologues will be spoken in English, the only language through which Magda/Coetzee can engage with a wider community of readers and/or viewers.

We know that Coetzee favours the kind of voice-over used in the Munk and Marker films, but we struggle to imagine how this will accompany the images. The voice we hear in the novel is Magda's voice, and so our first task should be to imagine her. She cannot be reduced to a conventional "character"; she is a figure in whom are crystallized a number of conflicting discourses, past and present. Her voice is presented by turns in the mode of parody and in the mode of sincerity. Should her monologue accompany the idyllic images of pastoral life filmed in classical mode, or should it accompany the "optical images"? Should the tone in either case be parodic or sincere?

Magda is both old-fashioned and modern, and her dress will have to vary accordingly. We know that she is thin, that she is not beautiful, but we have great difficulty imagining her face, and we wonder whether she should be shown in close-up at all; whether she should not be presented as a voice only, or in distant long-shots, in which the effect is created of a figure observed by herself as she acts out her fantasies, a figure "watched over gravely by a little ghostly double" (*Heart*, 40).

We go to a review of Munk's film for clues. The film brings together, in the present, the character Lisa, a former overseer in Auschwitz, and the character Marta, a former prisoner. The reviewer, James Price, says:

> What makes *The Passenger* such a novelty in the welter of Occupation films, is that the fiction does not degrade its subject-matter, though the fiction is the framework and the fictional figures are always in the foreground. Munk manages this in part by the way in which he has directed his actors. He has not allowed them to express feelings and emotions, because feeling and emotion are already expressed in the archetypal situation of prisoner and gaoler. His two principal characters can therefore be seen as figures in a rite: each has a part to play in a pre-arranged scheme of things, and neither is strong enough or free enough to step out of the ring or speak directly to the other.[37]

Perhaps we *will* have to imagine Magda in close-up, in order to produce the effects necessary to fiction, the effects which we have already indicated are necessary in encouraging a mimetic response in viewers. But, like Munk's women characters, she will not show emotions through facial expressions. Her feelings can be voiced, and the most extreme expression of her passions – the killing of the father, the disposal of his body, Magda's laying down of stones to form words in Esperanto, and the rape by Hendrik – can be filmed in long-shot.

---

[37]   James Price, Review of *The Passenger* [Pasazerka], *Film Quarterly* 18.1 (Autumn 1964): 42–6, at 46.

While visualizing these sequences, we were reading Jayamanne's analysis of the function of the gag in Chaplin's films. We were attracted in particular by her analysis of the violently impulsive activities of the child/clown/machine – of how the speed and rhythm of these activities disturbs conventional perceptions of time, thereby disrupting cause–effect relations and violating conventional subject–object relations.[38] We talked about how Magda the child/insect/machine could be imagined in the same way, with her bursts of frenzied repetitive activity fracturing the continuities of narrative and of history. Seeing Magda's movements performed in the rapid, disjointed manner of Chaplin performing slapstick, we were surprised by the way this allowed us to feel – somewhat shockingly – not only the horror, but also the hilarity of these sections of the novel, and we wondered if this was simply perverse.

At the same time, we received Cliff Bestall's responses to our questions about his screenplay of *Life & Times*. This is what Bestall says:

> Despite the problem of working with a character who was mainly constructed as an uncommunicative, silent individual, I was excited by the visual and filmic possibilities. I'd come from a background of fine art and performance art – a genre which I thought the film could incorporate. I thought of Chaplin, Buster Keaton. … A black figure in brilliant sunlight stepping through a crop of pumpkins whispering murmurs of paternal love got me.[39]

This was the basis of the draft with which Coetzee was delighted, the draft which, in Bestall's words, Coetzee said "was better than the book". This reassured us that our imaginings were not merely an aberrant – or irresponsible – reading.

The scenes which present the acts of rape by Hendrik cannot be imagined in this way, however. These scenes present us with particular difficulties, given that the novel was written in the mid-1970s, while we are trying to imagine it for audiences in the twenty-first century. It would be irresponsible to present the successive acts of rape as anything other than Magda's fantasies. Unlike the rape of Lucy in *Disgrace*, they cannot be seen as representing any kind of claim to power on the part of the servants on the farm, and must be shown as metaphors for Magda's desire to connect in a way that is different from that demanded by apartheid. Her desire is stunted and deformed by apartheid and by pre-apartheid relations between races in South Africa, so that she is not capable of imagining it outside the brutal and patriarchal terms imposed on her by history. These scenes need to be filmed with the camera positioned so as to give the sense of Magda's experiencing of the rape, and not Hendrik's. Again, there should be a sense that these scenes are observed – if not constructed – by Magda as narrator.

The final scenes, in which Magda attempts to commune with the sky-gods, could be presented in Chaplinesque fashion, with Magda shown in fast motion

---

[38] Jayamanne, *Toward Cinema and Its Double*, 181–200.
[39] Bestall, personal communication.

building words and lewd signs in stones. The quotations from the novel could be given in male voice-over, and, for those familiar with the work of Godard, might be seen as referencing a technique often used in his films, rather than as simply a literary device borrowed from the novel. Other devices that might be seen as alluding to Godard's work would be the unexpected changes of genre and mode (mimicking, also, the changes of genre in *The Story of an African Farm*), and the division of the entire film into numbered segments.

We imagine the time given to the black leader between segments would increase steadily towards the end of the film, until, in the final segment, Magda's voice, over black leader, speaks the words that are necessary to bring to a halt the narrative time set in motion by her monologue:

> I have uttered my life in my own voice throughout, what a consolation that is, I have chosen at every moment my own destiny, which is to die here in the petrified garden, behind locked gates, near my father's bones, in a space echoing with hymns I could have written but did not because it was too easy. (*Heart*, 138)

The tone here is elegiac, as the narrating voice submits to the ultimate authority of time as death. For, as Coetzee has said, "Historicizing oneself is an exercise in locating one's significance, but is also a lesson, at the most immediate level, in insignificance. It is not just time as history that threatens to engulf one: it is time itself, time as death".[40]

Our attempt to think and feel through the formal devices of Coetzee's novel, to understand them better through film theory and criticism, and to experience them in a sensory way by imagining them translated into the audio-visual medium of film, is of necessity incomplete. It represents a gesture toward an alternate mode of reading, but one which cannot, in the end, escape from language to the realm of the visual and the auditory. As it turns out, the adaptation to screen of *Disgrace* is being released as this book goes to press, and so we will conclude with a brief commentary on this adaptation.

Coetzee awarded the rights to film *Disgrace* to the Australian team of Steve Jacobs (director), and Anna Maria Monticelli (script writer and producer), on condition of retaining script approval. Coetzee apparently "sent back some suggestions – really only three or four minor things",[41] and was persuaded to allow Monticelli to change the ending (Torrance 2009).[42] Jacobs and Monticelli

---

[40]   Coetzee, "Kafka" interview, 209.

[41]   Steve Jacobs, cited in Karl Quinn, "Honour from Disgrace", Review of *Disgrace*, *The Age* (17 June 2009), at www.theage.com.au/news/entertainment/film/honour-from-disgrace/2009/06/16/1244918034964.html (viewed 2 October 2009).

[42]   Kelly Jane Torrance, "Beyond: The movie machine a 'Disgrace'", *Washington Times* (2 October 2009), at www.washingtontimes.com/news/2009/oct/02/beyond-the-movie-machine-a-disgrace/ (viewed 2 October 2009).

had previously made only one film together, *La Spagnola* (2001), and the question that arises, from our perspective, is what it was about these filmmakers and their film that might have persuaded Coetzee to hand over the task of adaptation to them. Coetzee may have wanted to strengthen his affiliation with his newly adopted country by choosing Australian filmmakers, but, beyond this, Jacobs and Monticelli's film must have made a favourable impression on him. Jacobs has said:

> He saw our film *La Spagnola* and appreciated that. I think he believed that we would not shy away from some of the issues in *Disgrace,* because we executed the mother-daughter relationship in *La Spagnola* with quite a clinical and, in a way, objective and [un]sentimental eye. Although he wasn't involved in the project once we got approval of the script.[43]

La Spagnola, written by the Moroccan-born Monticelli, tells the story of a Spanish woman migrant struggling to survive in Australia, and apparently "draws from her own experience and memories as a '60s immigrant child".[44] Much of the dialogue is in European languages, and the film was submitted (but not accepted) for the award of best foreign language film to the 74th Academy Awards. The setting is a bleak borderland between industrial and rural Australia, and the story of the Spanish woman's stormy relationships with her husband and daughter has to be understood in relation to her alienation from the society around her; and as a dramatization of the bigger issue of the clash of cultures. The themes, and the way in which the drama works on a metaphorical level to suggest something beyond the immediate, would thus seem to be compatible with Coetzee's oeuvre.

More importantly, one has to ask what it is about *La Spagnola*'s aesthetic that may have attracted Coetzee. Analysis of the film by Rose Capp is useful in this respect:

> According to Jacobs, in *La Spagnola* "the mundane and the supernatural on occasion collide". Interiors and exteriors are thus given a highly stylised treatment which the director has described as a "quirky naturalness". Rather than offering an environment "without distraction", the contrived nature of the production design tends to distance rather than engage the audience from the central drama. While clearly mining Almodóvar territory, *La Spagnola* bears

---

[43]   Steve Jacobs, cited in Anders Wotzke, Interview with *Disgrace* director Steve Jacobs, *Cut Print Review* (14 June 2009), at http://cutprintreview.com/interviews/interview-steve-jacobs-disgrace/ (viewed 4 October 2009).

[44]   Rose Capp, "*La Spagnola*: Spanish Mission Fails to Conquer", *Senses of Cinema* (2001), at http://archive.sensesofcinema.com/contents/01/16/spag.html (viewed 2 October 2009), citing Steve Jacobs' production notes.

something of the overheated quality and distinctive aesthetic of the Spanish director's work but none of the sophistication.[45]

The place of *Disgrace* (the adaptation) in the context of recent Australian cinema has been recognized by one reviewer, who argues that "despite the South African background and setting, *Disgrace* is an unmistakably Australian film", and goes on to claim that Coetzee's "literary voice" melds "seamlessly with the kind of blunt and unsentimental truth-telling that has defined Australia's unique brand of poetic realism since it first emerged during the Australian New Wave of the '70s and '80s".[46] The Australian New Wave might be characterized as a stylized realism that borders on surrealism and that simultaneously deals with and distances itself from darker issues though comedy. This is, as Capp points out, how *La Spagnola* works, alternating between "scenes of melodramatic intensity and exaggerated farce. Harrowing scenarios of abandonment, violence or attempted abortion are quickly succeeded by broadly comic moments".

This transgressive attitude towards genre and the effect of estrangement might be said to suit Coetzee's mode of writing, and to lend itself to the simultaneous embodied and rational approach that we have argued is necessary to the appreciation of his work. Few would associate Coetzee's work with comedy, although, as we have pointed out in relation to *In the Heart of the Country*, there are elements that can be read as comic. In *Disgrace* Lurie reaches a point in the composition of his opera when he switches to a toy banjo as his instrument, and realizes that "it is not the erotic that is calling to him after all, nor the elegiac, but the comic".[47] One imagines, then, that the black comedy of *La Spagnola* might have been one of its attractions for Coetzee.

The adaptation, in fact, does not deliver on any of these potential filmic approaches. This is understandable, given the difficulties of finding distribution channels for alternative cinema – even as it is, distribution in the US was difficult,[48] and the film ran for less than two weeks in New York. Perhaps in an attempt to promote the film's general appeal, Jacobs insists upon the universality of both the novel and the film, saying:

> It's definitely universal. I mean, that's why the book has done so well. I believe
> films like this could be done in areas that have been through long traumatic
> periods, like Palestine or Northern Ireland or the Balkans. ... You know,

---

[45]   Ibid.

[46]   Wade Major, "*Disgrace*", review of *Disgrace* (the film), *Box Office* (18 September 2009), at http://boxoffice.com/reviews/2009/09/disgrace.php (viewed 30 September 2009).

[47]   J.M. Coetzee, *Disgrace* (London: Vintage, 1999), 184.

[48]   Michael Cieply, "Independent Filmmakers Distribute on Their Own", *New York Times* (12 August 2009), at www.nytimes.com/2009/08/13/business/media/13independent. html?_r=1&hp%C2%A0 (viewed 2 October 2009).

anywhere where rivalries and histories have locked people into conflict that can't
be resolved. So when I read the book I didn't solely think "oh, this is about South
Africa". Of course, it does focus on aspects of the country, but I'm not qualified,
nor would I ever presume to be, to make a statement about South Africa.[49]

But the novel *is* about South Africa. In a paper we are currently working on we
draw on Lindiwe Dovey's recent theorizing of certain modes of African cinema
through Adorno's concept of mimesis,[50] and argue that the novel stages an
encounter between different modes of rationality, and that this encounter has a
specific historical and geographical location. This location is in the Eastern Cape,
for a long time referred to as "the Border", where Europeans and black Africans
engaged in fierce battles over the territory. The filmmakers, however, chose the
more spectacular Western Cape as their setting. Coetzee's only comment on the
film has been to say that "Steve Jacobs has succeeded beautifully in integrating
the story into the grand landscape of South Africa. The lead actors give strong
and thoughtful performances".[51] Given Coetzee's cryptic way of offering critique,
what appears to be approval is probably a mark of his disaffiliation from the
role of landscape in the film, and dissatisfaction with the choice of international
actors such as Malkovitch and the well-known French-Cameroonian actor Eriq
Ebouaney. In its representation of a physical and human reality, the adaptation of
Disgrace is a great deal more accurate than *Dust*, but, like *Dust*, does not evoke
the appropriate mimetic response.

Coetzee gave his approval to Monticelli's ending, which switches the final and
the penultimate scenes from the novel, but said that he preferred his own ending.[52]
In the film's ending, Lurie looks from a distance at Lucy working on the farm
shared with Petrus, and then goes down to join her, implying his accommodation
to this new order. In the novel's ending, Lurie gives over to be euthanized the
lame dog with which he identifies. Coetzee's ending emphasizes the significance
of Lurie's work with the dogs, underplayed in the adaptation and misunderstood
by reviewers as a reference to animal rights (Wotzke 2009).[53] In the novel, Lurie's
work with the dogs carries a complex philosophical discourse concerning the
construction of the human self in different contexts. It has to be recognized that
film as medium has at its disposal very few ways of representing the discourse of
philosophy, and that films attempting to do this would not be likely to get funding.
It is this that makes the adaptation of Coetzee's novels so difficult, and raises
questions about his seeming ambivalence in relation to this enterprise: in the

---

[49]   Wotzke, Interview with Steve Jacobs.

[50]   Lindiwe Dovey, *African Film and Literature: Adapting Violence to the Screen*
(New York: Columbia University Press, 2009).

[51]   J.M. Coetzee, cited in Quinn, "Honour from Disgrace".

[52]   Torrance, "Beyond: The Movie Machine a 'Disgrace'".

[53]   Wotzke, Interview with Steve Jacobs.

end, why is it that Coetzee attempts to retain some control by insisting on script approval, but gives the novels over to be made into something other?

Chapter 4

"The Language of the Heart": Confession, Metaphor and Grace in J.M. Coetzee's *Age of Iron*[1]

Michael Neill

Apartheid ... set for itself the task of reforming – that is to say deforming and hardening – the human heart. Apartheid will remain a mystery as long as it is not approached in the lair of the heart. If we want to understand it, we cannot ignore those passages of its testament that reach us in the heart-speech of autobiography and confession.

J.M. Coetzee, "Apartheid Thinking"[2]

[T]his enterprise of self-construction.does it yield only fictions? Or rather, among the fictions of the self, the versions of the self, that it yields, are there any that are truer than others? How do I know when I have told the truth about myself?

J.M. Coetzee, "On the Question of Autobiography"[3]

One of the fates of confession since Rousseau – of secular confession at least – has been to spin itself out endlessly in an effort to reach beyond self-reflection to truth. Only later does the realization dawn that getting to the real self (finding the Mystery I) is a life's task, like cleaning the Augean stables.

J.M. Coetzee, "Breyten Breytenbach"[4]

---

[1]   An earlier version of this essay appeared in Colin Gibson and Lisa Marr, eds, *New Windows on a Woman's World: Scholarly Writing in Honour of Jocelyn Harris* (Dunedin: University of Otago English Department, 2005), 515–43.

[2]   In J.M. Coetzee, *Giving Offense: Essays on Censorship* (Chicago: University of Chicago Press, 1996), 163–84, at 164.

[3]   David Attwell, "On the Question of Autobiography: Interview with J.M. Coetzee", *Current Writing* 3 (1991): 117–22, at 117.

[4]   J.M. Coetzee, "Breyten Breytenbach and the Reader in the Mirror", in *Giving Offense*, 215–31, at 231.

True Confessions

Early in 1976, the year of the Soweto students' uprising, in which more that 600 young people were to be killed by the South African security forces, I found myself listening to a terrible confession. I was on a flight from London to Hong Kong and had made the mistake of helping an older passenger with her hand-luggage: I was immediately concerned that my gesture could license the kind of intimacy which it is best to avoid on long-distance flights, and which, as soon as I heard her heavy Afrikaans vowels, I felt especially anxious to evade; but, wedged against the window by her ample frame, and shamefully wanting the courage to express my real feelings about the society from which she came, I could find no means of escape. She introduced herself as Connie, a florist from Jo'burg, and for the next eight hours (ignoring my conspicuous efforts to bury myself in literature and sleep) exposed me to a remorselessly self-justifying monologue on the sufferings of white South Africa, leavened only by photographs of her hideous floral creations. As I contemplated the splendours of a poodle "four feet high and made entirely out of white carnations", Connie said: "I expect you have heard there is trouble in my country? Of course it's not true – there are just a few *tstotsis* (criminals, you know). I had one just laast week trying to interfere with my caar – so I shot him."

"You *shot* at this guy?"

"No," indignantly, "I shot him dead. I was brought up on a faarm, I know how to shoot."

Then she told me how God has protected her: "If you ever have any trouble, ask the Old Man upstairs – he has never let me down."

Her tone was by turns confiding and truculent; and at first I thought it demanded a response – that she wanted to be told that it was alright – alright to kill a man for "interfering" with her property. But, as the monologue continued, it became apparent that no such reassurance was sought: my role was simply that of a sounding board; for hers was a confession that appeared to confer its own absolution, simply by virtue of the fact that it had been uttered.

This was to be the first of several such encounters; and, to an outsider like myself, there were few more eloquent expressions of the pathology of apartheid than the drive to confess, which sometimes appeared to turn every white South African, regardless of political allegiance, into a kind of Ancient Mariner, frantic with the desire for unburdening. Amongst supporters of the regime, this would result in angrily defensive tirades, which it was difficult not to read as speaking to their own repressed anxiety and guilt; amongst liberals – or even amongst more radical dissenters – it produced a more abject style of apology: one calculated to persuade the listener of the speaker's distance from a criminal regime that, so long as it survived, nevertheless seemed able to enforce a repellent complicity. In either case, listeners would be left with the uneasy feeling that, despite their having provoked an outburst of appalling confidence, they were ultimately irrelevant to it. It was as if their attention, like that of Coleridge's hapless wedding guest, was necessary simply as a release for a discourse that remained essentially inner-directed.

Reflecting on the compulsive nature of such narratives, the South African critic David Schalkwyk, in an essay published after the collapse of the apartheid regime, suggested that confession had become "the inevitable condition of all white South Africans whatever their personal feelings, beliefs, or even actions".[5] Schalkwyk's essay was devoted to the prison writings of the poets Breyten Breytenbach and Jeremy Cronin; but the phenomenon he observed had become a distinguishing feature of the remarkable literature that emerged from the decade of crisis preceding the release of Nelson Mandela in 1990 – the uneasy time of "Waiting" so brilliantly analysed by the American anthropologist Vincent Crapanzano.[6] Famously dubbed "the Interregnum" by Nadine Gordimer,[7] this was a period still haunted by the fantasies of apocalypse that had fuelled some of the most powerful fiction of the 1970s;[8] but, while the shadow of the *dies irae* remained, the most characteristic writing took a rather different turn: whether one thinks of such displays of autobiographical abjection as Breyten Breytenbach's *True Confessions of an Albino Terrorist* (1985), Christopher Hope's *White Boy Running* (1988), Rian Malan's *My Traitor's Heart* (1989), or of the most personal essays in André Brink's *Mapmakers* (1983), or of novels like Brink's *States of Emergency* (1988), and Gordimer's *Burger's Daughter* (1979) and *My Son's Story* (1990),[9] the literature of this phase was dominated by the confessional voice.

In the prominence which they gave to confession, these writers might be thought to have anticipated (and perhaps even helped to create the climate for) the elaborate rituals of public contrition, supervised by the Truth and Reconciliation Commission, through which the post-apartheid state successfully averted the South African Day of Judgement. But in the self-reflexive intensity with which their best work held the motives, truth-status, and efficacy of confession up to question, they also prepared the way for a moral critique of confessional politics of the kind advanced in Coetzee's novel of the post-apartheid world, *Disgrace* (1999).

---

[5] David Schalkwyk, "Confession and Solidarity in the Prison Writing of Breyten Breytenbach and Jeremy Cronin", *Research in African Literatures* 25 (1994): 23–45, at 42.

[6] Vincent Crapanzano, *Waiting: the Whites of South Africa* (London: Granada, 1985).

[7] Nadine Gordimer, "Living in the Interregnum", *New York Review of Books* (20 January 1983), 21–9.

[8] See, e.g., Nadine Gordimer's *The Conservationist* (1974) and *July's People* (1981); J.M Coetzee's *Waiting for the Barbarians* (1980) and *The Life and Times of Michael K* (1983); and André Brink's *Rumours of Rain* (1978) and *A Dry White Season* (1979).

[9] On the special prominence of 'confessional autobiography" in South African fiction from the period of the State of Emergency in the late 1980s, see M. van Wyk Smith, "Waiting for Silence; or, The Autobiography of Metafiction in some recent South African Novels", *Current Writing* 3 (1991): 91–104, at 92.

Confession, as the nature of the Commission's process reminds us, is always an ambiguous business: inspired as they were by the theology of Archbishop Tutu, the Commission's hearings were poised somewhere between judicial process and sacramental rite, reflecting the double nature of confession itself. The term, after all, can refer impartially to the voluntary admission of sin, or to the involuntary declarations of guilt extracted by the power of an interrogator or torturer – one directed towards atonement and absolution, the other aimed at indictment and punishment. To the confessant, however, arraigned before the bar of conscience, the one may often feel very like the other. In Nadine Gordimer's *Burger's Daughter* (1979), Rosa Burger, recalcitrant child of anti-apartheid radicalism, is haunted by the sense of being "[a]lways ... addressed to someone" so that even her dreams feel as if "performed before an audience".[10] The nature of that audience shifts, as her first-person narrative unfolds, to include former lovers, members of the Communist Party, political comrades, and the constant shadowy presence of state security; but by the end of the novel we discover that the real object of her address, from the very beginning, has been her missing father, Lionel Burger, dead hero of the struggle. Thus Rosa's narrative can be seen to constitute a secular version of confession, through which the prodigal daughter seeks absolution from the patriarch whose law she has (in spite of her own commitment) transgressed. Caught between her simultaneous need for an audience to hear her confession, and weary longing to escape the confessor/interrogator's remorseless attention, Rosa articulates a version of the more urgent anxiety that devours the abject narrator of Breytenbach's prison memoir, as he begs "May I be your humble servant, Mr Investigator? Listen to me. I shall confesss."[11]

The burlesque title which Breytenbach gave to this most remorselessly self-reflexive of confessional narratives, *The True Confessions of an Albino Terrorist*, served to ironize not merely the poet's scandalous desertion of his white Afrikaner *volk*, but the conspicuous parade of sincerity on which the moral claims of his chosen genre depend. Breytenbach's narrative is addressed to a normally silent "Mr Investigator" – also called "Mr Interrogator", "Mr Investerrogator", "Mr Confessor", "Mr Eye" and "Mr I"– a shifting figure who (in Schalkwyk's words) "is constituted variously.as the reader, Breytenbach's wife, his alter ego, his Security Police interrogators, a Supreme Court Judge, and the black South African activists who dismiss Breytenbach for being a naive and expedient sell-out".[12] Yet in this psychological mirror-maze, where seemingly opposed identities elide into one another, there is in the end no real interlocutor but the writer himself – the self-indicting inquisitor who is made to identify himself at the end of chapter 4, "I Found Myself Confronted By", in a section entitled "(Recapitulation)":

---

[10]   Nadine Gordimer, *Burger's Daughter* (Harmondsworth: Penguin, 1979), 16

[11]   Breyten Breytenbach, *True Confessions of an Albino Terrorist* (London: Faber, 1984), 14.

[12]   Schwalkwyk, "Confession and Solidarity", 26.

I must sniff out. I must uncover ... I must allow it to reveal itself. The secret secrets ... Do you mind that I ask, I ask, I ask. Don't you know it's necessary? That it can *never* be any different? That it has been like this from the beginning of time – you and I entwined and related, parasite and prey? Image and mirror-image ... You make me accept myself. You make me feel that I know I *am*! Come, I'm your father confessor. Together we are the embodiment of the reality of my thoughts, my wishes, my anguishes, my existence ... Through you I see that the looking-glass is true. You bring me to my knees. Because you are you and I am I, I am saved.[13]

The self being voiced here, as Schalkwyk puts it, is simply "an externalized projection of an internal revulsion, a revulsion at precisely his sick sincerity, his fawning desire to please: his sense of being shaped at every turn by master-others of his despised cultural and personal heritage".[14] To make matters worse, because this confessor "has power but not moral or spiritual authority",[15] the process of confession can lead nowhere: for the lapsed Calvinist Breytenbach, there is no possibility of atonement or absolution, only the endless interrogation of (and by) a tormented (and tormenting) conscience.

The dilemmas of Breytenbach's and Gordimer's confessants point up the paradox that lies at the heart of the confessional impulse, that it both requires and abhors an audience: *con*fession, after all (as its Latin root would suggest) is as much a social as a personal act – an "uttering *with*". In the ritual of confession, the presence of an auditor is necessary for the cathartic reckoning to be made at all – both as an implicit guarantor of sincerity, and as the formal vehicle of release from the burden of sin; yet the truths that must be disclosed are by definition shameful (even "unspeakable"), and the absolution which the speaker craves is, in the end, an entirely private matter. Moreover the very presence of an audience compromises the truthfulness of a confession, since it demands a rhetoric, a theatricalized display of sincerity[16] – one that, at some point, always seeks to lure the sympathetic auditor into guilty complicity, and (tacitly at least) into that acknowledgement of a common creed which is one of the other meanings of "confession". This, of course, is why, in the world of tabloid journalism, "true confessions" have come to stand for the most fraudulent kind of self-exposure.

---

[13] Breytenbach, *True Confessions*, 57–8.
[14] Schwalkwyk, "Confession and Solidarity", 27.
[15] Ibid.
[16] This is the inherent paradox that Derek Attridge describes in *J.M. Coetzee and the Ethics of Reading: Literature in the Event* (Chicago: University of Chicago Press, 2004), when he writes: "for Coetzee, as for Dostoevsky, confession is never simple or direct, it is always what Derrida calls a circumfession, an avoidance as well as an admission, a staging of confession as well as a confessing" (136–7). On the problematics of truthful self-revelation, see Lionel Trilling's indispensable *Sincerity and Authenticity* (London: Oxford University Press, 1972).

In the Roman Catholic tradition, which remains the paradigm of efficacious confession, the paradoxes that threaten to undo the veracity and integrity of the process are symbolically accommodated through the studied privacy of the confession box. Invisible, anonymous, emptied of personality, the priest is there to *hear* the confession, but the confession is not really made *to* him: it is made to God, who alone can confer the absolution that confession is designed to secure, and for which the priest serves simply as a medium. In this ritual form, the truth of confession is ultimately guaranteed by the presence of the Almighty who is able to hear, behind the formulaic utterances of the confessional, the unmediated language of perfect sincerity. It is this claim to absolute nakedness before God that makes absolution possible. Outside the Catholic dispensation, however, since the confessional impulse is always rhetorically compromised and is without any secure guarantor of truth, absolution is impossible. But that in no-way diminishes the need to confess – if anything, it exacerbates it; which is why the Ancient Mariner is seemingly doomed to make his tormented confession again and again and again.

No one has explored the agonizing repetitions and recursiveness of secular confession with more subtlety than J.M. Coetzee: his interest in it was evident in several of his earlier fictions, including *Dusklands* (1974), *In the Heart of the Country* (1977), *Waiting for the Barbarians* (1980) and *Foe* (1986); it was the subject of a substantial critical essay, "Confession and Double Thoughts: Tolstoy, Rousseau, Dostoevsky", published in 1985;[17] and it is crucial to the narrative design of his most openly political novel, *Age of Iron* (1990), in which the novelist explores the very issues of complicity and collective guilt that the public confessional of the Truth and Reconciliation Commission would later allow the mass of white South Africans to put to one side. In this novel, Coetzee's use of the confessional mode is distinguished not merely by the self-reflexive qualities that he shares with Breytenbach and (to a lesser extent) Gordimer, but by a fastidious and exacting scepticism about both the motives and the efficacy of confession. This scepticism must have been shaped, at least in part, by Coetzee's somewhat anomalous position in the white South African world: although his surname links him to the predominantly rural Afrikaans-speaking community, with its strong Calvinist tradition, the novelist was raised in an urban, English-speaking family, and educated at a Catholic school.[18] Whilst he nowadays acknowledges

---

[17]   J.M. Coetzee, "Confession and Double Thoughts: Tolstoy, Rousseau, Dostoevsky", *Comparative Literature* 37 (1985): 193–232. The significance of this essay for an understanding of *Age of Iron* and the novel that succeeded it, *The Master of Petersburg* (1994), is briefly examined by Dominic Head in *J.M. Coetzee* (Cambridge: Cambridge University Press, 1997), 138–43, 149–51. A more extensive discussion of the motif of confession in Coetzee's writing will be found in Attridge, 135–7 and chapter 6. Attridge, however, makes only passing reference to the confessional element in *Age of Iron*.

[18]   In one of several interviews published in *Doubling the Point: Essays and Interviews*, ed. David Attwell (Cambridge, MA: Harvard University Press, 1992), 335–43, Coetzee,

no particular religious affiliation, his writing seems indelibly marked by this divided inheritance. This is what seems to underlie the deep scepticism about the expressive power of language – its capacity to speak the world – that informs his bare, scrupulous prose: and the other face of this scepticism is the longing, repeatedly expressed by his characters, to master a kind of speech that will allow them to utter their hearts: "As for language," says Paul Rayment, the French-Australian protagonist of *Slow Man*:

> "English has never been mine in the way that it is yours. Nothing to do with fluency. I am perfectly fluent, as you can hear. But … [p]rivately I have always felt myself to be a kind of ventriloquist's dummy. It is not I who speak the language, it is the language that is spoken through me. It does not come from my core, *mon coeur*."[19]

The desire for such purity of utterance, for someone who (as Rayment says) "was once a pukkah little Catholic boy",[20] is driven by needs that are ultimately confessional; and Coetzee's writing is marked by a recurrent yearning to find some secular equivalent for the Catholic sacrament of confession and absolution. Yet the very impossibility of that desire means that the confessional impulse is constantly frustrated by an awareness of the sleights and deceits that lurk in the crevices of language: and the result (as I shall try to show in the latter part of this paper) is an equally powerful nostalgia for the salvific promise held out by a Calvinistic notion of arbitrarily conferred grace that derives from the other side of Coetzee's theological inheritance.

In "Confession and Double Thoughts", Coetzee explores the paradoxes at the core of secular confession "in which problems of truth-telling and self-recognition, deception and self-deception, come to the forefront".[21] Starting with the *Confessions* of St Augustine, Coetzee reflects at length on the moral ambivalence and psychological evasions that compromise the confessional process, especially

---

while acknowledging his inevitable "complicity" in a "gang" from which he felt neither able nor morally entitled to withdraw, yet pointed out: "No Afrikaner would consider me an Afrikaner … In the first place because English is my first language, and has been since childhood … In the second place because I am not embedded in the culture of the Afrikaner (I have never belonged to a Reformed Church), and have been shaped by the culture only in a perverse way" (341–2).

[19] J.M. Coetzee, *Slow Man* (New York: Viking, 2005), 198. Elizabeth Curren elaborates the same point later in the novel: "you speak English, you probably think in English, yet English is not your true language. I would even say that English is a disguise for you, or a mask … As you speak I can hear the words being selected, one after another, from the word-box you carry around with you, and slotted into place. That is not how a native speaks, one who is born into the language." A native, she insists, will speak "[f]rom the heart. Words well up and he sings them, sings along with them. So to speak" (230–31).

[20] *Slow Man*, 156.

[21] "Confession and Double Thoughts," 195.

when it is cut loose from its theological underpinnings. Citing Spengler, he argues that the Protestant abolition of its sacramental framework, meant that confession must inevitably "tend to be 'unbounded'":[22] to be effective "[c]onfession ... can be made only to an adequate confessor"; so when "there is ... no confessor empowered to absolve", the confessant finds himself tormented by doubts as to whether his narrative "can ever lead to that *end of the chapter* whose attainment is the goal of confession".[23] The result is a kind of psychological *mise en abyme* in which the confessant endlessly interrogates not only his own truthfulness, but even the sincerity of that interrogation itself. In this respect, confessional narratives can be thought of as secular descendants of those anxious self-inquisitions through which the Calvinist sensibility sought for the signs of grace and the proof of salvation. In each case the confessant is liable to become trapped in a recursive spiral of self-accusation and "double thought"; and just as the Calvinist was tormented by the knowledge that the inward apprehension of grace might be indistinguishable from the damnable sin of "security", so the fictional confessants described by Coetzee can never be sure of "the difference between a 'true' moment of self-forgiveness and a moment of complacency."[24] As a result, he argues, citing a group of stories by Dostoevsky, true confession cannot come either from "the sterile monologue of the self", or from "the dialogue of the self with its own self-doubt", but can only be achieved through "faith and grace".[25] "Against the endlessness of skepticism," Coetzee remarks, in a gloss on his own essay, "Dostoevsky poses the closure not of confession but of absolution and therefore of the intervention of grace in the world."[26] The end of confession, the essay concludes, "is to tell the truth to and for oneself";[27] since, however, any firm conviction of grace remains elusive, beyond the reach of the will, it appears that "the impasses of secular confession [may point] finally to the sacrament of confession as the only road to [such] self-truth" – and hence to the absolution for which the confessant, however hopelessly, always yearns.[28]

In *Age of Iron* (published five years after "Confession and Double Thoughts", but written between 1986 and 1989), Coetzee revisited the "impasses of secular confession" through the consciousness of Elizabeth Curren,[29] a retired university teacher who introduces herself with the revelation that she has been diagnosed

---

[22]   Oswald Spengler, *The Decline of the West*, trans Charles F. Atkinson (London, 1932), cited in Coetzee, "Confession and Double Thoughts," 195.
[23]   "Confession and Double Thoughts," 195.
[24]   Ibid., 230.
[25]   Ibid., 230.
[26]   Interview with David Attwell, in *Doubling the Point*, 243–50, at 249.
[27]   "Confession and Double Thoughts", 230.
[28]   Ibid., 230.
[29]   Strictly speaking, as Attridge has pointed out, the narrator should be referred to as "Mrs Curren", since (apart from the initials "E.C.") that is the only name given her in the text (*Ethics of Reading*, 94–5, fn. 3). Attridge acknowledges, however, that Coetzee

with terminal cancer. Set in the Capetown of 1986, at the height of the low-level rebellion orchestrated by the young township "Comrades", this novel seemed to mark a departure from the allegorical obliqueness with which its author had hitherto addressed the political crisis in South Africa. Caricaturing the moribund white regime as "a bad-tempered old hound snoozing in the doorway, taking its time to die",[30] *Age of Iron* is self-consciously a document of the "interregnum" – that time of uneasy "waiting" which is mirrored in the disturbingly arrested moment at the end of Part 3 when the narrator waits for the police to gun down the armed schoolboy-revolutionary hiding in her house: "[a] hovering time, but not eternity. *A time being*, a suspension, before the return of the time in which the door bursts open and we face.the great white glare" (160). Mrs Curren's house (a metonym for the country as a whole) is itself imagined as "tired of waiting for the day, tired of holding itself together ready to die" (13); and Elizabeth Curren herself, is a creature *"in limine"* (85): brooding on the proximity of extinction, she imagines herself as one of Vergil's shades, hovering by the Styx:

> All the days you have known me. I have been standing on the river-bank awaiting my turn. I am waiting for someone to show me the way across. Every minute of every day, I am here, waiting. (64)

To her, indeed, death and judgement, the *dies irae* (102), seem not merely imminent, but imm*a*nent, their presence figured by the censorious presence of her black housekeeper, Florence, and by the enigmatic silence of the tramp, Mr Vercueil, who haunts her like some banally diminished Angel of Death. If "the country smoulders" with the fire of revolution, Mrs Curren's sickness mimics its condition: "'Look at me!' I want to cry. 'I too am burning!'" (36).

Age of Iron, then, as its title suggests – drawing on a classical myth about human decadence and anarchic self-destruction – is a narrative of last things, a South African "thanatophany", as Mrs Curren herself calls it, a revelation of death. Significantly, however, the novel draws back from the sensational gratifications of apocalyptic ending – a move slyly foreshadowed by the rearrangement of the traditional mythic sequence when the narrator imagines that terminal age of iron may be succeeded by the "softer" ages of bronze, clay and earth (50). Playing on the literal meaning of apocalypse ("discovery, unveiling"), Mrs Curren writes

> I will draw a veil soon ... I will not show to you what you will not be able to bear: a woman in a burning house running from window to window, calling through the bars for help. (170)

---

has himself referred to his protagonist as "Elizabeth Curren", which indeed is how she is described on the dust-jacket of the first edition.

[30] J.M. Coetzee, *Age of Iron* (London: Secker & Warburg, 1990), 64. Subsequent citations will be by page number in the text.

Instead what she offers is confession: facing the certainty of ending, Elizabeth Curren is not merely writing her own death – but is also engaged in an act of moral accounting, making the "first confession" (124) that is also to be her final one; and it is this deeply private action, rather than the public events that occasion it, that is the real focus of the novel's attention.

The entire narrative is presented as a letter written to the absent daughter whom the narrator has chosen as her confessor; within that larger confession are a number of confessional moments in which Mrs Curren attempts to explain herself to a series of apparently reluctant and more-or-less uncomprehending audiences, including Florence and Vercueil, as well as the schoolteacher, Mr Thabane, and the angry mob that confronts her in the township of Guguletu. Explaining her need to confess, Mrs Curren tells her daughter:

> It is the soul of you I address, as it is the soul of me that will be left with you when this letter is over … that is what, reading, I hope you will glimpse: my soul readying itself for further flight. A white moth, a ghost emerging from the mouth of the figure on the deathbed. (118)

What she must do, to prepare herself for flight, is to discharge the burden of her own implication in the brutalities of a system she detests. Talking to her enigmatic *doppelgänger*, Vercueil, she acknowledges her complicity in a "crime … committed long ago … So long ago that I was born into it. It is part of my inheritance. It is part of me. I am part of it … Though it was not a crime I asked to be committed, it was committed in my name" (151). The only way to expiate that offence, she believes, will be through "as a full a confession as I know how", one in which "I withhold no secrets" (150). Expelled from her house, and forced to sleep beside the old tramp in a vacant lot, where she is exposed to the gaze of every passer-by, Mrs Curren imagines her condition as a figure for the absolute moral transparency she desires: "That is how we must be in the eyes of the angels: people living in houses of glass, our every act naked, our hearts naked too, beating in chests of glass" (151).

But for all this display of nakedness, the ultimate truth of Elizabeth Curren's self-revelation remains in doubt – for herself, and therefore for the reader. The confessions she attempts in the course of her narrative repeatedly fail: answering Mr Thabane's inquisition before the accusatory Guguletu crowd, she feels helpless before the unspeakable:

> "There are many things I am sure I could say … But then they must truly come from me. When one speaks under duress – you should know this – one rarely speaks the truth … These are terrible sights … But I cannot denounce them in other people's words. I must find my own words, from myself. Otherwise it is not the truth." (91)

Even her lengthy confession to Vercueil at the end of the third part is compromised by the uncertain role of her confessor: it is precisely because of his strange taciturnity, that Mrs Curren chooses the old man as "the one to whom I speak my heart, whom I trust with last things" (74); but his unresponsiveness may signal nothing more than indifference. Throughout her monologue on the empty lot, Vercueil remains silent, "his face hidden" (149), like a parodic version of a priest in the confessional; and even at the end he appears so impassive that she wonders if he is not asleep. "Is a true confession still true," she asks herself, "if it is not heard?" (151). This disturbingly self-reflexive moment, serves to reminds us that Mrs Curren's entire narrative takes the form of a confession that may not be heard, since it is constructed as a letter which she knows is unlikely ever to be delivered – a text, moreover, that we ourselves are not entitled to read since it constitutes a set of "private papers" whose author declares "I don't want them opened and read by anyone else" (28).[31] Of course, barely hidden behind his narrator at this point is the novelist himself, dryly reminding the reader of his metafictional game, whose recessive ironies destabilize our own relation to the text. Are we *hearing* this confession, or simply *over*hearing it? If we are licensed to hear it, does that make it "true" (even though it is part of a fiction); even if it is true, since the pretence is that it was never offered to us, are we bound to *mis*hear it? Does not our violation of these "private papers" in some way align us with the agents of surveillance and interrogation – thereby turning it into a very different kind of confession? Hell itself Mrs Curren imagines as a place of indiscriminate and interminable public apology where all privacies are annihilated:

> Perhaps that is what the afterlife will be like … a great crowded bus on its way from nowhere to nowhere. Standing room only: on one's feet forever, crushed against strangers. The air thick, stale, full of sighs and murmurs: *Sorry, sorry.* Promiscuous contact. An end to private life. (27)

Perhaps to defend itself against improper scrutiny, as well as to interrogate its own sincerity, Mrs Curren's letter is full of warnings about the reliability of confessional narratives, suggesting that the text we are reading may be as treacherous as the fraudulent messages conveyed by the "parade of politicians" whom she scrutinizes on television: "I am watching not the lie but the space behind the lie where the truth ought to be. But is it true?" (26). The space where the truth is conventionally hidden is to be found deep within – in the region of the heart, as we like to say – and confession, supposedly the utterance of a contrite heart, is meant to reveal it. The confessant, however, warns her reader to mistrust her: "This letter," she insists, early in the narrative, "is not a baring of my heart. It is a baring of something,

---

[31]   Coetzee's decision to dedicate the novel to his parents and his son, all three of whom had recently died, can seem like a further encoding of the suggestion that the book is meant for eyes that will never see it, and that our own reading constitutes a kind of unwarrantable eavesdropping.

but not of my heart" (13). What nevertheless seems to underwrite her sincerity is the fact that she is making a kind of deathbed confession, meant to be read by her chosen confessor only after her death, when "truth and love [are] together at last" (118). The imminence of death endows confession with an authority that promises to put its truth beyond question, since (as Coetzee expresses it in "Confession and Double Thoughts") "[t]he moment before death belongs to a different kind of time in which truth has at last the power to appear in the form of revelation".[32] Here Coetzee is discussing the case of Ippolit in Doestevsky's *The Idiot*, who claims that the terminal nature of his tuberculosisis means that he can have no possible motive for lying: the truthfulness of a confession made in the face of death is guaranteed because it "belongs to last things, it *is* a last thing, and therefore has a status different from any critique of it. The sincerity of the motive behind last confessions cannot be impugned, he says, because that sincerity is guaranteed by the death of the confessant."[33] In the same way, Coetzee has said, Elizabeth Curren's narrative "brings to bear against the voices of history and historical judgement … the authority of the dying"; and this authority, he suggests, is beyond question, since the power of the suffering body "is undeniable".[34]

In both cases, however, the guarantee of truthfulness proves to be less irrefragable than at first appears. In *The Idiot*, Ippolit's prognosis is exposed as completely unreliable; and in *Age of Iron* we have only Mrs Curren's word for the mortal nature of an illness that, as we shall see, often appears as much metaphorical as medical. Although her confession may seem to be rendered unanswerable when, in the novel's closing sentence, she gives herself to the cold embrace of Mr Vercueil, this proves to be a mere rehearsal for death rather than the real thing; for to read it otherwise would be to destroy the novel's foundational fiction – that it has been written as a letter from a living woman. If, moreover, Vercueil, resembles the Angel of Death, that is only because Mrs Curren, compulsive reader of signs that she is, has chosen to imagine him as "an angel come to show me the way" (153). But the closest she gets to fulfilling her wish to see him as he "really" is comes when she identifies him as "[j]ust a man." (165). In Dostoevsky's novel, Ippolit offers to make good his guarantee of authenticity by committing suicide; but the manipulative, rhetorical character of the gesture only serves to further undermine his claims: "The explanation, the privileged truth paid for with death," comments Coetzee, "is in truth a seed, a way of living on after death: it therefore casts into doubt the sincerity of the decision to die. The only truth is silence."[35] Mrs Curren imagines her words as just such a "seed": "These words, as you read them.enter you and draw breath again. They are, if you like, my way of living on" (120); and shortly afterwards she is forced to question the sincerity of her own decision to die,

---

[32]   "Confession and Double Thoughts," 224.

[33]   Ibid., 223–4.

[34]   Interview in *Doubling the Point*, 250, 248.

[35]   "Confession and Double Thoughts", 225–6.

when she sees it as if through Florence's eyes. She is thinking of her failed fantasy of dying as a suicide-bomber in an attack on Parliament, "the House of Lies":

> If dying in bed … in a purgatory of pain and shame, will not save my soul, why should I be saved by dying in two minutes in a pillar of flames? Will the lies stop because a sick old woman kills herself … If Florence were passing by, with Hope by her side and Beauty on her back, would she be impressed by the spectacle? Would she even spare it a glance? …
>
> What would count in Florence's eyes as a serious death? … Florence is the judge. Behind her glasses her eyes are still, measuring all … The court belongs to Florence; it is I who pass under review. If the life I live is an examined life, it is because for ten years I have been under examination in the court of Florence. (129)

"Examination" of this kind might seem designed to extract a very different kind of confession; but in fact it is part of Elizabeth Curren's "purgatory of pain and shame" that Florence seems deaf and indifferent to any such gesture: the only death that might seem "serious" to her would be one uncontaminated by the ambiguous motives of the confessional, one that "comes of itself, irresistable, unannounced, like a clap of thunder, like a bullet between the eyes" (129).

Nevertheless Mrs Curren can be distinguished from Dostoevsky's confessant by virtue of the sceptical self-awareness that forces her to question not only the truth of her own confession, but even the sincerity and seriousness of the death that ought to authenticate it. "A confessant who does not doubt himself when there are obvious grounds for doing so," Coetzee insists, "… is no better than one who refuses to doubt because doubt is not profitable"; thus, paradoxically enough, the only absolute "authority" that can be attributed to a secular confession is that which derives "from the status of the confessant as a hero of the labyrinth willing to confront the worst within himself".[36] Dominic Head is no doubt right to suggest that, when Mrs Curren describes her own writing as the "scratching and whining" of "a dog in the maze, scurrying up and down the branches and tunnels" (126), she is being invested with something of that heroic authority; but his conclusion, that her confession is also to be taken as "true", is much less secure. Head anchors this claim in Vercueil's "uselessness as a confessor" arguing that "because [he] does not respond … he cannot elicit or encourage double thought from her" with the result that – if only by a piece of "narrative artifice" – hers becomes a "notionally untainted confession … in which the self is alone with the self, without comfort or pity".[37] But double-thought, after all, is not necessarily elicited by the presence of a confessor; to the contrary, it is inseparable from that "dialogue of the self with its own self-doubt" from whose endless spirals only the sacramental sequence of confession, penitence and absolution could grant complete release.

---

[36] Ibid., 205.

[37] Head, *J.M. Coetzee*, 141, 143.

Head's conclusion, moreover, underestimates the significance of the narrator's engagement with her imagined reader(s). If she emerges as a "hero of the labyrinth" it is not only because she doubts the truthfulness of her own confession, but because she urges doubt upon her confessor: the more moving her language, the less, she suggests, it should be trusted. This is because rhetoric seeks to evoke sympathetic emotion in the auditor; and sympathy can only confuse the confessor's role. Thus the powerful evocation of her journey into Guguletu – presented as a kind of brutally degraded parody of an epic descent into the underworld ("Aornus this place: birdless ... Hades, Hell: the domain of ideas ... Why can hell not be at the foot of Africa?" – 83, 101)[38] – is accompanied by a warning:

> It is through my eyes that you see; the voice that speaks in your head is mine. Through me alone do you find yourself here on these desolate flats, smell the smoke in the air, see the bodies of the dead, hear the weeping, shiver in the rain. It is my thoughts that you think, my despair that you feel.To me your sympathies flow; your heart beats with mine. (95)

The sympathetic reverberation which Mrs Curren repudiates here resembles the response traditionally invited by humane literature – an emotional catharsis like that experienced by Miranda when she is exposed to the "direful spectacle" of shipwreck and death conjured up by Prospero's art: "I have suffered with those that I saw suffer" (*Tempest*, 1.2.5–6). But Coetzee's narrator insists that she is telling her story

> not so that you will feel for me but so that you will learn how things are ... So I ask you: attend to the writing, not to me. If lies and pleas and excuses weave among the words, listen for them, do not forgive them easily. Read all, even this adjuration, with a cold eye ... Do not read in sympathy with me. Let your heart not beat with mine. (95–6)

Sympathy can only blind us, she suggests, obscuring not just "the truth behind the lie", but the possibility that this truth itself may constitute nothing more than another artfully constructed falsehood.[39] Worse still, sympathy offers a dangerous

---

[38]   A little earlier she has used the same figure for Groote Schuur Hospital – ironically an institution made famous by the pioneering *heart*-transplant surgery of Christian Barnard – where she goes looking for an injured Comrade: "Hades this place, and I a fugitive shade" (64).

[39]   Mrs Curren's repudiation of sympathy may seem odd in the light of the insistence of her namesake, Elizabeth Costello, on the ethical indispensability of sympathy as a faculty, seated in the heart, "that allows us to share the being of another" (J.M. Coetzee, *Elizabeth Costello: Eight Lessons* (New York: Viking, 2003), 79) – but the potentially corrupting effects of sympathy are illustrated in her subsequent critique of a novel describing the execution of Hitler's would-be assassins.

palliation of the shame that Elizabeth Curren's confession is designed not simply to express, but to agitate and reinvigorate: the expression of shame, we might say, is her form of contrition; while the constant reanimation of shame (which, unlike guilt, assumes the offender's fearful transparency) is the penance she enjoins upon herself – even if it offers no reliable promise of absolution. After her visit to Guguletu, Mrs Curren goes on a second drive with Vercueil, a bottle of petrol beside her, contemplating self-immolation as a release from the "pit of disgrace" into which these shameful times have cast her (107); then, at the last minute, she finds herself reneging: "With relief I give myself back to the ordinary. I wallow in it. I lose my sense of shame, become shameless as a child" (109). But that moment of abandon offers no real release from shame – instead, like Breytenbach's confessant when he feels himself "ashamed of not having any shame left",[40] Mrs Curren finds herself tormented by "[t]he shamefulness of that shamelessness":

> that is what I cannot forget, that is what I cannot bear afterwards … It is like trying to give up alcohol. Trying and trying, always trying, but knowing in your bones from the beginning that you are going to slide back. There is a shame to that private knowledge, a shame so warm, so intimate, so comforting that it brings more shame flooding with it. There seems to be no limit to the shame a human being can feel. (109)

By a kind of cruel amphibology, at the very moment when Elizabeth Curren is on the "brink" of suicide (109) she finds herself gazing into a different abyss – one very like that evoked by St Augustine in his *Confessions*, and described by Coetzee at the beginning of "Confession and Double Thoughts": Augustine remembers a childhood transgression and recalls himself as "seeking nothing from the shameful deed but the shame itself … We were ashamed not to be shameless;" and Coetzee comments:

> the robbery brings shame to the young Augustine's heart. But the desire of the boy's heart (the mature man remembers) is that very feeling of shame. And his heart is not shamed (chastened) by the knowledge that it seeks to know shame: on the contrary, the knowledge of its own desire as a shameful one both satisfies the desire for the experience of shame and fuels a sense of shame. And this sense of shame is both experienced with satisfaction and recognized, if it is recognized, by self-conscious searching, as a further source of shame: and so on endlessly.[41]

In this vertiginous state, Augustine is denied the closure of absolution, since his mysterious desire for shame must reflect some shameful truth about himself that nevertheless remains, as Coetzee says, "inaccessible to introspection" – and

---

40 Breytenbach, *True Confessions*, 58.
41 "Confession and Double Thoughts," 193.

therefore incapable of confession.[42] In Mrs Curren's case, however much her shame is compromised by the corrupt satisfactions of her desire for it, she must on no account let go of it, since to abandon shame would be to withdraw from confession and surrender any possibility of absolution: as she tells Vercueil,

> I strove always for honour, for a private honour, using shame as my guide. As long as I was ashamed I knew I had not wandered into dishonour. That was the use of shame: as a touchstone, something that would always be there, something you could come back to like a blind person, to touch, to tell you where you were. For the rest, I kept a decent distance from my shame. I did not wallow in it. Shame never became a shameful pleasure; it never ceased to gnaw me. I was not proud of it, I was ashamed of it. My shame, my own. (150)

A little earlier, in one of several passages that echo Shakespeare's great chronicle of shame, *King Lear*, Mrs Curren tells Vercueil about the shooting of her *meid*'s son, the young Comrade, Bheki:

> I have imagined there could be no worse, and then the worse has arrived, as it does without fail, and I have got over it, or seemed to. But that is the trouble! In order not to be paralyzed with shame I have had to live the life of getting over the worse. What I cannot get over any more is that *getting over*. If I get over it this time I will never have another chance *not* to get over it. For the sake of my own resurrection I cannot get over it this time. (115)

Through this paraphrase of Edgar's "the worst is not, / So long as we can say, 'This is the worst'" (*King Lear*, 4.1.27–8), Elizabeth Curren chooses to embrace the abysmal: she repudiates the consolations of sympathy precisely because, in its abdication of the suspicion invited by every self-proclaimed "true" confession, such a response would permit her to yield to the damning moral indifference registered in that most heartless cliché of our times, "get over it." Then there could be no prospect of salvation, no "resurrection."

Speaking the Unspeakable: The Limits of Metaphor

In so far as the secular confessant's labyrinth of revelation and self-deception is a creation of "double thought", it is also an effect of language. Elizabeth Curren's confession is an attempt to render herself, as absolutely as possible, into words: "listen to me: can't you hear that the words I speak are real? Listen they may only be air, but they come from my heart, from my womb" – they are the progeny, as it were, of "[w]hat is living inside me, another word" (133). Thus she can imagine her letter as "my bleeding onto the paper here. The issue of a shrunken heart" (125).

---

[42] Ibid., 194.

Its words are nothing less than heart's blood; and traditionally a document written in blood could claim an absolute veracity, since the gap between signifier and signified was symbolically collapsed by words that were literally formed from the vital substance of the person out of whom they issued. Such a gesture makes sense, however, only as a kind of enacted metaphor; and the narrator's issue of blood (even as it tries to evoke an unadulterated directness of utterance) only succeeds in making a further metaphor out of that metaphor. The irony, by pointing up the irremediably metaphorical nature of all language, serves to remind us of how far secular confession is (in the favourite post-structuralist phrase) always/already compromised by the only medium available to it.

Nevertheless, the longing to achieve unqualified self-expression – to utter ("outer") oneself, as it were, utterly (to the outermost limit of utterance) – emerges as a recurrent motif in Coetzee's confessional writing; and it is no less intense for being recognized as chimerical. Thus Magda, the protagonist of his early novel *In the Heart of the Country* (1976), feeling herself imprisoned by the distortive language "of hierarchy [and] distance" that she calls her "father tongue", is consumed by an impossible nostalgia for a pure Adamic speech, a "language of the heart" whose figures would not be mere "signs of other things", but could somehow speak the things themselves – as they might in that "place where bodies are their own signs", that *Foe* (1986) describes as the "home" of the languageless Friday.[43] Only by means of such an instrument, Magda feels, might she escape into "a life unmediated by words" – a life thereby liberated from the solitude that belongs to those who are "the castaways of God as [they] are the castaways of history" (135). In *Age of Iron*, haunted as it is by a sense of the "unspeakable" (45) and a longing to find the "ground on which people are revealed in their true names" (93),[44] Elizabeth Curren presents her confession as an attempt to "speak [her] heart" (74), to embody herself in the very words she writes:

---

[43] J.M. Coetzee, *In the Heart of the Country* (Harmondsworth: Penguin, 1982), 97, 133, 135; *Foe* (London: Penguin, 1987), 157. Similarly in *Age of Iron*, Elizabeth Curren struggles to "speak her heart" (74), not just to the absent daughter to whom her confession is nominally addressed, but to Mr Vercueil, the enigmatic tramp whom she credits with access to "a language before language" (7). In *Slow Man*, where Paul Rayment is accused by Elizabeth Costello of keeping his heart "in hiding" (261), Rayment alternates between a nervous fear of "speak[ing] my heart too openly" (209) and an impotent longing to let "my heart speak" (225) which is vitiated by his sense of being "on foreign soil" (165). At one point, absurdly, he even imagines that learning Marijana's language might allow him to achieve this impossible ambition: "If only he could speak Croatian. In Croatian, perhaps, he would be able to sing from the heart ... Lesson one: the verb to love, *ljub* or whatever" (250–51).

[44] On *Age of Iron* as a "novel of naming", see Benita Parry, "Thanatophany for South Africa: Death With/out Transfiguration", *Southern African Review of Books* (January/February 1991): 16–11.

> day by day I render myself into words and pack the words into the page like
> sweets: like sweets for my daughter, for her birthday, the day of her birth. Words
> out of my body, drops of myself, for her to unpack in her own time, to take in,
> to suck, to absorb. (8)

The speech that Mrs Curren seeks to master is like that which, in a more grotesque
form, she attributes to Mr Vercueil, when he responds to her moralizing strictures
upon his idleness:

> With a straight look, the first direct look he has given me, he spat a gob of spit,
> thick, yellow, streaked with brown from the coffee, on to the concrete beside my
> foot ... *The thing itself*, I thought, shaken: the thing itself brought between us ...
> His word, his kind of word, from his own mouth, warm at the instant when it left
> him. A word, undeniable, from a language before language. (7)

Again the echo of *Lear* is deliberate. It is not simply that the tramp, like Edgar, is
"houseless" and "unaccommodated": each (however fancifully) is taken to embody
an absolute nakedness beyond the signification of "robes and furred gowns", and
hence to embody the pure presence of "the thing itself" (*Lear*, 3.4.106; 4.6.165).
Elizabeth Curren self-consciously constructs her own narrative as an attempt
to emulate the unqualified immediacy of Vercueil's utterance. She presents her
testament as *ossa* (bones), telling Vercueil that this is the "(Latin) word for a diary.
Something on which the days of your life are inscribed" (176). But in fact such
wordless, unmediated eloquence can amount only to a kind of silence – like the
stream of breath that issues from Friday's mouth at the end of *Foe*, or from Mrs
Curren herself as she yields to the deathly embrace of Mr Vercueil.[45]

Despite her impatience with the names of Florence's daughters – "Hope and
Beauty. It was like living in an allegory" (84) – and her nostalgic yearning for
"true names", the narrator is unable to resist the seductive translations of metaphor.
"[T]he truth" she writes, early in her confession, "is what makes me sick" (25);
and she can make sense of her cancer only as a physical expression of the shame
by which she feels consumed, another embodied metaphor: "Perhaps," she thinks
at the end of Part 2, "shame is nothing more than the name for the way I feel all
the time ... Shame. Mortification. Death in life" (78); and later she tells John "I
have cancer from the accumulation of shame I have endured in my life. That is
how cancer comes about: from self-loathing the body turns malignant and begins
to eat away itself" (132). But because the condition of shame is diagnosed as in
turn arising from the failure of love in "[a] land taken by force, used, despoiled,
abandoned ... a land ... not loved enough" (23), a land where "hearts are turning
to stone" (46), Mrs Curren thinks of her illness as a disease of the heart – a "heart

---

[45]   Of the latter passage, van Wyk Smith writes, "Suddenly we realise that the text we
have been reading is about a text of silence that can never reach us" ("Waiting for Silence",
104)

complaint", like that suffered by André Brink's significantly named protagonist, Martin Mynhardt, the industrial magnate in *Rumours of Rain*.[46] In Part 3, shortly before her confession to Mr Vercueil, her home is raided by the security police who are searching for the young comrade hidden in the maid's quarters; as Mrs Curren is being carried bodily from the house, she cries out in agony:

> "Put me down! ... I have cancer! Put me down!"
> ... "Where is the pain?" asked the woman, frowning.
> "In my heart," I said ... "I have cancer of the heart ... I caught it by drinking of the cup of bitterness ... You will probably catch it too one day. It is hard to escape." (142)

As it happens, the heart is one of the few organs in the body that is barely susceptible to cancer. Of course, the fact that Elizabeth Curren chooses to dramatize her distress by making it the symptom of such an improbable form of the disease does not mean that her cancer is no more than a metaphor, a thing of mere words. But she herself likes to think of it as a kind of word-made-flesh: "This is my life, these words, these tracings of the movements of crabbed [that is, cancerous] digits over the page" (120). The crabbed movement on the page mirrors the inward progress of her sickness, "the thing, the word, the word for the thing inching through my body" (36). Her cancer, then, is figured as a travesty of the Incarnation, an obscene pregnancy – just as the act of writing (reanimating one of the oldest tropes for literary creation) is imagined as a kind of drawn-out parturition. In the bitter wordplay of her conversation with a telephone operator from Lifeline, this is a narrative of "home deliveries" and Elizabeth is "having difficulty carrying things" (128). But in this parodic version of the mystery, what is being brought to birth is Death rather than Life:

> The sickness that now eats me is dry, bloodless and cold, sent by Saturn. There is something about it that does not bear thinking of. To have fallen pregnant with these growths, these cold, obscene swellings; to have carried this brood beyond any natural term, unable to bear them ... My eggs, grown within me. *Me, mine*: words I shudder to write, yet true. My daughters death, sisters to you, my daughter life ... Monstrous growths, misbirths: a sign that one is beyond one's term. This country too: time for fire, time for an end. (59)

> "I am sick too," I said. "Sick and tired, tired and sick. I have a child inside me that I cannot give birth to. Cannot because it will not be born. Because it cannot live outside me. So it is my prisoner or I am its prisoner. It beats on the gate but it cannot leave. That is what is going on all the time. The child inside me is beating

---

[46] André Brink, *Rumours of Rain* (London: W.H. Allen, 1978). In *Slow Man*, Paul Rayment imagines that the effect of his amputation and of his ensuing infatuation with his nurse Marijana has been to mutate him into "a heart case, *un cardiaque*" (165).

at the gate. My daughter is my first child. She is my life. This is the second one, the afterbirth, the unwanted." (75)

If Mrs Curren thinks of the "obscene swellings" in her body as physical symptoms of the shame aroused by her complicity in apartheid, she also sees them as metaphors for the morbid condition of the state itself. Thus her own suffering becomes a rhetorical instrument for re-invigorating what had become one of the most well-worn tropes of South African political discourse: the idea of apartheid as constituting a kind of cancer on the body of the nation – "a *malignant outgrowth* of the categorising thrust of social theory", as one critic expressed it.[47] No matter how powerful this device may prove, however, the novel's linguistic self-consciousness, combined with its resistance to the sympathetic emotions aroused by metaphor, necessarily invites a sceptical probing of the trope; and in this Coetzee was surely responding to the influential work of Susan Sontag.

Sontag's meditations on *Illness as Metaphor*, prompted by her own battle with cancer, were published as a book just a year before *Age of Iron*; but they had first appeared a decade earlier in the form of three extended articles in *The New York Review of Books* – a journal to which Coetzee himself has been a contributor since 1985.[48] It is from Sontag that Mrs Curren's notion of cancer as a form of morbid pregnancy appears to derive. Thinking of how the hearts of township children are "turning to stone" (46), becoming as hard as the tumour she locates in her own heart, Elizabeth Curren is reminded of the Voortrekker monument, and grimly remarks that the *Age of Iron* was born from "the age of granite" (47). She might be remembering Sontag's Alice James, "writing in her journal a year before she died from cancer in 1892 ... of 'this unholy granite substance in my breast'".[49] But if cancer is "degeneration, the body tissues turning to something hard", it is also, Sontag observes, "alive, a fetus with its own will"; thus

> Novalis ... defines cancer, along with gangrene, as "full-fledged *parasites* – they grow, are engendered, engender, have their structure, secrete, eat." Cancer is a demonic pregnancy. St Jerome must have been thinking of a cancer when he wrote: "The one there with a swollen belly is pregnant with his own death."[50]

For Sontag, such passages illustrate the way in which the very pathology of cancer, as a deformation of natural process has encouraged its use as a metaphoric vehicle

---

[47]   Van Wyk Smith, "Waiting for Silence", 93.

[48]   Susan Sontag, "Illness as Metaphor", *NYRB* 24.21–2 (26 January 1978): 10–16; "Images of Illness," *NYRB* 25.1 (9 February 9 1978): 27–9; "Disease as Political Metaphor", *NYRB* 25.2 (23 February 23 1978): 29–33.

[49]   Susan Sontag, *Illness as Metaphor and Aids and Its Metaphors* (Picador: New York, 2001), 13.

[50]   Ibid., 13–14.

by polemicists of all kinds: cancer's propensity to grow and multiply has made it a figure for the malignant spread of colonialism, for example, or for anxieties about the overgrowth and excess associated with Western affluence – as well as for the fears the spiralling disorder that such affluence may incite; its aggressive, but hidden assaults, combined with its capacity to proliferate throughout the body, have made it the metaphor of choice to describe all kinds of corruption and subversion; and it has been used again and again to demonize the presence of unwanted peoples. It has also, of course, become a routine metaphor for anyone wishing to express savage indignation – as when Sontag herself responded to the horrors of Vietnam, by declaring (in a phrase with particular resonance for South Africa) that "the white race is the cancer of human history". In political rhetoric, she argues, the cancer metaphor, because of its power to shock, is always "an incitement to violence" – potentially genocidal in its implications.[51]

Dedicating her essays to "liberation" from the "punitive or sentimental fantasies" concocted around illness in general, Sontag insists that "illness is *not* a metaphor, and that the most truthful way of regarding illness – and the healthiest way of being ill – is one most purified of, most resistant to, metaphoric thinking".[52] In the case of cancer, she maintains, political metaphors are rendered doubly dangerous by their malign tendency to combine with those psychological theories of disease that have sought to explain cancer as an outcome of inturned, baffled, or repressed emotion, "a disease of the failure of expressiveness" in which "[p]assion moves inward, striking and blighting the deepest cellular recesses".[53] Such an aetiology inevitably serves to make the patient culpable, helping to ensure that the "conventions of treating cancer as no mere disease but a demonic enemy make [it] not just a lethal disease but a *shameful* one".[54]

The thrust of Coetzee's novel, it seems to me, is to elaborate the political implications of Sontag's critique of disease metaphor: if the most truthful way of regarding illness is the one "most purified of, and most resistant to, metaphoric thinking", the same is true of thinking about politics. It is Mrs Curren's insistence upon seeing her cancer as metaphor for all that is most shamefully "unspeakable" about the regimen of apartheid South Africa (and her complicity with it) that makes her illness itself so shameful, so hard to bear. By the same token, it is also what leaves her ultimately bereft of effective speech in Guguletu, on that ground where metaphors will not serve, where it seems to her that "people [are] revealed in their true names" (93), but where she herself is unable find the words that will utter her own truth (91). For Elizabeth Curren, then, the compulsive nature of her drive to self-revelation offers no guarantee of its efficacy – rather the reverse. Corrupted *ab initio* by the fundamentally metaphoric nature of language, confession dresses itself in rhetoric that renders it incapable of the nakedness on which its claim

---

[51]   Ibid., 84.

[52]   Ibid., 3–4.

[53]   Ibid., 46.

[54]   Ibid., 57 (emphasis added).

to "truth" must depend. In the absence of sacramental guarantees, therefore, it can never achieve absolution. For salvation the secular confessant must look elsewhere.[55]

Intimations of Grace

> "What are you saying in your confession?"
> "What I said before: that I cannot afford to believe.'"
>
> J.M. Coetzee, *Elizabeth Costello*[56]

When Mrs Curren apologizes to the scornful Guguletu crowd by declaring that to speak of the "terrible sights" confronting her "you would need the tongue of a god" (91), she means that only a god, a *logos* incarnate, would be able to find words for such horror. But behind this abject declaration lies a text that further illuminates the failure of her confession: "Though I speak with the *tongues of men and of angels* and have not charity … I am nothing" (1 Corinthians 13:1–2). "Charity" here is love in its divine (or divinely inspired) form – *caritas* – the principle from which the bonds of human community themselves are formed; and its absence is what, the narrator has come to believe, accounts for the violent disintegration of her society: "the spirit of charity" as she tells Vercueil early in the novel, "has perished in this country". "What is the point of charity," she demands, "when it does not go from heart to heart? What do you think charity is? Soup? Money? Charity: from the Latin word for the heart" (19–20).[57] Of course this etymology, as she immediately acknowledges, is false – "*caritas* has nothing to do with the heart"; but (like "care", the equally fictitious "true root of charity" which she proposes as an alternative) it nevertheless gestures at a profound conviction: that in charity might somehow be found that elusive "language of the heart" on which Mrs Curren feels her salvation to depend – the pure utterance that might enable her to say "from a full heart … 'Save me!'" (67).[58]

---

[55]   For a rather different approach to Coetzee's protracted struggle with the treachery of metaphoric and figurative language – one that traces a way out of the impasse suggested here – see Jonathan Lamb's essay in this volume (Chapter 9).

[56]   Coetzee, *Elizabeth Costello*, 213.

[57]   At one point in *Slow Man*, Paul Rayment thinks of charity as the precondition of truthful expression: "Have a little charity," he wants to tell the novelist Elizabeth Costello, who may be writing his life. "Then perhaps you may find it in you to write" (162); and the link between charity and the heart is once again suggested through a series of quibbles on *core*, *care*, and *cardiaque* (165). See also Carrol Clarkson's essay in this volume (Chapter 2, pp. 48–52, 43–4, 55).

[58]   Unable to love, Elizabeth is equally unable to feel loved: charity, surely, is the name for what (in the absence of her own child) she yearns to receive from Florence; but "[w]hat I want from Florence I cannot have" (38). In St Paul's writings, Charity figures, alongside

Such plentitude of feeling, however, is something that cannot be willed. Only "[b]y doing what [she does] not want to do", Mrs Curren persuades herself, can she be saved: thus she must force herself to "love ... the unlovable", in the form of John, the violent young Comrade whom she takes into her house after Bheki's death. Yet try as she may, this charity seems beyond her; and this, she believes, is another symptom of her mortal sickness: "I cannot find it in my heart to love, to want to love, to want to want to love. I am dying because in my heart I do not want to live" (125). If she cannot love the boy, it can only be because she does not "with a full enough heart want to be otherwise"; and, in that case, may she not be incapable of love altogether – even for her own child: "Not wanting to love him, how true can I say my love is for you?" (125). In place of language that bespeaks a fullness of heart, all she can offer is this thin "bleeding onto the paper" that she calls "the issue of a shrunken heart" (125).

For Elizabeth Curren, then, there appears to be no escape from the reprobate condition in which she fears to die: "I do not want to die in the state I am in, in a state of ugliness. I want to be saved ... Why do I not call for help, call to God? Because God cannot help. God is looking for me but he cannot reach me. God is another dog in another maze ... Up and down the branches he bounds, scratching at the mesh. But he is lost as I am lost" (124–6). The "state of ugliness" to which she feels consigned is the outcast condition which a later novel identifies as *Disgrace*; and the only rescue from it (as the subdued wordplay in that title might suggest) would be through some apprehension of grace.[59] In the regime of Catholic confession, grace is attainable through an exercise of the will, through the sacramental performance of confession, penance and absolution; when, however, as Reformation Calvinists discovered, the syllogistic promise of the confessional ("If we confess our sins, he is faithful and just to forgive us our sins") is no longer

---

Faith and Hope, as one of the so-called Christian Graces: and there is an obvious irony in the fact that, of these three, only Hope figures in the "allegory" that Elizabeth discovers in the trinity of Florence and her daughters. This irony is compounded by the dream that begins the fourth part of Elizabeth's narrative, where Florence does indeed appear as an incarnation of Divine Love, but a figure of pagan terror, an inaccessible deity who does not even acknowledge the dreamer's presence: "Who is this goddess who comes in a vision with uncovered breast cutting the air? It is Aphrodite, but not smile-loving Aphrodite, patroness of pleasures: an older figure, a figure of urgency, of cries in the dark, short and sharp, of blood and earth, emerging for in instant, showing herself, passing. From the goddess comes no call, no signal. Her eye is open and is blank. She sees and does not see" (163–4).

[59]   In *Disgrace* the most obvious clue to the quibble occurs by way of an otherwise inexplicable detail at the beginning of chapter 21 when David Lurie's ex-wife mentions the friend whom she supposes to be living with his daughter, Lucy, and mistakenly identifies her as "Grace" – J.M. Coetzee, *Disgrace* (London: Secker & Warburg, 1999), 187. For an extended analysis of this novel as an account of Lurie's quest for a "state of grace", see Attridge, *Ethics of Reading*, chapter 7 , "Age of Bronze, State of Grace". Attridge's take on the novel is subjected to a rigorous critique in Myrtle Hooper's essay in this volume (Chapter 6).

sustainable; grace is put beyond the reach of will and answers to no such logic. It is imaginable only as a free and unmerited gift: in this, however, lies its great problem; for, since its dispensations are beyond reason, they are also beyond knowing – or at least beyond any knowing properly accessible to language. So, while confession implies dialogue, the knowledge of grace belongs to silence; it can be intimated, but not expressed. The state of grace can be glimpsed, perhaps, *through* words, but will always lie on the other side of them.

For all that, it is, I think, through a secular version of Calvinist grace that Coetzee imagines Elizabeth Curren's release from the "state of ugliness" and the endless labyrinth of confession without absolution. It is only as a manifestation of this mysteriously arbitrary principle that we can understand the significance of an enigmatic moment early in the second part of *Age of Iron* when the narrator, remembering her dead mother, imagines her ascending into the sky, as though in some vision of the Assumption, and finds herself begging for a gesture of acknowledgement: "mother ... look down on me, stretch forth your hand!" (50). Coming, as it does, after the failure of an appeal to Florence ("Absurd to imagine that Florence would hear me. And if she heard, why should she come?"), this, surely, is a plea for intercession and for *caritas*. No response comes, however. Instead there is a break in the text, followed by a passage in which Mrs Curren describes her longing for summer after four months of rain in a house bitter with the smell of damp – a longing that translates into a nostalgia for childhood, and a deep desire to recover its sense of "gratitude, unbounded, heartfelt gratitude, for having been granted a spell in this world of wonders" (51). Hardly has she written the words, than, inexplicably and without warning, this is precisely the emotion that overwhelms her: "Slowly, like a pomegranate, my heart bursts with gratitude; like a fruit splitting open to reveal the seeds of love. *Gratitude, pomegranate:* sister words" (51).[60]

If anything can account for Elizabeth Curren's epiphany, it is the act of writing itself that seems to produces her sudden apprehension of the mystery latent in the words.[61] "Gratitude", as this former classics professor surely knows, derives

---

[60]   Compare the moment in *Disgrace* when Lurie, remembering all the women in his life, feels (despite the deserved disgrace into which his mistreatment of them has finally cast him) is suddenly suffused with gratitude: "Like a flower blooming in his breast, his heart floods with thankfulness" (192). Though Hooper sees this epiphany as unearned (Chapter 6, pp. 132–3), it corresponds to what another of Coetzee's protagonists describes as "the experience of full being ... *joy* ... fullness, embodiedness, the sensation of being ... of being alive in the world" (*Elizabeth Costello,* 78).

[61]   Compare Attridge, *Ethics of Reading*, 145: "The "essential truth about the self" that is the goal of confession, then, is not just the revelation of what has been known all long by the author but kept secret for reasons of guilt and shame; rather, it is something that emerges in the telling, if it emerges at all. Nor can it be "read off" by the reader, as a series of facts hitherto unrevealed; it can be experienced only *in the reading*, or in certain kind of reading. The text does not *refer* to the truth; it produces it."

from the same root as "grace" – for which it is indeed a partial synonym; and that etymology is what links it in turn to the simile that figures her fullness of heart. The pomegranate is among the most ancient symbols of grace, interpreted in traditional exegesis of the Song of Solomon as a figure for the Virgin's pregnant womb, the vehicle of God's love to fallen humanity; and here its bursting ripeness briefly takes the place of the vile mock-pregnancy of shame, the obscene growth swelling in the narrator's body. The "seeds of love" discovered in this revelation belong to an order of feeling entirely different from Mrs Curren's willed effort to love the unlovable: instead the passage reaches back to the moment in Part 1, immediately after her meditation on charity, when she sat down at her piano and, in the music she played, recognized something like the elusive "language of the heart":

> I closed my eyes and played chords, searching with my fingers for the one chord I would recognise, when I came upon it, as my chord, as what in the old days we used to call *the lost chord, the heart's-chord* ... Then at last I went back to Bach The sound was muddy, the lines blurred, but every now and again, for a few bars, the real thing emerged, the real music, the music that does not die, confident, serene ... When the last bar was played I closed the music and sat ... contemplating the oval portrait on the cover with its heavy jowls, its sleek smile, its puffy eyes. Pure spirit, I thought, yet in how unlikely a temple! Where does that spirit find itself now? ... In my *heart* where the music still dances? Has it made its way into the *heart* too of the man in the sagging trousers eavesdropping at the window? *Have our two hearts, our organs of love, been tied for this brief while by a cord of sound?*[62] (21–2, emphasis added)

In the novel's final section, where the "cord of sound" becomes the "rope of words" that ties her to her absent daughter, the narrator will return to this intimation of plenitude, but this time in a passage of bare, stripped-down prose, which is the closest thing the novel can offer to a true heart-speech.

Before the narrative can reach this resolution, however, it must return to Mrs Curren's relationship with John, the boy she could not find it in her heart to love. Envisaging him as he lies in Florence's room, "with the bomb or whatever it is in his hand", waiting for the police to come for him, she has another of her visionary moments – a Transfiguration that corresponds to the earlier vision of her mother's

---

[62]   In *Disgrace*, music produces a similar intimation of grace for David Lurie at the end of chapter 20, as, in the course of composing his opera about Byron and Teresa Guiccioli, he suddenly hears, unbidden, the song of their daughter Allegra, and the wavering reply of her pitying father (186). Chapter 7 of Attridge's *Ethics of Reading* similarly treats *Disgrace* as a narrative whose protagonist finally "achieves something approaching a state of grace" (182). See also Attridge's discussion of Lurie's opera in the present volume (Chapter 1, pp. 35–7) and his comments on writing and grace in Coetzee's "As a Woman Grows Older" (2004) (p. 39).

Ascension. In it she imagines John (his name resonant with Revelation) looking forward to:

> the moment of glory when he will arise, fully himself at last, erect, powerful, transfigured. When the fiery flower will unfold, when the pillar of smoke will rise. The bomb on his chest like a talisman: as Christopher Columbus lay in the dark of his cabin, holding the compass to his chest, the mystic instrument that would guide him to the Indies, the Isles of the Blest. Troops of maidens singing to him, opening their arms, as he wades to them through the shallows holding before him the needle, that points forever in one direction, to the future. (137–8)

The effect of this triumphalist revelation upon Mrs Curren is startling and unpredictable; instead of drawing her into the inspirational frenzy of its apocalyptic rhetoric, it floods her with maternal compassion: "Poor child! Poor child! From somewhere tears sprang up and blurred my sight. Poor John ... battling now for all the insulted and the injured, the trampled, the ridiculed, for all the garden boys of South Africa" (138). We are meant, surely, to remember Lear once again: his reaching out to the Fool – "Poor Fool and knave, I have one part in my heart / That's sorry yet for thee" (3.2.72–3) – and his sudden outburst of sympathy for the outcasts of his kingdom, "Poor naked wretches ... that bide the pelting of this pitiless storm" (3.4.28–9).

Though she does not name it to herself, what Mrs Curren feels here is the same *caritas* that had seemed impossible only a few pages earlier; and it is what she will discover, in an equally sudden access of tenderness for Verceuil at the end of the book. Accepting this ragged outcast as her "shadow-husband", the narrator declares, "One must love what is nearest. One must love what is to hand, as a dog loves." (174). The "must" here is no longer one of moral obligation, like that which compelled her vain attempt to make amends for apartheid's betrayal of charity through a willing of love; instead it answers to an entirely spontaneous convulsion of the heart. What it produces in Elizabeth Curren is a *caritas* that claims no significance beyond itself, since it is offered to one whom she has learned to recognize as nothing more than "[j]ust a man. A man who came without being invited" (165). The point of her care is that it is given to (and invited for) a creature who, since he "does not know how to love" (180), can offer nothing in return – not even the bare consolation of ending, since her longing "for someone to show me the way across [the river of death]" (164) will not be answered by one who "cannot swim, does not yet know how to fly" (181).

In her review of the novel, Benita Parry reads this act of charity to Vercueil as ensuring that "in the disgraceful state of South Africa, [Mrs Curren] will die in state of grace";[63] and Coetzee himself, in an interview reflecting on both "Confession and Double Thoughts" and *Age of Iron*, appears to offer some support

---

[63]   Parry, "Thanatophany", 11.

for this interpretation: speaking of charity as an informing principle in his writing – one that serves to modify the ethical absolutism of politics – he suggests that "charity [is] the way in which grace allegorizes itself in the world". At the end of the interview, however, he appears to draw back from the implications of this remark: repudiating his interlocutor's suggestion that the novel comes "close to the Dosteoevskyan principle of grace" by offering a "promise of absolution" through Vercueil, he insists that its ending is "more troubled" than his interlocutor implies: "[as] for grace," he concludes, "no, regrettably no: I am not a Christian, or not yet."[64] But that characteristic moment of half-nostalgic irony ("regrettably ... not yet") hints at a glimpse of something else beneath the troubled surface. It is true that when, in the novel's bleak last sentence, Vercueil takes Mrs Curren in his arms, she remembers it as an embrace from which "there was no warmth to be had" (181); and this end, with its conspicuous refusal of the satisfactions of apocalypse, leaves its narrator in a state of grim suspension, without either absolution or its promise of salvation – waiting, as Graham Huggan describes her, in continued agony, "for a deliverance that may never come";[65] but that, it might be argued, is exactly what makes her surrender to silence an act of such graceful self-abandon.

---

[64]   Coetzee, Interview in *Doubling the Point*, 249, 250.

[65]   Graham Huggan, "Evolution and Entropy in J.M. Coetzee's *Age of Iron*," in G. Huggan and S. Watson, eds, *Critical Perspectives on J.M. Coetzee* (Basingstoke: Macmillan, 1996), 191–206, at 203.

Chapter 5

Disgrace as an Uncanny Revision of Gordimer's *None to Accompany Me*

Lars Engle

This essay responds to Derek Attridge's discussion of Coetzee and allegory in *J.M. Coetzee and the Ethics of Reading*.[1] In this book, Attridge offers strong illuminating descriptions of the experience of reading J.M. Coetzee's eight novels (through *Elizabeth Costello*) and his two memoirs – descriptions that occasionally take up the particular claims of other interpreters of Coetzee (most consistently those of David Attwell), but that also take a gentle categorical exception to the tendency of Coetzee's critics to read him as an allegorist. In doing this, the book also offers a general account of Coetzee's writing as exemplary of what Attridge calls the singularity of literature. In discussing Coetzee under this rubric, Attridge stresses the special ethical importance of the power of literature to express the particular apprehensions and intimations of situated human consciousness. In this, quite intentionally, Attridge takes on the strong tendency of much contemporary literary criticism to see the point of literature as some form of allegory of politics or philosophy – something that can lead either to praxis or to some general truth-claim. Attridge believes, by contrast, that "impulses and acts that shape our lives as ethical beings ... cannot be represented in the discourses of philosophy, politics, or theology, but are in their natural element in literature" (xi). He develops this intriguing general idea about literature quite concisely alongside his readings of Coetzee's novels, though he does not quite say that he arrived at these views through reading Coetzee's works. Indeed, he seems to have arrived at them in part through reading the works of Derrida and other theorists of engagement with the other, in part through his own long distinguished engagement with modernist literature, and in part through a special interest he has taken in lyric, as well as through his readings of Coetzee novels as they have appeared. It is clear, however, that he thinks one might well arrive at such views purely through experiencing Coetzee's writing in the way he has experienced it. Thus Attridge argues that allegorical reading in general, and allegorical reading of Coetzee in particular, are in a way misleading by being unliterary.

---

[1]   Derek Attridge, *J.M. Coetzee and the Ethics of Reading: Literature in the Event* (Chicago: University of Chicago Press, 2004). Page numbers will be given parenthetically in what follows.

Attridge's second chapter, "Against Allegory: *Waiting for the Barbarians* and *Life & Times of Michael K*", develops the anti-allegorical method of reading Coetzee's texts (and literary texts generally) that is at the heart of Attridge's idea of literary singularity. Noting the obvious ways in which both of these novels – the novels that gave Coetzee an international readership – seem to invite interpretation in which they are allegories of particular or general aspects of historicized human life, Attridge asks, "what happens if we *resist* the allegorical reading that the novels seem half to solicit, half to problematize …? [W]ould we have emptied them of whatever political or ethical significance they might possess?" (35). This is a hugely consequential question, and not merely for readers of J.M. Coetzee. Attridge knows this, and he compares what he is proposing about reading to what might be thought of as common ground between two famous essays, Susan Sontag's complaint about the predictable reduction of literature to banal generalizations in *Against Interpretation* (1966) and Donald Davidson's claim, in "What Metaphors Mean" (1978), that the meaning of a metaphor cannot be thought of as the predictable Venn-diagram-like intersection of previously known semantic fields, or as something beyond ordinary meaning that floats above it, but must rather be thought of as words working in an entirely normal way to do something very new. Basically, Attridge claims, and supports by admirably precise readings of brilliant passages from Coetzee's novels, that the *general* historical or ethical claims one can support by allegorizing aspects of the novels are far less interesting, precise and close to the experience of reading than the *particular* kinds of ethical investigation and puzzlement involved in the event of reading Coetzee. He calls this "literal reading", and he ends by saying that in his view "literal reading" and "literary reading" are inseparable. While Attridge connects this practice with such early and mid-twentieth-century exemplars as Richards, Leavis, Wimsatt and Burke, among others, he believes that his way of discussing literary singularity is more attentive to a variety of elements in reading that have been highlighted by the philosophically and culturally oriented criticism of recent decades: Attridge is thus, at least in his own view, not advocating a return to New Criticism, exactly (62). (He includes Empson on the list of twentieth-century critics he only in some ways resembles, but in many ways Attridge's set of attitudes *does* seem to me a return to what is remarkable in Empson's first two books of criticism – the simultaneous focus on the extraordinarily rich and unpredictable experience of reading, and the new and undetermined angles on social experience that free intense reading opens up.[2])

Obviously Attridge's general claims will not persuade unless his descriptions of particular passages can reveal something rich and particular in the experience of

---

[2]   For more discussion of Empson along these lines, see Lars Engle, "William Empson and the Sonnets", in Michael Schoenfeldt, ed., *A Companion to Shakespeare's Sonnets* (Oxford: Blackwell, 2006), 163–82, and Richard Strier, *Resistant Structures: Particularity, Radicalism, and Renaissance Texts* (Berkeley and Los Angeles: University of California Press, 1995), 13–26.

reading that gets glossed over in allegorical readings. Fortunately he consistently does this, and it is clear that Coetzee provides many opportunities to make such discoveries. Moreover, to the extent that Coetzee makes pronouncements about reading, Coetzee appears to agree with Attridge: Attridge quotes Coetzee's comment that in reading a novel as "playing the game you call Class Conflict or the game called Male Domination ... you may have missed not just something, you may have missed everything. Because ... a story is not a message with a covering."[3] Attridge concludes his chapter with the following summary comment:

> I am not against allegory ... in spite of the chapter's title; allegorical readings of many kinds have been and will continue to be of the greatest significance, ranging from allegories of actual history (where a novel is read as if it were about real people, places, and events) to universal allegory (where the novel is read as if [it] were about abstractions). But I am *for* reading as an event, for restraining the urge to leave the text, or rather the experience of the text, behind (an urge that becomes especially powerful when we have to produce words about it), for opening oneself to the text's forays beyond the doxa. If Coetzee's novels and memoirs exemplify anything, it is the value (but also the risk) of openness to the moment and to the future, of the perhaps and the wherever. Allegory, we might say, deals with the *already known*, whereas literature opens a space for the other. Allegory announces a moral code, literature invites an ethical response. (63–4)

What, then, is Attridge urging us to do? To continually open ourselves to surprise; not to create an allegory out of what we expect a text to say and select details to support that allegory; perhaps to chasten our own propensities to prophetic portentousness in the name of the exhilaration of reading. Critics would need humility if they were to confine themselves to "literal reading". And Coetzee is a propitious author to invoke while making a case for literal writing because the experience of reading Coetzee is (among other things) humbling. So much intelligence, so much concision, so much learning, so many surprises – what, besides our own desire to sound bigger than we are, tempts us to move toward reductive generalization?

That said, however, I believe that there is an aspect of the literariness of *Disgrace* that may both justify critics in reading it somewhat allegorically and explain some of the tendencies or hints toward allegorical writing I find in the novel. That aspect emerges as one explores its allusiveness to other texts, and several essays in this collection map this allusiveness – the fact that they overlap as little as they do points to the depth and breadth of Coetzee's intertextuality.[4]

---

[3]   J.M. Coetzee, "The Novel Today" *Upstream* 6.1 (1988): 2–5, at 4, quoted in Attridge, *Ethics of Reading*, 36–7. See David Attwell's essay in this volume for a similar use of this comment (Chapter 8, p. 164).

[4]   For example, Laurence Wright, "David Lurie's learning and the meaning of J.M. Coetzee's *Disgrace*" (Chapter 7); Derek Attridge, "Coetzee's Artists; Coetzee's Art" (Chapter 1).

My particular argument in this essay is that there is a good deal of revisionary allusion in *Disgrace* to Nadine Gordimer's 1994 novel *None to Accompany Me*, and that reading *Disgrace* as taking up issues about allegory from Gordimer is a way of seeing a certain kind of allegorization – a kind that interrogates allegory in ways Attridge has attuned us to – as part of the book's literary singularity.

Any great social change, however longed-for and prospectively imagined, creates a crisis for writers; a crisis of representation which is also a crisis of prediction, an attempt to find what will be the great shaping issues for a new period. The end of apartheid has evoked several outstanding novels already, novels that not only represent a rapidly reforming world but also try to find within the substantial symbolic resources of realist fiction evocative formulations of new situations and new relations. I will suggest below that J.M. Coetzee's *Disgrace* – a novel which shows signs of standing, for international readers, in relation to the end of apartheid as *Cry, the Beloved Country* stood to apartheid's beginning – in some ways rewrites Nadine Gordimer's end-of-apartheid novel, *None to Accompany Me*.[5] (It would, I think, be a miscategorization to call these *post* apartheid novels.) Gordimer's book offered readers compelling images of new South African possibility in what was on the whole a hopeful emotional register, and I will argue that Coetzee's novel rewrites Gordimer's in particular by noticing her somewhat schematic allegories of new possibility and suggesting that they might as realized be full of pain. Toward the end I focus on differences within similarities and meditate briefly on what this revision might mean in terms of the literary relations between South Africa's best-known (and, I think, best) contemporary novelists. But I should begin, obviously, by trying to persuade you that the similarities in fact exist. Coetzee's novel is more recent, more widely-discussed, and more controversial. Moreover, this volume addresses readers of Coetzee who may not be readers of Gordimer. So I'm going to assume your familiarity with the plot of Coetzee's *Disgrace*; let me, however, refresh your memories with a selective summary of events in *None to Accompany Me*. Since I believe Coetzee shows particular interest in the ways *None to Accompany Me* offers, within a realist frame, touches of politically prophetic allegory, I will stress such aspects in my summary.

None to Accompany Me is set in the period between 1990 and 1994 in which it was written. It incorporates extensive flashbacks from earlier in the lives of its major characters, and one of its aims is to present the rhythms of engagement and detachment through an adult lifetime in love and work. Vera Stark, the protagonist, seems to be exactly Gordimer's age: she was first married at 17 at the beginning of World War II (which would give her Gordimer's birth year of 1923), and is thus in her late 60s, divorced and remarried since just after the war to Bennet Stark. She and Bennet live in the house she received in the divorce settlement from her first marriage (her nameless first husband has emigrated to Australia). Bennet and

---

[5]   J.M. Coetzee, *Disgrace* (New York: Viking, 1999), cited by page number as *D* below. Nadine Gordimer, *None to Accompany Me* (New York: Farrar Straus and Giroux, 1994), cited by page number as *N* below.

Vera have two children (unless the eldest, her son Ivan, was in fact conceived in an impulsive coupling with her first husband – betraying Bennet, for whom she had betrayed the first husband – after his return from Egypt): Ivan, a banker in London who divorces in the course of the novel and has a teenaged son Adam; and Annick, Vera and Ben's daughter, who, having come out as a lesbian to her parents in the course of the novel, adopts an African child with her partner Lou at the novel's end. Vera is a lawyer who works for the Legal Foundation, which under apartheid helped or tried to help Africans resist expropriation and is now handling the claims of displaced Africans for return of expropriated lands. Bennet, who began as a sculptor and university English lecturer, joined an advertising firm, and in the 1980s founded a company called Promotional Luggage which manufactures and sells upscale suitcases bearing company logos. He did this to provide for his and Vera's old age, but Promotional Luggage goes bankrupt in the 1990s. Vera had a love affair in the 1960s with a German filmmaker, Otto Abarbanel – a man she imagines as a Jew (Bennet recognizes his last name as Sephardic), but who turns out to be a Hitler baby, bred as part of a Nazi eugenics project.

The lives of Vera and Bennet are cross-cut with the lives of African friends from the 1950s who have been in exile with the ANC: Didymus and Sibongile Maqomo. They return when the general amnesty is declared (Didymus, a lawyer, has been an important figure in Umkhonto we Sizwe, the ANC guerrilla force, and has been underground in South Africa part of the time), and they bring back with them Mpho, their teenage daughter (they also have older sons who do not appear, but who used to play with Ivan). Sibongile gets involved with the repatriation of exiles and with the ANC women's movement; Didymus serves the ANC executive in a variety of roles, but is not elected to the National Executive Committee at the party congress; Sibongile is. This places some strain on their marriage, as she is swept more and more fully into public life and he left more and more at home, where he is supposedly writing a history of the ANC in exile. Moreover, it becomes clear that he at one point during the 1970s or '80s conducted interrogations, probably involving torture, at the ANC camp for political prisoners or infiltrators in Tanzania: while not someone whom the party disavows, he takes part in a process of self-criticism that may seal off possibilities of a further political career for him.

Vera also has two important connections with African men through her work: with Oupa Sejake and with Zeph Rapulana. Oupa Sejake, a clerk in his 20s at the Legal Foundation who is studying at night to be a lawyer, by novelistic accident moves into the very flat in which Vera conducted her long and passionate affair with Otto Abarbanel a decade before – an affair to which, with breathtaking parental and heterosexual presumption, Vera attributes her daughter's lesbianism. Zeph Rapulana, a man in his 50s, meets her in the 1980s as the representative of a group of squatters filing a residency claim and becomes a black capitalist in the 1990s, buying a house in the white suburbs with an annexe Vera rents after she sells her own house. Oupa has an affair with Mpho, Didymus and Sibongile's daughter, who becomes pregnant and has an abortion that Vera arranges. Bennet's father has a stroke, comes to stay with Ben and Vera, has another stroke, and dies.

Oupa and Vera are both shot and wounded in a carjacking during a side trip to visit Oupa's wife and children during a Legal Foundation research tour. Oupa, shot in the chest, dies of septicaemia; Vera, shot in the leg, recovers.

Toward the end of the novel, Ivan's son Adam, getting in trouble in England after his parents' divorce, is sent to live with Ben and Vera in South Africa, where Vera successfully warns him off a budding affair with Mpho. Vera is offered, and after some hesitation accepts, a position on the Technical Committee to draft the new South African constitution. At the end of the novel, Bennet Stark has moved to England to live with Ivan; Adam has moved into an apartment of his own in Johannesburg; Vera, without consulting Ben, has sold the family home and moved to Zeph Rapulana's annexe. Sibongile is poised to become a government minister after the elections. Mpho goes to NYU to study drama.

So much for the plot. It sounds like a soap opera in this kind of summary, but then so does *War and Peace*: both novels, in fact, foreground characters who enjoy a charismatic closeness to centres of social power and negotiation – in this they differ from *Disgrace* and indeed from most of Coetzee's novels, with *Elizabeth Costello* and *Waiting for the Barbarians* as partial exceptions. *None to Accompany Me* reads austerely, despite this relative density of event. Since, no doubt like many readers of this essay, I have for many years steadily inscribed "avoid plot summary" in the margins of student papers, I summarize here with particular relish, given that tendentious recounting of plots turns out in fact to be one my favorite critical modes. Now let me try to expound the novel's allegorical dimension, which is fairly prominent in the novel on my reading of it.

Vera Stark (stark truth – the truth about her own life and the life of South Africa – "Nobody can con Vera" [*N* 12]) begins in the house she inherits from her divorce from a soldier of the British Empire. She ends in the servants' quarters of a house owned by a black capitalist. The allegory of a possible trajectory of white South Africans, from inheritors of empire to dependants of black enterprise, is clear enough. The gradual diminution of Vera's relation with Bennet can also been seen as a kind of allegory of the possibilities and limits of private life, a long-term theme of Gordimer's.[6] Bennet begins as an artist, a sculptor deeply interested in representing sexual feeling concretely: his triumphs as a sculptor are headless torsos of his wife's body – torsos which end up as "household gods" of feminine sexuality in his daughter's lesbian household (*N* 228). He also works early on as a university teacher of literature. These are both ways of making something public out of love (the first more honourable in the book's terms than the second). Bennet could never sculpt Vera's head successfully, nor can he keep up with her life; Vera wants to insist on the diffusion of her life into the public life she is part of and the variety of new relations she has taken on, Bennet

⁶ On this concern, which reflects itself in treatment of interior and exterior spaces, see Rita Barnard, *Apartheid and Beyond: South African Writers and the Politics of Place* (New York: Oxford University Press, 2007), pp. 10–11, 41–94; for a summary of Gordimer's treatment of the problem of "decent private life" in an apartheid setting, see my own "The Political Uncanny in the Novels of Nadine Gordimer" *YJC* 2.2 (1989): 101–27.

wants to hold on to what he had, and to serve capitalist mobility (advertising, designer luggage) in order to maintain what he has. Vera's affectionate dismissal of him is a judgment on decent private life given significance by love (something the novel in general as a form has always been thought to cherish and support): for Vera, as for Gordimer, it is not enough, or does not remain enough, to sustain a life-long course. Is her eye a cold one? Perhaps yes, but at the same time that it makes demands that relatively few of us could be confident we meet, it attractively displays the possibility of a life of multifarious movement and evolving commitment. Few novels I know are so clear and persuasive in such short space about relations between outward engagement and marriage, taking up Bennet and Vera, on one hand, and Didymus and Sibongile, on the other. The Maqomo marriage, which threatens to sink under Didymus's depression at being passed over by the ANC leadership ("I'm beginning to find it disgusting," says Sibongile with the terrifying frankness of female conversation in this book [*N* 132]) is rescued by external difficulties: Didymus is called back from inactivity by Mpho's unwanted pregnancy and then by the assassination of Chris Hani and the publication of a hit list with Sibongile's name on it. Even though his role in the new government is less than he would like, he accepts that he has one and soldiers on – literally in uniform as a pallbearer for Hani, and armed as a bodyguard for Sibongile. It seems possible that packing a pistol to protect his wife will reconcile him to life as an historian, oddly enough.

In other ways, the novel allegorizes the vertiginous shifts in perspective on the self and on what their political lives mean in altered contexts which events have made available to South Africans. Vera's affair with Otto Abarbanel, in which she thinks he is a Jew orphaned in the concentration camps but discovers that he is the child of a Nazi and an Aryan bathroom attendant adopted by Jews after the war, provides an example. In *None to Accompany Me*, as this minor example hints, adoptive affinities are at least as strong as genetic ones – to put it another way, the novel shows the sexual and familial bond to be less central than the bond of shared social purposes. Moreover, these shared social purposes get expressed partly in dealing with possible or actual babies: for example, Sibongile and Didymus protect their daughter by aborting her unborn child; Annick and Lou affiliate themselves with a new South African future by adopting a Xhosa daughter; the Nazi authorities a generation ago tried to breed good Aryans only to have them adopted and raised by Jewish survivors of the Holocaust. Ben ends up in the house of Ivan, who is probably not his son in genetic terms. And Vera ends up in the annexe of Zeph Rapulana's house.

The adoptive bond this represents – between adults – is a kind of non-sexual cross-racial partnership that Gordimer seems to be offering as an optimistic possibility in a new social order, also as a meditation on aging and developing beyond the sexual phase of one's life. Through her growing intimacy with Zeph, Vera realizes both the limitations on the sexual bond and the possibility of new bonds outside sex. Early in the novel, visiting the wounded Rapulana in his squatter encampment after it has been raided by a commando of white farmers – nine killed, fourteen injured – Vera reflects:

> To whom could she pose the very *inappropriateness* of any personal preoccupation arising from a situation where all individuality was in dissolution in terror and despair. Not the lover-husband to whom she used to tell – or thought she had – everything. Only to herself ... [F]inally, the bliss of placing the burden of self on the beloved turns out to be undeliverable. The beloved is unknown at any address, a self, unlike a bed, cannot be shared, and cannot be shed. (*N* 121)

Vera recognizes her alliance with Rapulana as "the beginning of some new capability in her, something in the chemistry of human contact that she was only now ready for"(*N* 122).

> Vera had never before felt – it was more than drawn to – involved in the being of a man to whom she knew no sexual pull. And it was not that she did not find him physically attractive; from the first ... [he] brought her reassurance she had not known she no longer found elsewhere with anyone. It was as if, in the commonplace nature of their continuing contact through the Foundation, they belonged together as a single sex, a reconciliation of all each had experienced, he as a man, she as a woman. (*N* 123)

As the capitalized word "Foundation" shows in this passage, the language of the novel itself approaches allegory: institutions have names designed for resonance. The ANC is called "the Movement", with a capital M. Vera works for "the Legal Foundation" with capital L and F and works on the legal foundation of a new South Africa when she serves on the technical committee to draft the new constitution. Sentences like the following underscore the pull toward allegorical generalization: "Now that the Act that put the Idea into practice has been abolished by the beginning of political defeat of that power, the Foundation has not, as might be expected, become redundant" (*N* 13).

One might then, illustrating the reductive brutality of allegorical interpretation in a way that risks buttressing Attridge's anti-allegorical stance, summarize the message of *None to Accompany Me* as follows:

South Africans, and especially white South Africans, must find a relation to the national and personal future which does not involve reproducing the relations of the past, even when those relations have (as in the sexual and genetic bonds uniting nuclear families) not in any evident way been wrong in themselves. The heterosexual, genetically united family, like racially homogenous patterns of land ownership, indeed all traditional dependencies with their attendant resentments and hostilities, must be loosened and at times cast off: new links, new forms of association, must be formed. Just as Vera in the final passage of *None to Accompany Me* takes pleasure in using her technical competence to staunch a flood in Zeph's house, while renouncing any sexual aspect to their relationship, Gordimer seems to signal her joy in using her own novelistic tools in this book to clear ground for a black-led South African future. The novel shows Gordimer's willingness to be as it were a draftsperson on the Technical Committee for the future. It is in this sense that *None to Accompany Me* seems a novel full of optimism and satisfaction. The committed political novelist may choose an allegorical mode deliberately. Indeed, if one accepts this way of summarizing the novel as message, Gordimer's willingness to subjugate a realist's focus on the particularities of situated individual consciousness to an allegory of collective optimism in itself bespeaks her eagerness to embrace new possibilities.

At the same time, *None to Accompany Me* records (in ways that prefigure *Disgrace*) the violence and vengefulness of this historical passage. Vera and Ben listen to the radio early in the morning:

> Some mornings, attacks on farms; a white farmer shot, the wife raped or killed, money and car missing. Taken. 'Taken' to mean the motive is robbery; as if robbery has a single meaning in every country at every period. Take cars, take money, take life. These mornings robbery means taking everything you haven't got from those who appear to have everything: money, a car to sell for money, a way of life with house and land and cattle. Otherwise, why kill as well as rob? Why rape some farmer's ugly old wife? No violence is more frightening than the violence of revenge, because it is something that what the victim stands for brings upon him. It is seldom retribution for a personal deed, of which innocence can be claimed. The rape has nothing to do with desire; the penis is a gun like the gun held to a head, its discharge is a discharge of bullets. (*N* 110–11)

It is my hope that, if your memories of *Disgrace* are relatively fresh, already you will be noting some general affinities in plot between the two novels. Each features an aging protagonist moving with reflective reluctance away from a life centred on eros and personal relationships toward a life centered on something else. In each, an aging parent sees in a child's lesbianism a possible reaction to the parent's heterosexuality. (It should be said that Coetzee, having David Lurie simply wonder on this score – Lucy is "[a]ttractive, he is thinking, yet lost to men. Need he reproach himself, or would it have worked out like that anyway?" [*D* 76] – handles the theme a lot more delicately than Gordimer does, perhaps having encountered lesbian reaction to Gordimer's treatment of it). Each features a new household, emblematic of new South African fates or possibilities, in which the idea of a nuclear family centred on a passionate heterosexual relationship and blood kinship is set aside in favour of a multiracial, partly adoptive family. In Gordimer, the new families are based on elective affinities: Annick and her partner Lou in Cape Town with their Xhosa daughter, and Vera's comradely tenancy in Zeph's servants' quarters in Johannesburg. In Coetzee, the new family is constituted out of mutual protection and opportunism: Petrus proposes to make Lucy his third polygamous wife, to protect her, provide a quasi-father for the mixed-race child who will be born as a result of her rape, and gain legal ownership of her farm, leaving Lucy as a tenant with possession of practically nothing, "like a dog" (*D* 205).

The Zeph-Petrus parallel here is key, because both are figures of black enterprise and uplift whose strategies are only gradually understood by their white associates.

When David Lurie agrees with Lucy's proposal that he occupy himself on the farm by helping Petrus, David remarks, "Give Petrus a hand. I like that. I like the historical piquancy. Will he give me a wage for my labor, do you think?" (*D* 77). Both Zeph and Petrus are non-violent, at times comforting, yet appropriative figures; both are people whose progress from dispossession to possession can, guardedly, be celebrated as what the New South Africa is supposed to be all about. Zeph gains membership on the boards of major Johannesburg companies and becomes a national economic advisor, while Petrus gains part-ownership of a small farm in the Eastern Cape, so if Coetzee is revising Zeph Rapulana he is also generalizing an elite case which is in many ways unrepresentative because so spectacular – schoolmaster-activist from rural location becomes urbane plutocrat shaping economic policy– into what could realistically be hoped to become a relatively common phenomenon: rural labourer/tenant becomes landholder and small-scale farmer, gains access to agricultural technology, and begins to acquire capital. And there are a number of passages in *Disgrace* where Coetzee seems to be simply heeding and exploring a concrete instance of Vera Stark's claim that land possession and land redistribution must be the key issues under a new regime.

> Petrus has borrowed a tractor, from where he has no idea, to which he has coupled the old rotary plough that has lain rusting behind the stable since before Lucy's time. In a matter of hours he has ploughed the whole of his land. All very swift and businesslike; all very unlike Africa. In olden times, that is to say ten years ago, it would have taken him days with a hand-plough and oxen. (*D* 151)

But in another way Petrus's rise also parallels Zeph's: in its awareness of the utility of threats and instances of racial violence. Here Coetzee has taken a fairly minor and fairly benign moment in Gordimer's novel and turned it into something large (perhaps taking a hint from Gordimer's discussion of rape, vengeance, and redistribution in the passage I quoted above). Relatively early in *None to Accompany Me*, Vera meets Zeph in a confrontation with the Afrikaner farmer who plans to make a profit from the thousands of black squatters living on one of his fields by getting the government to declare it a rural location and charge rent. Odendaal contemptuously dismisses Vera, speaking a mixture of Afrikaans and English. Zeph replies softly in Afrikaans: "Meneer Odendaal, don't be afraid. We won't harm you. Not you or your wife and children" (*N* 25). Vera thinks first of "the gift of the squatter leader's tolerance, forgiveness – whichever it was – was something the farmer didn't deserve"(*N* 26). Only later does she realize that

> she had not heard them aright on the stoep that day. The farmer heard [the three statements] and Rapulana the Odensville man heard them the way she did not, they understood what was being said. The words of tolerance and forgiveness so strangely coming from the Odensville squatter dweller, shaming her for the crude aggression of the farmer, were not tolerance and forgiveness but a threat. Remember, Meneer Odendaal, we are thousands on Portion 19, our Odensville.

We are there across the veld from you, every night. You have dogs, you have a gun, but we are thousands, and we can come across the veld to this house, this house where you and your wife and your children are asleep, and, as you said about us if we don't go from Portion 19, that'll be your funeral. (*N* 31–2)

In *Disgrace* Lucy has dogs, she has a gun, and her rapists use her gun to kill her dogs. Petrus, before and after the incident, which David comes to regard as in some way happening with Petrus's permission – particularly when it emerges that one of the rapists is Petrus's second wife's younger brother – has insisted that, though times are dangerous, Lucy is safe with him. At the end of the novel, Petrus offers Lucy his protection in a deliberately patriarchal conversation with David, the father whose incapacity to protect Lucy in the new South Africa has been so graphically demonstrated in her rape:

'I will marry.'
  'You will marry whom?'
  'I will marry Lucy.'
  He cannot believe his ears…
  'You will marry Lucy,' he says carefully. 'Explain to me what you mean. No, wait, rather don't explain. This is not something I want to hear. This is not how we do things.'
  We: he is on the point of saying, *We Westerners.*
  'Yes, I can see, I can see,' says Petrus. He is positively chuckling. 'But I tell you, then you tell Lucy. Then it is over, all this badness.'
  'Lucy does not want to marry. Does not want to marry a man. It is not an option she will consider. I can't make myself clearer than that. She wants to live her own life.'
  'Yes, I know,' says Petrus. And perhaps he does indeed know. He would be a fool to underestimate Petrus. 'But here,' says Petrus, 'it is dangerous, too dangerous. A woman must be marry.' (*D* 202)

To summarize, then. As I read it, *None to Accompany Me* suggests allegorically that the lifting of apartheid may, and perhaps needs to, promote new kinds of adoptive social relationship, involving new patterns of living and child-rearing, and new patterns of work. In this transformation, people like Vera and Zeph make use of and in a way exploit a violence they individually deplore. Gordimer locates hope specifically in the white lesbian raising a black child and in the white woman locating herself as a tenant of the newly successful black man. Coetzee, I believe, noticed this, and something very close to the same pattern returns, uncannily transformed, in precisely that aspect of *Disgrace* that readers find most politically disturbing: the independent lesbian Lucy's decision that perhaps it is her historical duty to accept, dog-like, her rape by black men and the increasingly strange familial arrangement that develops as she, pregnant after the rape, is assimilated into the growing Petrus household as a bywoner/concubine/wife/daughter and her biological father David is reduced to the status of a visitor.

It is typical, too, of the relations between the novels that David Lurie in *Disgrace* cannot rest with *None to Accompany Me*'s claim that the rape of white women on farms by black men unknown to them is simply revenge, that "the penis is a gun like the gun held to the head, its discharge is a discharge of bullets" (*N* 111). In what might be a somewhat more artful version of Gordimer's bald paragraph, David meditates on Lucy's belief that "'they *do* rape … They see me as owing something. They see themselves as debt collectors, tax collectors'" (*D* 158).

> *They do rape.* He thinks of the three visitors driving away in the not-too-old Toyota, the back seat piled with household goods, their penises, their weapons, tucked warm and satisfied between their legs – *purring* is the word that comes to him. They must have had every reason to be pleased with their afternoon's work; they must have felt happy in their vocation. (*D* 159)

The "not-too-old Toyota" might even be thought to echo Gordimer's harsh question "why rape some farmer's ugly old wife": Lucy, too, is not young but is "not-too-old".

But, again, as David continues to think of the issue after he sees Melanie acting at the Dock Theatre, revisits his own history of sexual encounters, and learns of Lucy's pregnancy, he revises his view: "They were not raping, they were mating" (*D* 199). *Disgrace* insists, in contrast to *None to Accompany Me*, on the emotional importance of biological parenthood.

Let me sketch, before closing, a couple of further ways, somewhat less specific perhaps, in which *Disgrace* seems to me to respond with guarded pessimism to the optimism of *None to Accompany Me*. Allegorically, the fate of David Lurie is a far more graphic reminder than that of Bennet Stark that the new South Africa is no country for old white men (in a passage I quote below, David paraphrases Yeats's "Sailing to Byzantium," which begins "That is no country for old men"). David receives public disgrace for the kind of crime white men have always gotten away with – exploiting his cultural authority to have sex with a younger darker women. At the same time, the archetypally over-punished colonial crime, the rape of a white woman by black men, goes unpunished. Now the crimes, failures, uglinesses of white men will be held to a most strict account, while the time for leniency for the crimes of blacks has arrived. Some of the pathos, and some of the power to disturb, in *Disgrace* stems from the uncomfortable awareness of readers that they come to care about David even as they recognize the wrongness of what he has done: that is, I think, one effect of the opening Cape Town segment of *Disgrace*. But throughout, Coetzee's treatment of the sexual offers a programmatic contrast to the relative buoyancy and grace with which Vera moves aside from and frees herself from the sexual, as opposed to the very explicit disgrace with which David Lurie makes the same transition. As I have suggested, David offers an uncanny revision of *None to Accompany Me*'s portrait of Bennet, the man committed to love who cannot shed that commitment as times change, whose sensibility is shaped by literature and art rather than politics, who cannot move with grace into a post-erotic existence. And, of course, Lurie's relation to his creator resembles Vera's to hers: both characters have roughly their authors' lifespans and aspects of their authors' lives without the novel-writing. This resemblance and others come into focus if we look at the last page of *None to Accompany Me* alongside *Disgrace*. The end of *None to Accompany Me*, like its beginning, shows us that in the rest of the rather drably written novel Gordimer has set aside rather than lost her capacity for extraordinarily detailed and evocative realist description – for writing, in Attridge's terms, that calls for literal reading:

> One winter night in that year a pipe burst, flooding outside Vera's annexe, and she put her leather jacket over pyjamas and went to turn off the main water control in the yard. The tap was tight with chlorine deposits and would not budge in hands that became clumsy with cold. She quietly entered the house. Vera always had access, with a second set of keys Zeph had given her; she kept an eye on the house while he was away on business trips or spent a few days with his family in Odensville.

So far, we notice again how Vera has taken on many of the roles of the trusted servant (in South African tradition, a "trust" that crosses racial lines, has clear limits, and plays a suspect role in mitigating a general racist order – these being issues Gordimer ventilates thoroughly in *July's People*). But there is also a gendered aspect to this relation, as the passage continues:

> The keys were also a precaution Zeph insisted on for her safety; if anything or anyone threatened her, a woman alone, she could come to him. The disposition of rooms in his house was familiar under her hands in the dark. She would not disturb him by turning on lights. She was making her way without a creak of floor-boards or any contact with objects to the cupboard in the passage between his bedroom and the bathroom where she knew she would find pliers.
> Without any awareness of a shape darker than the darkness she came in contact with a warm soft body.
> Breathing, heartbeats.
> Once she had picked up an injured bird and felt a living substance like that.
> Through her open jacket this one was against her, breasts against breasts, belly against belly; each was afraid to draw away because this would confirm to the other that there really had been a presence, not an illusion out of the old unknown of darkness that takes over even in the protection of a locked house. Vera was conscious of the metal tool in her hand, as if she really were some intruder ready to strike. For a few seconds, maybe, she and the girl were tenderly fused in the sap-scent of semen that came from her. Then Vera backed away, and

the girl turned and ran on bare feet to his bedroom where the unlatched door let
her return without a sound. (*N* 322–3)

Vera the tenant enters the master's house in the dark to borrow a tool. She
encounters, partly fuses with, another female body, nameless, headless, all breasts
and belly and smells of sex. Vera here encounters the version of her past self,
the lesbian household god, that Bennet sculpted, perfumed by the sexual relation
with Zeph Rapulana that a younger, not yet post-sexual Vera might well have had.
The new Vera fuses momentarily with the old Vera. But the new Vera now has
a purpose that trumps, and in this moment literally separates itself from, sex: to
handle a flood caused by a burst container. There is potential allegory here for her
work with the Technical Commission, as well as the obvious relation to her move
away from sexual life with Bennet and Otto to her essentially political adoptive
relation with Zeph. And after she exits the house she appears, in the book's final
sentences, to celebrate her new freedom:

> Vera came out into the biting ebony-blue of winter air as if she dived into the
> delicious shock of it. She turned off the tap with the satisfaction of a woman
> performing a workman-like task. Instead of at once entering her annexe she
> went into the garden, the jacket zipped closed over live warmth. Cold seared
> her lips and eyelids; frosted the arrangement of two chairs and table; everything
> stripped. Not a leaf on the scoured smooth limbs of the trees, and the bushes like
> tangled wire; dried palm fronds stiff as her fingers. A thick trail of smashed ice
> crackling light, stars blinded her as she let her head dip back; under the swing
> of the sky she stood, feet planted, on the axis of the night world. Vera walked
> there, for a while. And then took up her way, breath scrolling out, a signature
> behind her. (*N* 323–4)

What is her profit from this encounter? It sounds like exhilaration: "she came
out into the biting ebony-blue … as if she dived into the delicious shock of it".
She seems exhilarated by her own age, her dry wintry freedom from the sap of
sexuality which hangs on the girl, with the leafless trees and dried fronds "stiff as
her fingers". It is also a sense of intimacy with the underlying forms and essences,
rather than the lushnesses and growth points, of her world.

David Lurie's disengagement from and recollection of his own erotic past is
similar in structure but different in mood, governed as so much is in *Disgrace* by
David's literariness. He sees himself as a Yeats without a Byzantium to sail to: "He
sighs. The young in one another's arms, heedless, engrossed in the sensual music.
No country, this, for old men. He seems to be spending a lot of time sighing.
Regret: a regrettable note on which to go out" (*D* 190). But immediately the sight
of Melanie on stage sparks a moment of erotic vision for David, "images of women
he has known on two continents … Like leaves blown on the wind, pell-mell, they
pass before him. *A fair field full of folk*: hundreds of lives all tangled with his"
(*D* 192). The explicit quotation from Langland, suggesting that life is a pilgrimage

seeking grace, follows the covert quotation from the Paolo and Francesco episode in Dante, suggesting that erotic preoccupation is a damnable error. But David is grateful: "Like a flower blooming in his breast, his heart floods with thankfulness" (*D* 192). Then spitballs begin to hit him in the back of the head, and Melanie's boyfriend comes bearing a repetition of the same message David gave himself on the previous page via Yeats: "'Find yourself another life, prof. Believe me'" (*D* 194).

One could expand on the ways literary tradition functions in this section. "Until two years ago the Dock Theatre was a cold storage plant where the carcasses of pigs and oxen hung waiting to be transported across the seas" (*D* 190–91). So David has this encounter in a converted afterworld. He wishes to see in it an affirmation of lost passion, but Melanie does not oblige, and, if Ryan is right, Melanie would turn away from him as the shade of Dido turns away from Aeneas in his underworld visit, just as the unembraceable shades of David's past lovers recall Odysseus's vain attempt to clasp his mother's shade in the *Odyssey*. Rosalind misremember's Lucy's ex-lover Helen's name as Grace – a fascinating fact that Attridge makes much of; David is unable to see in Helen, "a large, sad-looking woman with a deep voice and bad skin" (*D* 60), a proper object of affection or of sexual desire for Lucy. He is, of course, utterly revolted by Pollux, Petrus's mentally defective brother-in-law, one of the three men who rape Lucy. But in classical myth Helen was the daughter of Zeus and Leda, the sister of the Dioscuri, Castor and Pollux, and while David cannot see grace in either, Lucy has obviously found grace in Helen and plans to accept her kinship with Pollux. These are literary allusions David does not seem to see, attentive as he is in general to literary allusion. But Coetzee surely intends us to think about them, and such thought will inevitably tend toward allegory, especially if we continue to pursue it (as in general I have been) along lines suggested by similarities between *Disgrace* and *None to Accompany Me*.

One might go further along these lines. Though David is himself a fount of literary allusion and himself a would-be allusive artist, there are zones of literary allusion in the novel unconnected with David's consciousness – for instance, the rich enigmatic evocation of books 24 of the *Iliad* and the *Odyssey* in the concluding chapter 24 of *Disgrace*. There David attends to the death and burial of Driepoot, the twenty-fourth dog to be sacrificed, having visited his daughter in a field of flowers, at first unseen by her, and reflected on life as a visiting grandfather, and having at the beginning of the chapter attempted to summon the frustrated shade of Teresa by his art. In *Odyssey* 24 the psychopomp Hermes leads the souls of the slaughtered suitors to the underworld, where the shades of Agamemnon and Achilles discuss the difficulties of accepting death when leaving duties of violent revenge unfulfilled; in the final panel of *Odyssey* 24 Laertes Odysseus and Telemachus confront the suitors' relatives as three generations united. Petrus is Lucy's suitor; he encroaches on her house; David, unlike Odysseus, cannot expel him or even expel Pollux (though he does violently attack Pollux); at the end David settles for grandfatherly visitation toward Lucy, the evocation of an undignified and forgotten passion in his Byron chamber opera, and dignified death and burial for dogs in what has become his central participation in new South African political life. In *Iliad* 24, aged Priam, led by Hermes, comes to ransom the corpse of Hector from Achilles, who has attempted to dishonour it and prevent its decent burial. In the course of their conversation Priam kisses and weeps over the hands of Achilles, saying

> "Respect the gods, Achilles,
> Think of your own father, and pity me.
> I am more pitiable. I have borne what no man
> Who has walked this earth has ever yet borne.
> I have kissed the hand of the man who killed my son." (24:539–543)[7]

Driepoot, in David's arms, going toward the operating table, "sniffs [David's] face, licks his cheeks, his lips, his ears" (*D* 220). Like Achilles, then, David accepts the caress of the being to whom he brings destruction; like Priam, he will deal decently with a corpse that others would dishonour – something David projects before coming to the decision that this must be Driepoot's day:

> He can save the young dog, if he wishes, for another week. But a time must come, it cannot be evaded, when he will have to bring him to Bev Shaw in her operating room (perhaps he will carry him in his arms, perhaps he will do that for him) and caress him and brush back the fur so that the needle can find the vein, and whisper to him and support him in the moment when, bewilderingly, his legs buckle; and then, when the soul is out, fold him up and pack him away in his bag, and the next day wheel the bag into the flames and see that it is burnt, burnt up. (*D* 219–20).

Achilles lifts Hector's body onto the wagon; Priam, led again by Hermes, wheels it back to Troy; and on the tenth day of the armistice Achilles grants, Hector is burnt: "Hector's brothers and friends collected / His white bones" (24: 849–50). While these literary connections are less direct than many that I and others in this volume have pointed out, they strike me as real; moreover, they strike me as exemplary of the mysteriousness of Coetzee's art. Is he mocking David, or himself, by offering in his chapter 24 diminished re-enactments of the ends of the original epic narratives in the history of Western literature? I do not think so, though I can see that a possible allegorical reading could be present in these re-enactments as part of lacerating self-irony. Rather, I would say that *Disgrace*, like *None to Accompany Me*, has undertaken a somewhat epic task, and that these hints toward Homer express both homage and recognition of a kind of kinship. Sheila Murnaghan, introducing *The Iliad*, comments that epic "recounts events with far-reaching historical significance, sums up the values and achievements of an entire

---

[7] Homer, *Iliad*, trans. Stanley Lombardo (Indianapolis: Hackett, 1997), 483

culture, and documents the fullness and variety of the world".[8] One might say that *None to Accompany Me* is *Odyssey*-like in its presentation of a transformed home and family marking the successful passage through a traumatic historical transition, while *Disgrace* is *Iliad*-like in closing on a note of decency about burial amid a holocaust of death and destruction and a recognition of the necessity of loss. But this is the kind of allegorical reading that I think Attridge is right to warn us against: a kind of whistling in the literary dark. It would be better to say that, for me, the literary event in chapter 24 of *Disgrace* involves recognizing that books 24 of the *Iliad* and the *Odyssey* are somewhere in the startling mix of responses evoked by pregnant Lucy amid her field of flowers, forsaken Teresa crying for her Byron, delighted Driepoot licking David while being carried towards the needle.

Disgrace is full of this kind of ironic movement, suggesting allegorical possibility but leaving the reader unsure how (or whether) to proceed with an allegorical reading. This feature of the novel enforces a question that, I am suggesting, Coetzee's reading of *None to Accompany Me* might plausibly have raised for him as a provocation: the question whether to read one's own experience in allegorical terms. "For a man of his age," the novel begins, then continues "fifty-two, divorced, he has, to his mind, solved the problem of sex rather well" (*D* 1). Like "it is a truth universally acknowledged", the beginning of this opening sentence seems headed toward something more general and sweeping than where it actually goes. But as the novel continues, David Lurie turns out to be, in many ways, a self-conscious, even self-dramatizing representative of an age, his age, which is no longer the age he can fittingly inhabit. A romanticist in a communication department. A libertine under a moralizing regime. His conversation with Lucy about his affair with Melanie Isaacs illustrates Lurie's tendency toward this kind of reading of his actions, and also Lurie's awareness that seeing oneself as standing for something larger than oneself can be dangerous:

> 'These are puritanical times. Private life is public business. Prurience is respectable, prurience and sentiment. They wanted a spectacle: breast-beating, remorse, tears if possible. A TV show, in fact. I wouldn't oblige.'
>
> He was going to add, 'The truth is, they wanted me castrated,' but he cannot say the words, not to his daughter. In fact, now that he hears it through another's ears, his whole tirade sounds melodramatic, excessive. (*D* 66)

The same sort of thing happens when he and Lucy discuss the later, in some ways parallel crime committed by the three African men who rape Lucy, burn David, and steal his car (parallel in that one of the sexual encounters Lurie has with Melanie involves his pushing his way into her flat and forcing himself upon her). Lucy comments, "'as far as I am concerned, what happened to me is a purely private matter. In another time, in another place it might be held to be a public matter. But in this place, at this time, it is not. It is my business, mine alone'"

---

8   Sheila Murnaghan, "Introduction", in *Iliad*, trans. Lombardo, xxi.

(*D* 112). Lucy repeatedly cautions David against trying to make her life mean something more than what it is, just a life in a particular place under particular conditions – the kind of life, *Disgrace* suggests, that animals live. We are more than animals in that we live in a construction of allegorical understandings of ourselves, but, *Disgrace* in part suggests, coming near death should mean leaving that construction, accepting its ramshackle contingency and indignity, submitting ourselves to a lack of control, not the wintry mastery Gordimer attributes to Vera at the end of *None to Accompany Me.*

In making a case for these similarities between these two novels as intentional revisions by Coetzee, I enter on fairly delicate ground. Without Coetzee's own commentary, which we are unlikely ever to get, it would be hard to be sure, and presumptuous to claim, that he was thinking about Gordimer's work when he wrote his own. Gordimer herself does not seem aware of similarities to her own work in *Disgrace*, or at least does not mention such similarities in the twofold reaction to *Disgrace* that Ronald Suresh Roberts quotes in his deauthorized biography, *No Cold Kitchen*. After *Disgrace* was published, she wrote to Coetzee describing David Lurie as "a wholly truthful, non-judgmental (you leave that to the reader) intuition of the present time". Six months later, however, she wrote to Philip Roth, praising his novel *The Human Stain* for its evocation of passion and contrasting it to *Disgrace*: in *Disgrace*, "this elegantly and powerfully written novel, there is no deep feeling (except, maybe, … self-disgust) no love, until there is the need to put down a stray dog, the feeling for which is the sole life-affirmative emotion for anyone or anything in the professor".[9] Obviously the way I have described relations between the two novels explains why Gordimer might not like *Disgrace*, even if she did not see those relations herself. *Disgrace* is a very different sort of novel from *None to Accompany Me*, and acceptance of the case I am making for a connection between the two works should not entail a diminution of either (in the way, say, a comparative reading of André Brink's fine novel *Rumours of Rain* alongside Gordimer's great novel *The Conservationist* may incline one to think slightly less of the former). Yet it is very tempting to approach some of the plot elements in *Disgrace* that lend themselves to political allegorization as revisionary allusions to allegorical elements of *None to Accompany Me*, a book that embraces its own political message-bearing. This would not rob these elements of *Disgrace*,

---

[9]   Ronald Suresh Roberts, *No Cold Kitchen: A Biography of Nadine Gordimer* (Johannesburg: STE, 2005), 550–51. The ellipsis is Roberts's. Given the extremely hostile attitude Roberts takes toward Gordimer by this point in the biography, it seems possible that what is left out might mitigate the conclusion he wishes to draw, which is that Gordimer "addressed Coetzee with forked tongue" (551). Surely, however, voicing to Coetzee the view that his book is a profound statement on the times and voicing to Roth that it strikes her as (by comparison with *The Human Stain*) loveless does not mark Gordimer as a snake or a hypocrite. Given that, as I have been arguing, *Disgrace* rather systematically offers a chilly minimalist reprise of plot elements of *None to Accompany Me*, one can understand why Gordimer would find the novel a cold "intuition of the present time".

I think, of the force as literary event they have for me – and, I believe, for many other readers – but it would create another layer of complexity to the life/art juxtapositions that are so lively and so strange in *Disgrace*. One of the strangest and deepest aspects of the end of *Disgrace* – David's characteristically wry and literary acceptance of the role of transracial grandfather to the child to be raised by Lucy as Petrus's *bywoner* – is both deeply idiosyncratic and original and also a revisionary rewriting of an admired rival's allegorically prophetic optimism. One could summarize the interaction I am speculating about allegorically as an exchange of famous literary aphorisms, in which Gordimer quotes Lawrence: "The novel can teach us how to live"; and Coetzee paraphrases Keats on Milton: "life to her is death to me". But in this case reading literally is a better idea than reading allegorically, particularly since Coetzee's way of evoking Gordimer's novel in no way dismisses the validity of Gordimer's projections for the South African future in hinting that they may be fraught with a lot of pain. Recognizing *None to Accompany Me* as a relevant subtext in *Disgrace*, and treating it as a subtext that stands for self-confident self-allegorization and optimistic political prophecy, adds one more layer of literary complexity to Coetzee's strange and beautiful work.

Chapter 6

"Scenes from a dry imagination": *Disgrace* and Embarrassment

Myrtle Hooper

"He could have thought …"

Unfolding in the media at the time I am writing are details of a sexual encounter being disclosed in a court of law trying a public figure for rape. The line of cross-questioning pursued by his defence over the past couple of days has been to establish that the act was consensual; in large part on the basis of what the man, at the time, understood, what he believed, what he thought. The logical slippage between belief and truth is one that ought to be challenged, as should the power dimensions underlying the assumption that if he thought she didn't object then it wasn't rape. The inexorable subtlety of the defence's questions are absent from the trial-by-sentiment taking place outside the courtroom, where supporters of each side are becoming increasingly entrenched in their views. The public standing of the man who is accused is attracting levels of attention in the press and amongst ordinary people that aren't often evoked by rape trials, even though – perhaps because – the predominance of rape in our society at this time is phenomenal. And we have yet to hear his side of things, his story of what happened in that bed on that night. This particular trial is serving, though, to dramatize some commonalities of rape trials. Prime amongst them is that, when unwitnessed, the nature and status of the event must be garnered from the usually opposing testimonies of the persons concerned. And that the power relations between them are shaped by structures, networks, dynamics beyond them. And that the urge, the impulse, the drive to get the meaning of the event is compelling for those who were not involved. In part this is prurience, the titillation of imagining the scurrilous exploits of people one does not ordinarily construe in sexual terms. In part, it is pity and wonder as to how so intimate an engagement could have become so non-mutual. In part, it is a patronizing identification with the victim – "If it had been me, I would have …" – identification that, paradoxically, underlies the cross-questioning presently being led by the legal defence – "so why didn't you just …?" In part, it is exasperation at a man's notion of consensual sex that goes no further than a woman not saying no. In part, it is abhorrence at the deep misogyny that defines the rights and powers of participants in a sexual act in such a way. And in part it is the very elusiveness of the meaning of the event, since the sexual act is a private act, even when associated with violence, even when put on public display by the laying of a charge of rape.

Perhaps the assumption of privacy is fundamental to the act of rape; or of getting a blow job off an intern; or of "consoling" and "tending to the physical needs" of the HIV-positive daughter of a dead friend; or of looking at a girl sitting on a motorbike "with knees wide apart, pelvis arched", and thinking "*I have been there*".

"Private life is public business"

A recurrent motif in Coetzee's novels of the 1990s has been that of privacy. In both *Age of Iron* and *Master of Petersburg*, this motif is reflected in the repeated phrase, "Nothing is private anymore". In *Disgrace* it is registered, briefly, in Lucy's reaction to "her" rape:

> "This has nothing to do with you, David. You want to know why I have not laid a particular charge with the police. I will tell you, as long as you agree not to raise the subject again. The reason is that, as far as I am concerned, what happened to me is a purely private matter. In another time, in another place it might be held to be a public matter. But in this place, at this time, it is not. It is my business, mine alone."
>
> "This place being what?"
>
> "This place being South Africa".[1]

Lucy's claim to privacy is understandable: her attempt is to keep things quiet, to keep the event to herself, as if in that way she can manage and control it. But, as in previous Coetzee novels, her claim is hollow. The consequences she elects to follow in due course take place in the public domain: she contracts a marriage of convenience with the neighbour who is, somehow, implicated in the act, in order to gain his protection and to ensure a degree of safety for herself in the community in the future. Lucy is a woman living alone in an isolated area and does not want further trouble. So her quietism is not unrealistic. Certainly there is often strong social pressure on a victim not to make a fuss, just to accept what has happened to her and to move on. In the legal case cited above, the complainant has described being visited by friends of the accused and by his lawyer, whose brief it was to prevail upon her to drop her case.

Nor is it inauthentic, psychologically, that a rape victim should blame herself for being raped, and construe the rape from the point of view of her rapist(s). As an act the rape of Lucy is clear-cut, and fits the stereotype of what rape "is" like: she is overpowered by three strangers against her will. Perhaps her unacknowledged goal is to make what has happened to her understandable; to retrieve some degree of autonomy; to know the terms in which she has to operate; and to manage this

---

[1]   J.M. Coetzee, *Disgrace* (London: Vintage, 2000): 112. All subsequent references to this edition.

knowledge. That is, to restore a balance of at least hermeneutic power. Yet in defending her decision not to lay charges Lucy goes a great deal further in her interpretation:

> "But isn't there another way of looking at it, David? What if … what if *that* is the price one has to pay for staying on? Perhaps that is how they look at it; perhaps that is how I should look at it too. They see me as owing something. They see themselves as debt collectors, tax collectors. Why should I be allowed to live here without paying? Perhaps that is what they tell themselves." (158)

Implicit in her use of "they" is the play of racial dynamics, since she is a white woman and her three assailants are black. Implicit in her interpretation is a political position, an attempt to understand and explain the personal crime in social terms, in terms of the shift in power in South Africa in a period of transition from the oppression to the liberation of the majority of its people. True, such a shift is not specific to South Africa; true, rape is widespread in societies undergoing such transitions, in societes in which one social group is seeking to dominate another, or to redress past imbalances of power. So Lucy's concept of "debt collection", of "tax collection", may not be completely outlandish. Yet her quietism *is* offensive, and not only to the women whose "place" it entrenches by confirming stereotypes. It is offensive in accommodating the bad behaviour of a few in terms that imply this is to be expected of the many. Its white liberal cringe translates a personal crime into a social phenomenon and so exculpates its perpetrators. And despite the phenomenal prevalence of rape in our society at this time, I would venture to believe that most ordinary people, most ordinary men, black and white, do not see rape as acceptable conduct, as decent behaviour.

My conviction, perhaps, is neither here nor there. More significant was the public reaction to the broader political implications of Lucy's position. When the novel came out, it drew substantial popular interest because the act of rape, in Lucy's conception of it, was seen as instantiating the violent crime endemic in our country post apartheid. And so a crude polemic emerged that confirmed the concerns of conservative whites about high levels of violent crime, and entrenched the resentments of politically conscious blacks at so racial a reaction. This public impact seemed to me deeply unfortunate. Such a polemic reinforces stereotypes and engrains prejudice, and makes it harder for ordinary black and white people to interact, to share terms of common understanding, to get on with the business of getting on with each other. It serves as one more interruption to hardwon progress towards an acceptance of diversity, of mutual respect, of living in accord. I found it disappointing that Coetzee had written this episode in this way that lent itself to the entrenchment of such vested ways of seeing things. He did not seem to me to be asking the question, "Can we live together?", but rather showing us that we can't – or that we can but at the cost of damaging accommodations, indecent compromises.

I encountered similar disquiet a couple of years ago when, like David Attwell, I workshopped *Disgrace* with a group of Grade 12 pupils. Some of them enjoyed the novel, found it "enthralling", "unputdownable". Some drew morals from it: simple ones, "pay attention and be obedient to your parents"; "being self-centred isn't the right thing to do"; "don't stalk women"; and more elaborate ones, "accept your children's decisions rather than try to control their lives as David Lurie and Mr Isaacs tried to do"; "very few people can be trusted; even those close to you can hurt you"; "we may need to integrate our cultures in South Africa"; "animals are a great comfort to humans when we are lonely and sad, and they do not judge you". Yet many did not like it: they had learned nothing from the novel, they said, and objected to its "incomplete ending", its "bad ending, where Lucy marries her rapist's friend". Several took issue with the novel's treatment of South Africa: it was "not depicted in a true South African style"; it offered a "bad outlook on South Africa, gives us a bad image", was "not a good reflection of South Africa and would give people overseas a bad view of the country"; it "used *apartheid* as an excuse for actions that were not relevant". The fact that Coetzee had left South Africa shortly after the publication of *Disgrace* did not help ameliorate their views.

Their reactions, like mine at the time, were tendentious in implicitly prescribing to the writer what he should – and should not – be saying in his fiction. Another instance of this "mimetic fallacy", as David Attwell calls it, occurred in the ANC's attempt to harness the novel as a kind of "expert witness" to testify that racism really does exist in our society. As Attwell reminds us, the relation between fiction and reality cannot be taken easily or simply for granted, not even in a realist paradigm. In an e-mail argument with an "ordinary reader" of *Disgrace* at the time, *Mail & Guardian* literary reviewer Shaun de Waal couches this in simple terms. For Coetzee "a fictional text is in fact a hypothetical space in which the writer can ask 'what if' questions ... the story is not an account of real events but an attempt to deal with the ramifications of all the 'what if' questions set in motion – narrative as well as 'moral' questions".[2] Fiction, in other words, affords a writer a space for exploration beyond the reach of the prescriptions of ordinary reality, and this is a space that needs to be respected, by ordinary readers as well as by experts. Granted. Yet to respect is not the same as to accept. No reader should have to forgo asking questions about the uses that writers make of this space, to forgo bringing ethical considerations to bear. I am not persuaded that, as Attwell seems to suggest, recognizing aesthetic practices to be "of a different order from utilitarian ones" renders fiction exempt from judgements about its content, sets it beyond the realm of normative views of "what social reality is or ought to be".[3]

---

[2]   Edited version of an e-mail discussion between Shaun de Waal and Di Kilpert, *Mail & Guardian On-Line* (20–24 October 2003), at www.chico.mweb.co.za/art/2003/2003oct/031024-coetzeeresp.html (accessed 16 May 2008, 18h43).

[3]   David Attwell, "J.M. Coetzee and South Africa: Thoughts on the Social Life of Fiction", *English Academy Review* 21 (2004): 105–17, at 163.

There are times when the pressure to judge literature normatively will be stronger than at others, and perhaps periods of social change, of social reconstruction, are more likely to produce the kind of question about "the message for the youth" that disconcerted Attwell than periods of established stability in which literary-intellectual life might more reasonably command moral space to play.

For me, in a three-decade academic career that continues to be conducted within South Africa, it has been more possible at other times than now to accommodate the demands of Coetzee's high literary self-consciousness. Living here, working here, being here, entails different kinds of relations with people than the hypothetical states of being postulated in his novel. In this place, at this time, the pronominal awareness I bring to my reading is deliberately oriented towards "you" not "they" or "them", because this is a way of rooting it, ethically, pragmatically. In *Disgrace*, it seems to me, Coetzee abjures the "you" more intensely and more far-reachingly than before. It is possible to read David redemptively, and this has been adroitly done in some of the critical interpretations I have recently seen. Yet in my eyes he is set up as a "me" – as an avatar of J.M. Coetzee. To read *Disgrace* without distaste, it seems to me, requires elisions that shut one's eyes to what is there; narrative compliance that forecloses scruples; critical reference beyond the text to received ways of reading Coetzee that sanction a solipsism both alienated and baleful.

Pamela Cooper's 2005 article, "Metamorphosis and Sexuality: Reading the Strange Passions of *Disgrace*",[4] is a case in point. Examining the "deployment of sexuality in the framework of allusion and under the aegis of myth", she argues that Coetzee "articulates change through sexuality, which becomes a kind of flexible but ambiguous trope for the wider historical changes he registers". She thus reads David in representative terms, and the novel in terms of process and development.

One of the temptations of reading at so general a level is to elide awkward or inconsistent detail. A striking instance occurs in her analysis of David's view of Melanie astride her boyfriend's motorbike: "Melanie, on the pillion, sits with knees wide apart, pelvis arched ...] Then the motorcycle surges forward, bearing her away" (28). What Cooper elides is David's reflection to himself: "*I have been there*". The elision is necessary so that she can read Melanie's sexuality in relation to her boyfriend rather than David; and, through reference to the myth of Europa, to Coetzee's reading of Lovelace, and to the archaic sense of the word as "abduction", to reassign the rape of Melanie to Ryan. And so to shift the focus from David's sexuality to male sexuality, to sexuality as trope, as a "code for or vocabulary of change".

Another is the tendency to complete and to elaborate Coetzee's narrative project in complicitous ways. Cooper follows David in seeing the rape of Lucy as conceptually distinct from his "not quite rape" of Melanie. A probably unintended

---

    [4]   Pamela Cooper, "Metamorphosis and Sexuality: Reading the Strange Passions of *Disgrace*", *Research in African Literatures* 36.4 (2005): 22–39.

effect of this is to entrench social and political hierarchies. Because Lucy's rapists are not white, not educated, not middle-class, their act of rape is available to be construed as "mating", as enacting "forces beyond their control". More consciously, Cooper goes on to sanitize and sanctify the rape: mooting it as spiritual, as mythic, as sacred, and Lucy's rapists as "angels or messengers", as aspects of the divine. Her take on Lucy herself is sanctimonious: that she has been "put in her place" by the rape, and that her pregnancy is a "moral act of endurance". And her emphasis on the displacement of the white phallus highlights the "chastisement" of David, his "shriveling" as the novel draws to a close (28), his effective castration (29), and the "dissolution", and by implication, bestiality, of his sexual encounter with Bev Shaw, who is "the 'dog' of contemporary slang designation" (37). The novel ends, she says, in the sexual despair of the older (white) man in South Africa, and, by implication, his withdrawal.

Although in its own terms Cooper's argument is compelling, I find myself resisting it for three reasons: one, her willingness to play fast and loose with detail; two, the teleology of her reading; and three, the critical excrescences of sanctifying Lucy's rapists, derogating Bev Shaw, and depersonalizing and generalizing the sexuality of David Lurie. It is on this last point that I wish to focus now.

The motif of privacy registered in Lucy's reaction to her rape is also registered in David's comment to her about the disciplinary hearing he faces following the rape allegation by his student: "Private life is public business" (66). And in fact it is the private world of David, not of Lucy, that the novel foregrounds and exposes. There is a certain irony in this: David is loath to make the public disclosure that would probably have been enough to fend off the respectable prurience that "wanted a spectacle", yet it is "his story" that is told in and by the novel. Broadly speaking, David is represented in terms of five interrelated dynamics: teaching, composing, fatherhood, ageing, sexuality. But it is sexuality that seems to me the core to his characterization, around which the others cohere. And given the narrative's present-tense third-person focalization of his consciousness, it is most acutely in the sexual domain that we see the self-obsession, the self-enclosure that characterizes him. Indeed, the strongest disquiet expressed by my Grade 12 pupils made this point: "the way he thinks about women is shocking and extremely descriptive"; "I didn't like the way he never explained the girl's position – it was very vague – one minute she's hot next she's not"; "I disliked the way David ... treated women and only thought about himself".

The "Rights of Desire"

Near the end of the novel (191–2), we get a moment of epiphany that offers a reflective overview of David's life of amorousness. It is involuntary: an "eruption", a "waking dream" that reveals itself "pell mell". It is also visual, in the first instance, releasing a stream of images that "pours down", that "pass[es] before him", that he calls a "vision". He is passive in its grip, holding his breath as he wills it to continue. The visual imagery becomes corporeal and visceral: bringing him a sense of entanglement; plunging him "into the ocean of memory"; flooding "his heart with thankfulness" like "a flower blooming in his breast". He labels the experience "hypnagogic", and speculates that he is being "led by a god". The images that stream before him are images of women he has sexually known. Although he deems all these encounters "enriching", his entanglement with them is in the past; their lives and his have diverged, and they exist now only within the realm of his memory. There is a strong sense of loss, of nostalgia, in his musing question, "What has happened to them, all those women, all those lives?" that echoes and amplifies the allusive *"fair field full of folk"*. There is also surprised hurt at the "jeering" of the newspapers at his "enrichment". At the same time, the qualification he places on it is both instrumental and reductive, "even the least of them, even the failures". Nor does he pause to wonder whether any of these women's lives have been correspondingly enriched by their encounters with him. In fact the epiphany is only possible because it is retrospective; because he is, in the moment of the present, alone. There is a marked disjunction between the profligacy, the plenitude of his past sexual encounters and this present solitude. In fact solitariness is fundamental to his character. To some exent this is an artefact of the present-tense focalization. Yet it is more than this too, and, as I have already indicated, has consequences for the ethos of the novel, and for ethical readings of David, and of *Disgrace*.

The epiphany occurs while he is sitting watching a play, amongst an audience of holidaymakers who are enjoying its risqué humour; his countrymen, amongst whom he feels alien, an impostor. Almost incidentally, he remembers another holidaymaker from years back, with whom he had sex (191). The memory is gradual; vague, at first, then specified detail by detail, becoming embodied, sensual, as he recalls the woman's soft feather-light hair between his fingers, and her long wiry legs, presumably under his hands or wrapped around his body. Although present to him in his memory, she is accorded no autonomy and the narrative carries no trace of her self. The woman thus exists in his mind predominantly as the tactile object of his actions. The memory is isolating, because he recalls only his own experience; because this recollection is self-centred, self-referential. He is free to savour the image of her, the memory of her, because it is distanced from him and hence preserved from any taint of reality.

This particular sexual encounter is distinguished by the fact that it occurs in the narrative past. The others, with the women mentioned in the epiphany, take place during the course of action of the novel. There are many. I wish to select a few to examine in detail, in order to correct – and to contest – the generalized reading of sexuality offered in Cooper's analysis. Two that occur early on in the novel set up a frame for a reading of the more important encounters that follow.

The first illustrates David's "solution" to what he dubs "the problem of sex". Soraya is a "hostess" with Discreet Escorts, whom he meets every week, at "a place of assignation, nothing more, functional, clean, well regulated", and for whose services he pays R400 a time. As the narrative concedes, by means of the tag "he imagines", Soraya's consciousness is not actually registered in his understanding of the relations between them. He settles for imagining, rather than finding out or knowing. In the absence of her point of view, his construction of their encounter is uncontested. The story he tells is quite evidently *his* story, not *the* story. And the serpentine image he chooses for their sexual relations reflects his sense of things, not a sense shared between them. The narration of this relationship thus allows, confirms, reinforces his aloneness, his isolation.

The second occurs after he sees Soraya in "real life" and transgresses the boundaries she has set up around the domestic sphere of being mother to two small boys. She then rejects him, and disappears. He tries out another hostess, "another Soraya", but finds her "coarse" (8). He then takes the new secretary in his department to lunch:

> Her name is Dawn. The second time he takes her out they stop at his house and have sex. It is a failure. Bucking and clawing, she works herself into a froth of excitement that in the end only repels him. He lends her a comb, drives her back to the campus. (9)

Unlike Soraya who, despite his desire for her, seems not particularly responsive, this woman's arousal is greater than his, and her deliberate pursuit of her own pleasure disgusts him. His self-centredness is evident in three things. One, he adjudges the event "a failure", with the point of reference quite clearly his own, not hers, not theirs. Two, he uses images for her that are demeaning and repellent. The phrase "bucking and clawing" implies a deliberate loss of human control, as the woman becomes horse-like, mare-like, and scratches like a cat of some kind, probably wild. The "froth of excitement" into which she works herself is non-specific. Does "froth" suggest foam on a wave, excitement that is transient, superficial? Does it, more portentously, suggest exudation, that she is foaming at the mouth, or somewhere else? Is there a hint of rabidity? And three, after the event, David "lends her a comb" in a deliberate reinstatement of order; and "drives her back" to the campus, enforcing retreat. His detachment after this is superior and patronizing: he takes care to avoid her, to put distance between them.

Midway through the novel, in a conversation about his leaving Cape Town, David's daughter puts a question to him: "What is your case? Let us hear it." He replies, "My case rests on the rights of desire ... On the god who makes even the small birds quiver" (89). It is true that this conversation is followed – and ironized – by the arrival of the intruders who rape Lucy and assault him. Yet by this stage the basis of his "case" has been demonstrated to us readers in the foregoing accounts of his sexual activities that I have considered, and most intensely in the encounter with his student Melanie Isaacs which leads to her accusation of rape.

"Not rape, not quite that"

This encounter takes place in the context of a relationship emerging between them, with co-operation and even initiative on her part. He propositions her, the first time he invites her back to his house for a meal, using the stale line that she is so beautiful that she has a moral obligation to share her beauty sexually with him. It does not work, on that occasion, but the next time he sees her he prevails upon her to let him make love to her. "Her body is clear, simple, in its way perfect; though she is passive throughout, he finds the act pleasurable, so pleasurable that from its climax he tumbles into blank oblivion" (19). The third and last time they have sex, he "feels a surge of joy and desire" when she "hooks a leg behind his buttocks to draw him in closer" and he feels the tension of the tendon of her inner thigh (29). The middle occasion, by contrast, is a disaster, a "failure":

> At four o'clock the next afternoon he is at her flat. She opens the door wearing a crumpled T-shirt, cycling shorts, slippers in the shape of comic-book gophers which he finds silly, tasteless.
>
> He has given her no warning; she is too surprised to resist the intruder who thrusts himself upon her. When he takes her in his arms, her limbs crumple like a marionette's. Words heavy as clubs thud into the delicate whorl of her ear. "No, not now!" she says, struggling. "My cousin will be back!"
>
> But nothing will stop him. He carries her to the bedroom, brushes off the absurd slippers, kisses her feet, astonished by the feeling she evokes. Something to do with the apparition on the stage: the wig, the wiggling bottom, the crude talk. Strange love! Yet from the quiver of Aphrodite, goddess of the foaming waves, no doubt about that.
>
> She does not resist. All she does is avert herself: avert her lips, avert her eyes. She lets him lay her out on the bed and undress her: she even helps him, raising her arms and then her hips. Little shivers of cold run through her; as soon as she is bare, she slips under the quilted counterpane like a mole burrowing, and turns her back on him.
>
> Not rape, not quite that, but undesired nevertheless, undesired to the core. As though she had decided to go slack, die within herself for the duration, like a rabbit when the jaws of the fox close on its neck. So that everything done to her might be done, as it were, far away.

The major question about this particular episode is lodged in the reflection that elides the act, "not rape, not quite that". The negative "not" obscures the closeness, the parity between the appositional phrase "quite that" and its reference "rape"; but the modifier "quite" serves to recast the differerentiation as analogy – in other words, "not quite … but very like". Nor is it entirely clear whose reflection this is: whether David's focalized consciousness is here cleaving with narrative comment, or cleaving from it.

In fact a fascinating modulation of focalization takes place through the passage. The judgements "silly, tasteless" that crop up in the description of Melanie's slippers in the first paragraph are quite clearly David's, insisting on the refinement of his tastes. Paragraph two is his attempt to recognize her point of view: the remark, "he has given her no warning", shows his awareness that his visit is in breach of the protocols of politeness; and, together with the observation "she is too surprised to resist", explains her failure to repudiate him. Although this seems to be an attempt on his part to engage imaginatively with her, it remains an ascription and hence imposes meaning on her. The attempt to engage is further circumscribed by his dramatization of himself as "the intruder who thrusts himself upon her". Nor does his awareness of his effect on her cause the compunction that would inhibit him, stop him from "thrusting" himself upon her, from "taking" her in his arms. Thus the next sentence abjures – or suppresses – agency. The words are clearly his, but their content is omitted in order to foreground their impact, their "thudding heaviness" on her "delicate" ear. The last sentence is an objective depiction of her reaction: she says no, she struggles, and she gives a reason for her refusal. Paragraph three then clearly reflects his experience: by means of description, "astonished by the feeling she evokes"; in free indirect discourse, "Something to do with ...", "Strange love!"; "Yet from the quiver ..."; and in assertion, "no doubt about that" – an overstatement that, paradoxically, undermines its certitude. Paragraph four offers an objective description of her actions and non-actions. Implied in it, however, are assumptions and expectations that measure her response: she might resist, but she does not do so; she might do various things, but all she does is this; she lets him do this, she even helps him; she slips under the covers herself. Two verbs in this paragraph are of particular interest. The repeated "avert" emphasizes both the determination and the impotence of her reaction to his onslaught. The active voice of the verb fixes agency firmly with her, where the nominal "aversion" (which is not used here) would have blurred it. The verb "let" is defined, in the *Concise Oxford*, as "not prevent or forbid; allow"; and "lets him" here emphasizes her passivity, her acquiescence with his actions upon her, his laying her out and undressing her. Its use works to erode the objectivity of his description since its tone is one of surprise that she should so comply. This surprise hints at his underlying assumptions and expectations about her, about women, about sexual conduct. Although he is "assured of certain certainties",[5] as it were, these are hollow. Without closer communication he cannot know what her response really is. Hence his subsequent astonishment at being accused of rape.

As focalization modulates in the passage, so a strand of similes and analogies indicate, and complicate, point of view. These images are significant in fixing how we see Melanie, and in disallowing a more sustained, sympathetic identification with her. Like David, we perceive her externally, objectively, and do not notice that his story is containing, and silencing, her story. When David thrusts himself on her and takes her in his arms, her limbs crumple, we learn, "like a marionette's". The feelings she evokes in him, which are intense enough to "astonish" him, have

⁵   T.S. Eliot, "Preludes", in *Collected Poems 1906–1962* (London: Faber, 1967).

something to do with "the apparition on the stage: the wig, the wiggling bottom, the crude talk". Once he has undressed her, she shivers with cold, and "slips under the quilted counterpane like a mole burrowing". Her reaction to sex is "to go slack, die within herself for the duration, like a rabbit when the jaws of the fox close on its neck". The images are used predominantly of Melanie, and so we read them as rooted in David's conception of her and of events. As with Soraya and with Dawn, he envisages her in animal terms, and the effect, although here it evokes sympathy, is to dehumanize and depersonalize her. She is certainly not construed, or rendered, as an active and willing sexual partner.

More disquieting, though, are the implications of death. For David, like Eliot's "young man carbuncular",[6] the act of sex entails a renunciation of both responsiveness and responsibility. David experiences feelings strong enough to "astonish" him – and, in the heat of the moment, he assures himself of the source of his passion ("from the quiver of Aphrodite ... no doubt about that") – but he does so in order to proceed in the absence of response from her. He is vaguely aware of this since we get a reasonably detailed account of her actions: "she does not resist", "all she does is", "she lets him", "she even helps him", "she slips", "she turns her back on him". Yet the dominant note is that of her deliberate passivity, her withdrawal, her dissociation. Without resisting, she "averts herself", "averts her lips", "averts her eyes"; she decides to "go slack", to "die within herself", so that "everything done to her" might be done "as it were, far away". Moles and rabbits are prey, it is true, yet the overrriding impression is not of David as huntsman, as predator, but of David as necrophiliac. Melanie is rendered, for the duration of the act of sex, as corpse, as dead body.

"This and even less than this"

Another significant sexual encounter occurs towards the end of the novel, after the rape of Lucy. David has begun to help her friend, Bev Shaw, in the work she does euthanizing stray animals. Although this encounter is initiated by Bev, it is preceded by an awkward conversation in which she asks him about his life in Cape Town. He describes himself in the present as being "out of the way of temptation", then realizes this is a "callous thing to say to a woman, even a plain one". Perhaps out of curiosity, or in compensation, he tries to "imagine" her in sexual terms, and on impulse "reaches out and runs a finger over her lips", a move to which she responds by kissing his hand, despite "blushing furiously". She then invites him to meet her at the clinic.

> Two blankets, one pink, one grey, smuggled from her home by a woman who in the last hour has probably bathed and powdered and anointed herself in readiness; who has, for all he knows, been powdering and anointing herself every Sunday,

---

    [6]   T.S. Eliot, The "Fire Sermon" section of "The Waste Land", in *Collected Poems 1906–1962* (London: Faber, 1967).

and storing blankets in the cabinet, just in case. Who thinks, because he comes from the big city, because there is scandal attached to his name, that he makes love to many women and expects to be made love to by every woman who crosses his path.

The choice is between the operating table and the floor. He spreads out the blankets on the floor, the grey blanket underneath, the pink on top. He switches off the light, leaves the room, checks that the back door is locked, waits. He hears the rustle of clothes as she undresses. Bev. Never did he dream he would sleep with a Bev.

She is lying under the blanket with only her head sticking out. Even in the dimness there is nothing charming in the sight. Slipping off his underpants, he gets in beside her, runs his hands down her body. She has no breasts to speak of. Sturdy, almost waistless, like a squat little tub.

Of their congress he can at least say he does his duty. Without passion but without distaste either. So that in the end Bev Shaw can feel pleased with herself. All she intended has been accomplished. He, David Lurie, has been succoured, as a man is succoured by a woman; her friend Lucy Lurie has been helped with a difficult visit.

Let me not forget this day, he tells himself, lying beside her when they are spent. After the sweet young flesh of Melanie Isaacs, this is what I have come to. This is what I will have to get used to, this and even less than this.

"It's late," says Bev Shaw. "I must be going".

He pushes the blanket aside and gets up, making no effort to hide himself. Let her gaze her fill on her Romeo, he thinks, on his bowed shoulders and skinny shanks.

It is indeed late. On the horizon lies a last crimson glow; the moon looms overhead; smoke hangs in the air; across a strip of waste land, from the first rows of shacks comes a hubbub of voices. At the door Bev presses herself against him a last time, rests her head on his chest. He lets her do it, as he has let her do everything she has felt a need to do. His thoughts go to Emma Bovary strutting before the mirror after her first big afternoon. *I have a lover! I have a lover!* sings Emma to herself. Well, let poor Bev Shaw go home and do some singing too. And let him stop calling her poor Bev Shaw. If she is poor, he is bankrupt. (150)

As with Soraya, his commentary on their conjugation is speculative, but here his tone is sneering as it was not earlier. The word "anointed" and the repetition in "powdering and anointing herself" has the clear corollary that he has spent the last hour doing no such thing, that he has seen no reason to ready himself in such a way. There is a throwaway quality to "for all he knows", but speculation gives way to assertion when he starts to relay what she "thinks". The bitterness of his tone is odd, given that what he says she thinks of him is, by his own admission, broadly true. He is active in setting things up – "he spreads", "he switches … leaves … checks … waits" – and in leaving her to undress alone, but he is also passive, even inert, going along with choices that have been predefined for him. And although he has, by his own account, slept with many women, many nameless, he baulks at her name, reducing and generalizing her by means of an indefinite article: "Bev. Never did he dream he would sleep with a Bev". Is her name common? Is the abbreviation low-class? Elsewhere he says it reminds him of cattle. The smallmindedness of this irritation perhaps indexes a larger resentment, perhaps at the "duty" imposed on him that he finds oppressive, perhaps at the fact that this is her choice, not his. Certainly his description of her is objective, dismissive: her head "sticks out" of the blanket, and there is "nothing charming in the sight". She is so ugly to him that even dim light does not help. Once under the blanket, his sense-impressions switch from visual to tactile, but he remains harshly conscious, passing judgements such as she has "no breasts to speak of", and she is "sturdy, almost waistless, like a squat little tub". The simile objectifies her, and the reiteration "sturdy ... squat" is overdetermined as well as disenchanted. He uses words to keep himself at a remove, to diminish and patronize her.

The terminology he uses to describe the encounter is abstract, analytic: "congress", "duty", "distaste", "accomplished", "succoured". The claim he makes that his "duty" is done without distaste is disingenuous, given his quite evident distaste. More belitting, though, is the projection onto her of what he understands to be her motivation. His assertions are a parody of her voice: they serve to impose his point of view as he speaks for her, instead of her, rather than to her. He shifts, then, to addressing himself about her: "Let me not forget this day". Nostalgia has become self-indulgence and self-pity. Where before the indefinite article of "a Bev" reduced and generalized her, now she is commodified as "this and even less than this". The contrast with Melanie Isaacs implies that her body is not-sweet and not-young, but the comparison treats both women as "flesh". The modal "will have to" measures his resistance to the fate he sees ahead of him. It also initiates self-scrutiny that points up his own "bowed shoulders and skinny shanks", that relishes his shortcomings as a Romeo because this cheats Bev of her romantic desires.

The session concludes with the brief embrace she instigates and he endures. Significantly, the word "let" is then used, twice. It links this passage with the "non-rape" of Melanie, putting him into the same, passive, role as Melanie, couching him as Bev's victim. Invoking the heroic literary figure Emma Bovary seems to make the contact endurable to him, because it reduces and diminishes her, by contrast, to "poor Bev Shaw". He corrects his condescension by reminding himself, "If she is poor, he is bankrupt" – and the comparison adroitly shifts the focus back to himself. Again we are asked to accept his reading of her motivations, her experience, her emotional state, without any corroboration from her. Throughout the passage there is a marked disjunction between bodily engagement and cognitive distance: she is held at bay, as it were, so that he can think about her, place her, locate her.

The Waste Land

A last very brief sexual encounter occurs near the end of the novel. After leaving the play mentioned earlier, in which Melanie is appearing, David is intimidated by her boyfriend. He retreats, cruises Main Street, and picks up a prostitute who approaches him.

> They park in a cul-de-sac on the slopes of Signal Hill. The girl is drunk or perhaps on drugs: he can get nothing coherent out of her. Nonetheless, she does her work on him as well as he could expect. Afterwards she lies with her face in his lap, resting. She is younger than she had seemed under the streetlights, younger even than Melanie. He lays a hand on her head. The trembling has ceased. He feels drowsy, contented; also strangely protective.
>   *So this is all it takes!*, he thinks. *How could I ever have forgotten it?* (194)

The "protectiveness" of the hand he lays on her head as she lies with her face in his lap is hypocritical, since, despite her youth and her intoxication, which are emphasized, the act is at his instigation. She is defined in terms of his need of her; the concern he registers about her intoxication has less to do with her incoherence than her capacity to perform "her work". His concluding comment too is abstracted of any human responsiveness, responsibility: it is celebratory, triumphant, as he reminds himself, with self-indulgent humour, of what he has "forgotten". What is striking in this passage is not so much what is there, but what is not; and that is any evidence of ethical valency. The act is presented as ethically neutral, and the narration assumes our complicity with it.

On Embarrassment

> An individual may recognize extreme embarrassment in others and even in himself by the objective signs of emotional disturbance: blushing, fumbling, stuttering, an unusually low- or high-pitched voice, quavering speech or breaking of the voice, sweating, blanching, blinking, tremor of the hand, hesitating or vacillating movement, absentmindedness, and malapropisms. As Mark Baldwin remarked about shyness, there may be "a lowering of the eyes, bowing of the head, putting of hands behind the back, nervous fingering of the clothing or twisting of the fingers together, and stammering, with some incoherence of idea as expressed in speech." There are also symptoms of a subjective kind: constriction of the diaphragm, a feeling of wobbliness, consciousness of strained and unnatural gestures, a dazed sensation, dryness of the mouth, and tenseness of

the muscles. In cases of mild discomfiture, these visible and invisible flusterings occur but in less perceptible form.[7]

Thus Erving Goffman. His account is unusual within sociological circles because it offers an objective, operational description of embarrassment. Yet it was Goffman's innovation to posit this as the "master emotion of modern life", as Thomas Scheff points out,[8] because it is "a phenomenon that requires a certain implicit mindful or cognitive grasp of social conventions and one's place within them", as Rom Harré explains.[9] It is intricately related to intersubjectivity, to the awareness of the other person or persons with whom one interacts.

In the context of this discussion of sexuality, we might see embarrassment as an inhibitor that prevents or interrupts or dislocates the "flow" of sexual passion. Yet because it involves recognizing the presence and the participation of the other party it also serves ethical functions. What makes David's sex with Melanie rape rather than "not rape" is the fact that he overrides his awareness that she does not want it. Although he is embarrassed by his encounter with Bev Shaw, this is because he feels sex with her is beneath him, that it belittles him, that he is being used by her. Hence his subsequent recourse to fellatio with a prostitute, in order to right the balance, to restore power and control. And this works because he is not embarrassed at using her in this way. What is important is that he should be reminded of what he has forgotten. Yet the absence of embarrassment is also conditional, because sex with a prostitute, like rape, has to take place in private. Public exposure would make it untenable. Embarrassment is important as a narrative principle as well, therefore, because it is through narration that what is private is rendered public; it is the narrative act that discloses, or exposes and so potentially mortifies, the one who would rather keep things quiet.

The "unblinking gaze"

In an illuminating reading of David Lurie, Derek Attridge finds, in the two tasks he undertakes in his state of disgrace, composing, and helping at the clinic,

> a dedication to a singularity that exceeds systems and computations: the singularity of every living, and dead, being, the singularity of the truly inventive work of art. … In this dedication we find the operation of something I've called *grace*, and perhaps – whatever ungainliness and awkwardness we associate

---

[7]   Erving Goffman, "Embarrassment and Social Organization" (1957), in *Interaction Ritual: Essays on Face-to-Face Behaviour* (Harmondsworth: Penguin, 1957): 97–112, at 97.

[8]   T.J. Scheff, "Goffman Unbound: A New Paradigm for Social and Behavioral Science", website at www.uab.edu/philosophy/SIGscheff.htm (accessed 30 August 2006).

[9]   R. Harré, Introduction to The Embarrassment Project: The Virtual Faculty Website, at www.massey.ac.nz/~alock/virtual/project1.htm (accessed 18 May 2008).

with Lurie ... even a touch of its derivatives, *gracefulness* and *graciousness*.
Where Coetzee differs from many others who have taken similar positions is his
unblinking acceptance of the non-instrumental nature of this stance.[10]

The focus of my present essay is the treatment of sexuality in the novel, and so I
shall not here move into a consideration of the themes of music and relations with
animals. Yet Attridge's observation has relevance for a discussion of embarrassment.
In his reading, we find the obverse of the prescriptiveness of the pupils' readings
of *Disgrace*, and of my own reaction to the text. As a critical stance it succeeds
in setting aside the demands of the real world; demands that include the urge for
justice where injustice has been done. The state of grace he sees David attaining
has nothing to do with the recognition of wrong, the anagnorosis we might hope
to find. Rather he emphasizes the restraint with which Coetzee-as-narrator treats
David, the patience, tolerance, forbearance, the respect he brings to his creation,
together with the "unblinking" gaze that he sees as morally inexorable. Implicit in
Attridge's reading is the suggestion that we, as readers, should accept and allow
this restraint, should respect the fictive space in which "what-if" questions are
posed and not necessarily answered. In his view, it seems, this is a higher ethical
stance to take than to press the rights and responsibilities that we would expect to
be met in the real world.

Yet it is worth weighing up what we renounce if we do. If we accept Coetzee's
terms, we must accept the weight and balance he gives to David's experience.
One of the narrative effects is an instrumental treatment of women, as setting,
as backdrop to that experience. And one of the most potent ways in which this
works is through David's imagery. I have examined the play of imagery in the
sexual encounters he has with various women. Despite the credit Attridge gives
to his "stumbling but tenacious endeavor to be a good father to Lucy" (179), this
operates also in relation to his daughter. One example occurs when he goes to visit
her near the end of the novel. He looks at her and sees the "milky, blue-veined skin
and broad, vulnerable tendons at the backs of her knees; the least beautiful part of
a woman's body, the least expressive, and therefore perhaps the most endearing"
(219). Lucy's kneepits may make David feel tender, but they mark her in our eyes,
and in ways that I think would not be comfortable for her. Another example is
the image he attaches to the rapists of his daughter. Having challenged her not to
accept the "stories" they might use to justify themseves, he himself imagines the
three men leaving the farm in his car, "their penises, their weapons, tucked warm
and satisfied between their legs – *purring* is the word that comes to him. They must
have had every reason to be satisified with their afternoon's work; they must have
felt happy in their vocation" (159). Attwell explains embodiment as one of two
limitations on the "autonomy and agency of the subject" in Coetzee's writing (16).
One of its manifestations, in several of the novels, is mortification of the flesh, and

---

[10]   David Attridge, *J.M. Coetzee and the Ethics of Reading* (Scottsville: University of
KwaZulu-Natal Press, 2005), 188.

underlying that, I think, the separability of parts, the partialling out of bits of the body. Hence the consideration David gives, at the start of the novel, to castrating himself. And hence his grotesque feline image of penises purring.

Writing about character, Thomas Leitch argues that omission, and hence reconstruction, are central to our reading experience. We "never know everything about any fictional character" he says; we recover characters "precisely by generalizing or extrapolating the exemplary thoughts we are given ... characters differ from people in being incompletely specified (how many characters are said to have armpits?)".[11] It is perhaps this metonymy that makes David's imagery so powerful. It is costly to others because it takes the form of relegating them, placing them, locating them, conceptually, existentially, iconically. David's imaging of Lucy's knees, of the rapists' penises, detaches them from the persons to whom they belong, and allows him to position himself, epistemologically, just in relation to these bits of their bodies. This limits their autonomy and agency, it is true (or perhaps reinscribes it in those particular body parts). It also reifies them and neutralizes any capacity they may have to embarrass him, to get him to see himself in their eyes.

What is missing in David is this sense that he is a person in a social world, with the ordinary reciprocities that this entails. I have complained above about the solipsism I find in his character. Here I will go further, and say that David is the way he is because Coetzee valorizes selfhood, and extreme forms of selfhood at that. There is a point at which subjectivity becomes self-enclosing and then it is very difficult for anyone else to engage – because relationship of any kind, of any degree, is seen as intrusion, as incursion, as encroachment upon the private space of the self. What is for the most part absent from Coetzee's rendition of his character is awareness of himself in the eyes of others, the sense that how they see him matters. Hence my sense, in reading *Disgrace*, of wandering in the wasteland of David's self. To push the point: I think the same dynamic coincides with, even instantiates Coetzee's relation with his reader. Coetzee's choice of present tense suppresses, or evades, the retrospective stance that invites reflection, that engenders opportunities for regret or repentance. His choice of third-person narration abjures the use of "I" that implicitly involves a "you", an addressee who can participate in a review of past actions, choices, conduct. David elects disgrace, in dramatic, histrionic, hysterical ways. But he eschews embarrassment – and Coetzee does not enable it – even disables it – on his behalf. The "unblinking gaze" that Attridge values in Coetzee seems to me a deliberate disinvitation. Coetzee holds up David as an avatar of himself, but in doing so he requires a suspension of ordinary rules of engagement, and the impression I get is of one regarding himself in a mirror. His challenge to his reader is to watch him without being embarrassed, without embarrassing him – to indulge the fiction, to let him live his life unto himself.

---

[11] Thomas M. Leitch, *What Stories Are: Narrative Theory and Interpretation* (University Park, PA, and London: Penn State University Press, 1986), 160, 158.

In discussing "the times" in *Disgrace*, Attridge argues that its temporal context is broader than South African society (165), and points out that, "in this new age, hitherto private details of sexual intimacy have become matter for daily public discourse, but rather than heralding a greater acceptance of sexual diversity and sexual needs, this shift marks an increase in puritanical surveillance and moralistic denunciation" (168). I do not, myself, think private details of sexual intimacy should be exempt from surveillance and denunciation when such intimacy is destructive or exploitative; nor do I see this caveat as puritanical or moralistic. A world in which individuals with power use privacy to cover over unacceptable or damaging sexual predations, an ethos that is beyond the reach of embarrassment, stands in need of the "administration" that David rebels against.

Contexts change, perhaps. For me a crucial gap in social emphasis has taken place between the readings of *Disgrace* by Derek Attridge and by David Attwell and my own reading now. One of its measures was the rape charge laid against our then ex-deputy president in November 2006, and tried in 2007. What the trial demonstrated very publicly was the pervasiveness of sexual violence throughout our society. Private and intimate the crime of rape might be, but its conceptual reach encompasses those in elevated positions as well as the lowest of the low. The accused, in this instance, was not found guilty. What the trial demonstrated disconcertingly was the hegemony of the discursive formations in which rape trials are conducted, and the genderedness of this hegemony. The intensest endeavour of the defence lawyer was to establish the possibility that the woman might have been unclear in the messages she conveyed; that the misunderstanding of the man she accused might have been justified. Hence the pressure on her to admit, "He could have thought I was not unwilling"; to warrant his interpretation, to centre it. And hence the triumph of the defence when she did so. What the trial demonstrated most disturbingly was the absence of any trace of embarrassment in these rhetorical maneouvres. In my reading of *Disgrace*, Coetzee stands in a relation to the sexuality of David that is not far removed.

Coda

One of the seminal readings that Pamela Cooper makes of the novel's treatment of sexuality involves the sanitization and the sanctifying of the rape of Lucy.

> The notion of "mating" – of ceremonial, impersonal impregnation at the behest of history – identifies rape as a pragmatic political act; it interprets sexuality, disturbingly, as both a primal biological compulson and the tool of new social patterns struggling into being. ... Lucy confirms this obscure prospect [of supra-historical forces] when she suggests that the men are rapists by vocation, that they "do" rape (158); her metaphor of a religious calling further depersonalizes the three while evoking biblical resonances (31).

Accurately read, though, the metaphor is not Lucy's – it is Cooper's. Lucy's metaphor, as we have seen, was one of "debt collection", with its grim implications of organized crime. Venturing beyond the novel into the real world, this week's statistics, in our country, at this time, are that one woman is raped every 23 seconds. Most of these women are not white, most are not the daughters of David. Their rapists are not religious and there are no biblical resonances in what they do. Rape is not a pragmatic political act; nor is it a primal biological compulsion or the tool of new social patterns. It is a social pathology. For the one in three women, children, grandmothers who will endure and perhaps survive it, it is a fact of life. For me, it is this context that makes both the disgrace and the sexual delectations of David seem like small fry; that makes Coetzee's narrative relation to David so hard to swallow.

Chapter 7

David Lurie's Learning and the Meaning of J.M. Coetzee's *Disgrace*[1]

Laurence Wright

One of the teasing characteristics of novels soused in literariness, like J.M. Coetzee's, is their tendency to leak, to bleed, into vast inchoate terrains of intertextuality. Trails of significance proliferate seemingly without end. The reader is constantly challenged to measure and assess their implications within or against the frail containing form of the story, much as Russian formalism taught us to keep *sujet* and *fable* in perpetual dialogue. However, it has become apparent that in all the dense thickets of commentary occasioned by Coetzee's most controversial novel, *Disgrace* (1999),[2] insufficient attention has been paid to the intertextual implications of David Lurie's learning, his scholarly preoccupations. In what follows, the status of the argument presented, which is concerned more with understanding than with evaluation, is debatable, perhaps even undecidable. Part intellectual background, part intertextual commentary, it comes closest to being a discussion of some of the things the character David Lurie might want us to think about, were he in a position to know that we are engaged in reading *Disgrace*.

Unless the reader attempts this kind of exploration, two of the most vexed issues freighting the novel's central fabulation: Lucy's curiously stoical, impassive response to her rape, together with her decision to stay on in South Africa; and David Lurie's sudden, seemingly inexplicable care for the doomed dogs, from their last moments at the animal shelter until he lovingly consigns their corpses to the incinerator, must remain opaque. In particular, the final words of the novel, "Yes, I am giving him up" (220), uttered in relation to the immanent "*Lösung*" of the little dog Bev Shaw calls Driepoot, will tend to taunt the reader, rather than illuminate.

Let us plunge straight into a particular train of enquiry: the matter of the intellectual history or genealogy supplied for the central focalizing figure of David Lurie. Evidence comes principally from skimpy but precise gestures towards his

---

[1] This paper was given as a plenary address at "Africa in Literature," the 15th International Conference of the English Academy of Southern Africa in association with SAWA, AUETSA, SAWAL and SAACLALS held at the University of Cape Town, 10–13 July 2005.

[2] J.M. Coetzee, *Disgrace* (London: Secker & Warburg, 1999). Subsequent citations will be by page number in the text.

various scholarly projects, past and present – a neat way of indicating an intellectual prologue and trajectory, without turning the text into a novel of ideas.

We learn that his first book was a study of Arrigo Boito's opera *Mefistofele* (1868; revised 1875). Two facts about this particular project seem relevant. First, *Mefistofele* is based on Goethe's *Faust* (both parts of the poem – Boito wrote his own libretto); and second, it is the only opera Boito ever managed to complete. His *magnum opus* was also his *solum opus*. Pronounced a failure when it opened, seven years later a revised version enjoyed considerable success. Thereafter Boito laboured unsuccessfully for 54 years to complete a second opera. Apparently deserted by his operatic muse, he nevertheless established an enviable reputation as a writer of libretti, Verdi's *Otello* being his masterpiece. It may be no coincidence that David Lurie's chamber opera remains immured in words (as far as the reader of *Disgrace* is concerned) and that much of Coetzee's own work comprises metatextual re-fictionalization of canonical texts. Lurie's study is called *Boito and the Faust Legend: The Genesis of Mefistofele* (4). As a fable, the Faust story – the ancient German story-complex in which a magician imperils his soul in his pursuit of knowledge, power and sensual satisfaction – presides over the life and career of David Lurie, as perhaps it does over scholarly and scientific pursuits in general. The question to which we must return is Why opera? Why music? Wouldn't Goethe's poem have sufficed?

His next venture is entitled *The Vision of Richard of St Victor*, in which David Lurie becomes preoccupied with one of the most important scholastic discussions of mystical transcendence. One passage from Richard (d. 1173) might still today be regarded as public property, as sufficiently well known to be recognized by non-specialist readers, and it comes from his work called *The Twelve Patriarchs* (also known as the *Benjamin Minor*):

> The full knowledge of a rational spirit is a mountain great and high. This mountain transcends the highest point of all mundane knowledges; from the height it looks down upon all philosophy, all knowledge of the world. What so excellent did Aristotle or Plato discover; what so excellent was a crowd of philosophers able to discover? … He who arrives at perfect knowledge of himself takes possession of the summit of the mountain.[3]

The visionary project of summiting the mountain of self-knowledge marks the first phase of Lurie's scholarly odyssey in the footsteps of Faust/Mefistofeles. Richard of St Victor's major work is *The Mystical Ark* or *Benjamin Major*, known to literary scholars mainly as the basis of the mystical psychology of Dante's *Paradiso*. In it Richard depicts the soul ascending through various stages of contemplation; through reason, imagination, and understanding, gradually

---

[3]　Richard of St Victor, *The Twelve Patriarchs; The Mystical Ark; Book Three of the Trinity*, ed. Grover A. Zinn, The Classics of Western Spirituality (London: SPCK, 1979), 133.

relinquishing all sensible objects of thought, until finally it contemplates that which surpasses reason, and may even be beside or contrary to reason. This is the condition of *mentis alienato*, or ecstasy, in which all memory of the present leaves the mind and simple, direct contemplation of truth is attained. In Richard of St Victor's version, this is the high mountain of ecstatic contemplation upon which Christ is transfigured, and one of the key moments in which the philosophy of Plato becomes assimilated to the teaching of the Gospels. Lurie studies it under the rubric of "eros as vision" (4).

Lurie's subsequent book, we are told, was a study called *Wordsworth and the Burden of the Past*. The title gestures to a famous short work by Walter Jackson Bate, entitled *The Burden of the Past and the English Poet* (1970). In post-apartheid South Africa, and in *Disgrace*, the past is an ethical and political burden in a particular sense, one deeply felt by David Lurie and his daughter. But it is also, and in a correlated way, a burden felt directly in the defining problem of the Romantic poet (and, perhaps, the post-apartheid white writer) as expressed by Bate, "*What is there left to do?*"[4]

Bate's book was very influential, not least in the reading – or strong mis-reading – to which it gave rise in the work of Harold Bloom, who has spent much of his scholarly life exploring the condition of Romantic belatedness, the feeling of having arrived after all the big statements have been made, yet needing desperately to be original in order to neutralize the "anxiety of influence".[5] To escape this condition, the Romantics resort to complex archaeologies of the self, and a deep preoccupation with responding adequately to the present moment, sporting an overt fictive reliance on fidelity to actual, present experience. We see something like the kernel of this project and its problems in the vignette presented of David Lurie's university class on Book 6 of *The Prelude*, where we encounter another mountain:

> "From a bare ridge," he reads aloud,
> > we also first beheld
> > Unveiled the summit of Mont Blanc, and grieved
> > To have a soulless image on the eye
> > That had usurped upon a living thought
> > That never more could be. (21)

He trails his uncomprehending students through the distinction between "usurp" and "usurp upon": "*Usurp*, to take over entirely, is the perfective of *usurp upon*; usurping completes the act of usurping upon" (21). This apparently inconsequential poetic moment presents a fleeting feeling of grief and estrangement accompanying

---

4   Walter Jackson Bate, *The Burden of the Past and the English Poet* (New York: W.W. Norton, 1970), 3.

5   See Harold Bloom, *The Anxiety of Influence: A Theory of Poetry*. (New York: Oxford University Press, 1973).

the realization that human perception is absolutely limited by the perceptual apparatus of the physical body. Such a moment marks a distinct step towards that philosophical egoism which later metamorphosed into the massive egotism seen in Romantic individualism – notably exemplified in the figure of Byron. In philosophical terms, this Mont Blanc episode gestures towards the Kantian revolution which prepared the way for Romanticism, in a sense underwriting its entire discourse.

Kant had proposed and defended radically new limits for what can and cannot be known by human beings. He confined knowledge to the sphere of actual or possible experience, to the empirical and conceptual deliverances of human sensibility and its mental and technological extensions. Whatever we know, we can know only according to our physiological and mental make-up as human beings. That there are other forms of sensibility (as in other life forms, dogs, for example) we cannot doubt. Similarly, that there is a reality beyond the reach of our own perceptual and conceptual apparatus we cannot doubt. But whatever its nature, this reality must remain permanently inaccessible.

Dismayed, though hardly surprised, by his class's failure to experience any "flash of revelation" concerning the Mont Blanc passage (21), David Lurie spells out some of its implications:

> " … Wordsworth seems to be feeling his way towards a balance: not the pure idea, wreathed in clouds [in other words, not the immediate mystical self-apprehension seen in Richard of St Victor, the beatific vision], nor the visual image burned upon the retina, overwhelming and disappointing us with its matter-of-fact clarity [i.e. not the "reality" delivered by empiricism, and exemplified in the realist novel], but the sense-image, kept as fleeting as possible, as a means towards stirring or activating the idea that lies buried more deeply in the soil of memory." (22)

The passage posits the coming together, the interaction and fleeting integration, of subject and object, noumenon and phenomena, in the act of perception – an act completed by the stimulation or reawakening of aboriginal memories of a Platonic reality through the process called *anamnesis*. What Kant ruled out as necessarily impossible, namely knowledge of that which is beyond the possibility of experience by human beings, the Romantic poets clung to with wistful determination.

The Mont Blanc passage also enacts the major philosophical equivocation of the Kantian revolution, a flaw so patent that subsequent generations have marvelled that so astute a thinker could ever have made it. The soulless image, we are told, "usurps upon" a living thought "that never more can be": in other words, there is here a vestigial awareness of two entities, not one: the percept and the "thing-in-itself". This corresponds to the contradictory Kantian assertion that our perceptions are caused by noumena of which they are the appearance, when all the while the deeper implication of the Kantian revolution should be that noumena are ultimately unknowable because permanently shrouded by the deliverances of human sensibility. We know phenomena only as mediated by our own forms of perception and intellection, and so phenomena are all we know. The second phase of Lurie's intellectual odyssey has here found its crisis.

David Lurie's current preoccupation is Byron, specifically Byron's relationship with Contessa Teresa Guiccioli, among the more equable and significant of his *embroglios* with women (a judgment sustained even in current biography[6]). The fullest account of the relationship is to be found in Iris Origo's book, *The Last Attachment* (1949), and of course in the Byron *Letters*.[7] I suspect, however, though it might be difficult to prove, that Coetzee's interest in Byron and Teresa was nurtured particularly, not by Iris Origo, but by the second volume of Peter Quennell's popular biography, *Byron in Italy* (1941), a work which did much to stimulate mid-twentieth century interest in Byron's life.[8] The book is very well written, perhaps not the least of its attractions for Coetzee, and it supplies the putative title for David Lurie's intended musical composition, "*Byron in Italy*, a meditation on love between the sexes in the form of a chamber opera" (4).

Following two years of sexual indulgence in Venice, in 1819 Byron took up with the young wife of Count Guiccioli, an affair which he decided was to be his "*last* love".[9] This is the relationship David Lurie sets himself to celebrate in his chamber opera – the *double entendre* is deliberate. Teresa was eighteen,[10] Count Guiccioli sixty and on his third marriage. The two had been married barely a year when Byron intervened to adopt – rather to his own surprise – the traditional role of the *cavaliere servente*, the lover who is tolerated by the husband provided decorum is observed. Most commentators on Byron's function in the novel simply note that Lurie's disgrace at the University and his departure for Salem parallel Byron's flight to Italy in the wake of his murky transgressions in England (15). True, but deeply inadequate. The plebian equivalent of Byron's Teresa in Lurie's life, the person, the arrangement, by which he claims to have solved what he calls "the problem of sex" (1), is the prostitute Soraya. Byron imperilled his relation with Teresa, the woman with whom he briefly came near to achieving some kind of equilibrium, when, on a visit to Bologna from Ravenna, the two decamped to Byron's house in Venice on their own, thereby impugning the honour of her husband.[11] David Lurie similarly destroys his convenient arrangement with Soraya when he attempts to invade her social world, having spied her out walking with her children and then seeing them eating together at Captain Dorego's in St George's Street (6). He even employs a private detective to track her down (9). In both

---

6   See Fiona MacCarthy, *Byron: Life and Legend* (London: John Murray, 2002), 355.

7   Iris Origo, *The Last Attachment* (London: Jonathan Cape & John Murray, 1949); *Byron's Letters and Journals*, ed. Leslie A. Marchand, Vol. 9 (1821–1822). (London: John Murray, 1979).

8   Peter Quennell, *Byron in Italy* (London: Collins Publishers, 1941).

9   See Quennell, *Byron in Italy*, 157.

10   Ibid., 186.

11   See, for example, Quennell, *Byron in Italy*, 160–61.

cases, a primarily sexual relationship, subterranean, unofficially tolerated but morally dubious, is forced into the open social world through impetuosity and scorn for public convention.

The implicit comparison between Byron, that grand European figure of scandal and taboo, and the insipid persona of David Lurie is both deliberately ludicrous and completely cogent. A suggestive passage from Quennell's *Byron in Italy* throws light on the juxtaposition:

> if moral standards are to be invoked (which, when we are dealing with Byron, proves very often an awkward and ineffectual business), as much disgrace attaches to escapades entered without love, affection and, in many instances, without real desire, as to a passion that engrosses the faculties of mind and soul. (168)

The relevance here may be purely adventitious, but its import is not. Lurie's sexual encounters in the novel are many and varied, but none rises above the banal. Byron's, in contrast, were often markedly zestful, even it could be said, euphoric. The choice of adjective is deliberate. In Goethe's *Faust* (Part Two), Byron surfaces unexpectedly in the figure of Euphorion, the allegorized offspring of Faust and Helen of Troy, their relationship supposedly symbolizing a hoped-for *rapprochement* between the Romantic and Classical ideals. (Think if you will of a fusion between the native visionary energies of Richard of St Victor – a synthesis of classical and mystical traditions – and Wordsworth's struggle to both escape and celebrate the confinements of the ego – the Romantic problematic.) The figure of Helen, supposed "cause" of the siege of Troy, whose beauty "launched a thousand ships", exemplifies a long tradition in which defence of female sexuality stands for the protective powers of civilization. As walled enclaves subject to siege, assault and occupation, the city's conquest or defeat is regularly troped in Western literature, both Classical and Romantic, as sexual possession – as the raping and pillaging that follows martial triumph. The rape of women signals the collapse of civility. In Salem (the very name unavoidably conjures stray associations with the 1692 witch trials in Massachusetts and notions of preserving a delusory peace), there actually is no need to breach defensive physical walls. Lucy willingly cooperates with Petrus, not sexually, but in terms of his ownership plans. Later, even after the gang rape, his symbolic irrigation pipes enter the African soil with her consent and support (139). Rape is always gratuitous from an ethical point of view, but here especially so. Lucy understands its aim to be "subjugation" (159). It is no accident that Lurie wants to put into Byron's mouth Aeneas's desolate words before Dido's fresco at Carthage depicting the destruction of Troy (162): *Sunt lacrimae rerum, et mentem mortalia tangunt* ("tears are shed for things even here and our mortal ways touch the soul".

In Goethe's poem Faust wins Helen, not through Romantic persuasion or Classical negotiation, but through powers of magical, supernatural intervention. She is one reward in his pact with Mefistofeles, part of Faust's egocentric fantasy.

And the offspring of this fantasy-brought-to life is the boy Euphorion, Goethe's critique of Byron.[12]

Like his real-life counterpart, even perhaps like David Lurie, Euphorion proves a very troublesome lad, and his unmanageable-ness centres on his errant sexuality, his freedom from restraint, as we see in this climactic episode from Part 2, Act 3:

> *Euphorion* (bearing a young girl).
>> Here I drag the little courser,
>> And to joy of mine will force her:
>> Now with rapture and with zest
>> Press I her unwilling breast,
>> Kiss her rebel mouth, that so
>> She my will and strength may know.[13]

This unconscionable rape destroys the idyllic relationship between Faust and Helen (any potential *rapprochement* between Classical and Romantic aspirations) and Euphorion dies like Icarus, attempting impossible flight, striving to transcend gendered sexuality through rampant indulgence.

The *basso profundo* of *Disgrace* is that, thanks to powerful biological drives expressed as sexuality (and whatever lies behind those drives), we all live subject to a state of potential disgrace, a disgrace servants of *eros* – those who yield to impulse, like Byron and David Lurie – evade mainly by chance:

---

[12]   Goethe's preoccupation with Byron, notably evident in the *Conversations of Goethe with Eckermann*, echoes David Lurie's own to a marked degree, as here:

> Goethe continued to talk of Lord Byron. "With that disposition," said he, "which always leads him into the illimitable, the restraint he imposed upon himself by the observance of the three unities becomes him. If he had but known how to endure moral restraint also! That he could not was his ruin; it may be said he was destroyed by his own unbridled temperament.
>
> "But he was too much in the dark about himself, and neither knew nor thought what he was doing. Permitting everything to himself, and excusing nothing in others, he necessarily put himself in a bad position, and made the world his foe … This reckless conduct drove him from England, and would in time have driven him from Europe also. Everywhere it was too narrow for him, with the most perfect personal freedom he felt confined; the world seemed a prison. His Grecian expedition was the result of no voluntary resolution; his misunderstanding with the world drove him to it."

(*Conversations of Goethe with Eckermann* (1836–48), trans. John Oxenford, ed. J.K. Moorhead (New York: J.M. Dent & Sons Ltd, 1930), 88)

[13]   Goethe, *Faust: Part Two*, trans. Philip Wayne (Harmondsworth: Penguin Books, 1959), 205.

He stood a stranger in this breathing world,
An erring spirit from another hurled;
A thing of dark imaginings, that shaped
By choice the perils he by chance escaped. (32)

This is Lurie teaching Byron's *Lara*, with Melanie and her boyfriend in front of him in the class, just as the scandal is about to break over the Cape Technical University. (Melanie is a Gretchen figure, in terms of Goethe's poem.) The sense of fundamental alienation, of originating somewhere else, of a source beyond "this breathing world" is very strong. Byron never escaped his Calvinist upbringing, and the concepts of unattainable grace, original sin and fallen angels form a constant backdrop to his poetry. But Byron's conception of the human situation goes beyond conventional Christian notions of the battle between spirit and flesh, beyond even Sidney's "erect wit" and "infected will",[14] as we see in the next excerpt from "Lara" that Coetzee has David Lurie ventriloquize for us:

He could
At times resign his own for others' good,
But not in pity, not because he ought,
But in some strange perversity of thought,
That swayed him onward with a secret pride
To do what few or none would do beside;
And this same impulse would in tempting time
Mislead his spirit equally to crime. (33)

Here we reach the crux of the Byronic hero's plight, be it Lara, Childe Harold, Manfred or even Don Juan (31): "dark imaginings" shape his conduct, and the impulse that unaccountably informs his acts of virtue is the same impulse that can and does "Mislead his spirit equally to crime". As Lurie puts it, "He doesn't act on principle but on impulse, and the source of his impulses is dark to him" (33).

We have travelled a long way from Richard of St Victor. "Vision as eros" (4) has become eros as vision. During his disciplinary hearing at the University, Lurie explains his actions to the committee as follows:

"I was not myself. I was no longer a fifty-year-old divorcé at a loose end. I became a servant of Eros."
"Is this a defence you are offering us? Ungovernable impulse?"

---

[14]   Philip Sidney, *An Apology for Poetry*, in D.J. Enright and Errnst de Chickera, eds, In *English Critical texts: 16th Century to 20th Century* (London: Oxford University Press, 1962), 3–49, at 9.

"It is not a defence. You want a confession, I give you a confession. As for the impulse, it was far from ungovernable. I have denied similar impulses many times in the past, I am ashamed to say." (52)

This, the first of two occasions where Lurie describes himself as "a servant of *eros*",[15] reflects much more than mere Wildean *savoir faire*.[16] The expression is not simply a fey euphemism for mundane sexual urges. *Eros* is more fundamental and inclusive even than modern tropologies centred on the notion of "desire" might suggest. For instance, we should recall that in Thucydides a powerful *eros* sends the Athenians on their fateful expedition to Sicily, a venture which eventually precipitates the collapse of Athens in the Peloponnesian war (404 BCE) and the end of classical Greek civilization. Eros in ancient Greek poetry is an overwhelmingly powerful but temporary impulse, what renaissance psychologists would later term an "Affection",[17] one that takes away an individual's better judgment and sense of independence. This surging, disruptive invasion of external energy, hints at a disgrace deeper than social or legal disgrace; a generic disgrace that troubles Lurie, Byron and I suspect, at some level, J.M. Coetzee; and it has to do with the power of an external force ("eros") to suborn the human will, indeed to become that will – and with society's inability to accommodate or even acknowledge this predicament. At various times, he is led to desperate ponderings on the possibility of self-castration (as in the historical instance of Origen – see 9), or concern for the plight of the next-door dog at his marital home in Kenilworth, beaten savagely by its owners for copulatory urges for which it is hardly responsible (90). He wants in some way to speak up for "the rights of desire" (89).

Such is the naive yet disturbing substance behind Lurie's admission to the disciplinary hearing. Immediately prior to the second passage from *Lara* that Lurie reads out from Byron's poem, we find Lara attempting some self-analysis:

> In wild reflection o'er his stormy life;   330
> But haughty still, and loth himself to blame,
> He called on nature's self to share the shame,
> And charged all fault upon the fleshly form
> She gave to clog the soul, and feast the worm;

---

[15] The second is at *Disgrace*, 89.

[16] Later Lurie reminds Lucy of the Blakean adage from *The Marriage of Heaven and Hell*: "Sooner murder an infant in its cradle than nurse unacted desires" (69).

[17] A telling vernacular definition of the Latin *Affectio*, as used by Cicero, appears in Thomas Cooper's 1578 *Thesaurus Linguae Romanae et Britannicae* (Hildesheim and New York: G. Olms, 1975):

> Affectio, Verbale. Cic.
> Affection: a disposition or mutation happening to bouie or minde: trouble of minde. Impetus, commotion, affectioque animi.

'Till he at last confounded good and ill,   335
And half mistook for fate the acts of will;

To confound intentional acts with the promptings of fate, to feel impelled to act
on impulses whose origins are dark to one, to feel that the same inscrutable force
external to one's being impels acts that are good and acts that are bad, or even
acts that are both good and bad (depending on how one looks at them): this is the
predicament shared by Byron and David Lurie and it marks the third stage of his
intellectual odyssey, the crisis with which the narrative of *Disgrace* opens and to
which his earlier intellectual explorations had been merely the prologue.

Elizabeth Lowry has correctly described the novel as an "anti-pastoral",[18]
meaning, I think, that the elaborately constructed parallels between town and
country, Cape Town and Salem, the university world of intellect and the rural,
ländliche one of practice, the artful/artless rape of Melanie versus the artless/artful
rape of Lucy – in fact the entire meaning-generating potential of the pastoral
complex – is here rendered inert, neutral. The traditional coinage is deployed,
but its symbolic value has been scuppered by flattening all tension, and most
hermeneutical differentiation between the two locales. Town and country suffer
under the same uniform ontological dispensation.[19]

Confronted with his social disgrace, with his inability to protect his daughter,
with his declining sexual attractiveness – and as a scholar of Goethe's *Faust* –
David Lurie ought, typically, to apply the routine romantic remedy which, in all
its belatedness and ambiguity, comes in the form of the doctrine of *entsagen*, or
renunciation, a teaching most closely associated with Goethe. This he deliberately
refuses to do (the final "blow-job" from the prostitute on the slopes of Signal Hill
underlines the point – see 194).

Entsagen might be described as the curbing of eros in both its intellectual
and sensual dimensions. Such a response, according to Max Weber's *Protestant
Ethic and the Spirit of Capitalism* (1904–5),[20] underlay much of the social energy
manifested in nineteenth-century industrial-capitalist development. It was also
Carlyle's answer to the Kantian revolution, borrowed from Novalis and Goethe
and elaborated in his extraordinary prose fantasia *Sartor Resartus* (1833): "Close

---

[18]   Elizabeth Lowry, "Like a Dog", Review of J.M. Coetzee's *Disgrace* and *The Lives
of Animals*, *London Review of Books* 21.20 (1999): 12–14, at 12.

[19]   Perhaps it might be more accurate to term the novel "anti [i.e. 'against"] pastoral"
rather than an anti-pastoral in the sense of its reversing the pastoral conventions. Despite the
odd reference to process (e.g., "Inexorably, he thinks, the country is coming to the city" –
175), *Disgrace* is more obviously dedicated to dismantling the pastoral than to subverting
it. The city is no refuge from the country.

[20]   Max Weber, *The Protestant Ethic and the Spirit of Capitalism*, trans. Talcott Parsons
(London: Allen & Unwin, 1976).

thy Byron; open thy Goethe".[21] This celebrated pronouncement of Carlyle's, though never quoted in the novel, hovers over *Disgrace* much as it did over mid-Victorian Britain, expressing what Lionel Trilling called "the manifest ruling intention of the age".[22] In South African terms, and for David Lurie in particular, *entsagen* might be seen as all too reminiscent of Calvinist puritanism, a rejection of *voluptas* closely related to the po-faced apartheid dissembling which disguised moral corruption of the most insidious kind.

Entsagen involves deliberate renunciation, self-abnegation, an acknowledgment and acceptance of limitation. In Goethe's version it issues in the attainment of Olympian detachment; in those of Novalis and Carlyle, the relinquishment of excessive self-consciousness. At one level, the doctrine is indeed a response to the post-Kantian predicament: the mind is forced to abandon the possibility of intellectual certainty, of unbounded knowledge, and becomes aware of its limitations and subject to increasing self-consciousness. This is a curbing of Faustian *eros* in its intellectual dimension. But at a deeper level, there is always a sexual accompaniment.

For the German Romantics and Carlyle, the *entsagen* teaching typically follows a failed romance, in literature as in life. In the case of Goethe, the doctrine was a belated response to a tepid physical relationship with his intellectual friend and companion Charlotte von Stein, during the busy Weimar years in government, between 1775 and 1786. On a visit to Italy, away from her, he underwent a sharp sensual awakening, followed by a troubling recognition of the heartless egoism of the sensualist, and returned to poor Charlotte espousing the doctrine of renunciation – a teaching important in all his later writings including, not least, his account of the Faust legend. Novalis invented his version of *entsagen* after the loss of his youthful love Sophie; Carlyle's Diogenes Teufelsdröckh in *Sartor Resartus* discovers the "Everlasting Yea" following the failure of his affair with Blumine.

But David Lurie's renunciation (if, indeed, it can be described as such) is precipitated not by failure of a particular relationship, as with his nineteenth-century Romantic precursors – Lurie in fact seems markedly unmoved by women as people – but by memories of the sensual specificity of his lovers (of Melanie at this particular moment) together with an intense awareness of his own declining sexual attractiveness. It is Eros, the god, the bodily power, that he serves, not specific women or even women in general; and Eros, the god, is abandoning him. In the final chapter, Rilke's famous injunction, *"Du must dein Leben ändern!"* ("you must change your life"), holds no appeal for him, is no longer relevant: "Well, he is too old to heed, too old to change. Lucy may be able to bend to the tempest, he cannot, not with honour" (209). Renunciation, in some form or other,

---

[21]   Thomas Carlyle, Thomas. 1871. *Sartor Resartus* [1833], in *The Collected Works of Thomas Carlyle*. (London: Chapman and Hall, 1871), book 2, chapter 9.

[22]   Lionel Trilling, *Sincerity and Authenticity* (Cambridge, MA: Harvard University Press, and London: Oxford University Press (1972), 56.

is indeed the only response, a response forced on him rather than welcomed. Like Faust, Lurie cannot repent.[23]

We are now in a position to explore the significance of the two key issues, Lurie's obsessive compassion and care for the expiring dogs; and why Lucy responds with such passivity, such resignation, such inertness, to her rape and her future on the South African smallholding.

We have noted the disabling ambivalence in Kant's treatment of the noumenal: his presumption that discrete noumena are the causes of our perceptions, when on his own assumptions this is precisely something we can never know. There is a further implication here. If our apprehension of a thoroughly differentiated world is indeed *caused by* things-in-themselves, then the noumenal must itself consist of multiple "things-in-themselves". This is again problematic on Kant's own grounds: multiplicity can be experienced only in relation to conceptions of space and time, and these Kant had shown to be subject-bound forms of sensibility and reflection. It follows ineluctably that differentiation itself is confined to the world of experience; there can be no knowledge of "things-in-themselves" independently of experience, as Kant had oddly assumed. The unknowable reality beyond all possibility of experience must be undifferentiated.

This powerful and mysterious move beyond Kant was taken by Schopenhauer,[24] and my contention in this essay is that the form of *entsagen* achieved consciously, if reluctantly, by David Lurie in *Disgrace*, and which is practised unconsciously by his daughter, Lucy, moves beyond the famous teaching espoused by the German literary Romantics. What Lurie discovers – and it *is* a discovery, not an intellectual insight – is the doctrine of *entsagen* as understood by Schopenhauer.[25]

Schopenhauer's *Weltanschauung*, achieved in the classical idiom of Western philosophy, postulates an undifferentiated, immaterial, timeless, space-less, cognitively inaccessible noumenon which presents itself to our variant perceptual constitutions as this differentiated phenomenal world of material objects and events (including each of us) in space and time. The vision is to an extent congruent with that

[23]   Eudo C. Mason, *Goethe's Faust: Its Genesis and Import* (Berkeley and Los Angeles: University of California Press, 1967), 319: "It is one of the laws of Faust's titanic nature that he should be incapable of repentance in the ordinary sense of the word."

[24]   See especially the Appendix on the "Criticism of Kantian Philosophy" in Arthur Schopenhauer, *The World as Will and Representation*, trans. E.F.J. Payne. 2 vols (New York: Dover Publications, 1965 and1969), 1:413–534. Coetzee's preoccupation with Schopenhauer is enacted in *Disgrace* rather than cited; but both *The Lives of Animals* (Princeton: Princeton University Press, 1999) and *Elizabeth Costello: Eight Lessons* (London: Secker & Warburg, 2003) are shot though with Schopenhauerian thought and feeling, as in Elizabeth Costello's discussion of Hughes's poems on the jaguar in the latter work: "In these poems we know the jaguar not from the way he seems but from the way he moves" (95). The publication dates of the two books, one before *Disgrace*, the other after, suggest that Coetzee's thought was running in these trammels while work on the novel was in progress.

[25]   See Schopenhauer, *The World as Will and Representation*, 1:378–98.

found in Vedic and Buddhist literature, something which impressed Schopenhauer enormously when he uncovered the parallels.[26] According to Schopenhauer – and here comes the major implication for *Disgrace* – the undifferentiatedness of the noumenal is crucial to understanding the basis of morality.

In the phenomenal world we exist as separate embodied individuals, as gendered humans and animals – not to mention mollusks, plants, rock formations and so forth; but noumenally, in the ultimate ground of our being, it is impossible that we should be differentiated. In relation to this ultimate origin, *we are one*; differentiation cannot apply. It follows that if we hurt another being, in this special sense we hurt ourselves. This, for Schopenhauer, is the ultimate explanation of compassion, altruism, disinterested concern for others – of those ethical behaviors which would make no sense were we actually the utterly separate beings our senses proclaim us to be. (One might question the epistemology here and still find the description telling in terms of moral awareness.)

Schopenhauer maintains firmly that this basis of moral insight, which gives rise to the possibility of ethical behaviour, "just because it is not abstract [in other words, because it does not belong to the world as representation], cannot be communicated, but must dawn on each of us. It therefore finds its real and adequate expression not in words, but simply and solely in deeds, in conduct, in the course of a man's [or woman's] life."[27] Lucy seems to have this sense of things as a given. David Lurie's experience at the animal shelter, in tandem with his attempts to come to terms with Lucy's rape, suggests (though it cannot communicate) the ripening of a comparable moral awareness. He discovers first hand what no course in "communication" such as the one he is forced to teach at the Cape Technical University could ever convey; no discourse grounded in phenomenal knowledge, no interaction in which a subject grasps or is grasped by an object, no self trying to come to terms with an "other" can ever apprehend. Such a realization should modify at a deep level the adequacy of interpretative approaches that read the novel simply as a reaction to the Enlightenment project, or to the cult of sentimentalism, as a puzzling treatise in post-coloniality, as an

---

[26]   For an intimation of this strain of thought in Schopenhauer's earliest work, see his *On The Fourfold Root of the Principle of Sufficient Reason* (1813), trans. E.J.F Payne (La Salle, IL: Open Court, 1974), 185–9.

[27]   Schopenhauer, *The World as Will and Representation*, 1:370. I have kept to E.J.F. Payne's rendering of the title of Schopenhauer's principal work, but the following comment by Konstantin Kolenda is worth noting: "The original German title *Die Welt als Wille und Vorstellung* was rendered by the translator as *The World as Will and Representation*, in preference to Haldane and Kemp's *The World as Will and Idea*. As Professor D.W. Hamlyn pointed out, the use of 'representation' in place of 'idea' is less misleading but not altogether felicitous; he suggested that perhaps a more neutral term, such as 'presentation', would come closer to what Schopenhauer meant by *Vorstellung*" (Preface, in *On the Freedom of the Will* by Arthur Schopenhauer, ed. Konstantin Kolenda (Oxford: Basil Blackwell, 1985), v–vi. at v).

exercise in empirical realism, as a questioning of the possibility of ethical action – or any of several other responses derived from what, elsewhere, Coetzee wryly calls "the games handbook".[28] Lurie's unbearably moving apology to the Isaacs family, mother and younger daughter, after the awkward meal in George, portrays his brave effort to supply from their own cultural repertoire a symbolic gesture he hopes will convey a meaning they need from him: "With careful ceremony he gets to his knees and touches his forehead to the floor" (173). The symbol has been offered; the meaning cannot be conveyed with any surety. But the gesture neither transcends nor negates the predicament of gendered sexuality: a few lines further we read, as he looks into the eyes of mother and daughter: "again the current leaps, the current of desire" (173).

This retreat into silent symbolism may seem a simple cop-out. It is not. Though we cannot know the noumenon as such, we know its manifestations, some beautiful, some terrible. The noumenon throws up earthquakes, hurricanes, tsunamis, fires, bestial ferocity. It engenders organic forms which persist for a while, and then retire to their noumenal source, returning and relapsing into energy like the dogs' corpses in the hospital incinerator. The noumenon is undifferentiated elemental energy, existing beyond the phenomenal world, quite outside the reach of the senses or their conceptual extensions and therefore permanently unknowable. Through our senses we are aware of each other as discrete phenomenal beings and therefore as objects of knowledge. But – and this is crucial – we also experience ourselves from the inside, immediately. This latter experience is not one of *knowledge* (that belongs to the world of representation and the senses) but of pure physiological will. All emotions and feelings are modifications of the will, of the body experienced from inside. As Lurie puts it, "What does he *know* of the force that drives the utmost strangers into each other's arms, making them kin, kind, beyond all prudence?" (194, emphasis added).

It is through this unknowable experience of our own inner existence as embodied will that we are able to empathize with other human beings; with other animals, other life forms, and other material formations. His daughter tells Lurie, "This is the only life there is. Which we share with animals" (74). The stolid Lucy's Wordsworthian namesake may be "A perfect Woman, nobly planned" (*Poems of the Imagination*, VIII), but the poet must also come to contemplate her "Rolled

---

[28]   J. M. Coetzee, "The Novel Today", *Upstream* 6.1 (1988): 2–5, at 3–4. A small selection of relevant work would be Jane Taylor, "The Impossibility of Ethical Action", Review of J.M. Coetzee's *Disgrace*, *Mail & Guardian* (23–9 July 1999), 25; Mike Marais, "The Possibility of Ethical Action", *Scrutiny2* 5.1 (2000): 57–63; Lucy Graham, "'Yes, I am giving him up': Reading Rape in Recent South African Literature", *Scrutiny 2* 7.1(2002): 4–15; David Attwell, "Coetzee and Post-apartheid South Africa.", Review of J.M. Coetzee's *Disgrace*, *Journal of Southern African Studies* 27.4 (2001): 865–6, and "Race in *Disgrace*", *Interventions* 4.3 (2002): 331–41; and Gareth Cornwell, "Realism, Rape, and J.M. Coetzee's *Disgrace*", *Critique: Studies in Contemporary Fiction* 43.4 (2002): 307–22.

round in earth's diurnal course / With rocks and stones and trees" (*Ibid.*, X).[29] Lucy does not stay on at Salem "for an idea" (105). Her crucifixion-like cry, "But why did they hate me so?" (156), is her one concession to the world as representation. We cannot *know* the world as will, but we can experience its effects in ourselves. From that basis we can learn, if not compassion, at least a disconcerting empathy, even for rapists and other violators. The body's response to the god *Eros* is both willed (permitted by us) and not willed (fated, ensured by our biological makeup); and in ethical terms, *eros* is one of the noumenon's most powerfully contradictory manifestations.

However, despite its aboriginal obscurity, according to Schopenhauer there *is* a medium through which we can have powerful if indirect access to the noumenon, where the world as will becomes intelligible – and that is music. In his hierarchy of the arts, music is supreme; not only supreme, but of a different order. Unlike the other art forms, music bypasses the realm of representation (except in moments of weak mimesis, of which Schopenhauer disapproves) and speaks directly to and through our inner being. Through music, in this case his imaginatively evolving opera, Lurie's attachment to the world as representation eventually thins to the symbolic measure of a fishing line:

> He is in the opera neither as Teresa nor as Byron nor even as some blending of the two: he is held in the music itself, in the flat, tinny slap of the banjo strings, the voice that strains to soar away from the ludicrous instrument but is continually reined back, like a fish on a line.
>
> So this is art, he thinks, and this is how it does its work! How strange! How fascinating! (184–5)

By yielding up all investment in the world as representation; sacrificing any sense of himself as a physical being in the world, and therefore all possibility of relatedness (including, in Lurie's case, his sympathetic relationship with the little dog, Driepoot, his last attachment), Lurie achieves an accommodation with the world as will. The German word *Lösung* means something like "solution" or "resolution". Musically, in the course of the novel what had been conceived as a chamber opera (retaining elements of dramatic representation, the present tense) thins to a duet, a musical dialogue, between Teresa in her fifties and the shade of the dead Byron, and finally to a one-sided, all-absorbing "inner duet" in which Lurie hears only the music of Teresa. The pattern, both musical and epistemological, culminates in the perfective – "an action carried through to its conclusion" (71) – after the final period. It may not be the blissful vision anticipated by Richard of St Victor ("vision" here would be quite the wrong word). But it has its completeness,

---

[29]   William Wordsworth, *The Poetical Works of Wordsworth*, ed. Thomas Hutchinson, rev. edn by Ernest de Selincourt (London: Oxford University Press, 1961), *Poems of the Imagination*, VIII, X.

perhaps as a form of *dis*-grace.[30] Just as Faust is finally absorbed by the "eternal feminine" (*das Ewig-Weibliche*) – the guise in which Lurie finally sees his daughter (see 218) – so David Lurie finds respite from the torment of gendered sexuality in relinquishing his physical being, upon which he can at least "hear", if not "know", the music of some kind of fullness.

We should not mistake the scope of Coetzee's thought in this book. There are two traditions in Western mythology concerning the rise of cities and civilizations. The visionary artists and heroes, such as Orpheus and Amphion, give rise to cities by means of music and eloquence.[31] David Lurie is a latter-day Orpheus, striving to hymn civilization into being, his modest chamber opera sadly reduced to the plonking of his daughter's banjo in the dog-yard at the animal shelter. "His own opinion", he tells us at the beginning of the novel, "… is that the origins of speech lie in song, and the origins of song in the need to fill out with sound the overlarge and rather empty human soul" (2). The more powerful counter-tradition, the tradition of Romulus and Cain, is that cities are founded or taken through cunning, treachery, siege and, yes, rape. Twins are fundamental to these foundation myths, a hint that the generative energy of the noumenon is ambivalent, if not downright amoral, in its manifestations. Cain, the tiller of soil and builder of the first city, slew his brother Abel, the pastoralist; Romulus killed Remus and went on to found Rome and rape the Sabine women (as a youngster pondering the meaning of the word "rape", Lurie saw a reproduction of Poussin's painting of this episode in a library book – see 160). In *Disgrace* we have a young rapist with the curious name of Pollux, wittingly or not taking part in Petrus's ambiguous scheme to assume his rightful place in the new South African scheme of things. Castor and Pollux, the so-called "heavenly twins", symbolize in Chinese astrology the twin energies of Yin Yang. There should be a place in *Disgrace* for Castor, the more spiritually- or intellectually-minded of the "heavenly twins". With terrible irony, the implication is that David Lurie, the artist-rapist, fits the bill.

---

[30]   I am grateful to Professor Ron Hall of Rhodes University for this insight.

[31]   The tradition of Orpheus and Amphion is well summarized by Vico in his oration 'On the Proper Order of Studies'(1707):

For no other reason, the very wise poets created their poetic fables of Orpheus with his lyre taming the wild animals and Amphion with his song able to move the stones, which arranged themselves of their own accord by his music, thus erecting the walls of Thebes. For their feats, the lyre of the one and the dolphin of the other have been hurled into the heavens and are seen among the stars. Those rocks, those oaken planks, those wild animals are the fools among men. Orpheus and Amphion are the wise who have brought together by means of their eloquence the knowledge of things divine and human and have led isolated man into union, that is, from love of self to the fostering of human community, from sluggishness to purposeful activity, from unrestrained license to compliance with law, and by conferring equal rights united those unbridled in their strength with the weak. (Giambattista Vico, *On Humanistic Education*, trans. Giorgio A. Pinton and Arthur W. Shippee (Ithaca and London: Cornell University Press, 1993), 130–31.

Chapter 8

J.M. Coetzee and South Africa: Thoughts on the Social Life of Fiction[1]

David Attwell

I

With *Disgrace* recently prescribed in the matriculation syllabus of the IEB (Independent Examinations Board) for 2002–2003, I found myself visiting a dozen or so schools in Johannesburg and KwaZulu-Natal to discuss the novel with pupils and teachers.[2] The decision to prescribe *Disgrace* was, of course, controversial; I was not wholly convinced it was a good idea, but was curious to gauge the response first hand. In many ways, I found the discussions lively and mature, suggesting that it was indeed possible for Grade 12 learners to debate issues like rape, sexual harassment, sexual diversity, and racialized crime in a responsible way.

Not that I doubted they could, although many parents would have felt happier if such matters were not on the classroom agenda at all. What troubled me more than what would be included, was what would probably be *left out* of a high school discussion of *Disgrace*: the novel's self-consciousness, its intertextuality; its reliance on the Romantic poets; its ironies around European cultural authority; its worldly tolerance of the excesses of Eros; its layered sense of history, including one in which current students are positioned as uncritical consumers of globalized culture; its dwelling on death, in the course of developing its particular ethical consciousness – everything, in other words, that gives the novel its intelligence once the obviously controversial material has been stripped away. On these grounds, I remain unpersuaded about the wisdom of the decision to prescribe *Disgrace*. If we are to prescribe Coetzee in the schools, the text to start with should be, I suggest, the first Booker Prize winner, *Life and Times of Michael K*,[3] in which the central conflicts and themes are both more clearly drawn and more obviously affirming.

---

[1]   This essay was written as a public lecture for the English Academy of South Africa, delivered in Johannesburg on 25 March 2004. It was conceived in part as a response to the ambivalent public debate that followed the award of the Nobel Prize to Coetzee in December, 2003 and proceeds from the view that Coetzee criticism has not, on the whole, sought to address a South African public. Extended extracts were published in the newspaper *The Sowetan* on 26 March, 2004.
[2]   J.M. Coetzee, *Disgrace* (London, Secker & Warburg, 1999).
[3]   J.M. Coetzee, *Life and Times of Michael K* (Johannesburg: Ravan Press, 1983).

A certain conversation after a lecture at a distinguished Diocesan school for girls confirmed my misgivings. I was approached by a pupil whose blazer bore insignia of achievement and responsibility at every level: academic colours, Junior City Council, captain of several teams, membership of cultural societies, prefect. She told me that she had warmed to the novel, and had even begun, as she put it, to see Coetzee's point of view, but she was still disappointed in one respect: *Disgrace* did not have a strong message *for the youth*.

I confess to having been tongue-tied. She was right; it *does not* have a strong message for the youth, and I regretted not being able to reassure her in her own terms. What foiled me was how to start a conversation, without seeming arrogant or dismissive, about whether the novel *ought* to have such a message; whether we should impose such demands on writers, specially writers of a late-modernist bent (imagine asking this question of Joyce or Beckett); whether, indeed, novels have messages at all, a possibility Coetzee himself has rejected with considerable laconic force: "a [novel] is not a message with a covering ... not a message plus a residue, the residue, the art with which the message is coated ... There is no addition in [novels] ... On the keyboard on which they are written, the plus key does not work" ("The Novel Today" 4).[4]

Later, it occurred to me that the public context implied by this encounter is not unlike the readership for West African fiction in a roughly equivalent phase of its history. In 1965, with Nigeria in the flush of independence (before the civil war), Chinua Achebe famously declared that a legitimate role for the novelist would be that of teacher. He illustrates the argument by citing the following letter from a young reader:

> Dear C. Achebe,
> I do not usually write to authors, no matter how interesting their work is, but I feel I must tell you how much I enjoyed your editions of *Things Fall Apart* and *No Longer at Ease*. I look forward to reading your new edition *Arrow of God*. Your novels serve as advice to us young. I trust that you will continue to produce as many of this type of books. With friendly greetings and best wishes.
> Yours sincerely, [etc.][5]

Achebe's response to this expectation, and more generally to the demands of his historical moment, was to use realist techniques to construct a comprehensive, quasi-anthropological image of Igbo society in the late nineteenth century as a way of recovering and valuing a past which had been denigrated in the colonial education system and in the novel of Empire (especially in Joseph Conrad and Joyce Cary, who featured in Achebe's early reading). "What we need to do," says Achebe in the same essay, "is to look back and try and find out where we went wrong, where the rain began to beat us."

---

[4]   J.M. Coetzee, "The Novel Today", *Upstream* 6.1 (1988): 2–5, at 4.

[5]   Chinua Achebe, *Morning Yet on Creation Day* (London: Heinemann, 1975), 42.

In its general terms, the kind of project Achebe offered his young countrymen could serve for young South Africans today. Indeed, learners in Grade 12 generally found it reassuring to have it pointed out that the episode in *Disgrace* involving Lucy's rape by black intruders was matched, structurally and morally, by David Lurie's abuse of the dark-skinned Melanie. The fact that Lurie's sexual carelessness is implicated in a history of colonial violence makes his and Lucy's suffering seem part of a wider historical pattern involving a return of the repressed. To this extent, Coetzee's novel is also about "where the rain began to beat us"; however, whilst Achebe was prepared to take on the responsibility of instructing the young, it is fairly obvious that Coetzee's emphasis has been elsewhere.

Perhaps young people have a right to expect instruction from serious fiction; perhaps that is what it means to study literature at school. However, it so happens that the general terms of this pupil's question are very widely distributed across South Africa, and are shared by pupils and adult readers alike. The controversies surrounding the publication of *Disgrace* reveal this: there was embarrassment that Coetzee had represented the universities badly by treating their current corporatization as implying a loss of intellectual power. There was dismay in one particular intellectual circle, led by Dan Roodt, about what was called "the Lucy syndrome", which would be an acceptance by whites that their current role would be one of atonement and self-sacrifice. At the other end of the political spectrum, there were reviewers like Aggrey Klaaste and Jakes Gerwel who were embarrassed about the portrayal of sexual violence and its implications for the representation of South Africa's post-apartheid democracy. There was, of course, the ANC's response in its submission to the Human Rights Commission's hearings into racism in the media – to which I will turn in a moment. Finally, there was a discussion in Cabinet, which also turned on how the country was being represented, after which Coetzee was informally given the dubious, though I am sure still welcome, reassurance that he was "not without his defenders". It would seem that, at a historical juncture in which the citizenry desperately wanted respect, above anything else, Coetzee gave them its opposite – he gave them the concept of disgrace. If Salman Rushdie shows how the dynamics of *honour* and *shame* operate in contemporary Pakistan, Coetzee focuses attention on *respect* and *disgrace* as a similar fault line in South Africa's post-apartheid culture.

At least, one might say, fiction is being taken seriously – we can be sure that the Bush Cabinet was silent on new fiction by Don de Lillo or Philip Roth. The problem, however, is that in South Africa *Disgrace* was taken seriously in all the wrong ways, ways that reveal the figure of the censor still standing in the shadows. The ANC's position is a case in point. Contrary to popular belief – and despite attempts by the official opposition, the Democratic Alliance, to embarrass the ANC following the award of the Nobel Prize – the ANC did not *directly* accuse Coetzee or the novel of racism. If the accusation is implied, it is not a controlled, deliberate implication; in fact, the ANC's submission to the HRC is rather poorly drafted and unfocussed in crucial respects. What is clear enough is that the ANC wished to use the celebrity of the novel (it had already won the Booker Prize) and of its author to provide a kind of expert witness to the prevalence and persistence of racism in South African society. Coetzee reveals what is there to behold, it says repeatedly, while refraining from saying that Coetzee *himself* holds the opinions being discussed; indeed, it is possible that the ANC may have been careful to avoid an accusation of philistinism. However, there is no indication of any awareness in its submission that the text they are quoting is a work of literature; no attempt in the ANC document to understand how fiction works. *Disgrace* is treated as piece of documentary, as providing access to a social truth without any acknowledgement that the truth it reveals is instantiated, contextualized, and frequently ironized, within forms of discourse which are being held up for scrutiny.

I could understand the objection that the ANC is, after all, a political movement and cannot be expected to pronounce reliably on literary matters. Indeed, if political parties in general were encouraged to express themselves about literature, the situation would be far worse than it is now, when they offer occasional opinions and get it wrong. However, the point I am making is that the ANC's political instrumentalism is representative of a situation which is endemic in South Africa, one that even now continues to dominate such public discussion of literature as we have.

A related, though not identical, example would be that of Colin Bower, whose ill-judged critique of Coetzee was published in *scrutiny2* with an extract appearing in advance in *The Sunday Times* – unluckily for all concerned, a week before the announcement of the Nobel. Bower's argument shifts from one insecure criterion to another, from what he perceives to be the tiredness of Coetzee's prose, to his supposed portentousness, to moral judgements about his accounts of sexuality, to the apparent lack of development in Coetzee's characters, and so on – all with dubious management of textual detail – but the strongest of Bower's objections are about Coetzee's apparent lack of connection to South African reality.

The first significant example Bower gives is from *Age of Iron*, where Bower objects to an episode in which the protagonist Elizabeth Curren's mouth is probed for gold fillings by street urchins as she sleeps under a bridge, as part of her Dantesque descent into the mode of life of her other-worldly and destitute companion, Vercueil. Ignoring the metaphoric power of the scene, Bower confesses to having tested its authenticity by speaking to a gold trader, pawnbrokers, a policeman, and a dentist, to find out whether they had ever heard of this practice in real life (7).[6] It is embarrassing that such naivety found its way into one of our academic journals: are we now going to teach our students that it is legitimate critical methodology to check the plausibility of fictional narration in the local dentist's rooms and the police station?

Apart from excellent articles by Maureen Isaacson, Lisa Combrink, Andre Brink and Shaun de Waal, in general the local media coverage of the Nobel Prize was also unfortunate, so much so that it was itself the subject of a media report in

[6]   Colin Bower, "J.M. Coetzee: Literary Con Artist and Poseur", *scrutiny2* 8.2 (2003): 3–23, at 7.

Sweden, which pointed out, amongst other things, that there was more coverage of Michael Jackson's arrest and Arnold Schwarzenegger's election in California. The emphasis fell constantly on Coetzee *the man* – his apparent reclusiveness, his suspicions of journalists, his decision to move to Adelaide, his supposed encounter with the ANC, and so on – at the expense of a serious attempt to come to terms with his work or even with the fact that the Swedish Academy had given it sustained attention and had reached what by all accounts was an easy consensus. My suggestion, once again, is that this substitution of the work for the man reveals a general inability or unwillingness in South African public life to deal with serious literature.

Why is it, then, that in South Africa the space between reportage and fiction is so frequently and dramatically closed down? Why does Coetzee himself feel compelled to say that "life inside a book is different from real life; not better, just different"? There may be several answers to this question. One answer might be philosophical, and suggest that the tradition of post-Kantian idealism, from which we inherit the notion that aesthetic practices are of a different order from utilitarian ones, is only thinly settled in the culture. But more brutal explanations are also plausible: the intellectual life itself is under-valued, and literary-intellectual life in particular is derided and trivialized. Some of this has a political history: "No More Lullabies", booms the title of a volume of poetry which began life in the revolutionary late 1970s, even though the poets of that period were more deeply invested in the aesthetics of the lyric poem than they cared to acknowledge.[7]

This is not a conflict between European or Euro-American or first-world perceptions of art, on one hand, and African or non-metropolitan or third-world perceptions, on the other. There is nothing inherently local, South African or third-world about the impulse to judge literature by its content, that is, by the extent to which it is faithful to some normative view of what social reality is or ought to be. As Susan Sontag points out in her essay "Against Interpretation," this impulse is as old as the theory of art itself in Western culture, having been formalized by Plato and refined by Aristotle. At the root of it lies the theory of mimesis as the basis of the distinction between form and content, which makes the content of art interpretable or transposable from its original figurative context to something else, where more prosaic value judgements prevail.[8] Indeed, when Achebe venerates the writer in the role of teacher, he is speaking in the Platonic tradition; or, to be

---

[7] Mafika Gwala, *No More Lullabies* (Johannesburg: Ravan Press, 1982). I have discussed the political environment of lyric poetry in the 1970s more fully in *Rewriting Modernity: Studies in Black South African Literary History* (Pietermaritzburg: University of KwaZulu-Natal Press, 2005; and Athens, OH: Ohio University Press, 2006).

[8] Susan Sontag, *Against Interpretation* (New York: Farrar, Straus, Giroux, 1966), 3–7. Sontag had recently visited Johannesburg, where she gave the inaugural Nadine Gordimer Lecture (entitled "At the Same Time") at the University of the Witwatersrand. It was her last public appearance.

more accurate, he is appropriating that tradition to serve the interests of a young and idealistic generation.

One would not wish to polarize Achebe and Coetzee; in fact, from their earliest work, they share a principled diagnosis of colonialism and its aftermath. Surely, though, there are many ways of constructing the relationship between literature and society, and, as I suggested earlier, there are roles for writers other than those of teacher, even at this stage of our democracy. In fact, one of the advantages of having a Coetzee in South Africa's national literature is to keep the culture open to experimentalism, complexity, difference, strangeness. In a prescient 1974 review in *Contrast* of Coetzee's first novel, *Dusklands*, Jonathan Crewe, a South African now known internationally as a scholar of Renaissance literature, said that with this novel Coetzee had brought the modernist novel to South Africa. This is not entirely true: that feat was accomplished by William Plomer in the 1920s with *Turbott Wolfe*, a novel with which Coetzee's writing has some affinities, especially in *In the Heart of the Country*. But the drift of Crewe's comments is correct because Coetzee has kept open a current between ourselves and a late twentieth-century self-consciousness about the language of fiction, one that has nourished the work of other writers, from Ivan Vladislavic to Zakes Mda, from Andre Brink to Zoe Wicomb. Moreover, we may have forgotten, after the discussion around *Disgrace*, that the experimentalism of *Dusklands* had the effect of shattering the numbed consciousness associated with apartheid's hegemony.

One of the persistent comments about Coetzee is his supposed silence on the issues around which the controversy turns, but if we attend to the writing we discover something different. Consider the following passage, which is taken from the final "lesson" in *Elizabeth Costello*, where the protagonist finds herself having to answer for her beliefs at the gate of heaven, before boards of examiners who resemble St Peter less than the bureaucratic officials of Kafka's *The Trial*. When Costello puts it to them that as a writer it is inappropriate for her to have beliefs, since her calling is to be a "secretary of the invisible" and thus to be open to any kind of prompting, she meets with scepticism and derision. Since this exchange is, in part, a meditation on the kinds of demands South Africa makes on its writers, it is worth citing at some length:

> "What about children?"
>   The voice is cracked and wheezy. At first she cannot make out from which of them it comes. Is it Number Eight, the one with the pudgy jowls and the high colour?
> "Children? I don't understand."
>   "And what of the Tasmanians?" He continues. "What of the fate of the Tasmanians?"
>   The Tasmanians? Has something been going in Tasmania, in the interim, that she has not heard about?
>   "I have no special opinions about Tasmanians," she replies cautiously. "I have always found them perfectly decent people."

He waves impatiently. "I mean the old Tasmanians, the ones who were exterminated. Do you have any special opinions about them?"

"Do you mean, have their voices come to me? No, they have not, not yet. I probably do not qualify, in their eyes. They would probably want to use a secretary of their own, as they are surely entitled to do." ...

"I said nothing about voices", says the man. "I asked you about your thoughts."

Her thoughts on Tasmania? If she is puzzled, the rest of the panel is puzzled too, for her questioner has to turn to them to explain. "Atrocities take place," he says. "violations of innocent children. The extermination of whole peoples. What does she think about such matters? Does she have no beliefs to guide her?"

The extermination of the old Tasmanians by her countrymen, her ancestors. Is that, finally, what lies behind this hearing, this trial: the question of historical guilt?

She takes a breath. "There are matters about which one talks and matters about which it is appropriate to keep one's peace, even before a tribunal, if that is what you are. I know what you are referring to, and I reply only that if from what I have said before you today you conclude that I am oblivious of such matters, you are mistaken, utterly mistaken. Let me add, for your edification: beliefs are not the only ethical supports we have. We can rely on our hearts as well. ...

"The aboriginal people of Tasmania are today counted among the invisible, the invisible whose secretary I am, one of many such. Every morning I seat myself at my desk and ready myself for the summons of the day. That is a secretary's way of life, and mine. When the old Tasmanians summon me, if they choose to summon me, I will be ready and I will write, to the best of my ability.

Similarly with children, since you mention violated children. I have yet to be summoned by a child, but again I am ready.

"A word of caution to you, however. I am open to all voices, not just the voices of the murdered and violated." She tries to keep her own voice even at this point, tries to hit no note that might be called forensic. "If it is their murderers and violators who choose to summon me instead, to use me and speak through me, I will not close my ears to them, I will not judge them."

"You will speak for murderers?"

"I will."

"You do not judge between the murderer and the victim? Is that what it is to be a secretary: to write down whatever you are told? To be bankrupt of conscience?"

She is cornered, she knows. But what does it matter, being cornered, if it brings what feels more and more like a contest of rhetoric closer to its end! "Do you think the guilty do not suffer too?" she says. "Do you think they do not call out from their flames? *Do not forget me!* – that is what they cry. What kind of conscience is it that will disregard a cry of such moral agony?"[9]

Characteristically, Coetzee's response to controversy and its underlying relations of power is to absorb it, as he does here, into his fiction, to enact the contestations and social conditions of possibility that history has bequeathed to him. This is what it means to write metafictional or self-reflexive fiction under conditions of historical extremity, and it is this combination of elements – a late-modernist and postmodern self-consciousness, which articulates the prevailing rules and conditions of meaning and therefore of its own practice – together with a fine-tuned understanding of the brutalities of life under colonialism and apartheid, that have made Coetzee the writer he is. Or rather, his sustained *response* to these conditions, his ability to play them out in compelling stories, has made him the kind of writer who has earned the respect of readers everywhere. If we are to try to open a space for a more receptive public debate around Coetzee, then we must try to consider the meaning and the value to us of this form of literary self-consciousness.

II

Another demonstration of Coetzee's metafiction was his Nobel Lecture which, following the practice established in the readings collected in *Elizabeth Costello*, took the form of a story. He introduced it by speaking about his childhood experience of reading *Robinson Crusoe*, then discovering only later in a children's encyclopaedia the existence of its author, Daniel Defoe. Where did Defoe come in, when Crusoe so clearly spoke in his own voice about things that really happened? The story, "He and His Man", takes off from this misunderstanding and develops an allegory of authorship in which the functions of the historical self and the writing self are split: Crusoe is cast as the historical self and Defoe – as Crusoe's "man" – is the self-who-writes. The same splitting of selves is apparent in the autobiographies, *Boyhood* and *Youth*, which are narrated in the third person, where "John" would be the historical self, and the narrator would be close to the self of writing, "his man". A puzzling element of the story's presentation is its epigraph, which is extracted from a passage in *Robinson Crusoe*, referring to Friday:

> But to return to my companion. I was greatly delighted with him, and made it
> my business to teach him everything that was proper to make him useful, handy,

⁹   J.M. Coetzee, *Elizabeth Costello: Eight Lessons* (London: Secker & Warburg, 2003), 202–4.

and helpful; but especially to make him speak, and understand me when I spoke; and he was the aptest scholar there ever was.[10]

In Defoe's novel, obviously, Friday is "his [Crusoe's] man," whereas in Coetzee's text, "his man" is Defoe himself. Since we read Coetzee through Defoe, however, we cannot fail to connect the Defoe figure, the writing self, with Friday, suggesting that around "his man'" there is a shadow of strangeness or alterity, perhaps the footprint on the beach which signals a common humanity but one that cannot be fully known. Why does Coetzee cast the writing self, then, in this light – or perhaps half-light? The reason is surely that he wishes us to understand something about the process of writing, that it is a process in which one enters into a space of otherness; or, to put it in terms Coetzee uses elsewhere,

> Writing, then, involves an interplay between the push into the future that takes you to the blank page in the first place, and a resistance. Part of that resistance is psychic, but part is also an automatism built into language: the tendency of words to call up other words, to fall into patterns that keep propagating themselves. Out of that interplay there emerges, if you are lucky, what you recognize or hope to recognize as the true.[11]

In Coetzee's text, then, Defoe and Friday merge as a reminder of the way the self-of-writing embodies counter-voices which enable the desired language, and possibly a form of truth, to appear. Why is this pact with alterity or strangeness so essential, why is it presented as a fundamental condition of literary language? Simply put, it is necessary because it is what drives the process of discovery: figuration and therefore transformation depend on the historical self's being willing to surrender to the sometimes counter-intuitive promptings of the writing self. There is little doubt in the story that the writing self, or "his man", is a particular manifestation of the historical self, meaning Crusoe, which is why "in the evening by candlelight he [Crusoe] will take out his papers and sharpen his quills and write a page or two of his man".[12] And yet, this self that is part of Crusoe and yet other to him, "his man", has powers that Crusoe lacks. Reflecting on a passage by "his man" in which he uses an image from the Apocalypse in a description of the plague, Crusoe muses:

> For he wields an able pen, this man of his, no doubt of that. *Like charging Death himself on his pale horse.* His own skill, learned in the counting house, was in making tallies and accounts, not in turning phrases. *Death himself on his pale*

---

[10]   J.M. Coetzee, *"He and His Man": The Nobel Lecture in Literature, 2003* (London and New York: Penguin, 2004), 1.

[11]   J.M. Coetzee, *Doubling the Point: Essays and Interviews*, ed. David Attwell (Cambridge, MA: Harvard University Press, 1992), 18.

[12]   Coetzee, *"He and His Man"*, 3.

horse: those are words he would not think of. Only when he yields himself up to this man do such words come.

The powerful turn of phrase emerges from the process of giving the counter-voices free rein. He and "his man" are indeed complementary parts of a composite selfhood and authorship, but the success of their partnership depends on preserving the distance and tension between them.

The closest they come to one another is when the reports that "his man" sends in are seen as ways of figuring Crusoe's experience. A number of these reports are drawn from other texts by Defoe, *A Journal of the Plague Year* (1722) and *A Tour thro' the Whole Island of Great Britain* (1724–26), which are assimilated into Crusoe's account of himself. In this way, the account of how people can continue their business without realizing that they are carrying the plague, becomes a figure for spiritual readiness. Reports of the practice of using decoy ducks in the Lincolnshire fens to lure birds from Holland and Germany, the guillotine in Halifax and the stories that surround it, become figures for Crusoe on his island discovering the craggy and inhospitable reaches of its coastline. The bleakness of the far coast, contrasted with the possibility of colonists taming it at some future time, stands for the contrast between "the dark side of the soul and the light". And so on: the gathering of empirical detail, in the realism of the reports sent in by "his man", come to serve as representations of the precarious and sometimes turbulent flow of feeling in Crusoe himself. In this way, Coetzee rewrites the founding moments of realism in Defoe as figuring the instantiation of the subject; the construction of the world by a troubled consciousness is foregrounded, at the expense of the details, or the data, which merely serve it. Although the reports of the writing self stand as figures for the subjective life of the historical self, and although they are intimately connected, the two can never meet or merge; a homecoming and reconciliation is impossible. In the language of the allegory, reconciliation would mean giving in to a homelier discourse, or perhaps giving up on the idea of figuration, and returning to a language without colour or contours. He and "his man", therefore, are fated to remain

> deckhands toiling in the rigging, the one on a ship sailing west, the other on a ship sailing east. Their ships pass close, close enough to hail. But the seas are rough, the weather is stormy: their eyes lashed by the spray, their hands burned by the cordage, they pass each other by, too busy even to wave.

To summarize: Crusoe – the historical self – needs the self-of-writing, the reports of "his man", because they are vehicles of transformation, and ultimately, of meaningfulness. It is in this sense that, as Coetzee puts it, "writing writes us".[13]

---

[13]   *Doubling the Point*, 18.

III

Defoe presented Crusoe as a real historical subject surrounded by a life-world made plausible by means of the accretion of detail. In doing so, as everyone knows, he helped to consolidate the English novel in a form which remained largely intact until the modernist turn of the late nineteenth century. As Defoe's heir, but also as the heir of modernism, Coetzee knows that the game is up, and that it is impossible to continue with Defoe's sleight of hand. He reverses the paradigm, therefore, presenting his own autobiography as fiction (*autre*-biography) and offering an allegorical story in which Crusoe is now the historical self, being written into meaningful subjectivity by an author somewhere in the wings. The key shift here is towards self-conscious modes of narration, and the performance of this self-consciousness. How do we, then, as ordinary readers, come to terms with this move?

At the risk of being unconscionably reductive, let me try to suggest some of the possibilities: instead of focusing on the social reality which is represented in the novels (in the manner, say, of George Eliot, or Dickens, or Balzac, or Tolstoy, although each of them, in some respects, are allegorists and fabulists too), Coetzee's fictions invite us to share the experience and point of view of a particular subject or consciousness: Eugene Dawn, Michael K, Susan Barton, Elizabeth Curren and David Lurie, among others. Moreover, this subject is anchored in a particular historical and discursive formation: the rationalism and the violence of eighteenth-century Dutch colonialism in the Northern Cape; American imperialism in Vietnam; master–servant relations on the Karoo farm; a magistrate administering the compromised justice of Empire; the seeming irrelevance of Classical culture in the South African State of Emergency; David Lurie facing the triumphant return of the repressed in post-apartheid South Africa. At the heart of these narratives is language, therefore: first of all, the voice of the central character – sometimes this is presented in the first person, sometimes in free indirect discourse – then, the contending forms of language and ideology circulating in the culture, within and against which the subject must define himself/herself. Frequently, this subject is the product of those discourses, but equally, as his or her agency comes into focus, there is a struggle and a yearning for a space outside of them – this is the struggle conducted by Michael K.

There are various conditions that challenge the autonomy and agency of this subject: I will mention two. One is the limitations of the culture which is the subject's inheritance, so that there is often a rivalling discourse which is present but not wholly understood: Eugene Dawn and the Vietcong, the magistrate bathing the feet of the barbarian girl, David Lurie and Petrus. Often, these failures of reciprocity bring longings for a common humanity – this is strongly the case in *In the Heart of the Country*. Sometimes, beyond the ethnographic differences, there is the more radical otherness of sheer blankness or silence, through which the subject realizes his or her vulnerability and mortality. This brings us to the second limitation on the subject's freedom: frequently, it is the inescapable reality of the body which is the ultimate connection between the self and history. In fact, bodies in Coetzee's writing frequently assert their own reality, and this physicality leads, in turn, to new ethical discoveries and relationships, based on the notion of a precarious but shared biological energy – David Lurie ministering to abandoned dogs, Elizabeth Costello reflecting on the lives of animals.

This mode of fiction has been present from the first sentence of the first novel: "My name is Eugene Dawn. I cannot help that. Here goes." The voice in history. Here is another memorable example:

> One thought alone preoccupies the submerged mind of Empire: how not to end, how not to die, how to prolong its era. By day it pursues its enemies. It is cunning and ruthless, it sends it bloodhounds everywhere. By night it feeds on images of disaster: the sack of cities, the rape of populations, pyramids of bones, acres of desolation. A mad vision yet a virulent one: I, wading in the ooze, am no less infected with it than the faithful Colonel Joll as he tracks the enemies of Empire through the boundless desert, sword unsheathed to cut down barbarian after barbarian until at last he finds and slays the one whose destiny it should be (or if not he then his son's or unborn grandson's) to climb the bronze gateway to the Summer Palace and topple the globe surmounted by the tiger rampant that symbolizes eternal dominion, while his comrades below cheer and fire their muskets in the air.
>
> There is no moon. In darkness I grope my way back to dry land and on a bed of grass, wrapped in my cloak, fall asleep. I wake up still and cold from a flurry of confused dreams. The red star has barely moved in the sky.[14]

How did Coetzee come to this particular gate as his entry into fiction – the power of the voice, or the mode of address? The fact that he delayed his writing until he could not delay any further, is relevant: there was rather circuitous preparation which took him through several branches of linguistic studies – stylistics, linguistic philosophy, structuralism, psychoanalysis, deconstruction – and through the history of the novel, part of which involved writing a PhD dissertation on Samuel Beckett, which examined Beckett's last English texts in an attempt to understand from the style why Beckett turned to French. What Coetzee was doing in these years, he has remarked, apart from avoiding the moment of reckoning, was searching for a position, or a way in. He found it in *Dusklands* in an act of explosive experimentalism which was part-autobiographical (the two novellas fictionalize his own historical positions, in South Africa and the United States) and part anti-colonial critique, of necessity a critique from within.

The experimentalism extends to a self-consciousness about his place in relation to the history and development of the novel, and to a refusal of ordinary realism, or what he calls "illusionism", which has the effect of reminding the reader of language's constitutive powers. This linguistic self-consciousness in Coetzee is

---

[14]   J.M. Coetzee, *Waiting for the Barbarians* (Johannesburg: Ravan Press, 1981), 133–4.

not simply a distraction from the narrative itself or a faddish self-absorption on the part of the author. As Robert Pippin suggests in an essay on the philosophy of abstract art, "subjectivity or reflection", a "critical and rational self-consciousness about the way we actively render the world intelligible" has become indispensable as a basic element of modernity. Pippin continues:

> Normative claims to knowledge, rectitude, spiritual life, or even claims *to be making art*, or that *that was good*, are now made with the self-consciousness that the authority of such claims can always be challenged and defeated (or such claims could simply die out, lose their historical authority) and must be in some way defensible to and for subjects if they are to be defensible at all.[15]

To foreground the constitutive powers of language and to stage the contestation Pippin is describing – as Coetzee does as in the example from *Elizabeth Costello* – is to be responsive to the inherent self-consciousness of modern life and to the claims of multiple voices in modern democracy. Similarly, one might argue that Coetzee's refusal to assume the role of superior interpreter of his own work is to support a democratic conception of how fiction and its meanings circulate within the culture. Commentators are fond of remarking on a certain aloofness in Coetzee's public presence, but he is, in fact, the most self-revealing of writers in his work, the difference being that the self-revelation is always combined with self-directed irony and an immensely accomplished control over the narrative and the nuances of language.

Since I began by wrestling with the question of finding appropriate homilies for the young, here are a few alternative ones: look for the subject, or the subjectivity in the work, locate that subject within the discourses of the culture being represented, and from that tension, try to understand the subject's ironies, longings, failures, triumphs of insight, linguistic implosions, and recoveries. There is seldom what we could call a positive philosophy that emerges from this struggle, but there is always an expansion of language, a breaking of rules, a rethinking of dominant categories, and a creativity which is constantly in search of a place not previously known or understood, potentially a place of transformation.

In moving to Adelaide, Australia, J.M. Coetzee has joined a long line of South African writers who have found their imaginative spaces elsewhere: Peter Abrahams, Lewis Nkosi, Dennis Brutus, Breyten Breytenbach, Dan Jacobson, Zakes Mda, and many others. We should remember that after Sharpeville he attempted emigration, first in London; then Austin, Texas; then Buffalo, New York. He came back not by choice, but by force of circumstance: an arrest in an anti-war demonstration meant the end of his efforts to gain permanent residence in the United States. The return set up conditions in which his fiction would frequently be about a subject longing for freedom from a historical nightmare, pushing at

---

[15]   Robert Pippin, "What Was Abstract Art? (From the Point of View of Hegel)", *Critical Inquiry* (Fall 2002): 1–24, at 17–18.

the boundaries of language, ethics and self-consciousness, moved by the idea of community but unable wholly to discover it, self-conscious about its authority and legitimacy, and, as a result of all this, investing in the power of verbal art to reinvent the possibility of a meaningful life. South Africa has been the grit in the oyster. The Australian provenance of *Elizabeth Costello*, *Slow Man* and *Diary of a Bad Year* will be distinctive and striking but it is unlikely to produce as rich a harvest.

Chapter 9

"The true words at last from the mind in ruins": J.M. Coetzee and Realism

Jonathan Lamb

In the short story "What is Realism", subsequently incorporated into *Elizabeth Costello* as "Lesson 1: Realism", we are quoted Robinson Crusoe's list of all that remained of his lost companions on the shore of his island: "three of their hats, one cap, and two shoes that were not fellows". "No large words," the narrator adds, "no despair, just hats and caps and shoes."[1] These naked particulars are offered as exemplary of a realist technique pioneered by Defoe which, in this short story, is defined as the realism of embodiment, "the idea that ideas have no autonomous existence, can exist only in things" (*EC* 9). In his essay on Defoe, J.M. Coetzee quotes the same passage from *Robinson Crusoe* and further characterizes this technique as a method of "bald empirical description" that is applied by Defoe with equal success to the extremes of experience, the mundane and the emergent. He calls it, "pure writerly attentiveness, pure submission to the exigencies of a world which, through being submitted to in a state so close to spiritual absorption, becomes transfigured, real".[2] When he goes on to say that Defoe is one of the purest writers in English, he distinguishes his achievement from what Catherine Gallagher has lately called "realist *fiction*", where a concept of the real is plausibly presented as the work of imagination; this is "*realist* fiction", where the facts of a journal or memoir are apparently unmediated evidence, authentic and not imagined.[3] Coetzee admires therefore the bravado of *Serious Reflections*, where the author rebuts his critics, beginning, "I Robinson Crusoe, do affirm that the story, though allegorical, is also historical" – an affirmation to which he sets his name: "Robinson Crusoe" (*SS* 17–18). Defoe's realism is the empiricism of Bacon, then, who asks that the mind be kept within the enclosure of particularity; of Locke, who admits no single idea into consciousness that has not come through the inlets of the senses; and of

---

[1] J.M Coetzee, *Elizabeth Costello: Eight Lessons* (London: Penguin, 2003), 4. Hereafter *EC* in text.

[2] J.M. Coetzee, *Stranger Shores: Essays 1986–1999* (London: Penguin, 2001), 19. Hereafter *SS* in text.

[3] Catherine Gallagher, "The Rise of Fictionality" in Franco Moretti, ed., *The Novel* (Princeton: Princeton University Press, 2006), 336–63, at 345.

the experimental scientists of the Royal Society, who established a rigorous parity between things, ideas and words as the criterion of the mathematical plainness of the prose of their proceedings. But Defoe has put this empiricism in the service of the imagination and of fiction; he made it all up, as Charles Gildon long ago pointed out. He has used realism to tell of things whose relation to history is illusory or at best allegorical. His work raises these difficulties: what is the status of an idea *about* the necessity of embodied or materialized ideas; how can that be materialized? And what possibly can be real about the ideas existing in things which themselves have only a fancied existence?

Throughout Coetzee's fiction there is evident his preoccupation with the problem of truth and how it might be elicited and stated. Often it leads him to scenes that literalize Bacon's metaphor of the torture chamber, in which reticent Nature is subjected to the vexations of art so that she may be induced to speak more freely. Michael K, with his wounded mouth and his very few words, is threatened with torture to see if that will fetch more information out of it. In *Foe* Friday's muteness allegedly has been inflicted by venal white men, whose violence it still attracts. Mandel subjects the narrator of *Waiting for the Barbarians* first to a mock hanging then to the strappado, suspending him with his arms tied behind his back so that his body's weight dislocates his shoulders. While he is bawling with agony his tormentors make jokes about the sounds that spill from him – "That is barbarian language you hear".[4] It seems important both for Coetzee's humanity and the austerity of his own prose that such scenes remain free of metaphor. In a discussion of the description of torture he makes the point that lyric metaphors sidestep the physical fact of pain by claiming a weird beauty for it. Citing the highly figurative descriptions of torture and prison in the work of writers such as Mongane Serote and Alex La Guma, Coetzee goes on to observe that they are not alone in being unhappy in their flights of fancy: "Presenting the world of the interrogator with a false portentousness, a questionable dark lyricism, is not a fault limited to South African novelists: the same criticism might be leveled against the torture scenes of Gillo Pontecorvo's film *The Battle of Algiers*" – where, if you remember, an Algerian prisoner is tortured by legionnaires to the accompaniment of baroque music.[5] Elizabeth Costello calls obscene the executions of the Wehrmacht generals in Paul West's *The Very Rich Hours of the Count von Stauffenberg*, where they are represented at length as a gross harlequinade (*EC* 158–9).

Coetzee wishes to assert the importance of bare facts in respect of the irrefragable authority of the sensate body, an authority that strides above all other earthly powers. He makes this claim on behalf of the body by closely attending to the circumstances of its pain. Such a body is therefore a stranger to figurative language, such as simile, metaphor, personification and especially irony. "Whatever else, the body is not 'that which is not' and the proof that it is is the pain it feels

---

[4] J.M. Coetzee, *Waiting for the Barbarians* (London: Penguin, 1980), 121.

[5] J.M. Coetzee, *Doubling the Point: J.M. Coetzee, Essays and Interviews*, ed. David Attwell (Cambridge, MA: Harvard University Press 1992), 366. Hereafter *DP* in the text.

… In South Africa it is not possible to deny the authority of suffering therefore of the body … The suffering body takes this authority: that is its power … [and] its power is undeniable" (*DP* 248). The authority of the suffering body, along with the authority of the eyewitness and the authority of literature itself may however be usurped by another force that makes its appearance as a personification. Coetzee admits as much when he quotes this description of a drunken man beating a donkey from Nadine Gordimer's novel *Burger's Daughter*. "'The infliction of pain [had] broken away from the will that creates it; broken loose, a force existing of itself, ravishment without the ravisher, torture without the torturer, rampage, pure cruelty gone beyond the control of the humans who have spent thousands of years devising it.'" (*DP* 367). Suddenly history (or is it History?) is invaded by forces beyond human control, and they are manifest as figures in an apocalyptic allegory: Rape, Torture, Rampage, Cruelty, cousins of Death, Plague, War and Famine. In this essay I want to judge whether any compatibility is possible between realism that refuses figurative language and the force of figuration which under certain circumstances overwhelms the univocal language of things.

In three essays all dealing with aspects of transparency in the prose of seventeenth- and eighteenth-century writers, published in the collection *Doubling the Point*, Coetzee tests the standard of empirical purity against a Whorfian hypothesis. He wonders whether the world of particulars disclosed by Defoe's kind of realism isn't determined by the structure of the English language, specifically the relationship between nouns and verbs (*DP* 183). He poses this question specifically in relation to Newton's attempts to handle the effects of gravity without first supplying himself with a conjecture that would account for them, Gravity itself as it were. Newton sought a method of bald empirical description that would yield only the facts he knew, not the suppositions (however buoyant) to which they might lead. Not wishing to meddle with hypothesis, then, it was for him "a question of finding the right words, and specifically of finding matter-of-fact nonmetaphoric words [capable of stating] in 'real' terms relations between elements of the physical universe … [a] translation from mathematics to 'real' language – language with 'real' powers of reference to the universe" (188). He was aiming at the universal language invented by scientists such as John Wilkins, and the "real Character" in which it could be written. But as soon as Newton moved from mathematical equations to English prose he found himself ambushed by metaphors which animated things and personified forces. Thus he found that a centrifuge "communicates" motion to the water it contains. Water responds by trying as hard as it can to "recede from the axis of its motion" (*DP* 188). Even when he resorted to passive constructions designed to elide the place of agency such as "the moon is continually drawn off from a rectilinear motion", Newton found agency implied, and sometimes he had to concede that matter seemed to move itself: "Particles are moved by certain active principles such as that of gravity" (*DP* 189). "Real" language turned out for him to be an unhappy compromise between a short passive, where the effects of gravitational force are seen as occult personifications of things such as machines and water, and the long passive, where the cause is identified (as gravity or attraction) but not accounted for. Thus the language and its referent are ironically distinguished by Coetzee in inverted commas as "real". He wonders if there is any way around this problem, perhaps by means of nominalization, a sort of super-passive in which description supplants causation: "Corrosion of unpainted surfaces takes place", for example. This is a statement in which the secret ministry of rust as Rust is neither performed nor implied (*DP* 192). He considers also a kind of idealism, the accidental product of the persistent failure to express the real in a simple ratio of things to words. The decay of metaphors such as Newtonian "attraction", for instance, produces a detritus of literalized figures from which springs (somewhat obliquely) an intuition of language as thought, a detour that takes us back to the non-referential purity of mathematical symbols (*DP* 193–4). "We are asserting that there exists a pure concept of attraction toward which the mind gropes via the sideways process of metaphoric thinking, and which it attains as the impurities of secondary meanings are shed and language becomes transparent" (*DP* 193)

These difficulties give an extra twist to Coetzee's estimate of Defoe's success, where the world is rendered *real* by means of language that *transfigures* it. Is this still bald empiricism, or does it suggest a degree of engagement with metaphors and figures, out of which transparent meanings emerge when secondary ones fall away? The best place to find an answer is in the story that advertises the issue. "Lesson 1: Realism" in *Elizabeth Costello* exhibits none of the writerly absorption in the delivery of detail that distinguishes Defoe's prose. The narrator explicitly raises the topic of realism at the outset, but not as one of his own ambitions. He mentions Defoe's contribution – the hats, cap and shoes – while giving an unabsorbed description of Elizabeth Costello's shoes, hair and skin. This takes place in a narrative whose schematic outlines are emphasized by frequent signals of transition and elision: "We skip ... We skip to the evening ... We skip the foyer scene", and so on. That "we" might be under no obligation to suspend our disbelief, the narrator adds, "The skips are not part of the text, they are part of the performance." Skipping, we are told, "plays havoc with the realist illusion", but that doesn't seem to matter, since what seems to be being performed is at most realist *fiction* such as Henry Fielding's, not *realist* fiction such as Defoe's (*EC* 16). And in the following astonishing example of the long passive, the narrator yields his or her place to the personification of Realism itself, the occult cause of its own effects: "Realism has never been comfortable with ideas ... So when it needs to debate ideas ... realism is driven to invent situations ... in which characters give voice to contending ideas and thereby in a certain sense embody them" (*EC* 9).

Elizabeth Costello is not treated by her public as Realism's creature, nor is it how she treats herself as a writer. She is an author who commands as transparent a language as she can. The author of *The House on Eccles Street* is praised for taking Molly Bloom out of the figurative prison or hive of number 7, and turning her loose on the streets of Dublin where things are more haphazardly and less metaphorically arranged. Costello is nostalgic for the days (presumably Defoe's) when things on streets or beaches and words on the page would stand up and be counted, "each proclaiming 'I mean what I mean'". "We used to believe that when the text said, 'On the table stood a glass of water,' there was indeed a table, and a glass of water on it" (*EC* 19). So when she begins her discussion of realism by reminding her audience of Kafka's story, "Report to an Academy", she is eager not to be suspected of a joke, or of what (in a later model of this story, "The Lives of Animals") she calls irony. She owns there to a literal cast of mind (*EC* 70), so she explicitly repudiates any suspicion that she might be using language figuratively, saying what she means by not saying it. "That was not how my remark ... was intended. I did not intend it ironically. It means what it says. I say what I mean ... I do not have the time any longer to say things I do not mean" (*EC* 62).

Whether she intends it or not, Costello employs a reversible proposition that recalls the Mad Hatter's tea-party in *Alice in Wonderland*. When the March Hare tells her she ought to say what she means, Alice replies, "I do, at least – at least I mean what I say – that's the same thing, you know."[6] Saying what one means, if what one means is a distinct idea derived from a sense impression, is Locke's version of bald empiricism and the "real" non-metaphorical language Newton desired. The word serves the idea. Meaning what you say, on the other hand, puts words first and they or the persons using them decide what they are saying. Meaning waits upon the word. Humpty Dumpty is the tyrannical exemplar of this option. He uses words such as "glory" and "impenetrability" and then suborns or coerces them to mean whatever he chooses.[7] He interprets nonsense very confidently on the same principle: "brillig" means four o'clock in the afternoon. Meaning what you say endows language with a limitless metaphorical potential, because any word can stand for any other, unconstrained by loyalty to definitions or to the reality of things on which they depend. If we go back to Costello's remarks in "The Lives of Animals" she seems to make a distinction along the same lines. She says twice that she says what she means, but she adds that her *remark* ("I feel like Red Peter") means what it says. The possibility that the remark means something different from Costello herself troubles the meaning of the word "like", which spins between the alternatives of "resemble" and "identical with." The first person pronoun is likewise disturbed, referring equally to Costello, Red Peter and the remark. Two years before Costello confesses, "I felt a little like Red Peter myself ... today that feeling is even stronger" (*EC* 62). Just how much stronger is left to the remark to say; and what the remark means by what it says is that "like" is not a trope but a literal case, an example of what Costello calls elsewhere limitless sympathy, the ability to know fully and exactly what it is like to be Red Peter, or any other creature. Regardless of the fact that this claim for resemblance or identity is driven by the association of a fictional non-human character with a "real" human author, Costello tries to rid it of irony, although it is to one of the great works of irony (*Gulliver's Travels*) that she owes the coalition of literalism

---

[6]   Lewis Carroll, *Alice's Adventures in Wonderland and Through the Looking Glass*, ed. Roger Lancelyn Green (Oxford: Oxford University Press, 1971), 61.

[7]   Ibid., 190–91.

and figure – of saying the thing which is by means of saying the thing which is not – as well as the fiction of a human bearing an animal identity.

In "Realism" Costello complains of "Report to an Academy", "We don't know and will never know, with certainty, what is really going on in this story: whether it is about a man speaking to men or an ape speaking to apes or an ape speaking to men or a man speaking to apes… or even just a parrot speaking to parrots" (*EC* 19). This freewheeling permutation of possible relations is owing to the failure of modern words to stand up and be counted; "like" thrives where *like* fails, spawning all sorts of incipient allegories. In "The Lives of Animals" Costello resorts to a more shapely series of analogies. If she is like Red Peter it is because Srinivasa Ramanujan, the South Asian mathematician, was like Sultan (the ape trained by Wolfgang Koehler in his laboratory on Tenerife) and because the Jews of the Holocaust were like sheep and cattle going to the slaughter. Each pairing of a human with an animal counterpart seems to reinforce the core figure, "like" as resemblance, so that she is only as it were like Red Peter. But in fact the pairings do what the remark says and make *like* literal. This conversion from figure to fact is signalled obliquely by means of two sets of equivalents, both leading to a third. Ramanujan was the finest intuitive mathematician of modern times but incapable of demonstrating what he thought because thought was his only language. Taken as a trophy to Cambridge, his relation to G.H. Hardy was analogous with Sultan's to Koehler, where two radically different ways of thinking, silent thought and explicit logic, were forced into conjunction, the one being used imperfectly to translate the other. Intuitions became the metaphors of reason. A *real* translation would have lain along a different axis: "How are we to know that Red Peter … shot in Africa by the hunters, was not thinking the same thoughts as Ramanujan was thinking in India, and saying equally little?" (*EC* 69). Alexander Pope was moving along this axis in *An Essay on Man* when he had an intuition about the relativity of human genius, and imagined Newton in heaven being shown off as a prodigy among the angels, who "Admir'd such wisdom in an earthly shape, / And shew'd a NEWTON as we shew an Ape".[8] Abraham Stern takes issue with what he regards as Costello's ill-judged simile when he says, "If Jews were treated like cattle, it does not follow that cattle are treated like Jews. The inversion insults the memory of the dead" (*EC* 94). He excuses his directness by recalling her own: "You said you were old enough not to have time to waste on niceties." But that is not what she said. She said she was an old woman who did not have time to say what she did not mean or to make remarks that did not mean what they said. It is plain that the inversion was fully intended, whether or not it insults the memory of the dead. She was not talking about resemblance when she mentioned Jews in cattle-trucks, or discussed the parallels between Ramanujan in Cambridge and Sultan in Tenerife; it was only the weakness of words that made it seem so. The human cases and the animal ones are thoroughly interchangeable. She (or her remark) was talking about the possibility of one creature being so fully like another it was

---

8   Alexander Pope, *Poems*, ed. John Butt (London: Methuen, 1963), 517.

capable of being treated in exactly the same way, even of changing into it. Her equation between saying what you mean and meaning what you say leads her in the direction of metamorphosis, where physical change is so sudden and absolute that it can only be expressed in what looks like a metaphor. Quintilian says, "In Metaphor one thing is *substituted* for another. It is a comparison when I say that a man acted 'like a lion,' a Metaphor when I say of a man, 'he is a lion.'"[9]

This is an issue Costello will directly engage under the heading of sympathy, when she advances from saying that she feels like Red Peter to saying she knows what it is like to be a bat or a corpse. In "Realism" her son John tells Susan Moebius, "My mother has been a man ... she has also been a dog" (*EC* 22). But the problem with these metempsychoses, and with the translations they require from intuitive thought into a "real" language, is that any consciousness of being (as Thomas Nagel points out in the essay cited by Costello, "What is it like to be a bat?") is arrived at via *something which it is like* to be a bat or a corpse, otherwise the claim for sympathy is just an anthropomorphic fiction. When Costello tries to deal with this intervening stage of metamorphosis, the likeness between human and animal being that allows the one to cross into the consciousness of the other, she becomes passionate. She is talking of her brief but intense intuitions of being dead as her warrant for all her other feats of sympathy:

> When I know, with this knowledge, that I am going to die, what is it, in Nagel's terms, that I know? Do I know what it is like for me to be a corpse or do I know what it is like for a corpse to be a corpse? The distinction seems to me trivial. What I know is what a corpse cannot know: that it is extinct, that it knows nothing and will never know anything any more. For an instant, before my whole structure of knowledge collapses in panic, I am alive inside that contradiction, dead and alive at the same time. (*EC* 77)

There are two things worth emphasizing here. The first is that the distinction (she as corpse or corpse as corpse) is not really trivial because it points to what Costello is actually doing, which is as self-reflective as Nagel could wish. That is, she is not just imagining herself dead, she is impersonating a corpse that she calls her self. The co-presence of the two elements that constitute the person of the corpse, the object represented and the power of representing it as something like what it is, this is what allows her to be dead and alive – or human and animal, or man and woman – at the same time. Adam Smith makes this point when, in a remarkable retreat from his first position on sympathy in *A Theory of Moral Sentiments* (namely that we cannot sympathize with the real pain of another's pain, we react only to what we imagine we would feel in the same situation), he says: "I not only change circumstances with you, but I change persons and characters. My grief, therefore,

---

[9]   Quintilian, *The Orator's Education*, ed. and trans. Donald A. Russell (Cambridge: Harvard University Press, 2001), 8.6.9 [3.429].

is entirely upon your account, and not in the least upon my own."[10] The advance measured here from hypothesizing one's own case of misery to actually inhabiting imaginatively someone's else's depends upon the double capacity of the person. Person effects the transfer from person to person, as Smith demonstrates when he says: "This imaginary change is not supposed to happen to me in my own person and character, but in that [that is, the person] of the person with whom I sympathise."[11] That extra person has to be there, representing the something that it is like to be the other person, a figure who effects the transfer and then disappears when it has fully taken place. Such a person is necessary when Robinson Crusoe prefers his claim to lordship of the island while making the transition back to civil society: "When I shew'd my self to the two Hostages, it was with the Captain, who told them, I was the Person the Governour had order'd to look after them … so I now appear'd as another Person, and spoke of the Governour, the Garrison, the Castle, and the like."[12] This is how he is able eventually to authenticate his history with his name, beginning, "I, Robinson Crusoe …."

Sympathy compasses two phases in each cycle. Its desire of metamorphosis is ideally expressed in the real unmetaphorical language ("I am literally like the other"); but arrives at its destination via a figure or a person, a metaphor without which identity cannot happen. Before the panic of being a corpse there is the consciousness of being dead and alive at the same time, when one's death is as it were impersonated. These are the impurities of secondary meaning that contaminate the real language, but they are necessary if it is ever to be uttered. For want of such a language, Ramanujan remained silent, and Newton was forced to experiment unsuccessfully with the passive mood. As far as Elizabeth Costello is concerned the metamorphoses such a language might represent are left as fictions, like Red Peter, or enigmas, like her silence at the end of the story. There she goes back to Ovid to explain to her son how terrible it would be to say what she means, or mean what she says: "When I think of the words, they seem so outrageous that they are best spoken into a pillow or into a hole in the ground, like King Midas" (*EC* 114). Like Red Peter, like King Midas, like Molly Bloom.

There is no shortage of persons to aid the transformation; and the fictionality of the object of sympathy is no impediment. Molly Bloom, a woman invented by James Joyce, is reinvented by Elizabeth Costello, a female author invented by J.M. Coetzee, another author. The fact that Red Peter is to be found in a fable by Kafka, or Midas in Ovid's *Metamorphoses* does no harm to the metaphor, but it raises questions about realism, especially the realism of embodiment, since these intervening persons do not belong to the real world, at least not directly. Red Peter

---

    [10]   Adam Smith, *The Theory of Moral Sentinments*, ed. D.D. Raphael and A.L. Macfie (Indianapolis: Liberty Classics, 1982), 317.

    [11]   Ibid., 317.

    [12]   Daniel Defoe, *The Life and Strange Surprizing Adventures of Robinson Crusoe*, ed. J. Donald Crowley (Oxford: Oxford University Press, 1983), 271.

reports from what he calls (in the Muirs' translation) "the thick of things".[13] The thick of things doesn't precede the invention of the character, it follows it. It is the consequence of an act of imagining, and it is evident in a disorderly accumulation of facts. Kafka is praised for his fidelity to these consequential facts: "That ape is followed through to the end, to the bitter, unsayable end ... Kafka stays awake during the gaps when we are sleeping" (*EC* 32). For Coetzee, Crusoe's world is transfigured and made real by attending to the exigencies that follow from inventing it, "the hundreds of little practical problems involved in getting the contents of the ship ashore, or in making a clay cooking pot" (*SS* 20). John calls this standard of realism zoo-keeping, not writing, and his mother (the literalist) shouts, "Do you know how many kilograms of solid waste an elephant drops in twenty-four hours? If you want a real elephant cage with real elephants then you need a zookeeper to clean up after them" (*EC* 33). This is a point John himself has made in a different register when thinking of the divinity of her authorship, her having been touched by the god: "He serves at her shrine, cleaning up after the turmoil of the holy day, sweeping up the petals, collecting the offerings, putting the widows' mites together, ready to bank" (*EC* 31). So the various persons drawn from fiction – Molly, Red Peter, Midas and even Elizabeth Costello herself – stand at the centre of a litter of things expressive of embodiment – not because they were first implicated in that clutter, but because it trailed in their wake.

Cleaning up is literal-minded fidelity to the thick of things that emerges from a fable or a fiction; it involves stripping out the figurative secondary meanings of the story so that the "real" may be experienced for what it is. This work is performed by someone who stands in need of a person, a necessarily fictional person, in order to know what these things were really like. Coetzee offers an exemplary performance of such work in his Nobel Lecture, "He and his Man", where he imagines himself as Robinson Crusoe ("he") with Defoe acting the part of "his man", the designation the "real" Robinson Crusoe reserved for Friday. His man brings reports of the thick of things, of decoy ducks from the Lincolnshire fens, and of curious machines of execution in Halifax. But his man also has a way with words. He says that living through the plague year in London was "like charging Death himself on his pale horse". "Crusoe" says: "Those are words he would not think of. Only when he yields himself up to this man do such words come."[14] He yields himself up frequently. In a dizzying circuit of figures he claims that the plague victim prancing naked in his agony in *Journal of the Plague Year* "is allegoric" of his own distracted motions on the beach of his island the day he saw the three hats, one cap and two shoes that were not fellows. Alone on his island, he is figured again in the *Journal* by the healthy man they tried to throw into the

---

[13]   Franz Kafka, *Metamorphosis and Other Stories*, trans. Willa and Edwin Muir (New York: Schocken, 1995), 183.

[14]   Coetzee, ["He and his Man":] *Lecture and Speech of Acceptance upon the Award of the Nobel Prize in Literature, Delivered in Stockholm in December 2003* (London: Penguin, 2004), 14.

plague pit at Mountmill ("And this too is a figure of him on his island"). The sight of the dead in the pit is like the footprint in the sand, "a figure for life itself, the whole of life". The cannibals on "Crusoe's" island figure the imitators and plagiarists who pester his man. As for his fit of palsy, which made him dream the devil was sitting on him in the shape of a dog, that "may be figured as a visitation by the devil, or by a dog figured as the devil, and vice versa, the visitation figured as an illness".[15] Thus the plague (or Plague) is finally restored via many figurative secondary meanings to the sphere of pathology, and the solitude of the island is reduced by the same sideways process of metaphoric thinking to the singularity of the real. So when it comes to the question, "How are they to be figured, this man and he?",[16] the answer seems to be identically, not as figures at all. Coetzee says in the essay on Defoe: "The castaway returned in late life to the country of his birth seems at this moment to merge with the sixty-year-old Londoner, Daniel Defoe, from whose head he was born" (*SS* 16). When Defoe issued a public testimony, beginning "I, Robinson Crusoe...", in order to assert the historical veracity of a memoir that might have been mistaken for an allegory, he acknowledged the commonalty of the first-person pronoun, and the experience of the real that went with it. In an effort to figure this intimate fellowship, Coetzee as Robinson Crusoe says that he and his man are the same, deckhands on ships going in opposite directions, and so busy with their work and blinded by spray they cannot see one another as they labour in the rigging. But now there is a third person in the mix, the new impersonator of Robinson Crusoe who casts Defoe as Friday, and himself as the person Defoe had claimed. But that does not matter since their work is what is important, and the wake it leaves.

The author has a life as the person of his own character, and the character in turn seizes the person of the author. Defoe yields to Crusoe and Crusoe yields to his man; Joyce yields to Molly Bloom as she yields to Elizabeth Costello. Costello yields to Red Peter and Midas, and Coetzee to her. Thus certain personifications emerge, such as Death on his pale horse and Realism, only to disappear as these yieldings open up new identities who literalize figures in the process of cleaning up the thick of things.

We can get closer to this effect by looking at a personification similar to Death on his pale horse. It comes in "Realism" when John wakes up beside Susan Moebius feeling very sad. He does not leave her room because he wants to sleep. "Sleep, he thinks, *that knits up the ravelled sleeve of care*", and he is astonished by the power of the metaphor, which he ascribes to the genius of Shakespeare. No zoo-keeping here: "Not all the monkeys in the world picking away at typewriters all their lives would come up with those words in that arrangement" (*EC* 27). But his unconscious has already come up with image that fixes the personification of Sleep and its accoutrements literally in the body of his mother:

---

15   Ibid., 17.
16   Ibid., 18.

> Out of her back, out of the waxy, old person's flesh, protrude three needles: not the tiny needles of the acupuncturist or the voodoo doctor but thick grey needles, steel or plastic: knitting needles. The needles have not killed her, there is no need to worry about that, she breathes regularly in her sleep (*EC* 26).

Sleep personified and the body of the woman merge. They form an image that performs like Defoe's three hats, one cap and two shoes, embodying meaning and feeling instead of figuring it. The arrangement of flesh and needles means only what it says, it has no allegorical dimension. However, it is necessary to add that, without a metaphor to which this embodiment might refer, it would lose its charge and become merely grotesque. The reader has to experience the slide between sleep-as-knitting and knitting-sleep, between the secondary meaning and the real words. The same slide or drift blends Costello's saying what she means with remarks that mean what they say. This connexion is never lost and is productive of an affinity between body and language that is persistently misunderstood by her interlocutors as sentimental ethics, and to some extent misunderstood by herself as the immediacy of sympathy.

I want to instance one more example of figuration which dramatizes most clearly the obstructions to metaphor-free language that challenge and refine Coetzee's brand of realism. The "Postscript" to Elizabeth Costello's eight lessons is Coetzee's version of Hugo von Hofmannsthal's *A Letter*, supposed to be written by the distracted Philip Lord Chandos to Francis Bacon. This letter is written by his wife Elizabeth Lady Chandos ("E.C.") covering much the same ground as the original. Chandos has been bewitched by the charms of metamorphosis, desiring to enter the glistening bodies of Narcissus, Proteus, Perseus and Actaeon. But this transformation has not occurred. Instead he has found his language degenerating, becoming resistant equally to abstract nouns and metaphors; meanwhile his attention has become focused on ordinary items randomly displayed, such as watering cans and dogs. These things have supplanted his speech, saying and meaning whatever is left to mean and say in a world of minimal symmetry. "Everything," he says, "seems to mean something" (*EC* 125). Central to Chandos's altered consciousness has been his powerful intuition of the death of the rats in his cellars, poisoned on his orders – the smell, the shrilling, the writhing heaps of bodies, the bared teeth, the desperate search for a way out.

His wife Elizabeth takes up the complaint from a very different angle. Everything experienced by her husband as an embodied meaning has turned for her into a metaphor, particularly the plague of rats which now stands as the metaphor of all metaphors. "It is like a contagion, saying one thing always for another (*like a contagion*, I say; barely did I hold back from saying, *a plague of rats*)" (*EC* 228). Everywhere in her letter this trick of speech protrudes, "I say," as if in a vain effort to keep the words from figuring whatever they want: "*Always it is not what I say but something else* ... words give way beneath your feet like rotting boards (*like rotting boards* I say again, I cannot help myself, not if I am to bring home to you my distress and my husband's, *bring home*, I say" (*EC* 228). The italics mark words that have turned into figures. "I say" is borrowed from Defoe, his way of affirming the real: "The decoy men ... fail not to go secretly to the pond's side, I say secretly", in *A Tour through the Whole Island of Great Britain*;[17] "It ended where it begun, in a meer common Flight of Joy, or as I may say, *being glad I was alive*", in *Robinson Crusoe* (89); or in *Roxana*, "No Pen can describe, no Words can express, *I say*, the strange Impression which this thing made upon my Spirits".[18] If Philip has been drawn into a world of speaking things, Elizabeth has been overwhelmed with multiplying metaphors and an infinitely extending allegory, caught as if in a mill race: "I yield myself to the figures, do you see, Sir, how I am taken over?" (*EC* 229). Most clearly demarcated then is the division between the bald empiricism of the language of things, and the inevitably figurative tendency of language itself (or at least the English language). Her resource lies in the meta-metaphor of contagion and plague, for no sooner does she yield to a figure, than the figure itself yields to another and is forced to say something else again:

> Yet as I am that (a wayfarer in a mill) I am also not that; nor is it a contagion that comes continually upon me or a plague of rats or flaming swords, but something else. *Always it is not what I say but something else.* (*EC* 228)

This time the something else rids itself of metaphor and figure, along with their intrusive secondary meanings, and approaches instead a literal statement of a real case, just as the pullulating figures of the plague return finally to cohere in sickness in the Nobel Lecture. This is the transfiguration of the real. Lady Chandos goes on to call this state of mind induced by self-cancelling figures her *rush*, as opposed to her *rapture*:

> The rush and the rapture are not the same, but in ways that I despair of explaining though they are clear to my eye, *my eye* I call it, *my inner eye*, as if I had an eye inside that looked at the words one by one as they passed, like soldiers on parade, *like soldiers on parade* I say. (*EC* 229)

If rapture is like being caught in a mill-race of figures, an uncontrollable allegory, rush appears to be the opposite, a way of reflectively controlling the meanings of words as they stand up and are counted, like soldiers on parade. When Elizabeth Costello reluctantly concedes that the inner reflective eye makes metamorphosis possible, that the something which it is like to be a bat or a corpse leads to the sensation of the illimitable sympathy with it, she experiences this rush. When Elizabeth Chandos finds that failures to say what she means on one level lead to success on another in her effort to mean what she says, she exemplifies Michel

---

[17]   Daniel Defoe, *A Tour through the Whole Island of Great Britain*, ed. P.N. Furbank at al. (New Haven: Yale University Press, 1991), 220).

[18]   Daniel Defoe, *Roxana; or, The Fortunate Mistress*, ed. David Blewett (New York: Penguin, 1982), 323.

de Certeau's definition of the happiness of glossolalia as "a transition from a can not say to a can say, by way of a can say nothing".[19] Her husband and she have been divided, he operating within the zone of saying only what things mean, and she in the zone of meaning only what her words say. They are reunited in the discovery of a strange univocality, his in things and hers in words. Between them they achieve a language suitable to an empiricism that can scarcely be called bald, since it comes about by means of the sideways process of metaphoric thinking, and the sacrifice of so many secondary meanings. She salutes Bacon as a man "known above all men to select your words and set them in place and build your judgments as a mason builds a wall with bricks" (*EC* 230) – a dead metaphor to be sure, but a lot safer than live ones that forced her to yield to a collapsing structure, and prevented her from bringing home, via the person of her husband, what was real and proper to her: what she meant to say.

---

[19]   Michel de Certeau, "Vocal Utopias: Glossolalias" *Representations* 56 (1996) : 29–47, at 32.

Chapter 10
Pity and Autonomy:
Coetzee, Costello and Conrad

Graham Bradshaw

"Pity" or "Compassion"?

> There is no limit to the extent to which we can think ourselves into the being of another.
>
> Elizabeth Costello, in *Elizabeth Costello: Eight Lessons*

> The trouble with criticism is that one can't say everything at once.
>
> F.R. Leavis, in conversation.

In Conrad's *Victory* (1915) Axel Heyst's philosopher-father certainly resembles Schopenhauer as a "destroyer of systems, of beliefs, of hopes",[1] but his philosophy includes nothing that corresponds with Schopenhauer's ethical teaching. This difference is most marked when we hear the elder Heyst's response, a few hours before he dies, to the question that the very unhappy young Axel "had asked – for he was really young then":

"Is there no guidance?"

His father was in an unexpectedly soft mood on that night, when the moon swam in a cloudless sky over the begrimed shadows of the town.

"You still believe in something, then?" he said in a clear voice, which had been growing feeble of late. "You believe in flesh and blood, perhaps? A full and equable contempt would soon do away with that, too. But since you have not attained to it, I advise you to cultivate that form of contempt which is called pity."

"What is one to do, then?" sighed the young man, regarding his father, rigid in the high-backed chair.

"Look on – make no sound," were the last words of the man who had spent his life in blowing blasts upon a terrible trumpet which had filled heaven and earth with ruins, while mankind went on its way unheeding. (134)

---

[1]   Joseph Conrad, *Victory* (London: Dent, 1948), 175. All subsequent quotations from Conrad's fiction are taken from the Dent Collected Edition.

The idea of cultivating "pity" as a "form of contempt" would have horrified Schopenhauer, whose main thesis in his 1841 monograph *On the Basis of Morality* (*Die Grundprobleme der Ethik*) was that "all virtues stem from pity".[2] But German philosophers like Kant, Schopenhauer and Nietzsche all use the word *Mitleid* when they are discussing pity or compassion, and this poses a problem for their English translators. In English, the words "pity" and "compassion" are often but not always interchangeable. So, although Conrad's much earlier *The Nigger of the "Narcissus"* (1897) provides a profound creative critique of Schopenhauerean ethics, it does not matter when Conrad keeps switching between the English words "pity" and "compassion";[3] but it would sound very strange if, in the passage from *Victory*, the elder Heyst had advised his unhappy son to cultivate *compassion* as a "form of contempt".

Of course the idea of cultivating *pity* as "a form of contempt" is in itself repugnant: as Bertolt Brecht observes in one of his best poems, even righteous anger disfigures the face – and so does any form of contempt. But, as the acerbic Heyst obviously knows – and in this respect he is closer to Nietzsche than to Schopenhauer – pity can include some element of detachment, or condescension: one can look *down* on a suffering person or creature, even when providing (or passing down) relief or assistance. Some writers, like Schopenhauer or Dostoevsky, would object to any such detachment as the meanly rational, emotionally rationed equivalent of a soup kitchen. But for other writers, including Plato, Montaigne, La Rochefoucauld, Kant and Nietzsche, such detachment is morally hygienic, a necessary safeguard against the kind of indiscriminate hysteria that so disables poor Stevie in Conrad's *Secret Agent*. As Dostoevsky's Ivan Karamazov says, our world is drenched in tears; but, as young Axel Heyst asks his father, "What is one to do, then?" When nothing we do can begin to be enough, how should we live our lives?

Human, All Too Human (*Menschliches, Allzumenschliches*, 1888) was the first book in which Nietzsche explicitly dissociated himself from both Schopenhauer and Richard Wagner, not least by attacking Schopenhauer's concept of *Mitleid* – which had also provided the ardently Schopenhauerean Wagner with the philosophical-metaphysical underpinning for *Parsifal*. In this attack Nietzsche aligned himself with that Western philosophical mainstream, from Plato through Kant, that regarded pity or *Mitleid*-as-pity, as an "infection". In his *Nachlass* or

---

[2]   Arthur Schopenhauer, *On the Basis of Morality*, trans. E.F.J. Payne (Indianapolis: Hackett,1965), 144. Schopenhauer constantly returned to this idea in his other writings, and his concept of *Mitleid* is presented with unforgettable passion and eloquence in book 4, chapter 47 of the greatly enlarged 1844 edition of his *magnum opus*, *The World as Will and Representation*, and in Chapters 8 and 9 of the second part of *Parerga and Paralipomena* (1851).

[3]   The younger Conrad read Schopenhauer attentively, and in *Conrad's Models of Mind* (Minneapolis: University of Minnesota Press, 1971) Bruce Johnson shows how *Nigger of the "Narcissus"* provides a creative critique of Schopenhauer's ethics.

notebooks, Nietzsche sounded more than ever like Kant when he warned that "Pity is a squandering of feeling, a parasite harmful to moral health", and then completed this sentence with a remark that he put in quotation marks but did not identify, doubtless because he was writing a note to himself and was unlikely to forget the author: "it cannot possibly be our duty to increase the evil in the world". As David E. Cartwright shows in his fine essay on "Kant, Schopenhauer, and Nietzsche on the Morality of Pity", both Nietzsche's quotation and his emphasis on pity as a pathological infection are taken from Kant's chilly argument that

> if another person suffers and I let myself (through my imagination) also become infected [*anstecken lasse*] by his pain, which I still cannot remedy, then two people suffer, although the evil (in nature) affects only the one. But it cannot possibly be a duty to increase the evils of the world or, therefore, to do good from pity.[4]

Kant's parenthetical, curiously accusatory reference to what would happen, if he were to "let" it happen "through my imagination", shows how he is presenting or locating his argument within the Western, post-Cartesian analytic tradition of *disembodied* thinking that so rigidly separates reason from imagination, cognition from emotion, and the mind from the body. Nietzsche is usually closer to Schopenhauer than to Kant in his refusal to separate these things, but Cartwright convincingly shows how regularly Nietzsche draws on Kant when discussing pity or *Mitleid*. We might suspect that there were complex, self-protective reasons for this, if we recall how Nietzsche would eventually be declared officially insane when he collapsed after rushing across a street in Turin to embrace a horse that was being cruelly flogged; we might even reflect that life was imitating art in Wildean fashion, if we recall the two horses that are flogged across the eyes in Dostoevsky, or poor Stevie's utter anguish in the cab-drive episode that Conrad inserted when preparing the book-version of *The Secret Agent*. It would be insentient to suppose that Nietzsche himself was being insentient when he subscribed to the Kantian view that pity or *Mitleid* is something we should "desire to be free from" because it is an "infection" that threatens our moral autonomy; in *Human, All Too Human*, Nietzsche approvingly quotes La Rochefoucauld's view that one should show pity, or *Mitleid*-as-*pity*, but "carefully keep from having it."

Whereas *Mitleid*-as-*compassion* is different, because it is something one *has*. At this point etymologies provide the appropriately Nietzschean backward inference, or genealogy. The English concept of *com*passion (*con*+*patior*) and the German concept of *Mit*leid (*mit*+*leiden*) both carry the idea of suffering or grieving *with* another suffering person or creature. This seems more nobly human but is also – in an awkward sense, that plagues Coetzee's Costello in *Elizabeth Costello* – more presumptuous. As Rainer Maria Rilke once observed, to suppose

---

⁴   David E. Cartwright, "Kant, Schopenhauer, and Nietzsche on the Morality of Pity", *Journal of the History of Ideas* 45.1 (1984): 83–98.

that one can imagine another person's suffering is to assume a greater insight than any novelist or dramatist has into a character he has created. And how enraging it can be, after losing a front tooth or a child, to be told, "I *know* how you feel!" As Elizabeth Costello reflects in Coetzee's most recent novel, *Slow Man*, care "is not love. Care is a service that any nurse worth her salt can provide, as long as we don't ask her for more."[5] But, although *compassion* presumes to be more loving than *pity*, it can also be less caring. To show *Mitleid*-as-pity, it may be enough to *see* another's grief or pain, but *Mitleid*-as-compassion, or what Elizabeth Costello calls "imaginative sympathy", presumes to imagine and *share* that pain.

Conrad's Stevie is so disabled by his sympathetic imagination that he cannot help himself, let alone others, whereas Kant is fearful of what "imagination" would do to him, if he "let" it. Although the Kantian fear that pity threatens one's moral autonomy looks back to Plato's *Republic*, it was massively reinforced by the Cartesian tradition of disembodied thinking. Costello fiercely opposes this fear and denigration of the imagination in her Appleton College lectures (which should not be confused with Coetzee's Princeton lectures) on "The Rights of Animals": for Costello the concept of "imaginative sympathy" is as crucial as it was for George Eliot. But it then gets Elizabeth into difficulties she could have avoided if she had chosen, like George Eliot, to emphasize *equivalence*, not *identification* and *sharing*. *Middlemarch* (1871–72) Is probably the most impressively philosophical of all nineteenth-century English novels, because it so rigorously exposes and explores the fundamental distinction between two kinds of "egoism". *Epistemological* egoism in unavoidable because every individual just *is* the centre of his or her universe: hence the famous first sentence of Schopenhauer's great work, "The world is my representation." Epistemological egoism then leads, all too easily or naturally, to *moral* egoism like that of Eliot's Bulstrode, Rosamund Vincy, Casaubon and even young Lydgate, when he chooses his wife as though he were choosing furniture, to adorn his life. In chapter 21 of *Middlemarch*, after several chapters that have encouraged the unresisting reader to take a profoundly sympathetic but exclusively Dorothea-centred view of her marital anguish, the reader is suddenly challenged by the momentous change in Dorothea's own attitude to her situation:

> We are all of us born in moral stupidity, taking the world as an udder to feed our supreme selves: Dorothea had early begun to emerge from that stupidity, but yet it had been easier to her to imagine how she would devote herself to Mr. Casaubon than to conceive with that distinctness which is no longer reflection but feeling – an idea wrought back to the directness of sense, like the solidity of objects – that he had an equivalent centre of self whence the lights and shadows must always fall with a certain difference.

---

[5]   J.M.Coetzee, *Slow Man* (London: Secker & Warburg, 2005), 154. Hereafter *SM* in text

Dorothea comes to see, or *imagine*, that even her emotionally desiccated husband has his own "intense consciousness within him", and his own "small, hungry, shivering self", from which he can never be "liberated". This is not "imaginative sympathy" in Elizabeth Costello's sense, because Dorothea does not "enter into" or "share", let alone love, her husband's hungry self and its moral egoism; but her imagination has helped her to recognize or "conceive" what Mikhail Bakhtin calls "a world of other consciousnesses with rights equal to those of the hero."[6] Kant fears that the "imagination" threatens our moral autonomy, but for George Eliot morality and our capacity to resist "moral stupidity" depend upon the imagination and our capacity to imagine "other consciousnesses" or "equivalent" centres of self.

Elizabeth Costello's deep hostility to the Cartesian tradition of disembodied thinking emerges most clearly in her lecture on "The Philosophers and the Animals" when she is attacking Descartes's idea that an animal lives as a machine lives:

> "*Cogito, ergo sum*," he also famously said. It is a formula I have always been uncomfortable with. It implies that a living being that does not do what we call thinking is somehow second-class. To thinking, cogitation, I oppose fullness, the sensation of being – not a consciousness of yourself as a kind of ghostly reasoning machine thinking thoughts, but on the contrary the sensation – a heavily affective sensation – of being a body with limbs that have extension in space, of being alive to the world. This fullness contrasts starkly with Descartes' key state, which has an empty feel to it: the feel of a pea rattling around in a shell.[7]

Since Costello's subsequent comparison of slaughter-houses with Auschwitz and death camps has drawn much hostile criticism, it is worth noticing that Jacques Derrida had also compared the slaughtering of animals with "genocide" in his essay "The Animal That Therefore I Am (More to Follow)", while making the Cartesian *ergo sum* link in the essay's title.[8] Derrida argues the need for "fundamental compassion" (395) when he writes of a "war" about "pity" that we have to *think*, because this war "concerns what we call 'thinking'":

> To think the war we find ourselves waging is not only a duty, a responsibility, an obligation, it is also a necessity, a constraint that, like it or not, directly or indirectly, everyone is held to. (397)

---

[6] Mikhail Bakhtin, *Problems of Dostoevsky's Poetics*, trans. Caryl Emerson (Minneapolis: University of Minnesota Press, 1984), 48.

[7] J.M. Coetzee, *Elizabeth Costello: Eight Lessons* (London: Secker & Warburg), 78. Hereafter *EC* in text.

[8] Jacques Derrida, "The Animal That Therefore I Am (More to Follow)", *Critical Inquiry* 28 (Winter 2002): 369–418, at 394.

However, because Derrida is so determined to go on attending to "difference, to differences, to heterogeneities and abyssal ruptures as against the homogeneous and the continuous" (398), he refuses to allow for *continuity* between other forms of animal life and our own. Instead, he insists that to deny or contest "the rupture or abyss between this 'I-we' and what we call animals" would be "asinine" (an interesting metaphor in this context) – whereas Elizabeth Costello insists on continuity in a way that asserts, all too proudly, what she, as a novelist, can do and is constantly doing, that "Philosophers" allegedly can't or won't do. She then gets into difficulties that (as her creator surely knows) emerge most clearly in her quarrel with Thomas Nagel's famously challenging essay, "What is it like to be a bat?"[9]

Of course Nagel never argues or supposes that animals live as machines live. He expressly allows that "conscious" experience "occurs at many levels of animal life", and he observes that "the fact that an organism has conscious experience *at all* means, basically, that there is something it is like to *be* that organism" (166). Bats resemble human mammals in feeling "some versions of pain, fear, hunger and lust", but bats (or most kinds of bat) perceive the world through sonar or echolocation, and we can't *imagine* what that is like because "bat sonar, though clearly a form of perception, is not similar in its operation to any sense that we possess" (168):

> Our own experience provides the basic material for our imagination, whose range is therefore limited. It will not help to try to imagine that one has webbing on one's arms, which enables one to fly around at dusk and dawn catching insects in one's mouth; that one has very poor vision, and perceives the surrounding world by a system of related high-frequency sound signals; and that one spends the day hanging upside down by one's feet in an attic. In so far as I can imagine this (which is not very far), it tells me only what it would be like for *me* to behave as a bat behaves. But that is not the question. I want to know what it is like for a *bat* to be a bat. Yet if I try to imagine this, I am restricted to the resources of my own mind, and those resources are inadequate to the task. (169)

Costello's reply to this invokes what she calls the "sympathetic imagination", and immediately generates more heat than light:

> Despite Thomas Nagel, who is probably a good man, despite Thomas Aquinas and René Descartes, with whom I have more difficulty in sympathizing, there is no limit to the extent to which we can think ourselves into the being of another. There are no bounds to the sympathetic imagination. (*EC* 79–80)

---

[9]   Thomas Nagel, "What Is It Like to Be a Bat?" in *Mortal Questions* (Cambridge: Cambridge University Press, 1987), 165–80.

A moment later she adds, as the acclaimed author of "the book called *The House on Eccles Street*":

> If I can think my way into the existence of a being who has never existed, then I can think my way into the existence of a bat or a chimpanzee or an oyster, and any being with whom I share the substrate of life. (*EC* 80)

Costello would therefore be no less confident about her ability to enter into the "being" or "existence" of Friday in *Foe* and the Namaqua women in *Dusklands* or the barbarian woman in *Waiting for the Barbarians* – or even the Jewish "Muselmänner" or "Muslims" described in Giorgio Agamben's *Remnants of Auschwitz*. The so-called "Muslims" were so called by other Jewish prisoners (no comment, it would take too long) because, although they were technically still alive, the horrors of the death-camps had destroyed their sense of self and their capacity to speak; they were then the most complete witnesses because they were incapable of bearing witness.

Costello's notion of thinking ourselves *into* the being of another – which, I have suggested, needs to be distinguished from George Eliot's concept of imagining an *equivalent* centre of self – figures no less prominently and provokingly in her discussion of the death camps:

> The particular horror of the camps, the horror that convinces us that what went on there was a crime against humanity, is not that despite a humanity shared with their victims, the killers treated them like lice. That is too abstract. The horror is that the killers refused to think themselves into the place of their victims, as did everyone else. They said, "It is they in those cattle cars rattling past." They did not say, "How would it be if it were I in that cattle car?" They did not say, "It is I who am in that cattle car." They said, "It must be the dead who are being burned today, making the air stink and falling in ash on my cabbages." They did not say, "How would it be if I were burning?" They did not say, "I am burning, I am falling in ash." (*EC* 79)

In an unwittingly ironic way all of Costello's examples of what these killers "did not say", or imagine, illustrate the force and wisdom of Nagel's distinction between imagining what it would be like for *me* to behave like a bat and knowing what it is like to *be* a bat – or a Muselmann, or Friday in *Foe*. Costello's jarringly confident notion that she can think her way into another's being until she *shares* it is presumptuous in the same way that the notion of *Mitleid*-as-compassion, or suffering *with* another (or "Other"), can be presumptuous.

Here too Nagel is right; to imagine the responses of a fictional character "who has never existed" is easier, less constrained by limited "resources", than imagining what it is like to be a bat or an oyster. When Costello is quarrelling with Nagel she allows herself more than one crack at "academic philosophers". Coetzee does not do that in the interview in *Doubling the Point* where he evidently agrees with Costello – up to a point:

> If I look back over my own fiction, I see a simple (simple-minded) standard erected. That standard is the body. Whatever else, the body is not "that which is not," and the proof that it *is* is the pain it feels. The body with its pain becomes a counter to the endless trials of doubt. (One can get away with such crudeness in fiction; one can't in philosophy, I'm sure.)[10]

Costello would never have added those worried parentheses. After another paragraph on how, in South Africa, the authority of the suffering body is not something that "one *grants*" but something that "the suffering body takes", Coetzee volunteers this extraordinary admission, which is all the more searing because he insists that it is also and entirely "parenthetical":

> (Let me add, *entirely* parenthetically, that I, as a person, as a personality, am overwhelmed, that my thinking is thrown into confusion and helplessness, by the fact of suffering in the world, and not only human suffering. These fictional constructions of mine are paltry, ludicrous defenses against that being-overwhelmed, and, to me, transparently so.)[11]

The more confident (though, in her own way, desperate) Costello declares:

> The heart is the seat of a faculty, *sympathy*, that allows us to share at times the being of another. Sympathy has everything to do with the subject and little to do with the object, the "another", as we can see at once when we think of the object not as a bat ("Can I share the being of a bat?") but as another human being. There are people who have the capacity to imagine themselves as someone else, there are people who have no such capacity (when the lack is extreme, we call them psychopaths), and there are people who have the capacity but choose not to exercise it. (*EC* 79)

That last sentence is depressingly true, and perhaps has a counterpart in Derrida's essay when he suggests that philosophers can be divided between those who look at animals and then just see "animals", and those who are also aware of the animals seeing them. But Elizabeth is still begging the question of whether our "imaginative sympathy" or "capacity" to imagine ourselves as someone or even something else, like a bat, amounts to sharing the being of another.

Coetzee's two lectures on "The Philosophers and the Animals" and "The Poets and the Animals" were originally given as his response to Princeton University's

---

[10]   J.M. Coetzee, *Doubling the Point: J.M. Coetzee, Essays and Interviews*, ed. David Attwell (Cambridge, MA: Harvard University Press, 1992), 248.

[11]   Ibid., 248.

invitation to deliver the 1997–98 Tanner Lectures, and were first published in *The Lives of Animals*, as part of the University Center for Human Values series, with replies by Marjorie Garber, Peter Singer, Wendy Doniger and Barbara Smuts.[12] The previous lecturers in this series were Charles Taylor, Antonin Scalia and Amy Gutmann – who introduces *The Lives of Animals*. Gutmann notes, reassuringly, that even though the fictional "form of Coetzee's lectures is far from the typical Tanner Lectures, which are generally philosophical essays", they "focus on an important ethical issue – the way human beings treat animals" (3). She also attempts, more uneasily, to explain and pay tribute to Coetzee's choice of a fictional form for his lectures by saying that "John Coetzee displays the kind of seriousness that can unite aesthetics and ethics" (3). When I first read that and tried to imagine Coetzee's response I found myself recalling Wittgenstein's response to the idea that aesthetics and ethics could ever be separated. In what survives of his lectures on aesthetics, Wittgenstein repeatedly emphasizes the need to consider aesthetic values in relation to ethical commitments to different, socially and culturally specific "ways of living". Writers as unlike each other as Dr Johnson, George Eliot, F.R. Leavis and Nietzsche or Bertolt Brecht would all have agreed that there are no purely aesthetic values, although they would not all have agreed that there are no external values. And yet, if we consider ethical values and some idea that we might all now support, like the belief that slavery is wrong, we had better allow that for some two thousand years philosophers from Aristotle to David Hume were arguing that some people or, still worse, peoples were "natural" slaves. The values in question – ours as well as theirs – are not external; they cannot, as Wittgenstein puts it, be "read off". As Coetzee himself puts it, they are "constructs" or "foundational fictions".[13]

If this is granted, Gutmann's distinction between fictional and philosophical "forms" for discussing "Human Values" becomes more tenuous, more like a house constructed upon a metaphysically condemned foundation – with one obvious exception that works to Coetzee's advantage: philosophers, especially modern English rather than "continental" philosophers, have been fond of arguing from trivial rather than humanly complex examples. Coetzee's decision to frame the "animal rights" issue in a fictional rather than a logically discursive form provided a salutary kind of "lesson" on the relation (not "unity") between aesthetics and ethics – just as his much earlier decision to eschew "realism" had provided a sometimes resented challenge to other South African novelists. His "lesson" challenged the entrenched post-Cartesian assumption that philosophers like David Hume, Bertrand Russell or Peter Singer *think* about philosophical issues and "ideas", whereas "creative" writers like William Blake, D.H. Lawrence or Coetzee are not really "thinkers".

---

[12]   J.M. Coetzee, *The Lives of Animals*, with introduction by Amy Gutmann (Princeton: Princeton University Press, 1999)

[13]   See above pp. 9–10, 17, 50.

Later, when these lectures became part – "Lesson 3" and "Lesson 4", *not* Chapters 3 and 4 – of *Elizabeth Costello: Eight Lessons*, the idea of a "lesson" inevitably shifted. Once eight somewhat uneven lessons on disparate matters and the "Postscript" to *Elizabeth Costello* are in question, not just two lessons on the same, terribly compelling question of how we humans treat other animals, it becomes or seems more disconcerting to pay such sustained attention to the novel's tense, old and unhappy protagonist without being sure how far her ideas are those of the author – but why? The answer to that question may provide another salutary lesson. As we shall see, *Slow Man*, in which Costello is older and still more weary and unhappy, provides further reasons for not thinking of her as Coetzee's *alter ego*. As we shall also see, *Slow Man* also explores the question of whether (as Dostoevsky, Bakhtin and others have certainly believed) fictional characters can become autonomous.

Moral and Fictional Autonomy

Most of the time you won't notice I am here. Just a touch on the shoulder, now and then, left or right, to keep you on the path.

Elizabeth Costello, in *Slow Man*

"I am not a young man in a novel."

Razumov, in *Under Western Eyes*

My Tatiana's married!

The startled, delighted Pushkin, writing to a friend

In late January 1910, after finishing *Under Western Eyes*, the exhausted Conrad had a complete nervous breakdown. Months later, he told Edward Garnett, "I feel as if I had somehow smashed myself."[14] He did not recover until early May, and some critics suppose that he never completely recovered. In an earlier, less severe collapse, Conrad had badly frightened his wife Jessie by raving in Polish, like the delirious, dying Janko in his story "Amy Foster", but now he was carrying on impassioned conversations with characters from his novel. "Poor boy," the commonsensical Jessie reported to one friend on 6 February, "he lives the novel, rambles all the time and insists that the Dr and I are trying to put him into an asylum"; on the same day, she wrote to another friend that "he lives mixed up in the scenes and holds converse with the characters. I have been up with him night and day since Sunday week and he, who is usually so depressed by illness, maintains he is not ill …"[15]

---

[14]   Zdzislaw Najder, *Joseph Conrad: A Chronicle*, trans. Halina Carroll-Najder (Cambridge: Cambridge University Press, 1983), 368.

[15]   Ibid., 357–8.

Common sense, which tells us that the earth is flat, also tells us that fictional characters can only ever say or do whatever their creators decide they will say or do. It then seems strange, or theoretically impossible, for any novelist to have long, excited conversations with his characters as though they were in some sense autonomous, or free. Very stern narratologists might even attribute Conrad's crack-up to this culpable failure to remember that "characters" are dependent *abstracta*: Jessie's "poor boy" had apparently forgotten the basic theoretical distinction between *external* and *internal* statements about "characters" and the fictional "world" they inhabit. Critical claims and theories about Conrad's creative "achievement and decline" frequently date his alleged "decline" from this devastating breakdown and then offer different explanations or speculations, which Zdzislaw Najder soberly appraises and usually rejects in his exemplary biography of Conrad – but Najder is not as fascinated as I am by these haunting glimpses of an author, at the end of his tether, having impassioned conversations with his own characters while insisting that he was not "ill" and refusing to allow his completed manuscript (which he had dated "22 January, 1910") to be sent off to the anxious publishers.

For Conrad at least, some of the characters in *Under Western Eyes* had evidently become sufficiently autonomous to have conversations with their creator. They could talk back. In Coetzee's *Slow Man*, Paul Rayment meets, talks and quarrels with his immediate or ostensible creator, Elizabeth Costello, although he can never think of her as his creator, and his creator's creator hovers in the background. Costello explains that she has come to Paul to discover what he will do next, while also insisting (more than once) that Paul first "came to" her. Coetzee, unlike his second "Elizabeth" or "E. C.", is playing with the question of whether, in the creative process, a fictional character can become autonomous; but *Slow Man* is also addressing, or speaking to and teasing our readerly sense of what the reading process involves – when, for example, an involved reader wonders why Thomas Hardy is being so cruel to Tess, whom he so obviously adores. Although Conrad's Razumov could not quarrel directly with his creator in the novel, he had grounds enough to ask, like Paul Rayment, "What is this that is being done to me?"

One way of explaining the strangely autonomous afterlife of those characters in *Under Western Eyes* who could talk back to their creator is to suppose that they had come to possess some kind of "extraordinary independence in the structure of the work", so that the character's voice becomes autonomous in some inescapably relative but still real sense, and then "sounds, as it were, *alongside* the author's word and in a special way combines both with it and with the full and equally valid voices of other characters."[16] These quotations are all taken from Mikhail Bakhtin's still controversial account of Dostoevsky's "polyphonic" or dialogical poetics, in which Bakhtin argues that "Dostoevsky – to speak paradoxically – thought not in thoughts but in points of view, consciousnesses, voices" (93). Characters like Raskolnikov, Stravrogin and Ivan Karamazov are "not only objects of authorial

---

[16]   Bakhtin, *Problems of Dostoevsky's Poetics*, 7.

discourse but also subjects of their own directly signifying discourse" (7). It is then "as if the character were not an object of authorial discourse, but rather a fully valid, autonomous carrier of his own individual word" (5) – although that word "autonomous" sits so strangely with "as if". When Garnett reproached Conrad for hating Russia in his novel, as in life, the deeply wounded Conrad replied that he had "lavished a 'wealth of tenderness' on Tekla and Sophia" and that "in this book I am concerned with nothing but ideas, to the exclusion of everything else"[17] – although these two claims also sit together strangely. Since the exclusive concern with "ideas" evidently did not exclude a "wealth of tenderness", Conrad's letter implies something unexpectedly like Bakhtin's account of the Dostoevskean hero as a *person born of an idea*: so, for Bakhtin, Raskolnikov is "the image of a fully valid idea" that *lives* "in uninterrupted dialogic interaction with other fully valid ideas – the ideas of Sonya, Porfiry, Svidrigailov, and others".[18] That might still seem strange, since the characters can only come into being within "the structure of the work". Anatoly Lunacharsky, one of the critics Bakhtin opposes, argued that the "unheard-of freedom of voices in Dostoevsky's polyphony, which so strikes the reader, is in fact an immediate result of the limitations of Dostoevsky's power over the spirits he has called into being".[19] In *The Master of Petersburg* the formidable Maximov asks Coetzee's "Dostoevsky" whether it is "practical to talk about ideas going about in the land, as if ideas had arms and legs".[20]

Certainly, the idea of an author having long, impassioned conversations with his characters wouldn't have seemed strange to Bakhtin, or to Dostoevsky himself, who assumed in his essay on Edgar Allan Poe that an author can proceed like a scientist conducting an experiment, placing his character in some deliberately contrived, extreme situation to see, or discover, how the character will behave.[21] Of course this scientific analogy makes no sense if we insist that everything a fictional character says and does must be determined by the author, but it applies very well to the kind of extreme experiment that Conrad was so deliberately setting up in *Under Western Eyes* when he ensured that Razumov, his sensitive and gifted "man with a mind", is also an illegitimate son with no family and no friends, who thinks of "Russia" as his only parent. Whether Conrad was also setting up

---

[17]   Najder, *Joseph Conrad*, 373.

[18]   Bakhtin, *Problems of Dostoevsky's Poetics*, 86.

[19]   Ibid., 35.

[20]   J.M. Coetzee, *The Master of Petersburg* (London: Secker & Warburg, 1994), 44. Hereafter *MP* in text.

[21]   Bakhtin, *Problems of Dostoevsky's Poetics*, 143–4. In *Einstein and Dostoevsky* (London: Hutchinson, 1972), the scientist Boris Kuznetsov, who was then President of the Russian Einstein Society, noted how Dostoevsky's account of Poe's quasi-scientific procedure better described his own way of setting up a provocative anacrisis like a scientist devising a laboratory experiment; the scientific analogy that impressed Bakhtin and Kuznetsov presupposes that the novelist can discover, *without* determining in advance, how his hero will behave.

Razumov – determining his doom, not discovering how he might behave – is a more complicated question.

It may be that, after his catastrophic breakdown, Conrad was not only talking with his seemingly autonomous characters but quarrelling with them, in ways that followed from his extraordinarily ambitious concern to present what he saw as distinctively Russian "modes of feeling" and thereby "render not so much the political state as the psychology of Russia itself" (vii).[22] The only comparably ambitious novel I can think of is Thomas Mann's *Doktor Faustus* (1947), which set out to present and diagnose what in the *psychology of Germany itself* prompted the nation's capitulation to Nazism. Mann greatly admired Conrad, and his procedure involved powerful but controversially diagnostic reinterpretations of German culture and of writers and artists like Nietzsche and Schoenberg; in this respect Mann was adapting Conrad's strategy in *Under Western Eyes*, when it so frequently recalls Dostoevsky. At one, relatively simple, level the Dostoevskean echoes appear to authenticate the Russianness of Razumov's compulsive urge to confess, and his readiness to slide into mysticism and fatalism. But the novel is also advancing its own diagnostic, radically un- or anti-Dostoevskean account of these Russian "modes of feeling", so that Conrad's treatment of Razumov's need to confess is closer to Coetzee than to Dostoevsky. Although Conrad's novel is never mentioned in Coetzee's profound essay on "Confession and Double Thoughts", which was arguably a landmark and turning point in his own development, Coetzee's essay provides the best commentary on why the driven, Dostoevskean intensity of Razumov's compulsive, almost promiscuous need to "confess" makes any truthful confession impossible.[23]

Any reader who is familiar with critical discussions of *Under Western Eyes* will know how frequently critics discuss Razumov's "confession" to Natalia as though only one confession were in question, and as though it delivered some kind of expiation on the model of *Crime and Punishment* or even "The Ancient Mariner". But, as Coetzee observes, confessions sometimes reveal "nothing so much as the helplessness of confession before the desire of the self to construct its own truth".[24] And if, as Coetzee also suggests, "The end of confession is to tell the truth to and for oneself" (297), that is something that the author of *Under Western Eyes* ensures that Razumov can never do. Critics have argued for many years about whether Anna Karenina falls or is pushed, but not about what Conrad does with and to the appallingly lonely Razumov to ensure that his character will carry his creator's sense of what it means to think "like a Russian", and to be subject to what the novel presents as historically determined "modes of feeling".

---

[22] Joseph Conrad, *Under Western Eyes* (London: Dent, 1947), "Author's Note", vii. Subsequent page numbers given in parenthesis.

[23] J.M. Coetzee, ,"Confession and Double Thoughts: Tolstoy, Rousseau, Dostoevsky", *Comparative Literature* 37 (1985): 193–232.

[24] Ibid., 297.

Razumov's confession – or, to be more attentive, his two (verbal and written) confessions – to Natalia are preceded by constant, morally and ideologically contradictory impulses to confess to utterly different characters at opposite ends of the political or ideological spectrum. Immediately after resolving to betray Haldin but before he has done so, Razumov suddenly longs "to pour out a full confession" to Haldin that would end in "an incredible fellowship of souls" (40). Immediately after that, indeed on the very same page, the "glimpse of a passing grey whisker" makes Razumov suddenly think of turning to Prince K——, the father who will not acknowledge Razumov as his illegitimate son but "had once pressed his hand as no other man had pressed it": "A strange softening emotion came over Razumov – made his knees shake a little" (40). His father leads him first to the detestable General T—— and then to the formidably clever and relatively liberal autocrat Councillor Mikulin, who recalls Dostoevsky's Porfiry in *Crime and Punishment* and anticipates Coetzee's Maximov in *The Master of Petersburg*. In Razumov's very first meeting with Mikulin, and "against his will", the idea of confessing "presented itself with such force that he had to bite his lip" (91); after this Razumov begins to write his journal, as yet another dangerously compromising form of confession. Later, when he thinks Mikulin "the only man in the world able to understand his conduct", the idea of, "as he termed it to himself, *confessing* to Councillor Mikulin flashed through his mind" (297) – before he asks himself, in some amazement, "Confess! To what?" *Why* this constant, compulsive urge to "confess", and to people as different as Haldin and Mikulin?

When Razumov finally confesses to Natalia that he betrayed her brother he cannot explain why, and when she begs for "the story" his confession is gestural: "It ends here," he says, pressing "a denunciatory finger to his breast" (354). But this is not his final confession, even to her. He provides the "story" Natalia wants when he sends her his journal, after adding some pages that are directly addressed to her and contain a distorted, self-demonizing account of his feelings when he first met her. The English narrator observes that these pages are sometimes "incoherent" (357); more significantly, the narrator hadn't trusted their testimony enough to incorporate it into his own earlier accounts of the first meeting. The pages abound in mystical and fatalistic references to "Providence" and "the power of destiny": Razumov tells Natalia that "It was only later on that I understood – only today, only a few hours ago" that she was "appointed to undo the evil" (358), and even writes that, although he is "not converted", the revolutionists "have the right on their side! – theirs is the strength of invisible powers. So be it" (361).

Although Razumov addresses Natalia as "You alone in all the world to whom I must confess" (361), he has already determined that he must next confess to the assembled revolutionists. This final confession is no more truthful than his account of his first meeting with Natalia, and is preceded by a parody of Dostoevskean melodrama. "He could have gone out at once," as the narrator drily observes, "but the hour had not struck yet" (362): Razumov is by now so helplessly driven by his fatalistic sense of "the power of destiny" (360) that he must wait until midnight – the hour when Haldin left Razumov's Petersburg lodgings. The "facts and the words" of that "evening in his past were timing his conduct in the present"; the intelligent, keenly sensitive "man with a mind" becomes "the puppet of his past" (362) – in accordance with Conrad's determination to present Russian "modes of feeling", and "the psychology of Russia itself".

So, when Razumov finally confronts the revolutionists, his way of talking about the alcoholic Ziemianitch shows how the very "form of his confession" is also "suddenly, unavoidably suggested by the fateful evening of his life" (365). Ziemianitch never speaks a word in the novel and is comatose the only time we see him; what matters, and makes him a kind of touchstone, is how others regard him. On the "fateful evening" when Haldin appeared in his lodgings and destroyed Razumov's life, Razumov had been disgusted by Haldin's vapid exaltation of Ziemiamitch as a "bright Russian soul". He is still more disgusted when he finally sees the insensible Ziemianitch, and beats him in a hysterical rage. Later, when he learns of Ziemianitch's suicide, Razumov starts sliding into mystical, fatalistic thoughts but can still – just – catch himself: "Hallo! I am falling into mysticism too" (284). In his final conversation with Natalia he can no longer catch himself: he repeats his own view that Ziemianitch "was a brute, a drunken brute", but also describes Ziemianitch as "a man of the people" who was "absolved" through the "efficacy of remorse" (352–3). By this time he can no longer resist "mysticism" and exclaims to Natalia, "That you are a predestined victim … Ha! What a devilish suggestion!" (347). This is the point of no return, when Razumov, "the man with a mind", becomes the "puppet of his past". When he makes his confession to the revolutionists he begins, "I now declare solemnly", and then describes Ziemianitch as "a man of the people – a bright Russian soul" – using Haldin's mystical language he had earlier abhorred, but can no longer resist. To borrow another phrase from Coetzee's essay on confession, Razumov's final, fatal confession is "in the service not of truth but of a deeper desire".[25]

I am of course rejecting those sentimental readings of *Under Western Eyes* that suppose that it finishes like *Crime and Punishment*. Razumov is neither "converted" nor "absolved". "The end of confession is to tell the truth to and for oneself", as Coetzee writes, but Razumov can never do that because he has had a complete breakdown and become the "puppet of his past". He is then too deranged to be *morally* autonomous – but when we say that a very dark paradox emerges. Conrad is pulling his puppet's strings to show what happens to a "man with a mind" who thinks "like a Russian". And yet what Conrad called a "wealth of tenderness" ensures that Razumov is no "puppet": as a character, he is unforgettably, quiveringly alive, and one of the few characters in Conrad who might seem autonomous in the Bakhtinian sense. Indeed, Conrad the novelist often brings Razumov to life most intensely in his moments of suffering and resistance, when the novelist is also working to undermine and finally destroy his character's moral autonomy:

---

[25] Coetzee, "Confession and Double Thoughts", 283.

> He had a distinct sensation of his very existence being undermined in some mysterious manner, of his moral supports falling away from him one by one.
>
> ... The idea of laying violent hands upon his body did not occur to Razumov. The unrelated organism bearing that label, walking, breathing, wearing these clothes, was of no importance to anyone, unless maybe to the landlady. The true Razumov had his being in the willed, in the determined future – in that future menaced by the lawlessness of autocracy – for autocracy knows no law – and the lawlessness of revolution. The feeling that his moral personality was at the mercy of these lawless forces was so strong that he asked himself seriously if it were worth while to go on accomplishing the mental functions of that existence which seemed no longer his own. (76–8)

In late January 1910, when Conrad had finished engineering Razumov's complete breakdown and had his own, the author and "his" character had much to discuss.

The implosive climax of *The Master of Petersburg* shows an author with much to discover, once his character begins to appear. Coetzee's Dostoevsky "unpacks his writing case, sets out his materials", and then sits feeling that he "cannot write, he cannot think" (*MP* 237-8). Although he is alone, he is also trying to make out and "confront" the character who seems to be sitting with him and will eventually emerge as Stavrogin in *The Devils*. This "sense of someone in the room beside himself persists: if not of a full person then of a stick-figure":

> For hours he sits at the table. The pen does not move. Intermittently the stick-figure returns, the crumpled, old-man travesty of himself. He is blocked, he is in prison.
>
>   Therefore? Therefore what?
>
>   He closes his eyes, makes himself confront the figure, makes the image grow clearer. Across the face there is still a veil, which he seems powerless to remove. Only the figure itself can do that; and it will not do so before it is asked. To ask, he must know its name. What is the name? (*MP* 237)

Stavrogin is named, but only in the chapter's title. Readers who already know Dostoevsky's novel will remember how, in the hours before his suicide, Stavrogin sat in his study, alone but confronting his demon or hallucination or even – since Coetzee's final chapter prompts this chilling double-take – creator. The unformed "figure" in Coetzee's novel comes to the author not as a formed invention but as a *revenant*, or crystallizing deposit that will incorporate different elements of Dostoevsky and Pavel; Coetzee's novel assembles different details that are to be creatively recycled in the novel his Dostoevsky has not yet written. The historical Dostoevsky's stepson Pavel outlived Dostoevsky, but in Coetzee's novel Pavel has died and the grieving Dostoevsky is chasing the "rumour of a ghost, the ghost of a rumour": he asks himself "Why", and replies to himself, "Because I am he. Because he is I" (*MP* 53). The most sinister "rumour" is that Pavel, like the student in *The Devils*, may have been murdered by the revolutionist Nechaev, but in

The Master of Petersburg as in *The Devils* we never learn the truth about whether Nechaev is a murderer or whether there even was a murder. The final chapter of Coetzee's novel suggests that his "Dostoevsky" has all the while been "chasing" an as yet uncreated fictional character.

When Coetzee's Dostoevsky realizes this he bitterly arraigns himself (and the creative process) for "betrayal", that is, for putting intimately personal matters to "another use":

> No longer a matter of listening for the lost child calling from the dark stream, no longer a matter of being faithful to Pavel when all have given him up. Not a matter of fidelity at all. On the contrary, a matter of betrayal – betrayal of love first of all, and then of Pavel and the mother and child and everyone else.
>
> *Perversion*: everything and everyone to be turned to another use, to be gripped to him and fall with him.
>
> He remembers Maximov's assistant and the question he asked: 'What kind of book do you write?' He knows now the answer he should have given: 'I write perversions of the truth. I choose the crooked road and take children into dark places. I follow the dance of the pen. (*MP* 235–6)

This is a very dark self-arraignment, and yet, in the terms of Bakhtin's account of Dostoevsky's poetics, the "betrayal" is also a liberation; giving up Pavel, which Dostoevsky guiltily regards as a "betrayal", is the necessary condition of Stavrogin's emergence or incarnation.

When, in the passage quoted above, Coetzee writes "He is blocked, he is in prison", it is not immediately clear whether the imprisoned "he" is the stymied Dostoevsky or the "figure" he cannot make out and bring into being. That confusion seems deliberate, indeed laden, but in English the use of third-person pronouns without a clear antecedent is a frequent source of confusion.[26] In *Slow Man* one attempt to forestall such confusion is very much a linguist's joke, since it involves authorial parentheses that are clearly not needed by or emerging from either of the two characters who are considering the frightful decision to amputate above the knee: "He (Dr Hansen) hopes that he (Paul Rayment) will come to accept the wisdom of that judgment" (*SM* 7). As readers, we expect writers to avoid the kind of ambiguity that these parentheses remove, but don't expect an author to bob in

---

[26]   To take a somewhat mischievous example, Stephen Greenblatt's interpretation of *Othello* in *Renaissance Self-Fashioning* is predicated on a demonstrable misreading of Iago's "he is too familiar with his wife". Iago's "he" obviously refers to Cassio, and "his" to Othello; but for Greenblatt the alleged "ambiguity is felicitous" because the "dark essence of Iago's whole enterprise" is to "play upon Othello's buried perception of his own sexual relations with Dedemona as adulterous". See Stephen Greenblatt, *Renaissance Self-Fashioning: From More to Shakespeare* (Chicago: University of Chicago Press, 1980), 233; and, for an unconvinced commentary, my *Misrepresentations: Shakespeare and the Materialists* (Ithaca: Cornell University Press, 1993), 196–8.

to remind us of his, and indeed our own, presence and activity. But which author bobs in here, Coetzee or Costello?

That question can sometimes be answered, if we work at it. In chapter 13, when Elizabeth enters the novel in person, her declared concern is to know what her character will do next; she is already considering a plot in which Marianna is a possible partner for Paul, since Paul has developed what Elizabeth regards and mocks as an "unsuitable passion" for Marijana. That these two names are so alike is an obvious intertextual contrivance: readers who know *Measure for Measure* and *If on a Winter's Night a Traveller* will recall Shakespeare's Mariana and her bedtrick, and Calvino's Marana. This is evidently Coetzee's not Costello's joke, since Elizabeth insists that the "other Marijana, the nurse woman, was not my idea": "Nothing to do with me" (*SM* 99).

Or, to take another, far more intricate example: in a first reading of *Slow Man* we cannot know what to make of this passage in chapter 2:

> Something is coming to him. A letter at a time, *clack clack clack*, a message is being typed on a rose-pink screen that trembles like water each time he blinks and is therefore quite likely his own inner eyelid. E-R-T-Y, say the letters, then F-R-I-V-O-L, then a trembling, then E, then Q-W-E-R-T-Y, and so on.
>
> *Frivole*. Something like panic sweeps over him. (*SM* 3)

When the word is not quite complete Paul is "trembling", and then feels "panic" when the word is completed in French, the language he spoke in childhood (he thinks he had a childhood). He recalls *frivole* later, but as something that had come to him earlier – "on Magill Road", when the accident took place, not in the hospital bed:

> Frivolous. How he had strained, that day on Magill Road, to attend the word of the gods, tapped out on their occult typewriter ...
>
> Yet *frivolous* is not a bad word to sum him up, as he was before the event and may still be. (*SM* 19)

Much later, when Costello asks him "How did you feel as you tumbled through the air?" he replies that he felt "sad": "My life seemed frivolous. What a waste, I thought" – and she mocks this: "Sad ... he feels sad. His life seems frivolous, in retrospect. What else?" The character then observes the author's lack of interest:

> What else? Nothing else. What is the woman fishing for?
>
> But the woman seems to have lost interest in her question. (*SM* 83)

I shall return to this later, in suggesting that *Slow Man* could also have been called *Slow Woman*; my immediate point is that it seems clear that Elizabeth was not typing "F-R-I-V-O-L" on the "occult typewriter".

After the amputation, when pain prevents him from sleeping, Paul reflects:

> *This* – this strange bed, this bare room, this smell both antiseptic and faintly urinous –
> this is clearly no dream, it is the real thing, as real as things get. (*SM* 9)

A few pages later, when Paul is still struggling with his pain, the narrational mode seems for a moment to shift as though the author – one of the authors – were correcting the character:

> Pain is nothing, he tells himself, just a warning signal from the body to the brain.
> Pain is no more the real thing than an X-ray photograph is the real thing. But of
> course he is wrong. Pain is the real thing ... (*SM* 12)

But the completion of that last sentence restores the narrational mode, as if to reassure us that the author is not intruding his – or her – judgment:

> Pain is the real thing, it does not have to press hard to persuade him of that, it
> does not have to press at all, merely to send a flash or two; after which he quickly
> settles for the confusion, the bad dreams. (*SM* 12)

But then what of that earlier reflection, that this "is the real thing, as real as things get"? Phrases like "he tells himself" are fictional devices, not historical testimony; they are *written*. Paul's life as a fictional character starts when he flies through the air and is so terribly hurt. But since Paul thinks he is real and had a long earlier life that the accident ruined, Paul the character is telling himself that the hospital horrors are as real "as things get in the real world". Every reader knows that this is not the real world, and that the ward and Paul's shock, pain and horror are only as "real" as "things" in a *novel* can get – perhaps all the more "real" and powerfully affecting because, as we are reading it, the novel is reminding us that although the fictional horrors and pains are not real they are all too familiar in the real world.

Consider the question Paul asks when he comes to in the hospital:

> He awakes in a cocoon of dead air. He tries to sit up but cannot; it is as if
> he were encased in concrete. Around him whiteness unrelieved: white ceiling,
> white sheets, white light; also a grainy whiteness like old toothpaste in which his
> mind seems to be coated, so that he cannot think straight and grows desperate.
> "What is this?" he mouths or perhaps even shouts, *What is this that is being done
> to me?* (*SM* 3–4)

Many readers might ask the same question, when they realize that "Paul" is not only in hospital, he is coming into being as print on the otherwise unrelieved grainy whiteness of the page. Another trick is in question, but since the word "trick" is so trivializing – Renaissance readers might have spoken of a "conceit", and felt *admiratio*, or "wonder" – it is worth remembering how one of the most harrowing moments in drama turns (all the more harrowingly) on a trick, when

Lear is protesting against what is being *done to him*, and even tries to negotiate with his creator:

> *Lear.*   She's dead as earth ...
> *Kent.*   Is this the promis'd end?
> *Edgar.*   Or image of that horror?
> *Albany.*   Fall and cease.
> *Lear.*   This feather stirs; she lives! If it be so,
>   It is a chance which does redeem all sorrows
>   That ever I have felt.[27]

Of course this kind of reflexivity constantly recurs in Shakespeare, as when Hamlet speaks of this distracted globe (his skull, Earth, the distracted audience in the Globe). Here, the broken Lear's tortured idea of a *redeeming chance* (Is anyone in charge?) turns into the hopelessly unanswerable *"Why* should a dog, a horse, a rat, have life, / And thou no breath at all? (306–7; my emphasis), which later turned into the old examination chestnut, "Why does Cordelia die?" – a question with too many answers. In the play's "world" Cordelia dies because she is hanged, and because too much time passes when Edmund invites his loquacious brother to "speak", and because it is then too late, though only just too late, when the "great thing by all of us forgot" is remembered. A very different answer to the question "Why does Cordelia die?" emerges if we reflect that she does not die like this in any of Shakespeare's sources: Shakespeare has decided that she must die in his play, and die in what so pointedly is but is also not an "accident".

   In the contingent, undetermined world that we like to call "real" accidents happen all the time, but it is extraordinarily difficult to present accidents in works of art in a convincing way because readers or spectators know that works of art are worked, and then ask *why* this "accident" is happening: if that question has an answer the "accident" was no accident. Wanting to know why a fictional accident happens reveals the extent to which we think about what an *author* is doing even when, and sometimes because, we are intensely engaged with fictional characters and their "world". We wait impatiently for Lydgate to meet Dorothea, for Levin to meet Anna Karenina, and wonder why their creators are postponing these encounters. We wonder why there are so many clearly contrived coincidences in *Dr Zhivago* and so many cruel coincidences in *Jude the Obscure*. In other words, we think about the author's relation not only to his or her characters, but to us. This involves setting up astonishingly complicated "mental spaces", but, as Barbara Dancygier argues in Chapter 12 of this volume, that is what we constantly do in "real" life.

   "Think how well you started," Elizabeth Costello complains to Paul: "What a sad decline ever since! Slower and slower ..." (*SM* 100). The excellent start in

---

[27]   William Shakespeare, *King Lear*, ed. Kenneth Muir (London: Methuen, 1966), 5.3.260–61, 263–7.

question was the accident that launches the novel: "What could be better calculated to engage one's attention than the incident on Magill Road", she asks – referring to the accident as an "incident" because from her authorial and self-congratulatory point of view this "incident" was no accident but a finely "calculated" start. When Costello goes on to refer to Paul's "sad decline ever since" she is referring to what she regards as Paul's "unsuitable passion" for Marijana. She already has her own plotty "alternative to propose", when she urges Paul to "Forget about Mrs Jokic and your fixation with her" (*SM* 95). The "other Marijana, the nurse woman", she insists, "was not my idea" (*SM* 99), but

> Marianna has possibilities, with her devastated face and the remorseful lust that grips her. Marianna is quite a woman. The question is, are you man enough for her? (*SM* 100)

As this sales pitch suggests, there is a profound contradiction between Elizabeth's offers of freedom or autonomy:

> It does not have to be this way, Paul. I say it again: this is your story, not mine. The moment you decide to take charge, I will fade away. (*SM* 100)

and her attempts to direct or propel the character, though with a canny sense of how much better it will be if the character *seems* autonomous:

> Most of the time you won't notice I am here. Just a touch on the shoulder, now and then, left or right, to keep you on the path. (*SM* 87)

She then bullies Paul into agreeing to meet with Marianna, and "bullies" seems the right word if we notice how she does nearly all of the talking in this chapter and Paul feels unable to oppose her or her plotty "alternative":

> He ought to say something sharp, but he cannot, it is as if he is drugged or bemused. (*SM* 98)

So it goes on, until her creator finishes the chapter by recalling *Foe* as well as *The Tempest*:

> "Answer me, Paul. *Say* something."
>   It is like a sea beating against his skull. Indeed, for all he knows he could already be lost overboard, tugged to and fro by the currents of the deep. The slap of water that will in time strip his bones to the last sliver of flesh. Pearls of his eyes; coral of his bones. (*SM* 100)

When Paul makes love with Marianna he very naturally feels, "What a pleasure, and how unexpected, to have the freedom of a woman's body again", but, like Shakespeare's Angelo when he has slept with his Mariana, Paul never wants to repeat this experience – not because he resembles Angelo in any other respect but because he loves the adorable Marijana, who was "not" Elizabeth's "idea" ("Nothing to do with me"). In the next chapter he feels that he has been "unfaithful" (*SM* 125) and subjects Elizabeth to a long angry "tirade":

> "You treat me like a puppet," he complains. "You treat everyone like a puppet.
> You make up stories and bully us into playing them out for you." (*SM* 117)

Costello the novelist's projected, plotty plot then goes bung, but Costello's unhappiest moment as a character comes later, when she is urging Paul to take Emma Bovary as a role model and give his "passion" for Marijana "a whirl" (*SM* 228–9).

Elizabeth Costello had shown how the courageous, unhappy Costello can recognize and confront profound moral issues; but *Slow Man* shows how, like most people who are strong on moral issues, Costello prefers to choose her own. Earlier, when she was urging Paul to "forget" Marijana and try Marianna, her proposed "alternative", she warned that his "unsuitable passion" could only end unhappily (like *Emma Bovary*). Now, when she selfishly urges Paul to "give it a whirl" Costello is no longer concerned with whatever may happen to Marijana and her family, or to Paul: she just wants Paul to *do* something, anything, whatever it takes, for her to get her novel. Paul very naturally longs to be Marijana's lover but is far more concerned than Elizabeth not to do anything that would hurt the Jokics family; when Elizabeth learns of Paul's wish to become a kind of family "godfather", she mocks him again. To do that would just be, in her view, another way of doing nothing. She cannot see that to do that would be doing something, and something that might to some extent answer to Paul's love for Drago as well as his mother, and to his gnawing sense that his childless life has been "frivolous", "a waste". Some novelists might be drawn to this as a subject – not D.H. Lawrence, who blamed Anna and Vronsky's failure on Tolstoy and would not have returned Isabel Archer to her husband, but perhaps Henry James, who would probably have wanted Lady Chatterley to return to her husband, or even, for more complicated reasons, J.M. Coetzee. But Elizabeth has been trying and failing to write a different novel, full of "incident" and "passion".

She cannot succeed, firstly because the "accident" that she regards as a finely calculated "incident" was also – to recall Bakhtin's important concept of "eventness" – an *event*, charged with different, contingent possibilities in the present (how it is *presented*), and for the past (how the *re*presentation might be explained), and in the future (where the event has different possible outcomes). Coetzee's preferred mode of present-tense, third-person but intensely focalized narration is of course perfectly adapted to represent what Bakhtin calls "eventness". In *Under Western Eyes* the range of possible futures for Razumov contracts as soon as he finds Haldin in his lodgings; after this crucial event, the character's fate is determined by Conrad's diagnosis of this novel's "world". But Paul determines that his future will not be determined by "the Costello woman". To recall Dostoevsky's essay on Poe again, the extreme situation into which Costello has contrived to place Paul admits different possible outcomes, some of which Costello cannot foresee. She resists, mocks or cannot handle – cannot *imagine* – Paul's emergent feelings for Marijana and Drago, or his growing sense that his life has been "frivolous", "a waste". Instead, she keeps telling Paul that he is slow, cold, uninteresting – charges that critics recycle without looking more closely at Costello as a character, as well as an old-fashioned novelist whose novels Paul cannot read. Paul is then driven to become more autonomous because his ostensible creator *cannot* bring him into being.

So Paul has to work out his own way of expressing his love for Marijana, not by trying to take the woman he wants but by trying to give her and her children what they need. This may not work, life being what it is, but Marijana herself shows that it can be done when she warms and transforms every life she touches. The novel that then emerges is utterly unlike the novel Costello has been trying and failing to write, and comes to its jubilant climax when little Ljuba gives Paul "a smile, the first she has ever given" and says, "You aren't Rocket Man, you're Slow Man!" – and then "breaks into giggles, and embraces her mother's thighs, and her face" (*SM* 258).

By this time Costello has discovered, by witnessing, what her increasingly autonomous character wants to do, and be. She then proposes to him, asking him to become her companion and live with her in Melbourne. He rejects her, in a dialogue that turns on issues I discussed in the first part of this essay. "If all else fails", Elizabeth says, "I will check myself into a nursing home. Though the kind of care I seek is, alas, not provided in any nursing home I am aware of":

> "And what kind of care might that be?"
>
> "Loving care."
>
> "Yes, that is hard to come by nowadays, loving care. You might have to settle for mere good nursing. There is such a thing as good nursing, you know. One can be a good nurse without loving one's patients. Think of Marijana."
>
> "So that would be your advice: settle for nursing. I disagree. If I had to elect between good nursing and a pair of loving hands, I would elect the loving hands any day."
>
> "Well, I do not have loving hands, Elizabeth."
>
> "No you do not. Neither loving hands nor a loving heart. A heart in hiding. That is what I call it. How are we going to bring your heart out of hiding?- that is the question." (*SM* 261)

I would have liked to describe *Slow Man* as a sometimes grave, always tender and witty Bakhtinian comedy about the conditions of "real", as well as fictional, moral autonomy, but Coetzee's attitude to Bakhtin is critical: "what is missing in Bakhtin", he writes, is any "clear statement" that Dostoevskean "dialogism (or its Bakhtinian near-synonym 'polyphony')" is "a matter not of ideological position, still less of novelistic technique, but of the most radical intellectual and even spiritual courage".[28] Coetzee is paying tribute to the way in which, to take an obvious and exemplary instance, Dostoevsky's creative summoning of a character like Ivan Karamazov went far beyond the intentions, plans and sketches that are recorded in his *Notebooks* for *The Brothers Karamazov*. In *Narrative and Freedom: The Shadows of Time*, Gary Saul Morson shows how Bakhtin's concern with the autonomy, or relative but real freedom, of fictional characters also had an urgent moral and political, anti-determinist and therefore anti-Marxist, dimension that Bakhtin could not treat explicitly in his study of Dostoevsky; to deny contingency or "eventness" is to surrender moral autonomy and responsibility.[29] This may go some way towards answering Coetzee's charge, at a rather general level, without being enough to resolve the question of how "fully valid, autonomous" characters or "voices" exist within a complex authorial design – like Ivan Karamazov and like Falstaff and Hamlet in their plays, or Shylock and Caliban in their five scenes apiece. Bakhtin always and rather perversely resisted the Shakespearean precedent proposed by Russian critics like Lunacharvsky, who also maintained that, unlike Shakespeare, Dostoevsky was unable to control his own characters or creations; that issue can only be addressed by considering the novel or play as a complex design, and it is not enough to insist, like Bakhtin, that Dostoevsky was unique.[30]

After thumbing through some of Costello's novels and the index of a critical study called *A Constant Flame: Intent and Design in the Novels of Elizabeth Costello*, the unimpressed Paul Rayment wonders, "What is wrong? Cannot she make up characters of her own?" (*SM* 119). "Intent and design", indeed! Costello brings Paul into being, but only to a point where he resists her plans for a novel packed with "passion" and "incident"; and then, perhaps because her imaginative impatience slows her down, the novel she could not write turns into Coetzee's *Slow Man*.

---

[28]   J.M. Coetzee, "Fyodor Dostoevsky", in *Stranger Shores: Essays 1986–1999* (London: Secker & Warburg, 2001), 145.

[29]   Gary Saul Morson, *Narrative and Freedom: The Shadows of Time* (New Haven: Yale University Press, 1994).

[30]   Bakhtin, *Problems of Dostoevsky's Poetics*, 32–6.

Chapter 11
Slow Man and the Real:
A Lesson in Reading and Writing

Zoë Wicomb

In J.M. Coetzee's "As a Woman Grows Older", Elizabeth Costello questions the point of her life's work as a writer. Her daughter, Helen, argues that it is of value "not because what you write contains lessons but because it *is* a lesson",[1] a pronouncement that asserts the heuristic value of reading. *Slow Man*, a novel that makes extraordinary demands on the reader, would seem to offer such a lesson. The text abounds with references to lessons, in which lessons are ostentatiously delivered by characters, present themselves in the unfolding of events, or are disparaged as in Paul Rayment's dismissal: "one can torture a lesson out of the most haphazard sequence of events".[2] This essay, in its attempt to engage with the problem of reading *Slow Man*, suggests that the novel's insistent cross-mixing of reference and phenomenalism is a heuristic device for alerting the reader to the complex relations between author, narrator, and character. It is as a lesson in reading, which is to say re-reading, that *Slow Man* demands the reader's active tracking of the relationship between representation and the real, or rather, levels of the real, and offers insights into the business of writing.

I start with a moment in the text where the character, Paul Rayment, reads the author-character Costello's notebook and finds in it references to his own thoughts. Thus it would seem that he is not an autonomous subject, but rather the product of her imagination. For Paul:

> the mind threatens to buckle ... Is this what it is like to be translated to what at present he can only call *the other side*? ... There is a second world that exists side by side with the first, unsuspected. One chugs along in the first for a certain length of time; then the angel of death arrives ... one tumbles down a dark hole. Then, hey presto one emerges into a second world *identical with the first*, where time resumes and the action proceeds – flying through the air like a cat .... (122)

---

[1]   J.M. Coetzee, "As a Woman Grows Older" *The New York Review of Books* 51.1 (15 January 2004): 11–14, at 6.

[2]   J.M. Coetzee, *Slow Man* (London: Secker & Warburg, 2005), 198. Subsequent page numbers given in parenthesis.

Paul's experience mirrors that of reading the novel. If the story of a man who comes through an accident with an amputated leg chugs along according to our expectations of verisimilitude, the entry of Costello disrupts mimesis, and in its intimations of other levels of reality disorientates the reader. The italics of "*identical with the first*" not only alerts us to graphology, the material aspect of writing, but also to Paul's sensation of "flying through the air like a cat" as a repetition, a re-presentation from the opening paragraph of the novel which we earlier had read as a real event of an accident, or rather, the representation of a real event. Thus the reader, like Paul, is cut loose, as another level of reality is established within the fictional work itself. If the first was presented as a world which we as readers enter, then Paul's "reality" turns out to be that of another world, another level into which he enters through writing.

We should not have been so surprised. Immediately after the accident Paul's emerging consciousness is described in terms of an attempt at writing:

> a letter at a time, *clack, clack, clack*, a message is being typed on a rose-pink
> screen that trembles like water each time he blinks … E-R-T-Y, say the letters,
> then F-R-I-V-O-L, then a trembling, then E, then Q-W-E-R-T-Y, on and on.(3)

We witness the physical aspect of writing, the letters arranged on a keyboard from which the writer taps out words. The letters, "E-R-T-Y", are meaningful, but whilst sounding like a suffix, it is not the correct one, and the word FRIVOL remains incomplete, or followed by an E (*frivole*) hints at Paul's French origins. The letters, Q-W-E-R-T-Y, constitute a shift back to the very beginning of the first line and the first consecutive letters of the keyboard, a pronounceable sequence, although arbitrary in terms of meaning. It speaks thus of beginnings, of the raw material of writing, the real thing in the world from which meaning is made, and from Paul's point of view of the difficulty of coming into being as a character through writing.

The question of whose writing only arises once Costello arrives, and that is when the text demands a re-reading, one that points to an ambiguity: the character appears both to be writing himself and to being written. If Paul thinks that the screen is his own inner eyelid, the word "screen" is also an early reference to photography where a screen in the process of picture-making is the surrogate surface for framing and focusing a previewed image. It is that which interposes between the phenomenological subject and its representation, here still trembling in the process of being formed. Re-reading also highlights an early comment, easily overlooked, on the text being focalized through a character whose fictionality is established as a character in a novel that is necessarily structured by temporality: "From the opening of the chapter, from the incident on Magill Road to the present, he has not behaved well, has not risen to the occasion: that much is clear to him" (14). Much later, when Costello quizzes Paul on how it felt at the time of the accident, she supplies the cliché of death as an apprehension of the whole of your life flashing before you. Paul confirms the experience as a death of sorts:

"My life seemed frivolous", he replies (83). But can we trust the duplicitous author's declared ignorance of how it felt? Does her question not confirm Paul's identity as an already-written character?

We are, of course, not unfamiliar with such self-reflexivity. Every schoolgirl understands the mimetic doubling in Ted Hughes's "The Thought Fox" where the efficacy of the imagination is illustrated in terms of an unambiguous author who is at one with his creation, so that the fox "enters the dark hole of the head" and "the page is printed".[3] There the act of writing is shown to be so complete, the imagination so replete, that the text proclaims a merging of the real and the represented. Paul, however, fails to act and thus to embody characterness; his story cannot be written, and Coetzee's wary representation references a subject in the real world who is not yet fully transformed or animated into a character whose actions should drive the story. In other words, imagination and the writing process is shown to be agonistic. The Paul who rises out of unconsciousness experiences the world as a death – "dead air"; "transported"; "encased in concrete"; "whiteness unrelieved" (3) – and only authorial labour can bring him to life. Elizabeth Costello appears at both the beginning and end as midwife: "Push!" she says in this droll representation of the birth of a text that exists at yet another level of reality (83; 204). Thus she asserts the ambiguities and the lack of clear distinction between their roles. She chides Paul: "Think how well you started. What could be better calculated to engage one's attention than the incident on Magill Road. ... What a sad decline ever since! Slower and slower, till by now you are almost at a halt" (100). Costello, the author, is also both character and midwife who assists in the birth of the text, and Paul, the character, appears at various levels of reality to be pre-authored, expected at some level to be co-author of the text, or to be self-authored, a representation of the way in which a writer finds her character taking on a life of his own, departing from the idea from which he originated.

Italo Calvino's discussion in "Levels of Reality in Literature" is helpful in making sense of the head-spinning conundrum. He speaks of the "layers of subjectivity and feigning that we can discern underneath the author's name, and the various 'I's that go to make up the I who is writing. ... The author-cum-character is both something less and something more than the 'I' of the individual as an empirical subject".[4] Such unpacking and refraction of authorship is of course already referenced in the hybrid genre of Coetzee's own *Boyhood* and *Youth* where "confessing in the third person"[5] also asserts the author's fictionality and alludes to the fluid relationship between author and character, which is also to say between author and the empirical world.

---

[3]   Ted Hughes, "The Thought Fox" (1957), in *The Norton Anthology of Poetry* (New York: W.W. Norton & Co., 1983), 1323.

[4]   Italo Calvino, "Levels of Reality in Literature" in *The Uses of Literature* (New York: Harcourt, Brace & Co., 1986), 101–24, at 111.

[5]   Derek Attridge, *J.M.Coetzee and the Ethics of Reading: Literature in the Event* (Chicago: University of Chicago Press, 2004), pp. 138–61.

In my attempt to reconnect *Slow Man* with things-in-the-world, including texts (for what else can a reader do), and resorting once again to similitude, that which structures the reading and interpretation of texts, I alight upon another contemporary work that produces a similarly vertiginous experience: Rachel Whiteread's sculptures, her trademark architectural scale objects, like "House" in London. What links their works is the concept of substitution, and I will go on to argue for substitution as a key device in Coetzee's articulation of the real. In Whiteread's "House" she substitutes for a real house on the Roman Road in London a casting of its interior, which demands that the viewer reimagine the original, real house from its negative. For the viewer such disclosure of normally concealed space is analogous to Coetzee substituting for a narrative the interior, normally hidden mechanisms and problems of writing a novel. Both works as I will discuss later, find a common emblem in photography.

The following commentary on Whiteread's practice precisely captures the experience of reading *Slow Man*. "Casting," Fiona Bradley notes, "like photography, combines that which is present with that which is absent/other – the residue of the original which advances and retreats in the mind of the viewer",[6] a phenomenon also experienced by Paul as he struggles with consciousness, or with being written. Whiteread does not cast objects, but rather the space they occupy, the negative space inside them, so that the sculptures, occupying different kinds of relationships with the "real" object, also reference different levels of the real.[7] The condition of entropy that according to Paul Rayment rules the world (119) is experienced by the reader of *Slow Man* where Coetzee dramatizes the real difficulties that beset the writer trying to produce a story from an initial, inchoate idea. In the process of doing so, the house of fiction, like Whiteread's architectonic cast object, is turned inside out. Coetzee's Marianna, the blind woman with whom the blindfolded Paul has sex, wears her dress "inside out, with the dry-cleaning instructions protruding like a bold little flag" (36). This I consider as emblem for *Slow Man* which, staging the writer's problem of how to proceed with a story and with a character who necessarily arrives inchoate, turns itself inside out, leaving its scaffolding intact and laying bare its own uncertain procedures, its own construction. Thus like the viewer of Whiteread's "House" *in situ* of a thing turned inside out in its casting, the reader of this novel must negotiate between the presence of the given text and absence of a narrative promised at the beginning and expected through the conventions of fiction. The real then is experienced at

---

[6]   Fiona Bradley, "Introduction", in *Rachel Whiteread: Shedding Life* (Liverpool: Tate Gallery Liverpool, 1997), 8–17, at 11.

[7]   A subsequent Whiteread work, the Holocaust memorial in Vienna's Judenplatz, is derived from a cast of the interior of a library. The resulting monolithic cube is an impenetrable structure of shelves turned inside out so that the spines of the books face inward, and what is normally concealed on the bookshelf forms the surface of the sculpture. The sculptural conundrum is that of a bookshelf turned inside-out, but in terms of a library, the structure is one of outside-in, a reversal of "House".

different levels and from different angles, demanding what Roland Barthes calls a "cubist reading" of the realistic portrait.[8]

Whiteread makes material that which normally exists as structured space. If the cast replaces what is lost – for in making the cast of a house, or bed, or bookshelf, she has to destroy the real object – *Slow Man* too trades in flamboyant substitutions, offering dizzying levels of reality for the reader to negotiate. Costello's entry or eruption into the narrative voids the first level of reality, casting off the stabilizing muffler of realism. She comes as a weary *deus ex machina* who, it turns out, is not up to the job, so that ultimately we are given multiple crossings over and are steered through a continuous slippage between reference and phenomenalism. And as Costello's position in the narrative shifts, fictionality turning inwards asserts itself more emphatically and leaves the reader to orientate herself within the various levels of reality.

The interpretation of signs is of course interwoven with the representation of reality, and in *Slow Man* we do not have to hunt for signs: they are given, but rather than referencing things in the world, they refer to the novel itself. Towards the end of the novel Costello tells Paul, "Your missing leg is just a sign or symbol or symptom, I can never remember which is which, of growing old, old and uninteresting" (229), a dismissal which at a first reading I find reasonable and set aside as unremarkable. Events in the novel are after all bracketed by reference to signs. There is the flag of Mariana's dress label at the beginning, and at the end the substitute for a substitute, a recumbent bicycle, with orange "pennant", or flag, built by the nurse's son, Drago, as substitute for the prosthesis that Paul refuses (255). These signs of signs, literally flagged in the text, would seem to indicate the infinite regress of sign reproducing the object that is represented by the sign. Or so an early reading suggests.

In this story then of Paul Rayment, the amputee who develops a passion for his nurse Marijana, Costello is introduced as an agent to deal with the unsuitability of the passion, and thus to move on a story that threatens either to go in an unsuitable direction or to grind to a halt. Through substituting in loud post-colonial fashion for the discreet author of European realism, Costello throws into question the very nature of mimesis. And one of the hermeneutic keys that is paradoxically flagged is substitution, a concept which structures the novel and at the same time admits to a problem within substitution: Costello herself has to be narrated; as a character who interrupts a narrative, she cannot replace the narrative agent employed by Coetzee, but rather, existing as she does at another level of reality, she is at the same time supplementary, and would seem to illustrate what Derrida discusses as the

> internal division within *mimesis*, a self-duplication of repetition itself, *ad infinitum* ... Perhaps then there is more than one kind of *mimesis*, and perhaps it is in the strange mirror that reflects but also displaces and distorts one *mimesis*

---

[8]   Roland Barthes, *S/Z* (New York: Hill & Wang, 1975), 61.

into another, as if it were itself destined to mime or mask *itself*, that history – the history of literature – is lodged, along with the whole of its interpretation. Everything would then be played out in the paradoxes of the supplementary double: the paradoxes of something that, added to the simple and single, replaces and mimes them, both like and unlike.[9]

I now list some of these substitutions in the novel, in events as well as in its emblems, and attempt to show how they relate to representation, including the connection with language itself, from textuality right down to the level of the symbol, the letter which may or may not be a phoneme.

1.   Costello substitutes for an author who must solve the diegetic problems of the story as if they were events in the real world. But why? Readers are after all familiar with "unsuitable passions" and their consequences in fiction; we do not, like the naive natives in Jane Campion's *The Piano*, lunge at a character on stage to prevent him from chopping off another character's hand. Yet, here sophisticated readers who, according to Paul de Man, would not dream of trying "to grow grapes by the luminosity of the word 'day'"[10] are boldly confronted with the slippage between reference and phenomenalism as a given. But, in a further resort to similitude, we should also remember wincing as the mute central character in *The Piano* has her fingers chopped off "for real" towards the end of that narrative.

2.   The visual relationship between Costello and Coetzee's names is enigmatic and supports the first substitution; it is also a reminder of the graphic aspect of writing. The crucial role of substitution in making visible similitude in poetic parallelism, where a degree of repetition coexists with difference, is visible here at the level of the letter. The patterning in the following,

$$\underline{C}\,\underline{O}\,\underline{E}\,\underline{T}\,\underline{Z}\,\underline{EE} -$$
$$\underline{C}\,\underline{O}\,\underline{S}\,\underline{T}\,\underline{E}\,\underline{LL}\,O,$$

with its repetitions, substitutions and centrally positioned chiasmus (the crossed Es and phonic repetition/difference in "S" and "Z") serves to foreground the author function – as well as what Calvino calls "the layers of subjectivity and feigning underneath the author's name".[11] The S/Z axis reminds us of Barthes's focus on the process of reading and the crucial role assigned to intertextuality in the production of meaning, although chiasmic reversal also cautions against uncritical

———
9   Peggy Kamuf (ed), *A Derrida Reader: Between the Blinds* (Hemel Hempstead: Harvester Wheatsheaf, 1991), 176–7.
10   Paul de Man, *The Resistance to Theory* (Minneapolis: University of Minnesota Press, 1986), 11.
11   Calvino, "Levels of Reality in Literature", 111.

reading of Barthes. The final or extra "O" then could be read as supplementarity in Costello or as ellipsis in Coetzee, grammatical ellipsis itself being a form of substitution in which an item is replaced by nothing. Discourse analysis shows that lexical substitution and ellipsis assume crucial roles in achieving textual cohesion; it is also worth noting that ellipsis leaves specific structural slots to be filled from elsewhere in a text. The character, Paul, on whose cooperation the author is so abjectly dependent, would seem to be a strong candidate.

3.   When Costello arrives and recites/repeats the opening paragraph of the novel – this time in italics – the disruption of mimesis is also achieved through verbal substitution. The lexical item, "tumbles" (*through the air*), substitutes for "flies" (81), and later in the same exchange, in free indirect discourse, Paul offers a further substitution: "[s]oaring through the air" in plain text (83). Such minimal substitution indicates repetition with a difference, and italics are repeatedly used in the text to flag supplementarity.

4.   Phonology alerts us to the theme of forgery in the homophonic Fauchery photographs. Drago substitutes the digitally doctored photographs for the originals. Specifically, a Jokic grandfather substitutes for one of the Irish/Cornish miners, and Ljuba substitutes for one of the children in front of the settlers' mud and wattle cabin, a scene of poverty that Paul finds particularly poignant. Through substitution Drago inserts the Croatian immigrants into the Australian national memory so that the photograph literally binds the past with the future. I will return to photography as a device in Coetzee's exploration of the real.

5.   Prosthesis, or the substitution of a real leg for an artificial one, which Rayment refuses, is (like Whiteread's house) present in the story as an absence. Attention is drawn to the word as early as page 7 when Paul repeats after the doctor: "'[P]rosthesis,' he says, another difficult word". Prosthesis is also a linguistic term for the addition of a letter or syllable at the beginning of a word to facilitate pronunciation, or for prosodic reasons – a supplementarity that complicates the question of reference in phonology. In addition, linguistic prosthesis is known as, or substitutes for, the word prothesis (ellipsis of the "s"), which has a second meaning that relates directly to *Slow Man* as a display text. Prothesis means setting out in public, and refers to the Eastern Orthodox church where elements of the eucharist are set out at the credence table, where bread and wine substitute for the body and blood of Christ; in other words, where the real is transformed. It is then through language and wordplay that one mimesis is displaced into another, and the doubling effect of substitution serves to highlight ambiguities within the notion of the real. Transformation in the eucharist relies of course on belief, a commodity in the shape of suspension of disbelief that is required for the successful reception of a fictional text. And for the writer, the pursuit of an inchoate idea too is an act of faith: what is required is belief that the surprising or seemingly irrational events

or images that arise in the act of writing will eventually link with other elements in a meaningful way.

6.   Costello's solution to Paul's unsuitable passion is to substitute Marijana with Marianna, the dejected, blind woman. The difference between speech and writing is evoked: the names sound the same so that Costello has to specify – Marianna "with two *ns*", thus drawing our attention to print and representation, rather than to the women of phenomenalism. Thus through substitution the text refutes a simple relationship between the thing and its representation: the inchoate Marianna clearly does not occupy the same degree of reality as the woman she substitutes for. Her shadowy nature, her improbable behaviour, as well as the bizarre blindfolding suggest a character whom the author fails to develop and thus has to abandon; her fictionality is encoded in Paul's first encounter with what he calls "the crone leading the hastily clad princess in an enchanted sleepwalk" (36).

7.   The name, Marianna, recalls substitutions in *Measure for Measure* where Angelo, who substitutes for the Duke, pursues his illicit desire for Isabella. The Duke engineers the substitution of Isabella with the "dejected" Mariana (of one "n"), and the sexual act that takes place in the dark echoes Paul Rayment, blindfolded and manipulated by Costello, having sex with another dejected Marianna, whose name with the double "n" points to substitution that is also the supplementary double of mimesis. As the Mari(j)an(n)as displace one mimesis into another, Paul's offer of money to the Jokics is shown to substitute for Angelo's mercy-for-sex. Angelo's callous sexual behaviour is again echoed later in *Slow Man* when Paul confesses that he once took to bed an unattractive employee who had fallen in love with him: "I left a note for her: a time, a place, nothing else. She came and I took her to bed" (200). Costello, substituting the unattractive "rugby player" for Marijana, is appalled by this story. She asks:

> "Your rugby player had enough love for two, you say. Do you really think love can be *measured*? That as long as you bring a case of it, the other party is permitted to come empty-handed – empty-handed, empty hearted? Thank you Marijana (Marijana with a *j* this time), for letting me love you … Thank you for letting me give you my money. Are you really such a dummy?" (202, my italics)

These variations on the name of Mariana illustrate Barthes's point about the proper name acting as a magnetic field for the semes,[12] its meanings accrued through a variety of intertexts. Perhaps the most pertinent of these is the echo of the name in Calvino's character, Marana, translator in *If on a Winter's Night a Traveller*. If *Slow Man* does not endorse that text's desire to absorb experience into a totalizing concept of language, or its overarching concern with the role of the reader, it nevertheless alludes to the Marana who produces counterfeit texts,

---

12   Barthes, *S/Z*, 67.

substitutes manuscripts, and mixes works and authors. Marana believes that "the author of every book is a fictitious character whom the existent author invents to make him the author of his fictions". The first person narrator in *If on a Winter's Night*, could be seen to be identical with Calvino, explains that Marana is interested in him "first, because I am an author who can be faked; and second, because he thinks I have the gifts necessary to be a great faker, to create perfect apocrypha".[13] The question of real and fake which is overtly addressed in *Slow Man* will be discussed later.

*   *   *

From a post-colonial perspective, intertextuality as a way of reading offers more than an openness of the text and the productive role of the reader; it operates also as a form of substitution aimed at re-presentation. *Slow Man*'s dramatization of the problem of what to do with characters who arrive inchoate and for whom a history has to be created is also staged via intertexts from the author's own oeuvre – the introduction of textual echoes, images, and repetition of strategies from, for instance, *Foe* and *Elizabeth Costello*.[14] Similarly, not only do Rachel Whiteread's analogous sculptures revise and re-present buildings or objects, but there is, as Stuart Morgan notes, "a strong sense of interplay between separate sculptures … .a rich dialogue ensues between one piece and the next".[15] In other words, both artists plunder events and images from their previous works in order to revisit the questions of authorship and the ambiguous relationship between representation and the real.

For *Slow Man* on the whole, the internal, hidden mechanisms of producing a narrative and the research that precedes writing substitute for a narrative. Having turned itself inside out, the novel reveals its halting construction which substitutes for the story and at the same time constitutes the story. Substitution then, is multi-functional: serving the interest of the real, and by definition a version of the original, it is staged in the text at a variety of levels. In its shifting relationship with language and representation, substitution insists on engagement with the real which is, however, shown to be heterogeneous, shifting, elusive and illusionary. Again, Whiteread's house which substitutes for a real house, and which allows for the viewer's *simultaneous* apprehension of both the house of phenomenalism and

---

[13]   Italo Calvino, *If on a Winter's Night a Traveller* (London: Picador, 1982), 142.

[14]   *Elizabeth Costello* was preceded by a real performance in 1996, when Coetzee on invitation by PEN International in London delivered what promised to be a talk on the subject of "What is Realism?" On that occasion, Coetzee the real author/speaker substituted the genre of the lecture with a story about a fictional Australian writer, Elizabeth Costello, who delivers an acceptance speech on the subject of realism.

[15]   Stuart Morgan, "Rachel Whiteread", in *Rachel Whiteread: Shedding Life*, 19–28, at 23.

the not-house work of art is helpful here. The representation is at the same time supplementary; it supervenes upon the real; these works while insisting upon the real at the same time do not allow the traditional notion of the real as that which is distinct from and which precedes mimesis. Instead, we see Derrida's paradox of the supplementary double: "something that added to the simple and single, replaces and mimes them, both like and unlike".[16]

If substitution in the above instances point variously to replacement, reversal, ellipsis, trickery, ambiguity, excess, or supplementarity, it is also significantly bound up with transformation. The linguistic shift from prosthesis to prothesis references transformation, instantiated in the first place in the figure and name of Paul Rayment, the boy from Lourdes where miracles of healing are available for believers. His very name, Paul, speaks of the conversion of Saul on the Road to Damascus, and there is the promise of further transformation into a fully fledged character who will transcend the flaws of the gloomy, hesitant and abject amputee. Costello has come to save him from himself, but this amounts to little more than nagging him to act: "'This is your story. The moment you decide to take charge I will fade away.'" Her offer of the blind Marianna "is like a sea beating against his skull. ... The slap of water that will in time strip his bones of the last sliver of flesh. Pearls of his eyes; coral of his bones" (100). In spite of Paul Rayment's name referencing Prospero's magic garment, the promise of Shakespearean transformation fails as the sexual act amounts to no more than manipulation by Costello who lacks Prospero's magical omnipotence. Moreover, since Paul resists his author, Marianna too cannot be fully animated into a character, so that the event constitutes a dark cul-de sac in the narrative. But the promise of salvation persists. In Marijana's last visit as a nurse, Paul laments the fact that he is too *labile* (210) for her taste. That, he says, is the word she is hunting for. But labile has another meaning: not only liable to lapse (as is Angelo in *Measure for Measure*) but also liable to undergo displacement in position or change in nature and form – another reference perhaps to prothesis and the eucharist table. In other words, Paul is aware of the potential for transformation that co-exists with the drive to lapse, its mechanisms achievable within language and representation. And yet, the promise of transformation is not kept: when Paul says goodbye to Costello there is no salvation, no resolution on offer. *Slow Man*, after all, remains a novel about the failure of an author to transform her raw material into a credible work of fiction.

The concept of reality to which every representation necessarily refers is also overtly discussed by the characters. Costello arrives as a doubting Thomas, taking Paul's hand to establish his and also her own reality. There are numerous occasions when Paul questions reality: "'Now let me ask you straight out Mrs Costello: Are you real?'" Her reply, "'Of course I'm real. As real as you'" (233), is within the realm of fiction perfectly acceptable. At the same time it confirms the work as fiction, that which is separated from empirical reality and is commonly discussed in terms of a self-reflecting mirror. Not surprisingly then, the cloth that

16   Kamuf, *A Derrida Reader*, 177.

Paul had draped over the mirror in his house has been removed by Costello; this he discovers after she has left when he once again covers the mirror. Later he tells Marijana that everyone should be more labile: "'we should shake ourselves up more often. We should also brace ourselves and take a look in the mirror, even if we dislike what we will see there'" (210). In other words, the reflection is not congruent with what we think of as our "real" selves, thus a lesson inheres in such an act of looking. When Costello repeatedly comments on the Jokics' house with its Japanese garden, – "'So real! ... So authentic! ... Who would have thought it!'" (242) – Paul, who exists on a different level of reality, assumes that she is being ironic. For the reader, however, it is surely a reference to the protean nature of representations, the propensity of fiction to slip beyond the author's control, and to beget further fictions. The Jokics as characters, who arrive via Mrs Putts – that is, not in Costello's original scheme (99) – have, unlike Paul, taken off, and represent a level of reality at which even the author must marvel. The fiction, turned in upon itself, cannot be cut adrift from referentiality; even the illusionary must refer to the world of things, so that the simulacral nature of a Japanese garden in an Australian suburb does not detract from its reality. Costello's problem is that she cannot achieve the same level of reality for her character Paul: "'I stay on,'" she says, "'because I don't know what to do about you'" (155).

The inherently reproductive nature of fiction is shown to have a number of consequences. The disconcerting level of reality introduced by Costello's arrival in the text is followed by a further disruption: the character of Drago moves centre stage to oust Costello, who after all has no story to tell other than to lament the impossibility of advancing with Paul's story. When Paul casts her out, we are also reminded of the first level of mimesis: she is only another fictional character making mischief among characters, rather than omniscient author. She may have arrived with a history for the Jokics, but Miroslav, in telling his history to Paul, adds details that Costello appears not to know. It also transpires that she knows nothing of Paul's childhood; he had come to her "with no history attached" (195). She is a representation of an unreliable author/character, who, for instance, forgets her own story about sleeping rough. It is clearly the case that the story *does* have reference independent of Elizabeth Costello, and that there is another level of mimesis, although these levels, shifting and sliding as they do into each other, are not stable.

The scene by the riverside where she feeds the ducks (an ironic allusion perhaps to The Ugly Duckling's tale of misrecognition and misreading which passes for a tale of transformation), and where a couple pass by in a swan-shaped pedal-boat, offers something of a commentary on the text and its narration. The swan is fake, and although there are indeed "real" people sailing by in a "real" pedal-boat of plastic, the spectacle points to the simulacral, so that we question the nature of this reality. In this scene Costello and Rayment's self-reflexive discussion overtly raises the question of the real. The complexity of a phenomenalist position is sketched out by her: "'let me tell you what you see, or what you tell yourself you are seeing. An old woman by the side of the River Torrens feeding the ducks. ...

But the reality is more complicated than that, Paul. In reality you see a great deal more – see it and then block it out'" (158). Here levels slide into each other as Costello attributes the text to Paul whom we remember is not only character, but also focalizer, the agent who substitutes for the narrator, so that she quotes back at him the opening words of that chapter, "*'He finds her by the riverside...'*", this time represented in italics. In the following, she alludes to a reciprocal relationship between reality and representation; writing does not only imitate, it animates and vitalizes the world:

> it is not good enough. It does not bring me to life. ... it has the drawback of not bringing you to life either. Or the ducks, for that matter, if you prefer not to have me at the centre of the picture. Bring these humble ducks to life and they will bring you to life. (159)

In attributing the text to Paul, Costello suggests that he as focalizer/narrator is another substitute for the author. Calvino's question: "How much of the 'I' who shapes the characters is in fact an 'I' shaped by the characters?"[17] is pertinent. Costello herself has not produced any of the text we read; like all the other characters she too has to be animated through the fiction, and as representation of an author she can only be apprehended through the narration. In the process of writing, characters animate each other, and author and character are interrelated: "'You were sent to me,'" she explains, "'I was sent to you. Why that should be God alone knows'" (161). In this reciprocity, they are both versions of the author function, albeit at different levels of reality, but it is also the promise of intersubjectivity, whether Paul likes it or not, that is asserted, as well as its crucial role in the world-disclosing function of the sign – as Habermas in his argument against postmodernism would have it.

*   *   *

The real in *Slow Man* is bound up not only with substitution, but also with the story's exploration of photography. It is in dialogue with *Camera Lucida* where Barthes speaks of photography as "the Real in its indefatigable expression" precisely because it is never distinguished from its referent. Contrary to the imitations of painting or discourse, he states, it is "the *necessarily* real thing which has been placed before the lens, without which there would be no photograph ... I can never deny *that the thing has been there*".[18] In other words, substitution of the thing by the image does not impinge on the real; rather, the photograph tells for certain (as opposed to writing) what has actually been; it has an evidential force and "its testimony bears not on the object but on time"[19]. This is echoed by Paul

---

[17]   Calvino, "Levels of Reality in Literature", 113.

[18]   Roland Barthes, *Camera Lucida* (London: Vintage, 1993), 76.

[19]   Ibid., 87.

who explains to Drago about the collection of Fauchery photographs which on his death "will become public property. Part of our historical record" (177). Moved by one of the images, Paul speaks of the way in which:

> this distribution of particles of silver that records the way the sunlight fell, one day in 1855, on the faces of two long-dead Irish women, an image in whose making he, the little boy from Lourdes, had no part and in which Drago, son of Dubrovnik, has had no part either, may, like a mystical charm – *I was here, I lived, I suffered* – have the power to draw them together. (177)

What is valorized here is the real, its transformation through photography that not only recalls the actual subjects of the past, but has affective value in the present.

But Barthes himself allows for a chink in his certainty about photography as evidence of the real. There is a foreshadowing of Drago's digital trickery, when Barthes laments the "sensation of inauthenticity" in a portrait photograph where he sees himself as subject become object, a micro-version of death: "others … turn me into an object, they put me at their mercy, at their disposal, classified in a file, ready for the subtlest deceptions", he complains.[20] When he finds the same photograph on the cover of a pamphlet he is distressed by the artifice of printing. It is such artifice, updated by digital technique, that drives the story of *Slow Man* to its ending. Drago has doctored the Fauchery photograph leaving Paul with the substituted forgery, and Costello takes him to the Jokics' house where Marijana is outraged by his demand for the original: "'What is this thing original photography? You point camera, click, you make copy. ... Camera is like photocopier. So what is original? Original is copy already.'" Paul's reply addresses the complex relationship between the real and representation:

> "That is nonsense Marijana. … A photograph is not the thing itself. Nor is a painting. But that does not make either of them a copy. Each becomes a new thing, a new real, new in the world, a new original." (245)

In linking representation with renewal and by implication devaluing the notion of authenticity and origin, Coetzee also avoids the reductive divide between the referential, that is to say Barthes's "*necessarily* real thing", and the simulacral of poststructuralism. Instead, the real is presented as renewable, substitutable, supplementary, and characterized by slippage between reference and phenomenalism. (It is such renewal that Habermas sees as a way out of the infinite regress of the sign.)

Costello's proposal that she and Paul live together comes with further elucidation of the relationship between the real and representation: "'You can tell me more stories …'" she says, "'which I will afterwards tell back to you in a form so accelerated and improved that you will hardly recognise them'" (232). This is

---

[20]   Barthes, *Camera Lucida*, 14.

not as preposterous as it sounds. Paul's account is already a reworking of original events, and what is writing but an endless re-production of words that takes shape also through substitution. Paul's question aptly explains the process: "'Isn't the whole of writing a matter of second thoughts – second thoughts and third thoughts and further thoughts?'" (228). By accelerating and improving his stories, she would be addressing Paul's ponderousness, the characteristic that prevents him from acting.

*   *   *

The final section of the novel directly tackles the question of writing and the relationship between author and character. Costello laments the burden of being "'an old woman who scribbles away, page after page ... damned if she knows why. If here is a presiding spirit ... then it is me he stands over, with his lash'" (233). Art is the tyranny that binds the author to her own creation, to a character who must be animated into action. Costello's description of the partnership, "'For me alone Paul Rayment was born and I for him. His is the power of leading, mine of following; his of acting, mine of writing'" (233) contains the linguistic figures I listed earlier in my sketch of substitutions – chiasmus, parallelism, ellipsis. The absolute authority of the author is relinquished in favour of a figural reciprocity: it is the character with his origins in the real world, who, once animated, takes off and cooperates in producing the diegesis of fiction; in other words, he too ideally assumes an author function. And the notion of animation that introduces a magical, irrational element into creativity, is a long way from Barthes's death of the author.

But Paul Rayment cannot act in the way his author wants him to. The scene at the Jokics' house confirms his resistance to the fiction. Marijana says of Drago's gift, the recumbent: "'It suits you. You should give it a whirl'" (257). Not only is Marijana's own fictionality underlined in the classical posture of thought she adopts in propping up her elbow and holding her chin, but her words establish fiction's relationship with other fictions. They echo Costello's earlier urging that he should act, be less of a tortoise. She chides him: "'*We only live once*, says Alonso, says Emma, *so let's give it a whirl*! Give it a whirl Paul. See what you can come up with'" (229). And in choosing Emma Bovary and Don Quixote as models, with their actual words re-presented in italics, Costello references Calvino's "Levels of Reality in Literature" where the same characters are cited. But Paul resists; he won't be a real character, the subject of a novel, just as he will never use that one-off, custom-made, original construction which is the recumbent.

Such oscillation between fiction and the real is also enacted in the forgery which turns out to be a joke. Indeed, on page 259 where Paul and Costello discuss the visit to the Jokics, the word "joke" occurs nine times, as if we are in danger of forgetting the phonological link with the Croatian family name. Costello, who appeared to have foreknowledge of the trickery, now reveals that the photograph has not disappeared and thus that Drago's manipulation cannot strictly speaking be called a forgery. We may be tempted to ask whether the entire event is not fake, unreal. There are after all discrepancies such as Marijana's comment that Paul should give up the idea of being their godfather, before she reads the letter in which he proposes this. But by now we know that to question whether event or character is real is meaningless in this narrative conundrum with its multiple reflections that converge and collapse on the reader. The simple distinctions between reality and representation as well as between the real and the simulacral have been refracted; we can be certain only of being engaged in reading a fiction that has as its subject the plight of an author writing a fiction that cannot be fleshed out to imitate reality. What is also dramatized is the intersubjectivity between author and character, who always to some extent originates from an existing character whether in fiction or in the real world. The autonomy and omnipotence of the author is itself shown to be a fiction, which is not to say that the author is dead and that the text is constructed entirely by the reader, but rather that a complex web of relations hold between the real and the represented, between the author and the character he or she has animated.

Marijana urges Paul to live with Costello as an antidote to his gloom. She points out that in Croatian the word *glumi* means pretend, not real, the suggestion being that taking up Costello's invitation would be entry to the "real", which is to say into fictionality. But for Paul pretence does not pose a problem. For instance, on their return trip from the Jokics, Costello claims to recognize Drago as one of the young men who flash by on their motorcycles. Paul knows that it is too much of a coincidence but he does not insist on being realistic: "let them pretend nevertheless that the one in the red helmet was Drago. Theatrically he sighs, 'Ah Drago, ah for youth'" (262). And within this dissimulation a truth emerges: the connection between Paul's gloom and the real raises the question of youth's antithesis – the wrecked body that Costello had so cavalierly dismissed as a sign or symbol. It is hard to believe that, as reader, I had so readily and perversely accepted the dismissal. The absence of a leg, which for Paul is the real presence of a stump that the reader encounters in all its raw physicality, could be discussed in terms of what Hal Foster calls traumatic realism, one of the conceptual shifts in contemporary art "from reality as an effect of representation to the real as a thing of trauma".[21]

Costello's final offer to Paul of joining her in Melbourne is of herself as nurse, a substitute of sorts for Marijana. Paul declines; he will not be transformed or redeemed. He chooses to remain a one-legged inchoate character, and they part with sardonic reference to the flags they could attach to their comic vehicles. Costello's flag, he says, would be mottoed as *malleus maleficorum*, a reference to the multi-authored fifteenth-century Counter Reformation text that advocated the persecution of witches, and particularly targeted midwives as the most dangerous

---

[21]   Hal Foster, *The Return of the Real: The Avant-garde at the End of the Century* (Cambridge MA: MIT Press. 1994), 146.

of witches. In other words, a wry comment on the role of the writer, whose task it is to bring characters into being. It is also a wry inversion of the idea of art as apotropaic: how could animation into art avert evil influence or bad luck when an accident at the first level of mimesis had turned Paul Rayment's leg into obscene stump and had tumbled him into another level of fiction, into the hands of the writer/midwife? Paul's refusal then could be read as an assertion of traumatic realism, a refusal to unite the imaginary and the symbolic against the real. In his discussion of trauma discourse, Hal Foster cites Kristeva on the body as primary site of the abject, which she defines as a category of (non-)being, of neither subject nor object, a condition that Paul the amputee claims for himself against Costello's importunities, against her insistence on textuality. Foster's description of appropriation art that pushes illusionism to the point of the real is pertinent to this novel turned inside out : "Here illusionism is employed not to cover up the real with simulacral surfaces, but to *un*cover it in uncanny things".[22] In contemporary art practice, Foster identifies a bipolar postmodernism in which the real, repressed in poststructuralism, returns as traumatic. Both the textual model of culture and the conventional view of reality are dismissed by artists who wish to "possess the obscene vitality of the wound and to occupy the radical nihility of the corpse".[23]

It is the fact that the referent adheres, says Barthes, that makes photography unclassifiable, and thus a condition of disorder. Such entropy also inheres in the fact that no matter how long he contemplates the photograph, it teaches him nothing – there is an arrest of interpretation because of the certainty *this-has-been*.[24] Rosalind Krauss finds Barthes's comments on photography pertinent to a reading of Rachel Whiteread whose congealing of space into a rigidly entropic condition also strips it of any means of being "like" anything. However, her words on the monochrome plaster of Whiteread's casts that "announce their own insufficiency, their status as 'ghosts'"[25] uncannily describe *Slow Man* and its characters. Krauss, by way of commenting on Whiteread, cites Barthes on photography as a kind of death, both structured and asymbolic, in other words paradoxical, which leads him to say, "I have no other resource than this irony: to speak of the 'nothing to say'".[26] If photography's absence-as-presence takes me back to entropy and the concern with death in both Whiteread and *Slow Man*, it also brings me to the irony of an arrest in interpretation: *Slow Man* offers itself as prothesis, lays out on the credence table its own hermeneutic. It waves its flags; there is ultimately nothing hidden; I can only describe what-has-been-read.

22   Ibid., 152.
23   Ibid., 166.
24   Barthes, *Camera Lucida*, 6.
25   Rosalind Krauss, "X Marks the Spot", in *Rachel Whiteread: Shedding Life*, 74–81, at 81.
26   Ibid., 76.

Chapter 12
Close Encounters:
The Author and the Character in
Elizabeth Costello, Slow Man and
Diary of a Bad Year

Barbara Dancygier

Authorship appears to be one of the more contested concepts in contemporary criticism and narratology. While the existence of a body and a mind responsible for the words of a text is tacitly assumed to be the boring fact of extra-textual reality, the relationship between the agency of a writer and the text she or he authors is becoming more and more elusive. The tendency to background the author's assumed intentions and, by the same token, to foreground the text and its situation in some cultural and social context is shared by narratologists and literary theorists, but authors themselves express their own opinions on the matter only occasionally.

It is thus quite striking to note that the three most recent novels by J.M. Coetzee address the question of authorship directly, through their narrative choices. Exploring the boundary between fact and fiction, these are novels about the multiple agencies involved in producing fiction, where the "author" does not necessarily have total control over the characters or the plot. In this essay, I propose a reading of Coetzee's view of various authorial sources of fictional narratives, as emerging from *Elizabeth Costello, Slow Man* and *Diary of a Bad Year*.[1] The analysis will rely on recent work in cognitive science and cognitive poetics uncovering the conceptual underpinnings of the processes of meaning construction. [2]

---

[1]   J.M. Coetzee, *Elizabeth Costello* (London: Secker & Warburg, 2003); *Slow Man* (London: Secker & Warburg, 2005); *Diary of a Bad Year* (London: Harvill Secker, 2007).

[2]   I will rely primarily on the theory of mental spaces and conceptual integration (or blending), introduced in the following: Gilles Fauconnier, *Mental Spaces* (1985), 2nd edn (Cambridge: Cambridge University Press, 1994) and *Mappings in Thought and Language* (Cambridge: Cambridge University Press (1997); Gilles Fauconnier and Mark Turner, "Blending as a Central Process of Grammar", in Adele Goldberg, ed., *Conceptual Structure, Discourse, and Language* (Stanford, CA: CSLI Publications, 1996), 113–30, "Conceptual Integration Networks", *Cognitive Science* 22.2 (1998): 133–87, "Principles of Conceptual Integration", in J.P. Koenig et al., eds, *Discourse and Cognition* (Standord, CA:

All three novels offer penetrating thoughts on the balance between the author and the character and on the very nature of fictional narratives. Coetzee constructs these novels as commentaries on the relationship between fact and fiction and on the role of fiction in our lives. Built into the very structure of the novels, the conceptual constructs proposed force us to rethink the basic assumptions about narrative discourse and reconsider the well-established understanding of authorship. Puzzling and disturbing as these ideas are, they will contribute to modes of thinking about narrative studies for years to come.

Putting Someone in a Book

One of the emerging themes of contemporary prose is questioning the traditional understanding of fiction.[3] Putting aside the narratological concept of verisimilitude,

---

CSLI Publications, 1998), 269–83, and *The Way We Think: Conceptual Blending and the Mind's Hidden Complexities* (New York: Basic Books, 2002); Mark Turner and Gilles Fauconnier, "A Mechanism of Creativity", *Poetics Today* 20.3 (1999): 397–418; and Seana Coulson, *Semantic Leaps: Frame-shifting and Conceptual Blending in Meaning Construction* (New York and Cambridge: Cambridge University Press, 2001). The theory has been applied in a number of different disciplines of social sciences, but it has proved to be an exceptionally rich and powerful tool in literary analysis. It has been used in the analyses of poetry and drama, in English and other languages (e.g., Masako Hiraga, *Metaphor and Iconicity: A Cognitive Approach to Analysing Texts* (New York: Palgrave Macmillan, 2005)), and has opened new perspectives on the interests of stylistics (see Mark Turner, "Compression and Representation", *Language and Literature* 15.1 (2006): 17–29; Elena Semino, "Blending and Characters' Mental Functioning in Virginia Woolf's *Lappin and Lapinova*", *Language and Literature* 15:1 (2006): 55–73; Barbara Dancygier, "Preface: What Can Blending Do for You?", *Language and Literature* 15.1, special issue ed. B. Dancygier (2006): 5–15). It has also proved a revealing tool in the analysis of the narrative: see Todd Oakley, "Conceptual Blending, Narrative Discourse, and Rhetoric", *Cognitive Linguistics* 9.4 (1998): 321–60; Jose Sanders and Gisela Redeker, "Perspective and the Representation of Speech and Thought in Narrative Discourse", in G. Fauconnier and E. Sweetser, eds, *Spaces, Worlds, and Grammars* (Chicago: University of Chicago Press (1996), 290–317; Mark Turner, "Double-scope Stories", in David Herman, ed., *Narrative Theory and the Cognitive Sciences* (Stanford: CSLI Publications, 2004), 117–42; Barbara Dancygier, "Identity and Perspective: the Jekyll-and-Hyde Effect in Narrative Discourse", in Michel Achard and Suzanne Kemmer, eds, *Language, Culture, and Mind* (Stanford: CSLI Publications, 2004), 363–76, "Visual Viewpoint, Narrative Viewpoint, and Mental Spaces in Narrative Discourse", in Augusto Soares da Silva, Amadeu Torres and Miguel Gonçalves, eds, *Linguagem, Cultura e Cogniçao: Estudos de Linguistica Cognitiva*, (Coimbra: Almedina, 2004), vol. 2, 347–62; "Blending and Narrative Viewpoint: Jonathan Raban's Travels Through Mental Spaces", *Language and Literature* 14.2 (2005): 99–127, and "Narrative Anchors and the Processes of Story Construction: The Case of Margaret Atwood's *The Blind Assassin*", *Style* 41.2 (2007): 119–38.

    [3]   Post-classical narratology, as David Herman calls it (see his *Story Logic: Problems and Possibilities of Narrative* (Lincoln, NE, and London: University of Nebraska Press, 2002)

the boundaries between fictional stories and characters on the one hand and the non-fictional ones on the other are openly broken more and more often, and crossed with impunity all the time. From a linguistic and cognitive point of view, the status of such a boundary seems highly suspicious. Even if specific events are made up and words spoken by the characters have never in fact been spoken, there is always the level of narrative construction where realistic or even real details of time, place, or somebody's life constitute an important part of a fictional story. Being an author of works deeply rooted in the realities of his own time, Coetzee could not fail to acknowledge the shadiness of the fiction/fact boundary.

At the same time, Coetzee is also known as an author of writings which are better seen as essays or commentaries, expressing his (often passionate) opinions on important issues of our time, such as the emergence of postcolonial literature or the relationship between humans and animals. When the book *Elizabeth Costello* appeared, Coetzee's own recognition of the potential overlaps between fact and fiction was given a new form. Instead of publishing a collection of his own essays, perhaps with revisions, under his own name, he created a character, Elizabeth Costello, and made her an author of fiction. However, in the book, the reader does not get introduced to any of Costello's fictional writings, but follows her instead through a series of invited lectures, bearing a striking resemblance to some of Coetzee's essays (and acknowledged as such in the notes). The puzzling situation created that way was that Coetzee himself shares the authorship of the essays with his alter ego, Elizabeth Costello, while being the unquestioned author of the book about her which introduces her as the fictional author of the texts he himself wrote

and *Narrative Theory and the Cognitive Sciences.* (Stanford, CA: CSLI Publications, 2003)), is relying in more and more ways on mental phenomena and human cognition. Starting with the very concepts of "story" and "discourse" (as discussed by Seymour Chatman in 1978. *Story and Discourse: Narrative Structure in Fiction and Film.* Ithaca: Cornell University Press, 1978) and *Coming to Terms: the Rhetoric of Narrative Fiction and Film* (Ithaca: Cornell university Press, 1990)), through stylistic and linguistic analyses of represented speech and thought (see Ann Banfield, *Unspeakable Sentences: Narration and Representation in the Language of Fiction* (Boston: Routledge and Keegan Paul, 1982); Geoffrey Leech and Mick Short, *Style in Fiction.* London: Longman, 1981);, Elena Semino and Mick Short, *Corpus Stylistics: Speech, Writing and Thought Presentation in a Corpus of English Writing* (London: Routledge, 2004); and, Lieven Vandelanotte, *Speech and Thought Representation in English: A Cognitive-Functional Approach* (Berlin and New York: Mouton de Gruyter, 2008), to the very concept of authorship and narratorship (especially as described in Wayne Booth, *The Rhetoric of Fiction.* Chicago: Chicago University Press, 1961); Mieke Bal, *Narratology: Introduction to the Theory of Narrative*, trans. Christine van Boheemen (Toronto: University of Toronto Press, 1985); Michael Toolan, *Narrative: A Critical Linguistic Introduction*, 2nd edn (London: Routledge, 2001); or Gerard Genette's classic study, *Narrative Discourse: An Essay in Method*, trans. J.E. Lewin (Ithaca: Cornell University Press, 1980)), most of the widely used terms describing the nature of narrative fiction are coming under discussion again from the point of view of various models of cognitive studies.

in reality. The same writer later appears as a character in the next novel, *Slow Man*. While it is tempting to see her also as the novel's author,[4] I will argue that her role is in fact more complex.

The tricky nature of the author/character and fact/fiction boundary is still more pronounced in Coetzee's most recent book, *Diary of a Bad Year*. The text experiments with "simultaneous" presentation of three narrative strands: the book of Opinions to be published in German, by an author whom we know as Señor C., Señor C.'s private comments on the situation surrounding the writing of the book, and the story of many of the same events told by his typist, Anya. These partly independent texts are allocated to three separate sections of each page, so that they can be read in any sequence the reader finds appropriate. The story, like *Elizabeth Costello*, also has a well-known author as a character, and his links to Coetzee are more specific (initials, interests, country of birth, authorship of *Waiting for the Barbarians*, among others). Various reviewers indulge in attempts to decide whether Señor C is in fact Coetzee or just someone very similar, but any such attempt is doomed to failure and beside the point. The puzzle to be solved is not that of identity, but of the idea of authorship. The author/character relationship first questioned in *Elizabeth Costello* is pushed a step further here, as if the writer were pulling the curtains hiding his identity just a bit further apart, but the narrative effect is similar and provokes the same kind of questions. The real difference is that *Diary* is more explicit in its commentary on the authorial choices, thus highlighting the points made earlier in the narratives of *Elizabeth Costello* and *Slow Man*.

There are many ways to describe the irony of such a construction of authorship.[5] In what follows, I will use the concepts introduced by the theory of mental spaces and conceptual integration, to attempt to explicate numerous ways in which fiction and fact can be talked about as one, while remaining conceptually separate in the reader's and writer's mind. The theory argues that a significant part of our understanding of colloquial language expressions requires that we construct and manipulate mental objects called mental spaces. When a speaker describes someone's opinion of her, as in *I think he suspects I'm not ready to get married*, she is using specific expressions, such as verbs *to think* and *to know* or negative forms, to prompt for the setting up of interconnected mental spaces. There is, first of all, her *think*-space (as distinct from what she conceives of as her factual knowledge), which contains a representation of another person's *suspicion*-space, which in turn calls up a space wherein the speaker is ready to marry, but embeds it in a negative space. Complex as this discussion may seem, it does nothing more than explicate the way the speaker actually conceptualizes the situation, with its various subjectivities, and the emergence of the intersubjective construct which allows the hearer to find out what both parties concerned think about the idea of

---

[4]   See the essays in this volume by Derek Attridge and Carrol Clarkson (Chapters 1 and 2, respectively).

[5]   See also Zoë Wicomb's essay in this volume (Chapter 11).

marriage, as well as of each other's ideas about it. The example is quite appropriate to our topic, because, among other things, it captures the awareness of the speaker, the hearer and "him" that their beliefs about each other's minds may be different from reality – clearly, the suspicion will not cause the break-up of the relationship until the negative approach to marriage becomes known, and it may also turn out that the speaker is wrong, and "he" is already planning to inform his family about the expected wedding.

Perhaps even more importantly for the argument to follow, we have no difficulty in establishing the participants profiled in any of the spaces and we can readily construct links which give us access to information about any specific participant in any of the mental spaces. That is, "I" is clearly identified as the speaker in the reality space where the conversation is occurring, the "thinker" in another space, the object of suspicion (rather than suspecting party) in yet another one, then as the person whose readiness is under discussion, and who would marry "him" if or when the obstacles are removed. The mechanism of constructing cross-space links, known as Access Principle, allows us to maintain a coherent understanding of the network of the spaces set up. As should become clear in the discussion to follow, the concept of intersubjective construal of meaning and of access which allows various subjectivities involved to keep track of each other's roles in the narrative construction is crucial to Coetzee's concept of authorship.

Mental spaces may be set up by specific expressions, called space builders, which also decide on the initial structure of the space. If we set up a space using the word *yesterday*, we are referring to a past situation, possibly further restricted in terms of spatial features, participants, and so on. For comparison, if we set up a mental space using the verb *think*, we are also assuming that there is an identifiable "thinker" in whose mind the space is to be envisaged. At a higher level of narrative discourse, we can also talk about mental spaces, narrative spaces to be exact, which are characterized by a much richer structure than ordinary spaces in conversation. For example, a novel such as *The Great Gatsby* is constructed via several major spaces which are responsible for important subplots or parts of the story. There is, then, the main narrative space where Nick tells the story, but there is also the space of Daisy's past (before she marries Tom), the space of Gatsby's past, or the space of Daisy and Tom's married life. Each space contributes to the entire story in its own way, while maintaining its own structure, temporal and spatial features, and so on. What elegantly links the spaces together, and in effect prompts for the coherent story told by the novel as a whole, is, among other things, the identity of characters across spaces, so that we include the murky past of James Gatz in our understanding of Jay Gatsby, use Nick's relationship to Daisy to account for his judgment, and so on.

Furthermore, we can describe narrative spaces as narrative constructs, identifying their teller (narrator), the teller's reliability, or the characters involved (for, example, Jordan Baker is not a character in any space other than Nick's narrative). Returning now to *Elizabeth Costello*, she is planted in the text (I hesitate to call it a novel) as a character, as an author of other texts (novels among them), but, by virtue of writing what Coetzee wrote earlier, she is also linked to Coetzee as a real author of *Elizabeth Costello*. The construction is somewhat dizzying. There are Coetzee's essays written in the 'outer" space of contemporary writing, and there is the "inner" space of the "novel" where those very essays are written by Elizabeth Costello. However, since she is linked via the relation of identity across spaces to Coetzee as an author of the essays <u>and</u> the "novel" in which she is a character, she may by the same token be the author of the novel in which she is the character of an author.

The concept that best explains the possibility of actually reading *Elizabeth Costello* without being indefinitely confused about who is the author of what is that of "blending". What the text invites us to do is merge the two spaces, so that authorship is now attributed to the blended identity of someone sharing Coetzee's and (so to speak) Costello's roles. The blend profiles an identity which is neither the real author nor the fictitious author, but has crucial characteristics of both of them. By the same token, though, the "reality" space in which *Elizabeth Costello* is a book we can read is blended with "fiction" space in which Elizabeth Costello is a character. The reality and fiction are undistinguishable.

Exotic as this construction may seem, it is commonly described via a colloquial expression – *to put someone in a book*. The expression *book* here stands for the narrative (or other textually constructed) space, with identifiable boundaries separating it from the space of "reality". Using a person existing in reality (complete with proper name, family ties, native language, and so on) as a character in a book (with the necessary changes, such as a different name or background) is constructing a blended identity which has features of both. The advantage of being able to say something revealing about the reality by extracting pieces of it and putting them into fiction is what authors rely on quite often – thereby constructing the now familiar reality/fiction blend, wherein events and behaviours are interpreted as relevant to both of its input spaces – the reality space and the fiction space. In the case of *Elizabeth Costello*, the benefits are quite clear – not only do we get to read the essays which Coetzee chose for us, all in one place and somewhat updated here and there, but we also have them put in a personal context, so that they are now personal statements of passionate belief, uttered by an exhausted and discouraged, but still indefatigable, author. In view of Coetzee's writing persona (or implied author) often being perceived as distant and unfeeling, the manoeuvre of blending his thoughts and words with the emotions of a character exhausted with oversensitivity and pain of seeing evil in the world presents him, as an author, in a different light.

Elizabeth Costello then appears in the next novel, *Slow Man*. She is the same kind of character – an older woman, famous novelist, lonely, tired, and still compelled to keep writing. But in this novel, she gets involved in the life of a man, Paul Rayment (more about their relationship below). Her role in his life is very difficult to describe, but he keeps on accusing her of studying him so that she could then "put him in a book" – which he finds unfair and in a sense demeaning. Paul protests against his real (in the space of the novel) life being blended into some fictitious character's life. He wants his identity to remain all in one space, the space of his life story.

In view of the fact that Paul obviously thinks being "put in a book" is a degradation from the level of full humanity, how come the author of *Elizabeth Costello* does not? Is the author already a bit of a "lesser" human? After all, volumes have been written about implied authors, death of the author and so on, all of them giving more power to texts and readers. Is the character of Elizabeth Costello meant to counter that view? And if that is what we (readers) indeed think about authors – after all, they are never really there and we don't get to know them as people – is Elizabeth Costello there in the two novels to change our minds?

The question of the consequences of "putting someone in a book" also arises in *Diary*. Señor C.'s typist, Anya, does not want to be "used" in this way, and is further encouraged by her lover, Alan: "You have an identity, which belongs to you alone. It is your most valuable possession, from a certain point of view, which you are entitled to protect." Alan's view would seem difficult to question, if not for the fact that he and Anya are known to us only as characters in *Diary* – so which identity is it that needs protection? Obviously, once the text is "out there", the only identity there is is the one created by the narrative (not even the narrator) and any insistence on the separation of reality and fiction is impossible, whether for writers or for their characters. Quite clearly, Coetzee is "putting himself in a book" as well, but he does not seem concerned about his identity being in danger – there is only one anyway, created by the texts.

In what follows, I will discuss the ways in which Coetzee's recent texts explore the question of authorship, but first, we need to look more closely at Paul Rayment and his predicament.

The Body and the Mind

The novel *Slow Man* starts when the main character, Paul Rayment, is hit by a car when riding on his bike and has his leg amputated as a result. The disaster changes his life entirely – he is practically confined to his apartment, deprived of the company of friends and the ability (and will) to lead further active life. He lives alone, and requires professional home care.

As a result of the accident, Paul is immobilized in many ways. He cannot freely walk or ride his bike, but his condition of being "halt" (as it is often referred to in the text) extends over other areas of his life. Having had that tendency before, he is unwilling to take action and remains in the state of emotional and mental stasis. Paul's inability to move, and also to move on, seems to embody a commonly used conceptual metaphor, usually discussed as Life is a Journey.[6] The metaphor

---

[6]   I am referring here to "metaphor" in the sense of "conceptual metaphor", a mapping which projects conceptual structure from one domain to another, as discussed, among others, in George Lakoff and Mark Johnson, *Metaphors We Live By* (Chicago: Chicago

captures the fact that we commonly use the understanding of self-initiated motion through space in our understanding of a purposeful life. In life, as in a journey, we choose the path and the destination, encounter and overcome obstacles, and, in spite of being side-tracked at times, we continue to work our way towards the chosen goal. The very act of "moving on" describes us as active and in charge. For comparison, being stuck in one location is often mapped onto our being prevented from continuing towards the goal, whether because of obstacles or because of our own inability to decide on the right course.

Paul's physical condition is thus metaphorically also representing him as putting his life on hold. A good example of the correlation between his body and his mind is his adamant refusal to consider using a prosthesis, which everyone sees as a solution to at least some of the difficulties his accident has caused. The explanation he offers uses emotional and aesthetic arguments, rather than practical ones. An artificial limb is not acceptable, because, well, it is artificial. Paul refuses to enhance his condition (again, in all areas of his life) by restricting the options available to him to those within the natural boundaries of his present ability. In the same way in which some depressed patients refuse to seek help, because they are too depressed to take action, Paul refuses to move on, because he feels that it is not within his own personal and bodily control.

At the same time, his condition can be understood metaphorically in yet another way. Towards the end of the novel Elizabeth tells him:

> You have lost a leg, I know, and ambulating is no fun; but after a certain age we have all lost a leg, more or less. Your missing a leg is just a sign … of growing old, old and uninteresting. (229)

Indeed, age puts limitations on our ability to run our life in full control and makes attempting to reach new destinations difficult. Paul's condition, however painful, is metaphorically an impediment shared with others, whose bodies may have remained untouched. His refusal to accept it and "deal" with it seems even more unreasonable in view of the fact that old age is a condition everyone has to face sooner or later. Still, the comment reinforces the metaphorical understanding of Paul's condition as that of someone whose inherent disability extends over many areas of life.

The metaphorical understanding of Paul's predicament is probably available to any reader worth her salt. However, from the point of view of cognitive theories of language I am invoking here, this availability is remarkable. Observing that the same kinds of concepts underlie both colloquial examples such as *I'm stuck, I'm not getting anywhere with this, I'll overcome anything to get where I want to be,* and the very plot and characterization choices an author can make, is an important point about how conceptual mappings consistently manifest themselves in all kinds

University Press, 1980) and *Philosophy in the Flesh: The Embodied Mind and Its Challenge to Western Thought* (New York: Basic Books, 1999).

of uses of language – from the simplest, to the most complex. The observation is in no way an attempt to undermine the author's creativity and is not meant to reduce complex issues of narrative structure to the level of colloquial discourse. On the contrary, acknowledging the depth of conceptual correlations involved reveals the skill and creativity required to construct a narrative around a basic understanding of the experience of "life". At the end of the novel Paul is described by a child as "Slow Man" – an expression which also becomes the title of the whole story. All that has happened since the accident has not changed that – he is not "going anywhere", and even if he thinks he is, he is on the wrong track.

Writing and Acting

After the accident, Paul is treated in the hospital for a short time and then is allowed to return home and remain in the care of a nurse. After a difficult beginning, he is recommended to a nurse who comes every day, and attends to all his needs. She is Croatian and has immigrated to Australia with her family. Her name is Marijana.

After a short while Marijana becomes more than a nurse. She becomes an object of what Costello calls Paul's "unsuitable passion". Paul loves her, or so he thinks, and is becoming ready to declare his feelings. At the same time, the attachment somehow extends over Marijana's children, as he dreams of a happy family he never had. He is ready to help care for them, to assist financially, but also to become a member of the family.

His growing engagement in Marijana's life is becoming awkward, for, as the reader soon sees, there is no future for him and Marijana together. Still, Paul attempts to declare his feelings and the declaration is clearly disturbing Marijana's commitment and professionalism. It may have seemed for a brief moment that Paul is ready to act and start a new life after all, but it is quite obvious that he is making a very bad choice, a choice that "won't take him anywhere".

At this very point in the story Elizabeth Costello knocks at the door and enters his life. She takes residence in his apartment as a very unobtrusive guest. This in itself is strange and does not seem particularly convincing – would a man of Paul's character let a complete stranger into the house and let her stay without a really good explanation of the reason for her visit? All he knows is that she is a well-known writer, which somehow makes her respectable enough to be indulged. Still, Costello's presence in his house (and life) should not be taken too literally. She has a role to play, for sure, but her physical presence is described in such a vague manner (as opposed to detailed descriptions of Paul's or Marijana's actions) that it is difficult to take her intrusion so seriously.

When asked about the purpose of her visit, Costello says things like "I wanted to explore for myself what kind of being you are". When he is still puzzled, she explains, "You came to me. … In certain respects I am not in command of what comes to me." The expression "you came to me" becomes an important token of their relationship. Of course, in the basic spatial sense, she came to him, as he points out in one of their conversations, but she insists that it is the other way round. What the expression reminds us of is, again, related to a mental, rather than spatial or physical event. Ideas "come" to people, thoughts or images do, but this does not exhaust what seems to be intended here. Perhaps the closest equivalent would be the situation of coming to a professional for consultation or advice, and this seems to be what Costello has in mind, though Paul could only "come to her" in her mind, rather than because that was his choice. He is certainly not aware of choosing to seek Costello out.

Paul is in need of advice on how to write the story of his life. Costello appears at his door just as his story begins to take a dangerously unadvisable course with the intention of assisting him – "just a touch on the shoulder, now and then, to keep you on the path". In a way, what she says about his state shows her dissatisfaction with the choices he is making, but not necessarily out of a personal concern – she is, after all, a stranger. The way she describes it suggests that the story he is embarking on is not good enough in her professional opinion. "Two a penny, Mr Rayment, stories like that are two a penny. You will have to make a stronger case for yourself."

The reader of *Slow Man* has been given an earlier indication of the process of writing as part of the process of living. After Paul has been propelled through the air by the car that knocked him off his bike, he lies in a state of subdued consciousness. Here is how his mental state is described:

> Something is coming to him. A letter at a time, *clack, clack, clack,* a message is being typed on a rose-pink screen that trembles like water ... E-R-T-Y, say the letters, then F-R-I-V-O-L, then trembling, the E, then Q-W-E-R-T-Y, on and on. (2)

There is, then, the image of a standard keyboard layout, with the letters QWERTY in the top left corner, combined with the description of typing, suggesting that writing is happening. The word that is attempted is the adjective *frivolous*, whose significance so early in the novel is not clear. Later on (p. 19), Paul recalls the appropriateness of that description:

> Frivolous. How he had strained, that day on Magill Road, to attend the word of the gods, tapped out on their occult typewriter ...
>   Yet *frivolous* is not a bad word to sum him up, ... (19)

Even though the final word that at the moment may have been appropriate as a summation of his life, it is not clear at all who was writing. The uncertainty remains in place, also when a paragraph on page 14 opens with the following:

> From the opening of the chapter, from the incident on Magill Road to the present, ...

Who would be talking about the focal event of Paul's story as "the opening of the chapter"? Whose viewpoint is being surreptitiously implied here? The novel is written in the third person, but the narrator is not "on stage" anywhere else in the text. There are no further allusions to the process of writing. And yet, the exact words of the novel as we are reading it are known to Costello, who quotes the initial sentences of the text to Paul upon first arriving at his door, to somehow prove her right to enter his life. So she knows these words, and she also knows what happened to him since the accident, including his very private thoughts and desires. In other words, she knows all that the reader does, all that is contained in the text, but she is not familiar with any details of his life before the accident.

In fact, she not only knows the words, she is also evaluating the effectiveness of the words used. In chapter 20, Paul is looking for Costello, who has left the house, possibly for good. The chapter starts with the words "He finds her by the riverside". They start a conversation, in which she repeats the whole first sentence:

> *He finds her by the riverside, sitting on a bench, clustered around by ducks that she seems to be feeding* – it may be simple, as an account, its simplicity may even beguile one, but it is not good enough. It does not bring me to life. Bringing me to life may not be important to you, but it has the drawback of not bringing you to life either. Or the ducks, for that matter, if you prefer not to have me at the centre of the picture. Bring these humble ducks to life and they will bring you to life, I promise. (159)

The image of writing that emerges from this is puzzling. We are reading the words of *Slow Man*, assuming tacitly that they are all the author's words, and that the author exists in the reality space in which the novel eventually exists as an artifact. And yet, we are told that the words come from someone else, the character, or the protagonist, although he himself is not aware of writing them. The only hazy access to this process of writing that he has is in a state beyond consciousness, although even then it is not clear that he is involved as a voluntary agent in the writing that happens. The story written that way is available to someone like Costello – a professional who can see its merits, but not only in terms of the writing technique. She evaluates, among other things, how effective the story is in *creating* (definitely not representing!) life.

But she does write as well. When Paul looks at her notebooks in her absence, he finds comments on the minor occurrences in his house, descriptions of what happens and, disturbingly, of his reactions to what happens. The first time he reads her words he is not sure how to understand it (he even thinks briefly that he may have actually died in the accident and he now exists only in a story she writes). Towards the end of the novel, when it is already clear that Paul will not take the kind of action Costello expects of him and that he may remain somehow linked to Marijana's family, as a kind of adopted godfather, he reads more of Costello's notes. She describes a game of cards that he plays with Marijana's children and he takes it as a good sign – if she wrote it, then maybe it is the future of the story that she knows something about. After all, writers are said to be omniscient, at least as regards their characters' lives.

But Paul is wrong here. Costello herself teaches him that nobody's story happens because it was written by someone else. Nobody's destiny is predetermined by fate or gods in ways that a human being could not change. We have to write our own story by acting, and only action will bring us and the world we live in to life. The concept of defying the idea of our lives being "written" is not new, and many a heroic tale was created to substantiate the belief. One salient example of its meaning is found in the movie *Lawrence of Arabia*, where Lawrence risks his own life to save a man, against the advice of everyone around him, who all think the man's death was "written". Lawrence brings the man back safely (thus becoming the one for whom "nothing is written"), but then has to kill him to prevent a disturbance among the troops. Ali, his friend, seeing him shattered by the apparent futility of the earlier risky rescue, says to him: "You gave a life, you took it. The writing is still yours." Quite clearly, this comment supports what Costello is trying to explain to Paul. Not only because it assumes that acting is in fact controlling one's own fate by "writing it", but in suggesting that you can write your own story by acting in a way that defies expectations or routine – the way which "brings things to life".

It might seem, again, that Coetzee relies on otherwise available concepts to tell us that it matters to control the course of one's own life. However, in doing so, he actually reverses the idea of our lives being "written", which typically assumes that the control over what happens to us is, for the most part, not in out hands. The idea of writing and authorship constructed in *Slow Man* is clearly different – by acting the way he does (or not acting, as a matter of fact) Paul creates his story, but it is written elsewhere, whether on "the occult typewriter" of the gods, or by a disenchanted professional like Costello. Whoever the writer is, she has to take the cue from the actual "character", though she may try little additions or possible continuations – perhaps when it becomes clear where the story is going. This seems to be the case with Costello writing some variant of Paul's future – clearly, he has disregarded all her advice, so she may have to assume that he will take the poorly constructed and uninteresting story to the bitter end.

Whose words are we then reading on the page of the novel? The character's nature and thoughts determine to some degree what words will best describe him, but he is not engaged in the writing itself. When Costello first appears in Paul's house and quotes the initial sentences of the novel to him, he presumably recognizes his own story, although we can assume her to be the one who wrote the words taking her cue from his most inner thoughts. Indeed, how would it be possible for writers to represent their characters' thoughts if they didn't have access to them? They have been writing down people's thoughts for centuries now, and their uncanny ability to make these passages feel "real" comes from somewhere. While these questions are naive when posed just this way, the answers to them cannot be, so it may be easier to assume that writers write what in some sense is already real. At least, this is what Costello seems to be saying to Paul, in the very final scenes of the novel.

> For me alone Paul Rayment was born and I for him. His is the power of leading, mine of following; his of acting, mine of writing. (233)

This poses further questions about the concept of "a character". Literature teachers often swap anecdotes about students who over-speculate on the nature of the lives of literary characters they read about, and then have to be reminded that the characters never existed. In *Slow Man*, the "character" has to exist so that the author can write. The novel questions the ordinary concept of authorship, and redefines the status of the character and the novel as such in the process. Living one's life is writing one's story – whether it will ever be read by others is not important. Furthermore, the narrative construction in *Slow Man* in a way suggests that fictional stories are about real characters – if living precedes writing, then that seems to be the only conclusion. Consequently, all lives are lives of "characters", though, again, their stories may never be read. Only some become the kinds of characters that deserve being "put in a book". In the next section I will explore the novel's construction of "a character" and his relationship to the writer in more detail.

Being a Main Character

Elizabeth Costello appears in Paul's life just when he has blurted out his feelings to Marijana. Since their relationship is not likely to take off, Costello appears to intervene in the construction of the story Paul is living at the crucial moment. She is there to help, and she will not just go away, but she cannot create the story for him – once more, it is the character who "writes" the story, not the writer. She says:

> I say it again: this is your story, not mine. The moment you decide to take charge, I will fade away. (100)

And then later:

> I cannot advise, that must come from you. If I knew what came next there would be no need for me to be here … until you choose to act, I must wait upon you. (136)

Interestingly, she sees Paul's "unsuitable passion" and his offers to help financially with Marijana's son's education as *not* acting. Presumably, for a character to "act" is to prompt a twist in the plot that requires a true emotional involvement. Paul's lame attempts to let Marijana appreciate his love without scaring her away do not count, because they lack true commitment and passion. Characters in novels often do things we do not find reasonable or that we do not approve of, but, as Costello points out, referring to the classic characters like Emma Bovary, they let their passion drive their actions:

> Remember, Paul, it is passion that makes the world go round … give it a whirl,
> Paul. See what you can come up with. (228)

His response is another complaint about her attempt to just use him as an object of her writing. He still misunderstands her role. She does not need him to be able to write, but he needs her to live a life worth a tale, which she can then write. Costello's answer is another attempt to describe Paul's role:

> So that someone, somewhere might put you in a book. Someone, anyone – not
> just me. So that you may be worth putting in a book … Become major, Paul. Live
> like a hero. That is what the classics teach us. Be a main character. Otherwise
> what is life for? (229)

Clearly, the matter is not just the book we are reading, but any literary text. Literature, by telling the stories of those who truly deserve to be main characters, also establishes the standards for a life worth living – one which, even if never told in a tale, would be worth it. Paul, an anti-hero in every possible sense of the word, does not deserve to be "put in a book". But there he is – "slow man", passive and cold, uninteresting and uninterested, destined for oblivion – and yet quite clearly the main character. His role, however, does not seem to be to tell a good story with his life, but rather to facilitate an expression of the authorial view of authorship. The presence of Elizabeth Costello at his side, which is the presence of the author's alter ego, creates a story which is more of a comment on fiction as a category than on any particular life-story.

Costello, cautious to offer advice as she is, suggests a woman who, unlike Marijana, may prompt Paul into a narratologically useful direction. Her name is Marianna, and she "came" to Costello the same way Paul did. She lost her eyesight and, like Paul, has to start again with her body impaired in an important way. Her connection to the story is unusual. When still in hospital, long before Costello appeared, Paul saw her in the elevator – with large dark glasses and her dress inside out. She was the first person since the accident to arouse his sexual interest, but he then forgot her. Costello, who knows all his thoughts since the accident, reminds him of the encounter and suggests that the two of them could give the story the desired whirl. Marianna is, in her opinion, suitable, and, as far as anyone can tell, ready to experiment with her life in the way that Paul is not. "Why not see what you can achieve together, you and Marianna, she blind, you halt?" she says (96). Costello sees this suggestion as coming from Paul, not from her. She relies on Paul's hospital memory as a prompt, but also claims that Marianna knew him earlier. She considers Paul's memory as an important narrative cue that he provided, whether he realized it or not ("Nothing that happens in our lives is without a meaning, Paul, as any child can tell you. That is one of the lessons stories teach us." – 96). Thus Costello arranges a meeting, in which Marianna appears in the guise of a hired prostitute – just so that nobody's feelings are hurt if the relationship does not work.

It does not work, indeed. The question remains, however, why the two women Paul successively "puts into" his story (by singling them out, by considering, perhaps unconsciously, how they might contribute to the story) have almost identical names. In fact, they may both originate in a memory from the childhood spent in France, of the face he saw on postal stamps attached to packages of books – the face of Marianne, the symbol of liberty and national emblem of France. One can only guess what Costello would say if she heard about it, but she would probably repeat that nothing is without meaning and go on to stress that our memory preserves only the meaningful bits of events and situations, those that contribute to the story. The wonderfully flexible name, with its many spellings and national varieties, seems to suggest that any woman in Paul's life who bears that name fills the mystical gap created by his childhood longing and imagination. While Marianna is a false start and disappears, Marijana occupies a more significant spot in the story, but in the end, she is also an instantiation of the same dream. If Paul were truly passionate about her and dared to risk more, she would have become a character too – as Costello said elsewhere, bringing others to life has a wonderful advantage of bringing us to life. But in view of Paul's coldness and reserve she will not become fully alive for him, passionate and daring as she can be in her own life.

End of Story

The narrative constructions discussed above seem to be the novel's central point. As a story, with its plot and characters, *Slow Man* is not as complex as other works by Coetzee, and the impact on the reader seems less daring. Compared with the main character of *Disgrace*, for one, who also refuses to play by the rules set by others, Paul is strangely detached from what befalls him. His story, to use the novel's terms again, does not quite bring him alive, and leaves the rest of the story wanting in the power to reach our deepest selves. Considering the standards set up by the text, it should not be surprising. Paul does not engage with people enough, and does not push himself enough to touch us. When Costello repeatedly urges him to "Push!", to move further, to invest more power and conviction in his life, to give birth, in a sense, to a new life he deserves, forgetting the pain and risk all this involves, she is on the reader's side as much as her own. Paul disappoints, perhaps even angers those readers who are waiting for a tale worth telling.

Costello is not an endearing character either. She is demanding and exacting, and often reminds Paul of the personal price she is paying to assist him, but one cannot help noting that she should have given up on the hopeless character much sooner. Trying to help when help is not wanted and cannot even be understood or appreciated will not inspire gratefulness and companionship. Having given up on making Paul "major", companionship is what she asks for. Two aging people, without unrealistic expectations and soul-tearing demands, two writers of a shared story knowing that they have each failed in their respective tasks – this could be the end of their tale, their happy ending. But even that is too much of an emotional commitment for Paul. Also, he does not really care for the tale. It is not in his temperament to be a main character, and it is also not in his temperament to be a writer.

The last scenes of the novel close all the themes. Paul is given a new bike, constructed by Marijana's husband and son especially for him, to make him Rocket Man. But he will remain Slow Man. He will not have Marijana, he refuses the companionship offered by Costello, and he will not ride his new bike to avoid people staring at him on his strange vehicle. And that is all. He has not got anywhere and will not.

A Novel about Novels

As I suggested earlier, *Slow Man* may not be a successful story in the terms we typically apply to fiction. But perhaps it can be seen, instead, as a companion book to *Elizabeth Costello*. It is a clear presentation of a very specific view of fiction, one that defines the role of Costello as a writer, and, based on the blend we considered at the beginning, the writing credo of the actual author, J.M. Coetzee. *Slow Man* seems to fly in the face of the trend in recent narratology to distance fiction further and further away from its author, to repeatedly remind us that characters are partial constructs with no life beyond the words that describe them, and to invest readers with almost infinite power over the meaning of the text. These novels bring literature back where it started – into our very lives.

The concept of authorship in *Slow Man* relies primarily on revisiting the pre-existing assumption that fact and fiction are separate mental spaces. Indeed, the assumption is not only traditionally assumed in criticism, but also supported by linguistic forms such as counterfactuals or subjunctives. However, in both areas of inquiry, it is accepted that what is not factual still does rely on our understanding of how reality works. In other words, fiction may be just as believable as the fact, because it is structured by the same concepts and assumptions about likely events. As a result, the exasperation with which we might receive discussion of literary characters as if they were real people is to a degree unjustified, although we still need an explanation of why exactly fictional characters "feel" like real. Apparently, it is only natural to think about fictional people in the same categories we apply to real people and recent scholarship referring to the uncanny reality of fictional characters uses different concepts to explain it.[7]

In *Slow Man*, Coetzee presents a construction whereby Paul has to be real in order to have his story written as a novel. While we would probably not take the claim literally, we can take it to mean that fiction, to be convincing, needs that "real" quality, however elusive the concept may seem. There is a life situation which is the starting point of a story ("a halt man with an unsuitable passion") and the tale can develop from there as if it were real. Reality is necessary for fiction to exist, but understanding of reality often requires thinking in terms of fiction (planning different scenarios, considering options, and so on). The blend thus created is the mental space where literature is placed alongside other construals which rely on real elements as well as imaginary developments. Any literary creation is a blend of reality and fiction, if only in the sense discussed by Herman,[8] whereby stories can be seen as "tools" for thinking about reality and have an internal logic which is not inherently different from the logic which underlies the understanding of reality. However, even the wildest fictional story relies on our every day ability to set up and connect imaginary mental spaces.

Coetzee's next novel, *Diary of a Bad Year*, is significantly less focused on the role of the main character, but it also treats the story as an autonomous space, regardless of it being real or fictional. A story has a life of its own, largely independent of its author. When Anya asks Señor C. why he writes a book of "opinions" rather than "tell a story", which she assumes would be more effective, he answers: "Stories tell themselves, they don't get told ... That much I know after a lifetime of working with stories. Never try to impose yourself. Wait for the story to speak for itself." Later, in the "soft opinions", Señor C. makes it clear that he is not planning on writing more stories, since he is satisfied with "an idea of a story" and does not wish to take on the heavy burden of story-telling again. But his authorial autonomy exercised in not writing does not ban stories he could write out of existence – they will keep on "coming to him".

The non-fiction he does write (opinions on aspects of contemporary reality), eventually turns out to be deeply influenced by his humble "secretary", so that, to some degree, she is his co-author, while remaining a character in the novel. What is more, in the earlier part of the "story", Anya's portion of the narrative serves as a generic reader's commentary on the opinions expressed in *Diary* and in the rest of Coetzee's ouevre. At some point they exchange thoughts on what might dishonour (disgrace?) a thinking human being. While Señor C. initially seems to stand by Coetzee's oft-expressed idea that one is dishonoured by living in a

---

[7] For instance, Alan Palmer, *Fictional Minds* (Lincoln, NE: University of Nebraska Press, 2004), talks about social construction, while Lisa Zunshine, *Why We Read Fiction: Theory of Mind and the Novel* (Columbus, OH: Ohio State University Press, 2006), refers to the theory of mind.

[8] Herman, *Story Logic: Problems and Possibilities of Narrative* (2002) and *Narrative Theory and the Cognitive Sciences* (2003).

morally troubling world and being part of it, Anya proudly defends her honour as dependent on her own deeds only. The result is as conceptually disturbing as anything else Coetzee does when authorship is involved. The ostensibly non-fictional opinions, easily attributable to Coetzee himself, are presented in Señor C.'s text, but these and other thoughts are commented on by a fictional character, Anya. The character, in turn, presents Coetzee as imposing moral standards which are impossible to uphold in the real world – an opinion often expressed by his readers and critics. Clearly, the text evokes Coetzee as the author in the real world, and presents him as engaging in a discussion with his readers. In the text of *Diary*, he is thus present as the author in several spaces – that of Señor C. (Coetzee's new alter ego), of the author of *Diary*, and the author of *Disgrace* and other novels.

In this context, the question whether the "non-fictional" opinions in the top narrative stream are indeed Coetzee's or should be attributed to the fictional Señor C. is impossible to answer. As James Wood observes aptly in his review,[9] some of the stylistic choices in the Opinions are clearly below Coetzee's usual standard (he picks the phrase "It's *deja vu* all over again", and it is indeed not too graceful). Wood suggests that these might be changes introduced by Anya, but it is also possible to see these fragments as the ones where Señor C.'s fictional discourse "leaks into" the "real" author's thoughts. The Opinions could be real Coetzee's blog (if he has one) or they could have been written to look like it – in fact the latter is more likely.

The choice to graphically separate "pretend-non-fiction" from "pretend-fiction" on each page looks like another reminder that they are impossible to tell apart. Every story has different voices, but we are used to seeing them textually merged together into one flow of text. The solution chosen in *Diary* is different from all the other novels containing other "novels" as their sub-stories in that it presents them as independent and concurrent streams. As I argued elsewhere,[10] every novel requires assembly in the reader's mind – no story is ever told in its entirety and crucial information is often withheld till the last minute or left unsaid. In *Diary*, the process of this "narrative construction" is explicitly acknowledged and revealed. Here, as elsewhere, the reader is charged with "putting it all together", but it is done explicitly. Besides, the solution supports the centrality of the idea of the reality/fiction blend, because the novel as a whole cannot in fact be read as coherent if the three parts are considered as entirely independent. The seams may be showing, but *Diary* is still ostensibly one text, not three, and needs to be read as such.

---

[9]   James Wood, Review of *Diary of a Bad Year*, *The New Yorker* (24 December 2007)

[10]   Dancygier, "Narrative Anchors and the Processes of Story Construction"; and Barbara Dancygier, "The Text and the Story: Levels of Blending in Fictional Narratives", in Todd. Oakley and Anders Hougaard, eds, *Mental Spaces in Discourse* (Amsterdam and Philadelphia: John Benjamins Publishing Company, 2008).

Blending and authorship

Blending seems a suitable tool to capture the tension between reality and fiction without relegating it to the concept of their being "blurred". The boundaries, if any exist, are difficult to define but need to be understood, and understood clearly. Blends are described as mental constructs which create new conceptual configurations – they are said to have their own emergent structure, and Coetzee's concept of the space where stories belong also has structure of its own. The same is the case with any instance of literature as a reality/fiction blend – each combination is creative, original, and unique. However, a blend also informs the inputs which were used in its creation – and we would probably agree that literature informs our understanding of both fiction and reality. While literary texts rely on reality in different degrees (though they all do), interacting with reality often builds on fiction of different kinds (to mention only teenagers' movie-based concept of love or the role of movie violence in the emergence of real life violence).

Jointly, Coetzee's three novels redefine authorship as a blend. One input to the blend, which is not generally considered as having any part in authorship, is the character. The person "living a life", and consequently "eligible" to become a character, is an author who creates the plot and chooses the setting, without losing the role of the character. A character thus functions in a fictional space (let us say of the novel), but that space has been constructed as a narrative space because the character "lived" that story in some "reality" space. That reality space, in turn, has to be assumed to be real because it is implied by the fictional space we interact with as readers, but does not have to be (in fact, most of the time is not) identical with the reader's reality space. In a sense, any fictional space assumes the existence of a meta-space, such that it is the reality on which the fiction is based (historical context, patterns of human behavior, social norms, and so on), but this "assumed" reality is not necessarily recognizable as anyone's particular reality.

The writer provides the other input to the concept of authorship (in fact, I try to stick to the term "writer", as the task he or she has is to write the character's story, rather than create it in the sense in which an author would). The writer "takes cue" from the character (whether this refers to Paul acting or Anya talking), but chooses the words, at least to the degree that they accurately represent the character's thoughts and actions and "bring" everything "to life" (recall Costello criticizing the choice of words in Paul's story). The mental space where the writer conceived in this way resides is not the fictional story space (that is the domain of the character), and not in the character's or the reader's reality. The writer's space has to have the character's fiction space and the character's reality space embedded in it, so that the writer has access to both, but can also make some choices that the character did not make or made differently. However, none of these spaces profiles the actual author in the role he/she has been attributed in classical narratology. The author, as an independent subjectivity with total control over all the spaces contributing to the narrative, is no longer needed, and this claim seems to be one of the main points the construction relies on. The power of creating the narrative is distributed, rather than given into the hands of only one of the subjectivities involved. The narrative is thus by its very nature an intersubjective construct.

Slow Man (in combination with *Elizabeth Costello*) does two things at the same time. On the one hand, it sets up the configuration of narrative spaces discussed above as the standard understanding of the narrative. At the same time, however, it complicates it further by adding two projections. First, the real author is projected into the narrative space of *Elizabeth Costello* and blended with the character of Costello-the-writer. Then, the blended author-writer from one novel is projected into one of the narrative spaces of *Slow Man* – the one of the story "lived" by Paul. This creates a rather puzzling narrative construction whereby Paul "lives" his story and discusses it with "his" assistant writer, Costello, within the same space. The narrative-structuring power of the story one lives is thus highlighted and the cross-space consequences of Paul's choices become clear. Naturally, though, the reader might then be expected to begin to consider her "life" space as one where the narrative of her life is simultaneously being constructed – although, presumably, without the expert help of the writer.

This does not exhaust the embedding possibilities of this narrative network. The text of *Slow Man*, as the reader sees it, is a further blend of two narrative spaces. It is a text of Paul's "life", as Costello writes it, and of other "life stories" he may have created, had he followed Costello's advice. The bits and pieces she writes outside of the main narrative of *Slow Man* (which actually do not represent Paul's story as we learn it), the options she considers, the alternative subplots she convinces him to try and which he rejects (like the Marianna theme) – all of these are partial narrative spaces which exist outside of the main storyline and represent alternative stories or missing parts of the real story. Additionally, because of Costello's link to the actual author, Coetzee, the blend also includes the role of the actual author as the subjectivity behind Costello's professional expertise and sharing some of the narrative burden with her.

Slow Man as a whole is a very complex blend in which all crucial aspects of story construction appear together, but in a logically connected and narratologically revealing way. The blend distinguishes the reality on the character's side from that of the reader's side, and acknowledges the story-creating power of each. Furthermore, it disperses the contribution to the narrative and responsibility for it across all the spaces, from the actual author, through the inner-space writer (Costello), to the lowest level writer (Paul). As all blends, this blend seeks to construct an innovative and imaginative understanding of the narrative, but it also informs all the participant spaces. Among others, by attributing various partial narrative roles to the subjectivities profiled in different spaces and linked only in the blend, it highlights correlations which could not otherwise be acknowledged – like the character's role in creating the story or the writer's limited contribution.

By comparison, the blend in the *Diary* is somewhat less complex – one cannot but wonder whether the way it is written is because *Slow Man* was indeed the last "story" Coetzee/Señor C. wrote, or simply because some things needed to be said more explicitly. In fact, in a section of "opinions" he addresses the issue of authorship head on, rejecting the postmodern idea of authorship as a rhetorical effect and correlating it instead with the concept of "authority". He talks about the importance of Tolstoy's writings in his own life, attributing the power to the moral authority and story-telling skills which go beyond anything one could write off as a rhetorical trick. He also openly winks at his critics, admitting with disarming self-irony that they saw through the disguise when they said that he wasn't really a novelist, "but a pedant who dabbles in fiction". The disparaging sense of the phrase, however, disappears in this context, since in the three books under discussion here "dabbling" is exactly what Coetzee does, but only to show what fiction is and is not. At the same time, Señor C.'s disagreement with Anya over the moral consequences of living in an immoral world is now put in a somewhat different context – the text is explicitly asking whether the author of *Disgrace* has exposed his own moral wounds enough to ask us to expose ours. The character of Elizabeth Costello – pained to speak in a real, not fictional voice – seemed to have been constructed to convince us that indeed he has.

By making fiction a part of life and life a part of fiction, these books redefine the role of literature in our lives. It is not an independent domain, subordinate to life as such. It is, instead, its constitutive, indispensable component. The reader, though not present in any particular story, is "living" her own story, and should make it worth a tale. Readers are all characters by virtue of being human, but they are also writers. Actual writers have a greater role to play. They make choices, they listen to different characters, they choose the words. They are "like Atlas – holding up a whole world on [their] shoulders" (*Diary*). Authorship seen in this way is not the total power over the characters' lives – it is having the authority to speak in their stead.

*   *   *

The discussion above assumes a methodological perspective not entirely in the tradition represented by other essays in this volume. Indeed, the framework represented here is an interdisciplinary attempt to look at specific features of literary discourse through the lens of conceptual structure. The meaning of a text, however varied the possible interpretations are, is seen as emerging from the interaction of specific language choices and the meaning construction processes the human mind brings into reading. While this approach involves close engagement with the textual matter of literary discourse, it is primarily interested in uncovering conceptual mechanisms specific to the process of interpretation. In this view, the language of the text provides crucial, but not sufficient evidence, as interpretive processes rely in equal measure on the cultural frames evoked and on cognitive patterns characterizing creative and imaginary thought. What one can hope to learn from applying this methodology is not only a somewhat different view of the meaning of literature, but also a better understanding of human thought and the role of language in mediating the connection between the world and the mind.

Coetzee's recent novels provide a perfect example of all these processes at work. His linguistic choices are meticulous and crucially important, and his overt and covert references to the most central issues of the contemporary world leave no doubt as to his interest in addressing those issues. But he also crafts these texts as a running commentary on the nature of literary discourse and on the multitude of subjectivities whose minds collectively give it meaning. Quite explicitly, Coetzee presents himself as reflecting on the processes of reading and writing, and on the conceptual underpinnings of these processes.

Works Cited

Works by J.M. Coetzee

1963. "A Computer Poem." *The Lion and the Impala*, 2.1: 12–13. Dramatic Society of the University of Cape Town.

1974. "Nabokov's *Pale Fire* and the Primacy of Art." *UCT Studies in English* 5: 1–7.

1978. *In the Heart of the Country*. Johannesburg: Ravan Press.

1980. *Waiting for the Barbarians*. London: Secker & Warburg and Penguin. Reprinted 1981, Johannesburg: Ravan Press.

1981. "Time, Tense, and Aspect in Kafka's 'The Burrow'." Reprinted 1992 in *Doubling the Point*, 210–32.

1982. *Dusklands*. London: Secker & Warburg.

1982. *In the Heart of the Country*. Harmondsworth: Penguin. Reprinted 1981, Johannesburg: Ravan Press.

1983. *Life and Times of Michael K*. Johannesburg: Ravan Press; Harmondsworth: Penguin.

1985. "Confession and Double Thoughts: Tolstoy, Rousseau, Dostoevsky." *Comparative Literature* 37: 193–232.

1986. With Jean Sévry. "An Interview with J.M. Coetzee." *Commonwealth* 9: 1–7.

1987. *Foe*. London: Penguin.

1987. With Tony Morphet, "Two Interviews with J.M. Coetzee, 1983 and 1987." *TriQuarterly* 69, special issue: *From South Africa* (Spring/Summer): 454–64

1987. Jerusalem Prize Acceptance Speech. Reprinted 1992 in *Doubling the Point*, 96–9.

1988. "The Novel Today." *Upstream* 6.1: 2–5.

1988. *White Writing: On the Culture of Letters in South Africa*. New Haven and London: Radix, in association with Yale University Press.

1990. *Age of Iron*. London: Secker & Warburg.

1992. "Kafka." in *Doubling the Point*, 197–209.

1992. *Doubling the Point: J. M. Coetzee, Essays and Interviews*, edited by David Attwell. Cambridge, MA: Harvard University Press.

1992. "The Poetics of Reciprocity", interview with David Attwell in *Doubling the Point*, 57–68.

1994. *The Master of Petersburg*. London: Secker & Warburg.

1996. *Giving Offense: Essays on Censorship*. London and Chicago: University of Chicago Press.

1997. *Boyhood: Scenes from Provincial Life*. New York: Viking.

1998. *Boyhood: A Memoir*. London: Vintage.
1999. *Disgrace*. London: Secker & Warburg. Reprinted 2000, London: Vintage.
1999. "*History of the Main Complaint*", in *William Kentridge*, New York: Phaidon: 82–93.
1999. *The Lives of Animals*. Princeton: Princeton University Press.
2001. *Stranger Shores: Essays 1986–1999*. London: Secker & Warburg and London: Penguin.
2002. *Youth*. London: Secker & Warburg.
2003. *Elizabeth Costello: Eight Lessons*. London: Secker & Warburg and Penguin, and New York: Viking.
2004. "As a Woman Grows Older." *New York Review of Books* 51.1 (15 January): 11–14.
2004. ["He and his Man":] *Lecture and Speech of Acceptance upon the Award of the Nobel Prize in Literature, Delivered in Stockholm in December 2003*. London: Penguin.
2004. *Landscape with Rowers: Poetry from the Netherlands*. Princeton: Princeton University Press.
2005. *Slow Man*. London: Secker & Warburg and New York: Viking.
2007. *Diary of a Bad Year*. London: Harvill Secker.

Other Works

Achebe, Chinua. 1975. *Morning Yet on Creation Day*. London: Heinemann.
Attridge, Derek. 2009. "Sex, Comedy and Influence: Coetzee's Beckett," in Elleke Boehmer, Robert Eaglestone and Katy Iddiols, eds, *J. M. Coetzee in Context and Theory*. 71–90. London: Continuum.
Attridge, Derek. 2004. *J.M. Coetzee and the Ethics of Reading: Literature in the Event*. Chicago: University of Chicago Press. Reprinted 2005, Scottsville: University of KwaZulu-Natal Press.
Attwell, David. 2004. "J.M. Coetzee and South Africa: Thoughts on the Social Life of Fiction." *English Academy Review* 21: 105–17.
Attwell, David. 1991. "On the Question of Autobiography: Interview with J.M. Coetzee." *Current Writing* 3: 117–22.
Attwell, David. 2001. "Coetzee and Post-Apartheid South Africa." Review of J.M. Coetzee's *Disgrace*. *Journal of Southern African Studies* 27.4: 865–6.
Attwell, David. 2002. "Race in *Disgrace*." *Interventions* 4.3 (2002): 331–41.
Attwell, David. 2005. *Rewriting Modernity: Studies in Black South African Literary History*. Pietermaritzburg: University of KwaZulu-Natal Press. Reprinted 2006, Athens, OH: Ohio University Press.
Bakhtin, Mikhail. 1984. *Problems of Dostoevsky's Poetics*. Translated by Caryl Emerson. Minneapolis: University of Minnesota Press.
Bal, Mieke. 1985. *Narratology: Introduction to the Theory of Narrative*. Translated by Christine van Boheemen. Toronto: University of Toronto Press.

Banfield, Ann. 1982. *Unspeakable Sentences: Narration and Representation in the Language of Fiction*. Boston: Routledge & Kegan Paul.

Banville, John. 1990. *Doctor Copernicus*. London: Minerva.

Barnard, Rita. 2003. "J.M. Coetzee's *Disgrace* and the South African Pastoral." *Contemporary Literature* 14.2: 199–224.

Barnard, Rita. 2007. *Apartheid and Beyond: South African Writers and the Politics of Place*. New York: Oxford University Press.

Barthes, Roland. 1975. *S/Z*. New York: Hill & Wang.

Barthes, Roland. 1993. *Camera Lucida*. London: Vintage.

Bate, W. Jackson. 1970. *The Burden of the Past and the English Poet*. New York: W.W. Norton.

Bloom, Harold. 1973. *The Anxiety of Influence: A Theory of Poetry*. New York: Oxford University Press.

Booth, Wayne C. 1961. *The Rhetoric of Fiction*. Chicago: Chicago University Press.

Bower, Colin. 2003. "J.M. Coetzee: Literary Con Artist and Poseur." *Scrutiny2* 8.2: 3–23.

Bradley, Fiona. 1997. "Introduction," in *Rachel Whiteread: Shedding Life*. 8–17. Liverpool: Tate Gallery Liverpool.

Bradshaw, Graham. 1993. *Misrepresentations: Shakespeare and the Materialists*. Ithaca: Cornell University Press.

Breytenbach, Breyten. 1984. *True Confessions of an Albino Terrorist*. London: Faber.

Brink, André. 1974. *Looking on Darkness*. London: W.H. Allen.

Brink, André. 1978. *Rumours of Rain*. London: W.H. Allen.

Brink, André. 1979. *A Dry White Season*. London: W.H. Allen.

Brink, André. 1988. *States of Emergency*. London: Faber and Faber.

Brink, André. 1993. *The First Life of Adamastor*. London: Secker & Warburg.

Brink, André. 1993. *On the Contrary: Being the Life of a Famous Rebel, Soldier, Traveller, Explorer, Reader, Builder, Scribe, Latinist, Lover and Liar*. London: Secker & Warburg.

Brink, André. 1996. *Imaginings of Sand*. London: Secker & Warburg.

Brink, André. 1998. *Devil's Valley*. London: Secker & Warburg.

Brink, André. 2002. *The Other Side of Silence*. London: Secker & Warburg.

Brink, André. 2004. *Before I Forget*. London: Secker & Warburg.

Burchell, William W. 1967. *Travels in the Interior of Southern Africa* [1832]. Vol. I. Facsimile reprint. Cape Town: Struik.

Byron. 1979. *Byron's Letters and Journals*. Edited by Leslie A. Marchand. Vol. 9 (1821–1822). London: John Murray.

Byron. 1981. "Lara. A Tale," in *Lord Byron: The Complete Poetical Works*. Edited by Jerome J. McGann. Vol. 3: 214–257. Oxford: Clarendon Press.

Calvino, Italo. 1982. *If on a Winter's Night a Traveller*. London: Picador.

Calvino, Italo. 1986. "Levels of Reality in Literature," in *The Uses of Literature*. 101–24. New York: Harcourt, Brace.

Carlyle, Thomas. 1871. *Sartor Resartus* [1833], in *The Collected Works of Thomas Carlyle*. London: Chapman & Hall.

Carroll, Lewis. 1971. *Alice's Adventures in Wonderland and Through the Looking Glass*. Edited by Roger Lancelyn Green. Oxford: Oxford University Press.

Cartwright, David E. 1984. "Kant, Schopenhauer, and Nietzsche on the Morality of Pity." *Journal of the History of Ideas* 45.1: 83–98.

Chatman, Seymour. 1978. *Story and Discourse: Narrative Structure in Fiction and Film*. Ithaca: Cornell University Press.

Chatman, Seymour. 1990. *Coming to Terms: the Rhetoric of Narrative Fiction and Film*. Ithaca: Cornell University Press

Clarkson, Carrol. 1999. "Dickens and the *Cratylus.*" *British Journal of Aesthetics* 39.1: 53–61.

Clarkson, Carrol. 2003. "'Done because we are too menny:' Ethics and Identity in J.M. Coetzee's *Disgrace.*" *Current Writing* 15.2 (October): 77–90.

Clarkson, Carrol. 2009. *J.M. Coetzee: Countervoices*. Houndmills: Palgrave.

Conrad, Joseph. *Victory*. 1946. London: Dent Collected Edition.

Conrad, Joseph. 1947. *Under Western Eyes*. London: Dent Collected Edition.

Cooper, Pamela. 2005. "Metamorphosis and Sexuality: Reading the Strange Passions of *Disgrace.*" *Research in African Literatures* 36.4: 22–39

Cooper, Thomas. 1975. *Thesaurus Linguae Romanae et Britannicae* [1578]. Hildesheim and New York: G. Olms.

Cornwell, Gareth. 2002. "Realism, Rape, and J.M. Coetzee's *Disgrace.*" *Critique: Studies in Contemporary Fiction* 43.4: 307–22.

Coulson, Seana. 2001. *Semantic Leaps: Frame-shifting and Conceptual Blending in Meaning Construction*. New York and Cambridge: Cambridge University Press.

Crapanzano, Vincent. 1985. *Waiting: The Whites of South Africa*. London: Granada.

Dancygier, B. 2004. "Identity and Perspective: the Jekyll-and-Hyde Effect in Narrative Discourse", in Michel Achard and Suzanne Kemmer, eds. *Language, Culture, and Mind*. 363-76. Stanford: CSLI Publications.

Dancygier, B. 2004. "Visual Viewpoint, Narrative Viewpoint, and Mental Spaces in Narrative Discourse", in Augusto Soares da Silva, Amadeu Torres, and Miguel Gonçalves, eds. *Linguagem, Cultura e Cogniçao: Estudos de Linguistica Cognitiva*, 2 vols. Vol. 2, 347–62. Coimbra: Almedina.

Dancygier, B. 2005. "Blending and Narrative Viewpoint: Jonathan Raban's Travels Through Mental Spaces." *Language and Literature* 14.2: 99–127.

Dancygier, B. 2006. "Preface: What Can Blending Do for You?" *Language and Literature* 15.1 (Special Issue on Blending; Guest Editor: B. Dancygier): 5–15.

Dancygier, B. 2007. "Narrative Anchors and the Processes of Story Construction: The Case of Margaret Atwood's *The Blind Assassin.*" *Style* 41.2: 119–38.

Dancygier, B. 2008. "The Text and the Story: Levels of Blending in Fictional Narratives," in Todd Oakley and Anders Hougaard, eds, *Mental Spaces in*

Discourse. 51–78. Amsterdam and Philadelphia: John Benjamins Publishing Company.

Davidson, Donald. 1978. "What Metaphors Mean." *Critical Inquiry* 5: 31–47.

de Certeau, Michel. 1996. "Vocal Utopias: Glossolalias." *Representations* 56: 29–47.

De Man, Paul. 1986. *The Resistance to Theory* (Minneapolis: University of Minnesota Press.

De Waal, Shaun. 2003. *Mail & Guardian On-Line*. Edited version of an e-mail discussion between Shaun de Waal and Di Kilpert (20–24 October 2003) at www.chico.mweb.co.za/art/2003/2003oct/031024-coetzeeresp.html .

De Waal, Shaun. *Master in an Age of Iron*. At http://archive.mg.co.za/ MGArchive/.

Defoe, Daniel. 1991. *A Tour through the Whole Island of Great Britain* [1724–26]. Edited by P.N. Furbank et al. New Haven: Yale University Press, 1991.

Defoe, Daniel. *Roxana; or, The Fortunate Mistress* [1724]. Edited by David Blewett. New York: Penguin, 1982.

Defoe, Daniel. *The Life and Strange Surprizing Adventures of Robinson Crusoe* [1719]. Edited by J. Donald Crowley. Oxford: Oxford University Press, 1983.

Derrida, Jacques. 2002. "The Animal That Therefore I Am (More to Follow)". *Critical Inquiry* 28 (Winter): 369–418.

Dovey, Lindiwe. 2005. "African Film Adaptation of Literature: Mimesis and the Critique of Violence." PhD thesis, University of Cambridge , UK.

Dovey, Teresa. 1988. *The Novels of JM Coetzee: Lacanian Allegories*. Cape Town: A.D. Donker.

Eliot, T S. 1967. *Collected Poems 1906–1962*. London: Faber.

Engle, Lars. 1989. "The Political Uncanny in the Novels of Nadine Gordimer". *The Yale Journal of Criticism* 1.2:. 101–28.

Engle, Lars. 2006. "William Empson and the Sonnets," in Michael Schoenfeldt, ed., *A Companion to Shakespeare's Sonnets*. 163-82. Oxford: Blackwell.

Fauconnier, Gilles. 1994. *Mental Spaces* [1985]. 2nd edn. Cambridge: Cambridge University Press.

Fauconnier, Gilles. 1997. *Mappings in Thought and Language*. Cambridge: Cambridge University Press.

Fauconnier, Gilles and Sweetser, Eve, eds. 1996. *Spaces, Worlds, and Grammars*. Chicago: University of Chicago Press.

Fauconnier, Gilles and Turner, Mark. 1996. "Blending as a Central Process of Grammar", in Adele Goldberg, ed. *Conceptual Structure, Discourse, and Language*. 113–30. Stanford, CA: CSLI Publications.

Fauconnier, Gilles and Turner, Mark. 1998. "Conceptual Integration Networks". *Cognitive Science* 22.2: 133–87.

Fauconnier, Gilles and Turner, Mark. 1998. "Principles of Conceptual Integration", in Jean-Pierre Koenig et al., eds., *Discourse and Cognition: Bridging the Gap*. 269–83. Stanford, CA: CSLI Publications.

Fauconnier, Gilles and Turner, Mark. 2002. *The Way We Think: Conceptual Blending and the Mind's Hidden Complexities*. New York: Basic Books.

Foster, Hal. 1994. *The Return of the Real: the Avant-garde at the End of the Century*. Cambridge Mass: MIT Press.

Freeman, Margaret H. 2005. "The Poem as Complex Blend: Conceptual Mappings of Metaphor in Sylvia Plath's 'The Applicant'". *Language and Literature* 14.1: 25–44.

Freud, Siegmund. 1938. *Three Contributions to the Theory of Sex*, in *The Basic Writings of Siegmund Freud*. Translated and edited by A.A. Brill. New York: The Modern Library.

Fugard, Athol. 1996. *Valley Song*. London: Faber and Faber.

Fugard, Athol. 1999. *The Captain's Tiger*. London: Samuel French.

Fugard, Athol. 2002. *Sorrows and Rejoicings*. New York: Theatre Communications Group.

Gallagher, Catherine. 2006. "The Rise of Fictionality," in Franco Moretti, ed., *The Novel*. 336–63. Princeton: Princeton University Press.

Geertz, Clifford. 1971. *Islam Observed: Religious Development in Morocco and Indonesia*. Chicago: University of Chicago Press.

Genette, Gerard. 1980. *Narrative Discourse: An Essay in Method*, translated by J.E. Lewin. Ithaca: Cornell University Press.

Gibson, Colin and Marr, Lisa, eds. 2005. *New Windows on a Woman's World: Scholarly Writing in Honour of Jocelyn Harris*. Dunedin: University of Otago English Department.

Goethe. 1930. *Conversations of Goethe with Eckermann* [1836–48]. Translated by John Oxenford and edited by J.K. Moorhead. New York: J.M. Dent & Sons Ltd., 1930.

Goethe. 1949. *Faust: Part 1*. Translated by Philip Wayne. Harmondsworth: Penguin Books.

Goethe. 1959. *Faust: Part Two*. Translated by Philip Wayne. Harmondsworth: Penguin Books.

Goffman, Erving. 1967. "Embarrassment and Social Organization" (1957), in *Interaction Ritual: Essays on Face-to-Face Behaviour*. 97-112. Harmondsworth: Penguin.

Gordimer, Nadine. 1963. *Occasion for Loving*. London: Gollancz.

Gordimer, Nadine. 1974. *The Conservationist*. Harmondsworth: Penguin.

Gordimer, Nadine. 1979. *Burger's Daughter*. Harmondsworth: Penguin.

Gordimer, Nadine. 1981. *July's People*. Harmondworth: Penguin.

Gordimer, Nadine. 1983. "Living in the Interregnum". *New York Review of Books* (20 January): 21–9.

Gordimer, Nadine. 1984. "The Idea of Gardening". *New York Review of Books* (2 February): 3–6.

Gordimer, Nadine. 1994. *None to Accompany Me*. New York: Farrar Straus and Giroux.

Graham, Lucy. 2002. "'Yes, I am giving him up': Reading Rape in Recent South African Literature". *Scrutiny2* 7.1: 4–15.

Graham, Lucy. 2006. "Textual Transvestism: The Female Voices of J. M. Coetzee", in Jane Poyner, ed., *J. M. Coetzee and the Idea of the Public Intellectual*. 217–35. Athens: Ohio University Press.

Greenblatt, Stephen. 1980. *Renaissance Self-Fashioning: From More to Shakespeare*. Chicago: University of Chicago Press.

Gwala, Mafika. 1982. *No More Lullabies*. Johannesburg: Ravan Press.

Habermas, Jürgen. 1992. Postmetaphysical Thinking: Philosophical Essays. Cambridge, MA: MIT Press.

Hardy, Thomas. *Jude the Obscure*. Harmondsworth: Penguin, 1985.

Harré, R. Introduction, to The Embarrassment Project. The Virtual Faculty Website. http://www.massey.ac.nz/~alock/virtual/project1.htm.

Hayes, Patrick. 2006. "'An Author I Have Not Read': Coetzee's *Foe*, Dostoevsky's *Crime and Punishment*, and the Problem of the Novel". *Review of English Studies* 57: 273–90.

Head, Bessie. 1995. *The Cardinals*. London: Heinemann.

Head, Dominic. 1997. *J.M. Coetzee*. Cambridge: Cambridge University Press.

Herman, David. 2002. *Story Logic: Problems and Possibilities of Narrative*. Lincoln, NE, and London: University of Nebraska Press.

Herman, David, ed. 2003. *Narrative Theory and the Cognitive Sciences*. Stanford, CA: CSLI Publications.

Hiraga, Masako. 2005. *Metaphor and Iconicity: A Cognitive Approach to Analysing texts*. New York: Palgrave Macmillan.

Hofmannsthal, Hugo von. 2005. *The Lord Chandos Letter and Other Writings*. Introduced by John Banville and translated by Joel Rotenberg. New York: New York Review Books.

Homer. 1997. *Iliad*. Translated by Stanley Lombardo. Indianapolis: Hackett.

Horkheimer, Max and Theodor W. Adorno. 1973. *Dialectic of Enlightenment* [1947]. Translated by John Cumming. London: Allen Lane.

Huggan, Graham. 1996. "Evolution and Entropy in J.M. Coetzee's *Age of Iron*", in Graham Huggan and Stephen Watson, eds. *Critical Perspectives on J.M. Coetzee*. 191–206. Basingstoke: Macmillan.

Hughes, George. 2002. *Reading Novels*. Nashville: Vanderbilt University Press.

Hughes, Ted. 1957. "The Thought-Fox" (1957), in *The Norton Anthology of Poetry*. New York: W.W. Norton & Co.

Jayamanne, Laleen. 2001. *Toward Cinema and Its Double: Cross-Cultural Mimesis*. Bloomington and Indianapolis: Indiana University Press.

Johnson, Bruce. 1971. *Conrad's Models of Mind*. Minneapolis: University of Minnesota Press.

Kafka, Franz. 1995. *Metamorphosis and Other Stories*. Translated by Willa and Edwin Muir. New York: Schocken.

Kamuf, Peggy, ed. 1991. *A Derrida Reader: Between the Blinds*. Hemel Hempstead: Harvester Wheatsheaf.

Kant, Immanuel. 1929. *Immanuel Kant's Critique of Pure Reason* [1787]. Translated by Norman Kemp Smith. London: Macmillan,.

Kentridge, William. 2001. "Interview with Dan Cameron," in *William Kentridge*. 67–74. Chicago: New Museum of Contemporary Art in association with Harry N. Abrams.

Kolenda, Konstantin. 1985. "Preface", in Konstantin Kolenda, ed., *On the Freedom of the Will by Arthur Schopenhauer*. v–vi.. Oxford: Basil Blackwell.

Krauss, Rosalind. 1997. "X Marks the Spot" in *Rachel Whiteread: Shedding Life*. 74–81. Tate Gallery Liverpool.

Kuznetsov, Boris. 1972. *Einstein and Dostoevsky*. London: Hutchinson.

Lakoff, George and Johnson, Mark. 1980. *Metaphors We Live By*. Chicago: Chicago University Press.

Lakoff, George and Johnson, Mark. 1999. *Philosophy in the Flesh: The Embodied Mind and Its Challenge to Western Thought*. New York: Basic Books.

Langa, Mandla. 1987. *Tenderness of Blood*. Harare: Zimbabwe Publishing House.

Leech, Geoffrey and Short, Mick. 1981. *Style in Fiction*. London: Longman.

Leitch, ThomasM. 1986. *What Stories Are: Narrative Theory and Interpretation*. University Park & London: Penn State University Press.

Lombardo, Stanley. 1997. "Introduction" to his translation of Homer's *Iliad*. Indianapolis: Hackett.

Lowry, Elizabeth. 1999. "Like a Dog". Review of J.M. Coetzee's *Disgrace* and *The Lives of Animals London Review of Books* 21.20: 12–14.

MacCarthy, Fiona. 2002. *Byron: Life and Legend*. London: John Murray.

Marais, Michael. 2000. "The Possibility of Ethical Action." *Scrutiny2* 5.1: 57–63

Marais, Michael. 2006. "Death and the Space of the Response to the Other in J. M. Coetzee's *The Master of Petersburg*", in Jane Poyner, ed., *J. M. Coetzee and the Idea of the Public Intellectual*. 83–99. Athens: Ohio University Press.

Marks, Laura. 2000. *The Skin of the Film: Intercultural Cinema, Embodiment, and the Senses*. Durham and London: Duke University Press.

Mason, Eudo C. 1967. *Goethe's Faust: Its Genesis and Import*. Berkeley and Los Angeles: University of California Press.

Mda, Zakes. 1995. *Ways of Dying*. Cape Town: Oxford University Press.

Mda, Zakes. 2002. *The Madonna of Excelsior*. Cape Town: Oxford University Press.

Memmi, Albert. 1974. *The Colonizer and the Colonized*. London: Souvenir Press.

Morgan, Stuart. 1997. "Rachel Whiteread" in *Rachel Whiteread: Shedding Life*. 19–28. Tate Gallery Liverpool.

Morson, Gary Saul. 1994. *Narrative and Freedom: The Shadows of Time*. New Haven: Yale University Press.

Nagel, Thomas. 1987. "What Is It Like to Be a Bat?" in *Mortal Questions*. 165–80. Cambridge: Cambridge University Press.

Najder, Zdzislaw. 1983. *Joseph Conrad: A Chronicle*. Translated by Halina Carroll-Najder. Cambridge: Cambridge University Press.

Ndebele, Njabulo. 1985. *Fools and Other Stories*. Harlow: Longman.

Ndebele, Njabulo. 1994. *South African Literature and Culture: Rediscovery of the Ordinary*. Introduced by Graham Pechey. Manchester: Manchester University Press.

Novalis. 1997. *Philosophical Writings*. Edited by Margaret Mahoney Stoljar. Albany, NY: State University of New York Press.

Oakley, Todd. 1998. "Conceptual Blending, Narrative Discourse, and Rhetoric", *Cognitive Linguistics* 9.4: 321–60.

Origo, Iris. 1949. *The Last Attachment*. London: Jonathan Cape & John Murray.

Palmer, Alan. 2004. *Fictional Minds*. Lincoln, NE: University of Nebraska Press.

Parry, Benita. 1991. "Thanatophany for South Africa: Death Without Transfiguration". *Southern African Review of Books* (January/February): 16–11.

Pippin, Robert. 2002. "What Was Abstract Art? (From the Point of View of Hegel)". *Critical Inquiry* (Fall): 1–24.

Plato. 1970. "Cratylus," in *The Dialogues of Plato*. Translated by Benjamin Jowett. Vol.3:119–94.

London: Sphere.

Pope, Alexander. 1963. *Poems*. Edited by John Butt. London: Methuen.

Price, James. 1964. Review of *The Passenger* [Pasazerka]. *Film Quarterly* 18:1 (Autumn): 42–6.

Quennell, Peter. 1941. *Byron in Italy*. London: Collins Publishers.

Quennell, Peter. 1950. *Byron: The Years of Fame*. London: Collins.

Quintilian. 2001. *The Orator's Education*. Edited and translated by Donald A. Russell. Cambridge: Harvard University Press.

Rich, Adrienne. 1971. *The Will to Change: Poems 1968–1970*. New York and London: Norton.

Rich, Adrienne. 1975. "When We Dead Awaken: Writing as Re-vision", in *Adrienne Rich's Poetry*. Edited by Barbara Charlesworth Gelpi and Albert Gelpi. New York: Norton.

Richard of St Victor. *The Twelve Patriarchs; The Mystical Ark; Book Three of the Trinity*. Edited by Grover A. Zinn. The Classics of Western Spirituality. London: SPCK.

Roberts, Ronald Sureshi. 2005. *No Cold Kitchen: A Biography of Nadine Gordimer*. Johannesburg: STE.

Rodowick, David N. 1997. *Gilles Deleuze's Time Machine*. Durham and London: Duke University Press.

Rose, Arthur. 2006. "Taking Care in *Age of Iron* and *Slow Man*". Unpublished working paper, University of Cape Town.

Sanders, Jose and Redeker, Gisela. 1996. "Perspective and the Representation of Speech and Thought in Narrative Discourse", in G. Fauconnier and E. Sweetser, eds, *Spaces, Worlds, and Grammars*. 290–317.

Schalkwyk, David. 1994. "Confession and Solidarity in the Prison Writing of Breyten Breytenbach and Jeremy Cronin". *Research in African Literatures* 25: 23–45.

Scheff, Thomas J. *Goffman Unbound: A New Paradigm for Social and Behavioral Science*. Website at www.uab.edu/philosophy/SIGscheff.htm.

Schopenhauer, Arthur.1965. *On the Basis of Morality*. Translated by E.F.J. Payne. Indianapolis: Hackett.

Schopenhauer, Arthur. 1965 and 1969. *The World as Will and Representation*. Translated by E.F.J. Payne. 2 vols. New York: Dover Publications.

Schopenhauer, Arthur. 1974. *On the Fourfold Root of the Principle of Sufficient Reason* [1813]. Translated by E.J.F. Payne. La Salle, IL: Open Court.

Schreiner, Olive. 1995. *The Story of an African Farm*. London: Penguin.

Semino, Elena. 2006. "Blending and Characters' Mental Functioning in Virginia Woolf's *Lappin and Lapinova*". *Language and Literature* 15:1: 55–73.

Semino, Elena and Short, Mick. 2004. *Corpus Stylistics: Speech, Writing and Thought Presentation in a Corpus of English Writing*. London: Routledge.

Shakespeare, William. 1966. *King Lear*. Edited by Kenneth Muir. London: Methuen.

Sidney, Philip. 1962. *An Apology for Poetry*, in D.J. Enright and Ernst de Chickera, eds, *English Critical texts: 16th Century to 20th Century*. 3–49. London: Oxford University Press.

Smith, Adam. 1982. *The Theory of Moral Sentiments*. Edited by D.D. Raphael and A.L. Macfie. Indianapolis: Liberty Classics.

Smithson, Robert. 1996. *The Collected Writings*. Edited by Jack Flam. Berkeley, Los Angeles and London: University of California Press.

Sontag, Susan. 1966. *Against Interpretation*. New York: Farrar, Straus, Giroux.

Sontag, Susan. 1978. "Disease as Political Metaphor." *New York Review of Books* 25.2 (23 February): 29–33.

Sontag, Susan. 1978. "Illness as Metaphor." *New York Review of Books* 24.21–2 (26 January): 10–16.

Sontag, Susan. 1978. "Images of Illness." *New York Review of Books* 25.1 (9 February): 27–9.

Sontag, Susan. 2001. *Illness as Metaphor and Aids and Its Metaphors*. Picador: New York.

Sterritt, David. 1999. *The Films of Jean-Luc Godard: Seeing the Invisible*. Cambridge: Cambridge University Press.

Strier, Richard. 1995. *Resistant Structures: Particularity, Radicalism, and Renaissance Texts*. Berkeley: University of California Press.

Taylor, Jane. 1999. "The Impossibility of Ethical Action." Review of J.M. Coetzee's *Disgrace. Mail Guardian* 23–9: 25.

Thorold, Alan and Richard Wicksteed. [No date.] "Grubbing for the Ideological Implications: A Clash (More or Less) with J.M. Coetzee", Interview with J.M. Coetzee. *Sjambok*. A *Varsity* Publication. SRC, University of Cape Town.

Thucydides. 1988. *The Sicilian Expedition*. Translated by Percival Frost. London: Macmillan.

Toolan, Michael. 2001. *Narrative: A Critical Linguistic Introduction*, 2nd edn. London: Routledge.

Trilling, Lionel. 1972. *Sincerity and Authenticity*. Cambridge, MA: Harvard University Press, and London: Oxford University Press.

Turner, Mark. 2003. "Double-scope stories." In David Herman, ed., *Narrative Theory and the Cognitive Sciences*. 117–42. Stanford: CSLI Publications.

Turner, Mark. 2006. "Compression and Representation". *Language and Literature* 15.1: 17–29.

Turner, Mark and Fauconnier, Gilles. 1999. "A Mechanism of Creativity". *Poetics Today* 20.3: 397–418.

van Heerden, Etienne. 2002. *The Long Silence of Mario Salviati*. Translated by Catherine Knox. London: Hodder & Stoughton.

van Niekerk, Marlene. 1999. *Triomf*. Translated by Leon de Kock. London: Little, Brown.

van Wyk Smith, M. 1991. "Waiting for Silence; or, The Autobiography of Metafiction in Some Recent South African Novels". *Current Writing* 3: 91–104.

Vandelanotte, Lieven. 2009. *Speech and Thought Representation in English: A Cognitive-Functional Approach*. Berlin and New York: Mouton de Gruyter.

Verdi, Giuseppi and Arrigo Boito. 1994. *The Verdi-Boito Correspondence*. Edited by Marcello Conati and Mario Medici. Translated by William Weaver. Chicago: University of Chicago Press.

Vico, Giambattista. 1993. *On Humanistic Education*. Translated by Giorgio A. Pinton and Arthur W. Shippee. Ithaca and London: Cornell University Press.

Vladislavić, Ivan. 2004. *The Exploded View*. Johannesburg: Random House.

Weber, Max. 1976. *The Protestant Ethic and the Spirit of Capitalism*. Translated by Talcott Parsons. London: Allen & Unwin.

Wicomb, Zoë. 1987. *You Can't Get Lost in Cape Town*. London: Virago.

Wicomb, Zoë. 2000. *David's Story*. New York: Feminist Press.

Wood, Marcus. 2002. *Slavery, Empathy and Pornography*. Oxford: Oxford University Press, 2002.

Wordsworth, William. 1961. *The Poetical Works of Wordsworth*. Edited by Thomas Hutchinson; revised edition by Ernest de Selincourt. London: Oxford University Press.

Zunshine, Lisa. 2006. *Why We Read Fiction: Theory of Mind and the Novel*. Columbus, OH: Ohio State University Press.

Films Cited

Dust (1985). Director: Marion Hänsel. Belgium/Spain/South Africa. Produced
  by Man's Films (Belgium) and Daska Film International. 87 min. Distributor:
  Kino International (USA).
La Jetée (1962). Director: Chris Marker. France. Produced by Argos Films. 28
  min. Distributor: New Yorker Films (USA).
The Passenger (1963). Director: Andrzej Munk and Witold Lesiewicz. Poland.
  Produced by Zespol Filmowy. 62 min. Distributor: Hen's Tooth Video (USA).
Le Petit Soldat (1960). Director: Jean-Luc Godard. France/Switzerland. Produced
  by Les Films Georges de Beauregard, Société Nouvelle de Cinématographie
  (SNC). 88 min. Distributor: Winstar Video (USA).

Index